REAL INTERNATIONAL
CRICKET

REAL INTERNATIONAL
CRICKET

A History in
One Hundred Scorecards

ROY MORGAN

First published by Pitch Publishing, 2016

Pitch Publishing
A2 Yeoman Gate
Yeoman Way
Worthing
Sussex
BN13 3QZ
www.pitchpublishing.co.uk

A CIP catalogue record is available for this book
from the British Library.

ISBN 978-1-78531-140-6

Cover scorecard: Papua New Guinea Women versus New Caledonia
Women, Pacific Games, 2015 (Pacific Games Council).

Front cover photo: Philadelphia versus the Australians, 1893
(courtesy C.C.Morris Cricket Library).

Back cover photo: Afghanistan squad in Argentina, 2009 (Asian
Cricket Council).

Cover: Design by David Olner (Olner Design), based on an idea by
Gillian Morgan.

Typesetting and origination by Pitch Publishing

Printed by TJ International Ltd, Padstow, Cornwall

Contents

Acknowledgements

My thanks to the following for variously providing valuable information, answering difficult questions and finding photographs and giving permission for their use: Dave Allen, Kathleen Burns, Barry Chambers, Abhishek Chauhan, John Elder, Ben Fox, Simone Gambino, David George, Tommy Graham, Martin Gray, Bianca Igas, Jørgen Jørgen, Barry Keane, Neil Leitch, Ingleton Liburd, Mazelan bin Anuar, Darren Matthews, Liam McCumiskey, Andrew Minogue, Ole Mortensen, Rangam Mitra, John Mountford, Ole Roland and Sevil Oktem.

Abbreviations

ACC	Asian Cricket Council
FMS	Federated Malay States
ICC	International Cricket Council
MCC	Marylebone Cricket Club
PNG	Papua New Guinea
SACBOC	South African Cricket Board of Control
SS	Straits Settlements
UAE	United Arab Emirates
USA	United States of America

The following are used in the scorecards:

R	Runs
B	Balls received
b	Byes
fow	Fall of wickets
lb	Leg byes
M	Maiden overs (in bowling analysis)
	Minutes batted (in batting analysis)
nb	No-balls
O	Overs
W	Wickets (in bowling analysis)
w	Wides
4s	Number of fours
6s	Number of sixes
*	Captain (in team list)
	Not out (in close-of-play scores)
†	Wicketkeeper

Statistics

Statistical information is correct to 31 December 2015 which was also the cut-off date for selecting the scorecards. Selection was made from a database of full or partial scorecards for 9,523 men's matches and 1,016 women's matches involving countries which either are or have been Associate or Affiliate members of the ICC or have not yet applied for membership. I would be pleased to know of any errors or omissions in the scorecards used.

1

Scorecards as snapshots in history

BOOKS BASED on a selection of 100 items have become so commonplace over the last decade that it is questionable whether another one can have any value. However, there may be some merit when the selection is used to illustrate history through a series of important events which may not, otherwise, be well-known. While selecting a series of cricket scorecards of Test matches is unlikely to add much to previously published material, the same is not true for matches played by lesser-known countries.

The history and achievements in the cricket world of countries like Denmark, Malaysia and Fiji are rarely publicised. Today, these countries, which total well over 120, fall into three groups: those where cricket is firmly established and which are Associate Members of the International Cricket Council (ICC); those where cricket is played in accordance with its Laws and which are Affiliate Members of the ICC; and those where cricket is played, but which are not members of the ICC. Scorecards of international matches involving these countries can tell us much about the development of cricket as a global sport.

One hundred scorecards have been chosen ranging in date from 1840 to 2015. They are arranged chronologically up to 2000, so that each scorecard, effectively, becomes a snapshot on a timeline. This approach supports a historical interpretation of how the number of countries playing international cricket has increased, which countries were important centres of cricket outside of the Test-playing community at which time and which went in and out of being accorded first-class status. The chapters cover the sequence of the Early Years, up to 1890; the Golden Age, from 1890 to 1914; the period between the two world wars, marked by consolidation in some countries and decline in others; the Shoots of Recovery, from the end of the Second World War to 1960; the 1960s and 1970s, when countries in east Africa and south-east Asia suddenly became attractive places for cricket tours by teams from the Full Member countries; and the 1980s and 1990s, when countries began to play each other across the world, instead of being restricted to matches against their near neighbours or in regional competitions.

For the period beyond 2000, the chapters are organised thematically to reflect the different formats in which the game is now played. With the dominance of one-day and T20 internationals, there are fewer multi-innings matches. One chapter is concerned with the struggle to maintain multi-innings cricket and the role of the ICC Intercontinental Cup in keeping the first-class game alive among the leading Associates and Affiliates. Another chapter covers the wonders of one-day internationals, ranging from instances where Associates and Affiliates outplay a Full Member country to cases of outstanding individual achievements. A third chapter on the Short Game presents scorecards of the most important T20 encounters. Between them, these three chapters encompass the period when cricket truly went global, with the largest-ever number of countries involved in international cricket and the largest-ever programme of women's internationals.

The scorecards are selected for a number of reasons. Some reflect the enthusiasm of the players and the hardships, particularly in the early years, that they were prepared to endure in terms of time, difficulties of travel and costs in order to play cricket. Some illustrate the work of pioneers in establishing the facilities required to support cricket. The roles of charismatic individuals like William Leach in Argentina, George Barber in Canada, John Udal in Fiji, Charles Lawrence in both Ireland and Scotland, and the Comte Jean d'Oultremont in Belgium were vital in providing the foundation on which others could build. Similar roles have been played more recently by Simone Gambino in Italy, Hossain Ali Saliman in Iran, James Kodor in Romania and Andy Grieve in Hungary.

Unfortunately, it has not been possible to reflect the efforts of all of these people in the scorecard selection. To do so would either have taken the number of scorecards beyond a hundred or reduced the importance of other criteria on which selection was based. These include matches which represent critical points in a country's cricket history, those that feature outstanding team or individual performances, particularly where several occur in the same match, and those distinguished by unusual events. Some scorecards are chosen to illustrate how the atmosphere at cricket matches, particularly for the spectator, has changed over time and differed from one part of the world to another.

By adopting a chronological approach, the scorecards show how cricket has evolved from a sport for amateurs who had their own professional careers as businessmen, doctors, solicitors or teachers, or who were so wealthy that they did not need another career, to one that encompasses, first, the middle-classes and eventually, anyone who was eager to play. The role of the military has declined from one where players represented those countries where they were garrisoned to virtually no presence at all today. The scorecards also document the change from cricket's early reliance in many countries on expatriates from Britain and Australia to today's dependence on players from the Indian subcontinent and, to a lesser extent, the Caribbean.

The greatest change over time has been in who is allowed to represent any given country. Until the 1970s, virtually anyone who was resident in the country at the time a match was played was generally eligible for selection. The result was great variability. Countries like Argentina relied largely on expatriates, whereas those like Malaya witnessed an increasing representation of players from the local population. Those like Denmark, The Netherlands and Bermuda had teams comprised almost entirely of nationals.

Since 1979, the ICC has set down criteria that players must satisfy in order to represent their country. The details of these have changed over time, but broadly, players must either be citizens or fulfil a residential qualification and contribute to the development of cricket in the country concerned. Italy, Greece and Samoa have all had players declared ineligible and been forced to field weakened sides in international tournaments. Although the intention is to encourage the spread of cricket from expatriates to the local population, its effect has been highly varied. Scorecards since the 1990s include many players who are not born in the country they represent, but are eligible for citizenship because one of either their parents or grandparents was. This has enabled countries like Croatia, Italy, The Netherlands and Ireland to find players of good standard born in Australia, South Africa or New Zealand to raise the quality of their national sides. In fairness, many of these players have participated in the domestic competitions in their 'new' country and helped locals to improve their cricketing abilities so that they have become good enough to represent their country.

In contrast, there are countries that rely on expatriates because little attempt has been made to interact with the local population. Recent scorecards for the USA are dominated by expatriates and contain hardly anyone born in the country. Teams from the United Arab Emirates also consist largely of players from the Indian subcontinent or whose parents came from there. Since the laws of the country prevent them or their descendants from becoming citizens, there is little incentive for them to encourage cricket among the local Arab population, a situation that contrasts with that in Kuwait and Oman, both of which have fielded citizens-only teams in international competition. Of course, the ICC's eligibility regulations apply only to matches that they recognise. They are not adopted in competitions like the South American Championships and some east European T20 tournaments, where countries can select anyone they choose.

A feature of the scorecards before the First World War is the inclusion of players described as the local equivalents of W.G. Grace. These include Herbert Dorning of Argentina, Leslie Balfour-Melville of Scotland, Robert Lambert of Ireland and John Dunn of Hong Kong. No other cricketer has achieved the status of a worldwide role model and been emulated in this way. In all cases, the assumption is that the analogy relates to the cricketing ability of the individuals, rather than to other aspects of his personality.

With the number of scorecards limited to 100, it impossible to include every country in the world where cricket either is or has been played. To partially offset this exclusivity, the Appendix lists all countries that have played international cricket and are not Full Members of the ICC, together with some key dates in their cricket history. The majority of the scorecards are for international matches between countries which are Associate or Affiliate Members of the ICC. Some, however, involve matches between an Associate or Affiliate country and either a Full Member country or a first-class side from a Full Member country. These are chosen because they represent an unexpectedly good performance, though not necessarily a victory, by the Associate or Affiliate team. A few involve matches between an Associate or Affiliate and a country which is not a member of the ICC, again because they represent an important event. Sri Lanka, Zimbabwe and Bangladesh are each represented by one scorecard which marks, arguably, their first important international result prior to their Full Membership.

Some of the scorecards relate to events that have been well-documented elsewhere and are very well known, like the loss of all but two of Hong Kong's team in the SS *Bokhara* disaster in 1892, the dismissal of the West Indians for 25 by Ireland in 1969 and various upsets in World Cup competitions when a Full Member country was beaten by an Associate one. It could be argued that nothing new is learned by presenting them here. Their exclusion, however, would omit vital moments in Associate cricket history. For this reason alone, they are included.

The scorecards cover a range of match formats, including multi-innings, one-day single innings, one-day internationals and T20. They also include examples from both men's and women's cricket. Where many details are unavailable, a basic scoresheet results, but with sufficient information from which to produce a match report. Each scorecard is accompanied by a report which gives details of the context of the match, the main happenings and any implications of the result for cricket in the countries concerned. The reports are based on those published in contemporary newspapers and a range of internet sources.

Overall, the aim is to demonstrate the wide variety that exists and has existed in the standards, facilities, playing conditions and attendance in cricket matches worldwide. There is just as much, if not more, enthusiasm for cricket outside of the Test-playing countries than within them and more opportunities for exciting and unusual events to occur. Some of these would be most unlikely to happen in Full Member matches today, or at any time. The players whose names appear in these scorecards are, of course, only a small proportion of those who, for well over a century and a half, have given up their time and, in may cases, their money, to support the cause of cricket across the world. Cricket as represented here is a men's and women's global sport. Those who restrict their interest to Test matches and the first-class game in the Full Member countries of the ICC can have only a very limited appreciation and understanding of cricket as a whole.

2

The early years to 1890

THE FIRST attempt at organising an international cricket match is generally attributed to the third Duke of Dorset, Lord John Sackville. He was an above-average cricketer of his day and a wealthy patron of the game. In 1783, he was appointed, at his own request, as the British ambassador to France at the Court of Versailles. During his five years in Paris, he organised casual matches among the locally-resident British aristocracy in which, possibly, a few members of the French aristocracy also took part. Relationships between the French and the British were strained at the time by the decision of the French to support the American colonists in the War of Independence. This created difficulties for the British aristocracy in Paris who felt they were being ignored by the British government.

Dorset endeavoured to improve matters by arranging a cricket match between the local aristocracy and a visiting English team to be played on the Champs-Elysée in August 1789. The match had the support of the British government through the then Foreign Secretary, the Duke of Leeds. Dorset contacted his friend, the Earl of Tankerville, to arrange a team. He was considered the only person with sufficient experience and resources to bring together a team and arrange transport at short notice. Tankerville sought the assistance of William Yalden, the landlord of the Cricketer Inn at Chertsey, and through him assembled a side made up largely of cricketers living in or around Chertsey. The team assembled at Dover on 10 August, but before they could cross the English Channel, they were met by the Duke of Dorset travelling in the opposite direction, supposedly escaping from the French Revolution.

According to this version of events, the French Revolution was the direct cause of the cancellation of what should have been the first international cricket fixture. The significance of these events to cricket history was recognised by a special fixture to mark their centenary. On 24 September 1989, MCC met the French national side on an artificial pitch at the Standard Athletic Club of Paris at Meudon, a match which France won by seven wickets, largely due to the batting of John Short, a former Irish international then working for the OECD in Paris.

Whether the above should be treated as a potential international fixture between England and France is somewhat debatable. Sir John Major, in his *More Than A Game: The Story Of Cricket's Early Years*, considers the whole story to be complete fiction. He argues that after having experienced the unrest in France and having warned British residents to leave Paris, the Duke of Dorset is unlikely to have invited a team of cricketers to the country. Further, rather than fleeing France ignominiously, as the above version implies, he had already requested the Duke of Leeds to terminate his appointment as ambassador in July 1879. It is not entirely clear whether his request was made before or after the Storming of the Bastille on 14 July or after many of the aristocracy chose to flee Paris on 17 July. However, it seems certain that his departure from Paris on 8 August and his subsequent arrival in Dover two days later was planned and not a last-minute act of desperation. After a journey of 144km from Paris, he reached Boulogne-sur-Mer on 9 August and took a night packet boat to Dover, arriving early the following morning.

Unfortunately, Major does not provide any evidence to support his view that the story is a myth and that the account presented by John Goulstone and Michael Swanton in *History Today* in August 1989, based on contemporary sources, is substantially incorrect. The request to Tankerville to organise a team was certainly made before conditions in Paris worsened. Otherwise Tankerville and Yalden would not have had long enough to find players with the necessary time and finance to undertake the venture and also willing to go, given the unstable political conditions. Had the match taken place, the players involved would have needed some three weeks to complete the round trip. The journey from London to Dover by stagecoach would have taken two days, with stops every eight to ten miles to change horses, a more prolonged rest at Rochester for lunch and sleeping overnight at Canterbury.

On arrival at Dover, there would have been a wait for favourable wind conditions for the Channel crossing which, itself, would have taken a minimum of three hours and possibly as long as 14. The journey from Calais to Paris would have taken a further two or three days. Only after the cricketers had arrived in Paris would the date of the match have been finalised. The players would have been allowed a few days for practice and there would undoubtedly have been many social engagements.

Dorset's request to end his ambassadorial appointment was not unreasonable after a term of nearly six years. It could well have been made regardless of the Revolution and would not have prevented him organising a cricket match. He could still have returned to Paris as a member of Yalden's team. Major describes Dorset's behaviour on reaching England as demonstrating that he had no knowledge of any cricket match. He dined with another of his friends, Horace Mann, and then, the following day, watched Kent play Surrey. All of this could equally well have occurred, however, after he had met with Yalden and his fellow cricketers to tell them that the match was cancelled.

Perhaps more important regarding its possible status as an international fixture is the standing of the two teams. It is unclear who the opposition in Paris would have been. It seems unlikely that more than a few, if any, French aristocrats would have been involved. The team would most likely have comprised selected British residents. Whether any would have resided in Paris for a sufficient time to be considered French, rather than British, is doubtful. The team that Yalden assembled was certainly experienced with seven having played at what is now recognised by the Association of Cricket Statisticians and Historians as first-class level. However, it was 1789 and the first-class careers of those players had ended by 1773. The side was therefore quite elderly and certainly not representative of the top English players of the time. To consider the event as a cancelled fixture between England and France is at best fanciful. Indeed, some contemporary descriptions give the match no more status than being William Yalden's XI versus the Duke of Dorset's XI. It is not entirely certain that the team would have even played a local team or whether, instead, they intended only to take part in exhibition matches at single-wicket or five-a-side.

Although the venture did not come off, the enthusiasm of the Duke of Dorset for assembling his own teams and organising matches was well-known. To attempt an overseas tour, albeit only across the English Channel, was, however, remarkably ambitious, given the travelling conditions of the day. It was to be 51 years before another attempt was made to arrange a match between teams from different countries. This involved St George's Cricket Club, New York, and Toronto Cricket Club in Canada.

St George's was founded as the New York Cricket Club by British expatriates on 20 September 1838, and changed its name to St George's Cricket Club, in honour of England's patron saint, on 23 April 1839. Although its founders were an iron merchant (William Jupe), a wool merchant (John Taylor) and an insurance specialist (Robert Bage), the club's membership was largely drawn from literary, artistic and theatrical circles. It was generally recognised as an exclusive club with membership restricted to British-born residents.

Perhaps as a result of this exclusivity, the club had difficulty finding opponents and no matches were arranged in 1839 or 1840 despite offering a challenge to any cricket club in the USA or Canada for a stake of US$100 per side. The club officials were therefore naturally interested when, in early August, a Mr Phillpotts, supposedly hailing from Toronto, proposed two matches against Toronto Cricket Club, the first in Toronto and then a return in New York, with each club to pay the others' expenses in travelling to their respective grounds. Although no definitive sum of money was agreed, Phillpotts indicated that the Toronto club would play for any amount between US$100 and US$5,000.

Officials of St George's immediately sent a letter, addressed to Phillpotts at the Toronto club, signifying their agreement. Phillpotts also gave the assurance that he would convey the details of the arrangements to his club and that no further correspondence would be necessary, except for St George's to confirm to the Toronto club that the first match should take place. On 13 August, St George's officials sent the confirmatory letter, indicating that they would leave New York for Toronto on the 29th of that month.

Travel from New York to Toronto required taking the regular stagecoach leaving every Tuesday, Thursday or Sunday morning for Rochester, via Auburn, which, with stops, was a journey of 55 hours. This enabled a connection with the ferry from Rochester to Coburg which departed at sunset every Monday, Wednesday and Friday, arriving at Coburg in time to take the 5.30am stage to Toronto. Accordingly, a party of 18 left New York as planned on 29 August and arrived in Toronto, somewhat travel weary, on 1 September.

Toronto Cricket Club had been founded in 1827 by George Barber under the name of York Cricket Club, York being the name of the original settlement. In 1834, York reverted to its Inuit name of Toronto and the cricket club followed suit. In August 1840, the first news of a possible cricket match against St George's was a short article on the arrangements, published on 22 August in the *Spirit of the Times*, a New York newspaper which reached Toronto on the 27th. Since the club had no official information about the proposal, its officials regarded it as one of many unauthorised articles which appeared from time to time in newspapers. The locals were therefore taken by surprise when the New Yorkers arrived. Equally, the players and officials of the St George's Club were astonished to find that their arrival was unexpected and that no arrangements for them had been made.

An official of each club went to the Post Office where the two letters sent from New York were found, but had not been forwarded on because they were addressed to Mr Phillpotts, who was known to be temporarily absent from the city. Having established that the contents of the letters matched the information provided by the St George's officials, a committee of Toronto Cricket Club was quickly set up to meet with the visitors. The committee, comprising Colonel McKenzie Fraser, Mr W.H. Boulton (vice-president of Toronto Cricket Club) and John Barwick, were instructed, on behalf of the Toronto club, to express their ignorance of the whole affair, apologise that the New Yorkers had received such a disappointment, offer to play a match for a stake of £50 (about US$250) per side and invite the visitors to a dinner after the game was finished. Not surprisingly, St George's accepted the arrangements and the match was played on 4 September at Caer Howell, formerly the country home of William Powell, son of an American loyalist. After Powell's death in 1834, Henry Layton bought the house and turned it into a country club with bowling greens, rackets court and a cricket ground which became the home of Toronto Cricket Club until 1894.

Clearly the whole event had been a hoax. Mr Phillpotts did not exist and was certainly not the Mr G.A. Phillpotts, a local cricketer, who later represented Canada in four international matches. Members of the St George's club confirmed, after meeting him, that he was not the same person they had dealt with in New York. Who the imposter was will never be known; nor will his motive for the deception. Was this someone who had a grudge against St George's Cricket Club, perhaps a person who had been refused membership? Was this someone obtaining revenge for a dispute with Toronto Cricket Club? Some contemporary accounts on the incident indicate that the perpetrator was identified and was known to members of the Toronto club, but his name was not revealed in order to protect other members of a well-regarded local family.

It was while officials from the two clubs were in New York that the possibility of a fixture involving players from other clubs was raised. During the winter of 1843/44, St George's issued a challenge to Toronto for such a match with a stake of US$1,000 per side, a huge sum of money at the time. Surprisingly, given the problems that arose in 1840, the challenge was made through a newspaper, the *New York Herald*, rather than direct communication between the two clubs' secretaries. Toronto accepted the challenge and on Saturday 21 September 1844, their players left the city for New York, crossing Lake Ontario and then linking up with the newly-built railway from Rochester to Albany, before transferring to stagecoach. Although no meals were served on the trains, which stopped at wayside taverns to allow refreshments to be obtained, the journey was undoubtedly more comfortable than that undertaken by the St George's team four years earlier.

The *Toronto Patriot* described the match as between Toronto and St George's, even though the Toronto side included James Wilson from Guelph and G.A. Phillpotts from Upper Canada College. The *New York Weekly Herald* referred to the match as between St George's and the Canadians, despite the St George's team including the brothers, John and Robert Ticknor, from Philadelphia Cricket Club, and James Turner and Samuel Dudson from the Union Cricket Club, Camden, New Jersey. It is not surprising that, in retrospect, the match has become recognised as being between the United States and Canada and, therefore, the first international match ever played. Even so, it is unlikely that any of the players knew they were involved in an international fixture or had allegiance to the country they are now associated with. The birthplaces of the majority of the players are not known but only one, John Beverley Robinson, was definitely born in North America; he was Canadian, having been born in Toronto. It seems likely that the remaining players were British by birth.

Although cricket in eastern Canada and the east of the United States in the 1850s was popular with both players and spectators and international matches were well-attended, the standard was undoubtedly very low. Just how low became clear in 1859 when a party of 12 of England's best professional players, under the captaincy of George Parr and drawn from William Clarke's All-England XI and John Wisden's United All-England XI, risked the rigours of crossing the Atlantic Ocean in late summer to undertake a tour. The idea of testing the strength of Canadian and American cricket against the best of England's cricketers was mooted during the USA–Canada match in 1856 and William Pickering, the English-born, Cambridge University blue and former Surrey player, but by that point a Canadian international, set about arranging the visit.

He corresponded with Robert Waller in New York, with respect to the American leg of the tour. Unfortunately, the search for funds coincided with what became known as the Panic of 1857 when an economic downturn threatened much of the investment in business and the railways. The failure of the Ohio Life Insurance and Trust Company on 24 August put pressure on the banks and borrowing money became very difficult. It was not possible to secure the money the English players requested. But the problems were short-lived and by 1859 the economy was stabilising. After the English cricketers reduced their demand by half it was possible to secure the sponsorship, a sum amounting to £1,300.

The tourists took just over two weeks, a week longer than normal, to travel from Liverpool to Quebec, first because of exceptionally rough weather and then a navigational error in thick fog as the ship approached Canada and entered the wrong estuary. From Quebec the party took a special train to Montreal for their first fixture. They thrashed a Lower Canada XXII by eight wickets. The tourists went on to beat a USA XXII by an innings and 62 runs, XXII of Canada by ten wickets, XXII of Philadelphia by seven wickets and a combined Canada-USA XXII by an innings and 68 runs. The weather for this last fixture, at Rochester on 21, 22 and 24 October, was so cold that the English players fielded in gloves and great coats and play on the second day was prevented by snow.

Worse was to befall the tourists, however, because during the return crossing of the Atlantic the jib-boom of the ship broke in a violent storm and, while the crew were attempting a repair, an anchor came loose and fell upon a sailor, breaking both his legs. He died from his injuries before the ship reached port. Nevertheless, the overall venture was a success for the tourists, as each returned home with a profit of about £90, which compared well with the £4 to £5 they earned for each match they played in England. For the Canadians and the Americans the visit showed just how much skill the local players lacked compared to their English compatriots. For many, this was the first time they had been exposed to either lob bowling or bowling of real pace. The accuracy of the English bowlers also contrasted with the inability of the locals to bowl a consistent direction, let alone pitch a good length.

The local press, particularly in New York, felt embarrassed by the humiliation of the American cricketers. Yet, the difference in standard between the locals and the tourists was not particularly surprising. Most of the locals were born in Britain and few had played top-level cricket before emigrating. At best they were on a par with local amateurs in England's smaller towns and rural areas, similar in standard to those representing say Buckinghamshire, Suffolk, Wiltshire or the Cambridge Town Club.

Results against the All-England XI also indicate that the standard of cricket in Scotland and Ireland at the time was probably similar to that in North America or, even, somewhat lower. A Scotland XXII met the All-England XI five times between 1849 and 1852 and were beaten on four occasions, two of them by an innings. An Ireland XXII lost to All-England three times between 1860 and 1869. However, on several occasions, the quality of the home sides was enhanced by the deeds of Charles Lawrence, one of the leading cricketers of his day. An all-rounder, he combined a sound, if defensive, batting technique with a wide range of bowling styles, from fast round-arm, to a slower medium-pace and even slower, but discerningly accurate, lobs. In addition to playing first-class for Middlesex and Surrey, he represented Scotland and Ireland at international level.

Against the All-England XI at Edinburgh in 1849 he took all ten wickets in the second innings for 53 runs, which still ranks as the best international bowling performance for Scotland. In all, Lawrence played four times for Scotland and seven times for Ireland. While in Dublin, he was employed by the Lord Lieutenant, the Earl of Carlisle, to construct a cricket ground at the Vice-Regal Lodge in Phoenix Park. This was the venue for many matches up to 1906, but is now a flower bed on the presidential estate. Lawrence was also an influential coach. He founded the United Ireland XI, based on the All-England XI, to promote cricket in Belfast, Cork and the rural areas of Ireland. He left Ireland in 1861, having been selected as a member of H.H. Stephenson's party of English tourists to Australia. He remained in Australia at the end of the tour as a coach with the Albert Club in Sydney and played a major role in developing cricket among the aboriginal population. He returned to England in 1868 as the captain and manager of the Aborigine side on its tour of Britain. Lawrence's contribution to Irish cricket was just one of many examples of the contribution of charismatic individuals to the advancement of cricket in a country of Associate or Affiliate status. He has been described as the 'Father of Irish cricket'. His contributions thus match those of George Barber, considered by some as the 'Father of Canadian cricket'.

Probably more so than in other Associate and Affiliate countries at the time, cricket in Ireland was largely the preserve of the wealthy and the elite. As a result, it managed to survive the effects of the Land War, 1879–1882, and the Plan of Campaign, 1886–1892, when landlords with British connections suffered harassment and many cricket clubs in the villages and small towns, which had relied on their support, folded. Many English clubs did not consider it safe to visit Ireland and what had been almost annual visits from MCC and I Zingari ceased. Enterprising cricketers of the upper class, however, were able to band together and in 1879 and 1888 organised tours to North America.

These were people like the Hones, an important Irish cricketing family, who could afford the costs of trans-Atlantic travel and did not need to worry about loss of income from being away from work. Reciprocal visits were made by Philadelphia, who played in Ireland in 1884 and 1889, and by Canada, in 1887. Ireland were thus engaged in international cricket with the Americas before they played their nearest Associate country, Scotland. The first meeting with Scotland was not until 1888.

The extent to which cricketers in the late 1850s and 1860s were prepared to go in order to fulfil 'international' fixtures was epitomised by the early contacts between the members of Hong Kong and Shanghai Cricket Clubs, both founded in 1851. The number of British people in both centres in the 1850s was under 1,000 and, in Shanghai, this had increased to only 1,300 to 1,500 by 1865. The census of December 1865 found that there were 2,034 Europeans and Americans in Hong Kong in a population of 125,504. Of these, 1,142 were men, 467 women and the remainder children. Since these undoubtedly included some who were not interested in cricket, there were only a few potential players. Matches were largely limited to 'pick-up' games between club members, or fixtures against either the military or the officers and crew of whatever ships were in port and willing to raise a side. The prospect of a game against another properly organised club was therefore appealing, even if it meant a round trip of some 2,560km and several days at sea.

There were already good contacts between club members because many were businessmen in the trading companies or *hongs* which had branches in both cities. As a result, following a challenge put out by Shanghai Cricket Club to their counterpart in Hong Kong, arrangements were made for a fixture in February 1866. For Shanghai's players, the match was important as an indicator of optimism for the future, as life was still adjusting to peace after the end of the Taiping rebellion. Although the last attack by the rebels on Shanghai was in September 1862, the threat of further disturbance remained until the uprising was quashed in 1864.

Although matches of this period would have been recognisable as cricket to people of today, there were important differences. The latest set of the Laws of Cricket were agreed in 1864, but it is not certain how quickly these were adopted overseas. The most important change to the Laws was to legalise over-arm as opposed to round-arm bowling. It is unlikely that any practitioners of over-arm would have played in these early matches since all would have learnt their cricket under the old rules. It was probably not until the 1870s that round-arm bowling even became the norm outside of the British Isles. What is also certain is that there were no boundaries. All hits had to be run for and if the ball went into the crowd, the spectators were expected to clear a path for its passage and not hinder the ball before it could be retrieved by a fielder. The position of long stop was still vitally important in the field. It was his duty rather than that of the wicketkeeper to prevent byes.

In the early 1860s, cricket in North America was disrupted by the American Civil War. The international series between the United States and Canada was not played in 1861 and did not resume until August 1865. Compared to the First and Second World Wars, however, the conflict was less detrimental to cricket. Although it was difficult to organise matches in the first summer, as men answered the call to military service and some grounds were requisitioned for military use, in subsequent years fixtures were arranged between clubs, fielding teams of players who were too young to serve. Some of these were designed to raise funds for various charitable and military causes. The commanders of the Unionist and Confederate forces encouraged impromptu matches between regiments or between officers and men, as a way of providing necessary relaxation.

Despite the atrocious conditions in which many of the battles were fought and the large loss of life, few cricketers of note became casualties. The most famous was Walter Newhall, who was drowned trying to cross the Rappahannock River in Virginia in flood. Cricket recovered surprisingly quickly after the end of hostilities and the late 1860s and 1870s was a time of rapid growth of the sport in New York and Philadelphia. With visits from English teams captained by E. Willsher in 1868 and R.A. Fitzgerald in 1872, cricket was increasingly taken up by the American-born, particularly in Philadelphia by the Newhall family. After winning two tournaments against Canada and a British Officers team in 1874 and 1875, the standard of Philadelphian cricket was on the rise. Sufficient funds were raised to attract the Australians on their way home from their 1878 tour of England and Philadelphia met them on equal terms in a three-day match beginning on 3 October.

In the 50 years since New York's cricketers first travelled to Toronto, cricket in the countries that eventually became Associate and Affiliate members of the ICC had made enormous progress. Matches between the United States and Canada were now annual events. A regular Interport series between Shanghai and Hong Kong was established, although the tragedy of the SS *Bokhara* had placed matches on hold. Ireland had met Scotland only once, but both countries had played against American and Canadian teams. In all these encounters the teams were undoubtedly of a good club standard, even though, in many instances, there was a very small pool of players from which to choose. The players were prepared to travel long distances and experience considerable hardships, let alone dangers, in order to further their love of the game. The greatest advance was in Philadelphia where cricket had become very popular with many matches attracting large attendances. By the early 1890s, Philadelphian representative teams were acclaimed as first-class and equal to the best of English amateur sides. These early days had laid the foundation for a Golden Age.

Club pioneers

After travelling for four days, the cricketers from St George's Cricket Club of New York arrived in Toronto to find that no one was expecting them. They had been the victim of a hoax and no match against Toronto Cricket Club had been arranged. Somewhat embarrassed, the Toronto club hastily organised a fixture to take place on Friday 4 September. The match began in very fine weather at 10am. Despite the short notice and it being a weekday, there was a sizeable crowd. The band of the 34th Regiment turned out to entertain the spectators and Sir George Arthur, His Excellency the Lieutenant Governor of Canada, honoured the occasion with his presence. Patrick Adams in his *A History of Canadian Cricket* suggests that the reason for Arthur's attendance was to show support for the loyalists in both countries rather than any desire to improve relationships between the USA and Canada. William Lyon McKenzie's attempt to form a Canadian republic had only been thwarted as recently as 1837. Support for the members of the St George's club was therefore politically appropriate since their players had closer links to Britain than to America.

Unfortunately for Toronto, the match proved very one-sided with St George's having the upper hand throughout. Batting first, Toronto ruined their chances of making a reasonable score by having five of their players fall to run-outs. Only one player reached double figures in a first-innings total of 52. Winckworth tried hard to retaliate with his fast round-arm and bowled six of the visiting batsmen, but Wild held firm for his 22 and received good support from Henry Russell and Wheatman. Toronto contributed to their deficit of 46 runs on the first innings by conceding 13 byes and 13 wides. They fared little better in their second innings with Groom's fast left-arm proving too difficult to handle. St George's were left to score nine runs to win, which they did without losing a wicket. The match was completed in one day, a combination of weak batting, inaccurate bowling and poor fielding accounting for the home side's downfall. Although not strictly an international, the match was the first to take place between teams from different countries. After the match, at 7.30pm, both sides enjoyed a banquet at Ontario House which, according to local accounts, removed any ill-feeling between the clubs. The following day, the sides joined together to form two XIs for a friendly game before the visitors began their arduous journey back to New York.

Attempts to arrange a return fixture failed in both 1841 and 1842. A game in Toronto the following year also fell through, but only after the New Yorkers had arrived in Toronto and both teams were assembled on the field on 25 July. Toronto objected to the inclusion by the visitors of three players from the Union Club of Philadelphia, who had been given honorary membership of St George's CC for the purpose of the fixture. The Canadians argued that the match was between players from the two clubs only and that outsiders were excluded. Neither side would relent and the match was abandoned.

The following day the visitors played against a combined Guelph and Upper Canada College side instead, losing on the first innings by 38 runs. Any enmity between Toronto and St George's must have been quickly resolved, however, because Toronto travelled to New York for a match on 13 and 14 September. Because of rain, the match extended into four days, finishing on 16 September with a victory for Toronto by four wickets. In addition, a single-wicket match was arranged between Henry Groom of St George's and David Winckworth of Toronto for a side bet of US$100. Winckworth won easily, scoring 21 runs to Groom's five and nought; Groom contributed to Winckworth's total by bowling six wides.

TORONTO CRICKET CLUB v ST GEORGE'S CLUB OF NEW YORK

Caer Howell, Toronto, 4 September 1840

St George's Club of New York won by ten wickets

TORONTO		R	B	M	4s	6s		R	B	M	4s	6s
R.R.Loring	c Wild	3					c Groom	3				
G.A.Barber	b Gill	1					run out	10				
Warren	b Gill	2					b Groom	0				
Bliss	run out	7					b Groom	9				
C.J.Birch	run out	10					b Groom	6				
J.H.Maddock	run out	9					b H.Russell	2				
D.Winckworth	run out	1					c Stead	0				
Marryatt	not out	6					(11) b Groom	7				
T.D.Harrington	c Gill	0					(8) c Green	1				
G.W.Girdlestone	run out	4					(9) not out	7				
J.G.Spragge	c Wright	0					(10) b Groom	1				
	b6 w3	9					b6 w2	8				
		52						**54**				

ST GEORGE'S CLUB OF NEW YORK		R	B	M	4s	6s		R	B	M	4s	6s
Gill	c Maddock	1										
W.Russell	c Barber	6										
S.Wright	b Winckworth	2					(1) not out	3				
H.Russell	b Winckworth	17										
R.N.Tinson	b Winckworth	0										
W.Wild	c Harrington	22					(2) not out	5				
J.Wheatman	b Winckworth	17										
G.Stead	b Winckworth	2										
H.Groom	b Maddock	1										
Wyvil	b Winckworth	0										
Green	not out	4										
	b13 w13	26					w1	1				
		98					(no wicket)	**9**				

St George's	O	M	R	W	nb	w		O	M	R	W	nb	w	fow
Gill				2										1
Groom											5			2
H.Russell											1			3
														4
Toronto	O	M	R	W	nb	w		O	M	R	W	nb	w	5
Winckworth				6										6
Maddock				1										7
														8
														9
														10

Umpires: W.H. Draper (Toronto) and W. Howe (St George's Club of New York)

Toss: not known

No bowling analyses were kept. Names of bowlers were not recorded unless the batsman was out bowled. Overs were probably of four balls.

R.R. Loring appears in the published scorecard as Goring, but there is no other record of a Toronto player by this name at the time whereas Robert Loring appeared for Toronto Cricket Club between 1835 and 1838.

Marryatt appears in some scorecards as Marriott.

Wyvil appears in the published scorecard as Wyville, but he is probably either H. Wyvil or W. Wyvil.

Wheatman appears in the published scorecard without an initial; he is probably J. Wheatman.

David Winckworth went on to play three matches for Canada and one for the USA, becoming the first player to represent two countries.

Canada win first international

What is now recognised as the first international cricket match ever played began at 10am on 24 September 1844, at the St George's Club ground, Bloomingdale Road, New York. This is now East 31st Street, near 1st Avenue, but what was then a rural area with a few farms. The starting time was not, as would be today, when the cricket actually commenced, but the time at which the players and officials were expected to assemble. Proceedings began by selecting the umpires, John Connolly of Toronto and Robert Waller from St George's. Agreement was reached on matters relating to the rules, in particular that there were to be no boundaries. All hits had to be run for. Finally, a toss was made, won by Robert Tinson, the American captain who invited Toronto to bat.

It was 11.40am before play began, by which time there was a crowd of nearly 3,000. Groom's left round-arm proved troublesome and were it not for some careful and stubborn batting by Winckworth, the Canadians would have been dismissed for a very low score. In keeping with the leisurely nature of the proceedings, when the Canadian innings ended for 62 at 2pm, an hour's rest was taken. By the time the United States began their reply, the crowd had reached some 5,000. Betting was considerable with reports in the *Toronto Herald* indicating that as much as US$100,000 was gambled on the outcome.

Turner, Robert Ticknor and Wheatcroft batted steadily for the Americans, but all three got out when looking well set. The home side were then the victim of two poor umpiring decisions, Wright being given out caught, when the ball rebounded from his knee and not the bat, and James Ticknor, dubiously adjudged leg before. Tinson anchored the innings, batting for an hour and a quarter. Phillpotts's wicketkeeping, Freeling's fielding and Winckworth's bowling were much admired. When play ended for the day, St George's had lost nine wickets for 61.

The second day was dull and wet and no play was possible. Instead of abandoning the match, however, the teams agreed to come back for a third day. Despite it being dull and cold, with a piercing wind, 4,000 people attended. Waller was unavailable to umpire because of a pre-arranged appointment in Philadelphia. Howard Russell took his place. The United States were also without Wheatcroft, who failed to turn up. The home side added only three more runs for the tenth wicket, but the visitors failed to capitalise and were dismissed for 63, leaving the Americans to make 82 runs to win. Turner batted for an hour and a half, but no one else could master the bowling of Sharpe, who took six wickets to take the Canadians to a comfortable victory by 23 runs. Twenty minutes after the match was over, Wheatcroft appeared, claiming that, given the weather, he did not expect there to have been any play. The Americans wanted the match to resume to allow him to bat. The Canadians, rightly, refused the request. With the large amount of money at stake, the *New York Herald* reported on 'ugly rumours' regarding Wheatcroft's non appearance and Waller's absence as umpire, particularly because he was the one responsible for the dubious decisions earlier in the match.

The Canadians returned to Toronto to be welcomed by a sizeable crowd, news of their victory having arrived before them. Alderman William Boulton, vice-president of the Toronto Cricket Club, who accompanied the team, had apparently made several thousand dollars on bets during the match, an outcome which seemingly enhanced his reputation. He was duly elected to the Legislative Assembly later in the year and went on to become Mayor of Toronto from 1845 to 1847 and again in 1858. This would not be the first time that an association with success in cricket laid the foundation for a political career.

UNITED STATES OF AMERICA v CANADA

St George's Club, Bloomingdale Road, New York, 24, 25 and 26 September 1844

Canada won by 23 runs

CANADA		R	B	M	4s	6s		R	B	M	4s	6s
D.Winckworth	run out	12					b Wright	14				
J.C.Wilson	b Wright	0					(7) b Groom	0				
C.J.Birch	c Bage b Groom	5					(5) c Turner b Wright	0				
G.A.Barber	b Wright	1					b Groom	3				
G.Sharpe	b Wright	12					(9) b Groom	5				
+G.A.Phillpotts	ht wkt b Groom	1					(8) b Groom	13				
J.B.Robinson	Lbw b [unknown]	1					(10) b Wright	4				
J.H.Maddock	not out	7					(2) b Groom	7				
Freeling	c Dudson b Wright	12					(11) not out	7				
F.French	b Groom	9					(6) b Wright	0				
W.Thompson	b Wright	7					(3) lbw b [unknown]	3				
	b9 w6	15					w7	7				
		82						**63**				

USA		R	B	M	4s	6s		R	B	M	4s	6s
J.Turner	b Winckworth	7					c Barber b Sharpe	14				
R.Ticknor	c Thompson b French	5					(4) b Sharpe	8				
G.Wheatcroft	b Winckworth	9					absent					
S.Wright	c Barber b French	4					(3) b French	3				
J.Ticknor	Lbw b [unknown]	0					(5) b Sharpe	0				
*+R.N.Tinson	st Phillpotts b [unknown]	14					Lbw b [unknown]	0				
J.Syme	c Thompson b French	1					(2) b Groom	11				
S.Dudson	c Freeling b Winckworth	4					(7) c Winckworth b Sharpe	0				
H.Groom	c Thompson b French	0					b Winckworth	0				
W.Wild	b Winckworth	10					(8) c Maddock b Sharpe	8				
R.Bage	not out	1					(10) not out	5				
	b7 w3	10					b3 w6	9				
		64						**58**				

USA	O	M	R	W	nb	w	O	M	R	W	nb	w
Groom	16			3						5		7
Wright	16			5						4		

Canada	O	M	R	W	nb	w	O	M	R	W	nb	w
Winckworth				4						1		
French				4						1		
Sharpe										6		

fow	Can (1)	USA (1)	Can (2)	USA (2)
1	3	15	11	25
2	17	15	24	30
3	20	20	31	36
4	36	25	31	36
5	37	30	31	36
6	40	31	32	36
7	40	42	32	51
8	57	44	45	51
9	66	55	53	58
10	82	64	63	

Umpires: J.H.Connolly (Canada) and R.Waller (USA)

Toss: USA

Overs were probably of four balls. No bowling analyses were recorded.

Close of play: 1st day – USA 61-9 (Wild 8*, Bage 0*); 2nd day – no play.

Match was originally scheduled for two days, but when no play was possible on the second day, it was agreed to extend the match into a third day.

R.Waller was unable to officiate on the third day; his place was taken by H. Russell (USA).

A.Marsh fielded substitute for G. Wheatcroft, who failed to turn up on the third day.

Wide of the mark

Following the challenge put out by Shanghai Cricket Club to their counterparts in Hong Kong, the two sides met in February 1866. Shanghai's team consisted mainly of businessmen. Francis Groom worked for Glover and Company, a typical *hong* with interests ranging from steamships and guns to tea. Henry Dent was a highly regarded businessman associated with the local offices of Dent and Company, a wealthy British firm specialising in silk and tea, with a base in Hong Kong, and, at the time, a rival to Jardine. Alfred Dent was a relative newcomer to Shanghai, aged only 22. He later became famous with his brother Edward for establishing the North Borneo Chartered Company. The Hong Kong side were similarly made up of professional and business people. Edward Pollard was a barrister, in his early forties; he had been the legal adviser to Thomas Sutherland when the latter founded the Hong Kong and Shanghai Banking Corporation. George Maclean worked as a merchant's assistant for Lyall, Still and Company, a trader of plate and plated goods which went bankrupt in 1867. Thomas Lane was a long-standing resident, having in 1850, with Ninian Crawford, established Lane Crawford, still one of the leading local department stores. Lane had been the tradesmen's representative on the ad hoc committee set up in 1851 to oversee the transformation of the southern portion of the Army parade ground into a cricket ground for the Hong Kong club.

None of the players were known for their ability on the cricket field. Although the match is now recognised as the first between the territories of Hong Kong and Shanghai in a series of what became known as the Interports, it was really no more than a game between two moderate club sides. Shanghai were the weaker because selection of their team was restricted to those who could take leave from their business for several weeks and afford the costs of the journey. Hong Kong could choose from all the players in their club who were available for all three days of the match. Shanghai were further disadvantaged by having to play cricket while acclimatising to the local conditions and adjusting to being on land again after several days at sea. Also, the timing of the match in February meant that is was about two-thirds of the way through Hong Kong's cricket season, but four months after the end of Shanghai's.

Shanghai won the toss and batted first but their players clearly had difficulty defending straight balls. Five of their first six batsmen were bowled. In a late partnership, Henry Dent and Hearne played with care and effected a recovery of sorts, sufficient to take the score above 100. Mackenzie bowled throughout the innings and picked up five wickets. Groom dismissed Hong Kong's top order relatively cheaply, but the later batsmen took advantage of some very weak bowling. The visitors' lob bowlers were unable to find a consistent line and length and conceded 41 wides. Starkey was the most impressive, hitting the ball hard and to great distances. His 99 included one eight and one seven. Clifford played attractively for his 71 and with Mercer and Wallace contributing dashing displays, the home team accumulated 430, a huge total for the time. Groom persevered and was rewarded with seven wickets. Despite the onslaught, Shanghai fielded well. McDonnell, at long stop, was particularly impressive, letting only one bye and it was generally agreed that this was not his fault.

Totally outplayed and demoralised, Shanghai capitulated in their second innings. Welsh defended his stumps with his usual obstinacy, but no one else could deal with Mackenzie, who, again, bowled throughout for a return of seven wickets. With Hong Kong winning by an innings and 264 runs, the *Hong Kong Daily Press* wrote, in a masterly understatement, that it 'could not be considered a very close match'.

HONG KONG v SHANGHAI

Hong Kong Cricket Club, Chater Road, Hong Kong, 15, 16 and 17 February 1866

Hong Kong won by an innings and 264 runs

SHANGHAI

Batsman		R	B	M	4s	6s		R	B	M	4s	6s
D.Welsh	run out	6					c Lane b Starkey	38				
A.K.McDonnell	b Mackenzie	6					run out	10				
W.Inglis	b Case	11					c Bird b Mackenzie	0				
J.B.Manson	b Case	1					b Mackenzie	3				
F.A.Groom	b Case	2					b Mackenzie	0				
A.Dent	b Mackenzie	1					run out	0				
K.C.Dow	not out	2					not out	0				
H.Dent	c Case b Mackenzie	23					c Clifford b Mackenzie	2				
H.R.Hearne	b Pollard	25					b Mackenzie	0				
T.Merry	c Davidson b Mackenzie	7					b Mackenzie	0				
T.G.Weston	c Mercer b Mackenzie	0					c Bird b Mackenzie	0				
	b6 lb2 nb3 w12	23					b3 lb2 w1	6				
		107						**59**				

HONG KONG

Batsman		R	B	M	4s	6s
E.H.Pollard	c Merry b Groom	4				
D.H.Mackenzie	c Manson b Groom	13				
G.S.Bird	b Groom	28				
D.Davidson	c A.Dent b Groom	45				
R.D.Starkey	b Manson	99				
T.Mercer	b Groom	45				
T.A.Lane	b Groom	16				
T.Clifford	lbw b Groom	71				
G.F.MacLean	lbw b A.Dent	12				
E.Wallace	not out	43				
A.M.Case	c Groom b A.Dent	4				
	b1 lb8 w41	50				
		430				

Hong Kong	O	M	R	W	nb	w	O	M	R	W	nb	w	fow
Mackenzie				5						7			1
Case				3									2
Pollard				1									3
Starkey												1	4
													5

Shanghai	O	M	R	W	nb	w		fow
Groom				7				6
Manson				1				7
A.Dent				2				8
								9
								10

Umpires: [unknown]

Toss: Shanghai.

No bowling analyses have been published.

Four balls per over.

Protest preferred to victory

The Australians had just completed a very successful tour of Great Britain when they met Philadelphia in a three-day match beginning on 3 October 1878. The Philadelphians included four brothers; Charles, Daniel, Robert and George Newhall, members of a great cricketing family. Charles was a right-arm round-arm fast bowler who, in his career, dismissed W.G. Grace more frequently than any other American bowler. George was a reliable batsman and wicketkeeper, Daniel, a stubborn, defensive batsman, and Robert, probably the best American batsman of the time.

The first day was sunny and unseasonably warm for early October and a good crowd of some 5,000 turned out. With such a large attendance, a recognised boundary was in place. Hits to or beyond the boundary scored three; a strike out of the ground was required for a six. The Philadelphian captain, George Newhall, won the toss and decided to bat, even though one of the openers, Brewster, had not arrived. When he did, he only just had time to change before he had to go to the wicket and, even then, the start of play had been delayed until 12.20pm. He and the Leicestershire-born John Hargrave began cautiously and put on 28 against Spofforth and Garrett. After a change of bowling, Brewster cut a ball from Allan straight to Murdoch at point. Allan then deceived Charlie Newhall, the ball bouncing off his left pad on to the wicket. George Newhall scored runs quickly, but after 40 was added, he gave Spofforth his second catch of the innings. Caldwell helped raise the score above 100 before he was given out stumped, apparently a rather dubious decision.

After lunch, Hopkinson fell without scoring. Dan Newhall joined his brother Robert and they thwarted the Australians in a partnership of 59. Robert was unusually careful, making sure that his feet reached to the pitch of every ball and striking it along the ground, even though he was renowned for long lofted drives. One such, off the bowling of Boyle, produced a sharp chance, but the ball passed through the bowler's hands to the boundary. Another chance was given when he drove a ball from wide of the leg stump straight to short leg, who was fortunate to avoid injury. The visitors tried seven bowlers before the partnership was broken, Robert Newhall being bowled while trying to drive a shooter. He had batted for two and a half hours. His innings included one four, a drive into the pavilion, and 17 threes for hits beyond the boundary, each of which, if the older regulations had prevailed and they had been run for, would have yielded at least four and, in some instances, five or six. Dan Newhall continued to score, including a drive out of the ground for six and four threes, before he ran out of partners, the innings closing at the end of the first day on 196.

The second day was also fine and sunny and the attendance was somewhere between 8,000 and 10,000, a surprisingly large crowd for a Friday. Play began at 11.34am and Philadelphia soon had a wicket, Charles Bannerman being caught behind without scoring. Despite this early success, Meade, who was returning to cricket after an absence of three years, proved expensive and was soon replaced. When Horan was run out and Spofforth caught by Robert Newhall, the visitors were in trouble at 17/3. This became 20/4 when Gregory was out without scoring. Alex Bannerman, well known for his stonewalling, then held the innings together in partnership with Murdoch, but they found the bowling of Charlie and Dan Newhall exacting. It was as much as they could do to survive, so scoring was very slow. Murdoch narrowly missed being stumped when the ball slipped out of George Newhall's hands. The latter made amends soon after by catching Bannerman off the bowling of Charlie Newhall. This ended a partnership of 72, the highest of the match. Lunch was taken with the score on 92/5.

Eating must have been a very sociable and leisurely affair because it was 3.20pm before play resumed. Bailey immediately gave a catch to Meade and Dan Newhall bowled Murdoch with one of his slow twisters, which just clipped the bails. In spite of contributions from Blackham and Boyle, the Dan and Charlie Newhall combination proved too much for the visitors. Not only did they take wickets, they made scoring runs extremely difficult. At one point, frustrated by persistent blocking of balls by the batsmen, Dan Newhall resorted to slow underarm, but without success. The Australian innings concluded at 5pm for only 150 runs, made at an even slower scoring rate than the Philadelphians had achieved.

Although 15 minutes remained before the close, it was decided to end play for the day. With the home side leading by 46 runs, the spectators were feeling pleased with the proceedings. The crowd were also fortunate that a potentially serious accident had been avoided when the second storey of the porch to the Germantown Club House began to sag under the weight of the large number of members present. However, it was quickly noticed from below. All except the official scorers were evacuated and some heavy two-by-fours of yellow pine, conveniently located at the back of the club house, were placed as supports under the porch.

The weather held fair for the third day, a Saturday. Many of the mill owners, knowing the local interest in the match, declared a half-day holiday. It is estimated that over 15,000 people attended. The start of play was brought forward one hour to 11am but the players and officials showed little concern for punctuality and it was 11.40am before Philadelphia began their second innings.

Alex Bannerman was unable to take the field for the tourists, as he had sprained his ankle the previous evening when getting off a railroad car at the junction of Ninth and Green Street. Haines acted as substitute. Philadelphia lost two quick wickets as the Australians changed tactics. In the first innings, they had bowled to a length with a close-in field; this time they placed their fielders in the deep and bowled for catches. In the second over of the day, Brewster gave a return catch to Allan. Next over, a ball from Spofforth to John Hargrave went high into the air and was caught. Surprisingly, the Australians appealed for leg before rather than the catch, an appeal which was rejected by umpire Henry Brown. The Australians immediately appealed again, this time for the catch, but this was turned down on the grounds that the previous appeal implied that the ball had not hit the bat. The tourists showed considerable dissatisfaction with the outcome and gave the impression that they intended to leave the field in protest. Reluctantly, they accepted the umpire's decision and continued to play. The incident was not expensive as Hargrave soon fell to a splendid stumping by Blackham.

Philadelphia failed to adjust their tactics and tried, unsuccessfully, to slog the bowling. Wickets fell regularly. Typical was Robert Newhall, who attempted to hit his first ball over the club house and a long, steepling catch was taken one-handed by Boyle. At 12.35pm Dan Newhall went down the wicket to one of Allan's slower tempters, missed it, and before he could get back into his ground, Blackham had taken the ball and removed the bails, only for Brown, the umpire, to rule not out. Blackham handed the ball to Gregory, the Australian captain, who immediately threw it to the ground and called his men off the field in protest.

This was one of several umpiring decisions which displeased the visitors, who were also unhappy with the way the local umpires generally seemed to applaud every run scored by the home side. The *Philadelphia Inquirer* summed up the Australian feeling; the visitors apparently left the field in 'high dudgeon'. Although this did not mean that the Philadelphian umpires were necessarily biased, it certainly fuelled the visitors' suspicions that the poor decisions were the result of either inexperience or incompetence. Any sympathy for the Australians, however, was tempered by the reputation they had gained in England for disagreeing regularly with umpiring decisions.

The action of the Australians displeased the spectators. Not only did they want to get value for their admission charge of 25 cents, they were furious that the delay was reducing the chances of a result in the match. The Australians demanded that Henry Brown be replaced before they would agree to resume play. The Philadelphians stated that, if that were to occur, then the other umpire, H.F.J. Freeman, should also be replaced, a condition which the tourists refused to accept. With an impasse prevailing, A.A. Outerbridge, the president of the recently-founded Cricketers' Association of the United States, informed the tourists they if they were not going to resume play, they should leave the ground immediately. He told them that there were thousands of spectators who had paid their entrance fee and wanted to be entertained and that they should get out of the way so that a new match with a scratch XI could be organised. Spofforth asked him to allow the Australians a minute or so for consultation. Outerbridge agreed to this, the Australian players took a vote and, with a majority of eight to three, agreed to continue the match.

Whether the above truly represents what happened is uncertain. There is an alternative story, perhaps true or perhaps part of a conspiracy theory, that Outerbridge informed the Australian captain that the cheque for US$2,500 that he had received that morning as the visitors' share of the gate receipts, had been stopped and that if the Australians did not return to the field, they would not get any receipts for the third day. A coach was available on a private estate backing on to the ground which they could use to slip away, should they wish, thereby avoiding the wrath of the crowd. Whatever took place in the pavilion, the outcome was that Gregory took his players back on to the field, with the same two umpires, after a delay of 70 minutes.

On resumption, at 1.50pm, Philadelphia quickly lost two more wickets before lunch was taken 15 minutes later. After a slightly faster repast than usual, the Australians returned to the field at 2.50pm and 45 minutes later had dismissed the home side for a mere 53 runs. Spofforth and Allan bowled unchanged throughout the innings, picking up five wickets each. Australia were left to make 100 to win and, after a very rapid turn round between the innings, began their quest at 3.38pm. With just over one hour and 20 minutes before the scheduled close at 5pm, the task was certainly feasible.

Charlie Newhall bowled faster and from a longer run-up than usual and proved quite dangerous. He knocked out the right stump to dismiss Spofforth. Horan then drove a ball from Meade into Bob Newhall's hands to put the Australians on 15/2. Charles Bannerman and Bailey were confident and the score rose with some hard hits to the boundary, each worth three. By five past four the score had reached 32. Dan Newhall then replaced Meade in the attack. The Newhall brothers troubled the batsmen and the scoring rate slowed. By 4.31pm the total had risen only to 41, leaving a further 59 to be made in 29 minutes. In the next five overs they made only one more run.

Charles Bannerman played a fast yorker from Charlie Newhall on to his stumps. Another yorker accounted for Bailey, before the match ended in a draw with Australia still needing 44 runs and with six wickets left. The crowd mobbed Charlie Newhall and carried him over their heads to the club house, accompanied by considerable cheering. The spectators celebrated the home side's performance, which had far exceeded anything the Philadelphians had previously achieved. The match is now recognised as first-class, making Philadelphia the first team from an Associate or Affiliate country to play first-class cricket.

PHILADELPHIA v AUSTRALIANS

First-class

Germantown Cricket Club, Nicetown PA, 3, 4 and 5 October 1878

Match drawn

PHILADELPHIA

		R	B	M	4s	6s		R	B	M	4s	6s
John Hargrave	c&b Spofforth	10					st Blackham b Spofforth	7				
F.E.Brewster	c Murdoch b Allan	15					c&b Allan	0				
C.A.Newhall	b Allan	3					(8) lbw b Spofforth	5				
R.S.Newhall	b Allan	84	150		1		c Bailey b Spofforth	0				
*G.M.Newhall	c Spofforth b Horan	13					(7) c Gregory b Allan	2				
R.N.Caldwell	st Blackham b Boyle	22					b Allan	8				
E.Hopkinson	c Gregory b Bailey	0					(10) c Bailey b Spofforth	5				
D.S.Newhall	not out	31			1		(5) c Boyle b Spofforth	7				
+T.Hargrave	b Allan	1					(3) st Blackham b Allan	9				
E.T.Comfort	b Allan	3					(9) b Allan	4				
S.Meade	b Allan	0					not out	0				
	b8 lb6	14					b6	6				
		196						**53**				

AUSTRALIANS

		R	B	M	4s	6s		R	B	M	4s	6s
C.Bannerman	c G.M.Newhall b Meade	0					(2) b C.A.Newhall	27				
A.C.Bannerman	c G.M.Newhall b C.A.Newhall	46										
T.P.Horan	run out	5					c R.S.Newhall b Meade	0				
F.R.Spofforth	c R.S.Newhall b C.A.Newhall	4					(1) b C.A.Newhall	4				
*D.W.Gregory	b C.A.Newhall	0										
W.L.Murdoch	b D.S.Newhall	37					(5) not out	0				
G.H.Bailey	c Meade b C.A.Newhall	0					(4) b C.A.Newhall	24				
+J.M.Blackham	b D.S.Newhall	20					(6) not out	0				
T.W.Garrett	b C.A.Newhall	1										
H.F.Boyle	c T.Hargrave b D.S.Newhall	30										
F.E.Allan	not out	4										
	w3	3					b1	1				
		150					(4 wickets)	**56**				

Australians	O	M	R	W	w	nb		O	M	R	W	w	nb	fow	Ph (1)	Aus (1)	Ph (2)	Aus (2)
Spofforth	24	8	51	1	-	-		18.3	7	24	5	-	-	1	28 (2)	3 (1)	2 (2)	8 (1)
Garrett	13	5	26	0	-	-								2	28 (3)	10 (3)	19 (1)	15 (3)
Allan	20	4	27	6	-	-	(2)	18	6	23	5	-	-	3	33 (1)	17 (4)	19 (3)	53 (2)
Boyle	19	6	39	1	-	-								4	73 (5)	20 (5)	19 (4)	56 (4)
Horan	10	2	24	1	-	-								5	110 (6)	92 (2)	27 (5)	
Murdoch	10	2	10	0	-	-								6	119 (7)	92 (7)	37 (7)	
Bailey	4	1	5	1	-	-								7	178 (4)	102 (6)	44 (6)	
														8	188 (9)	103 (8)	44 (8)	
Philadelphia	O	M	R	W	w	nb		O	M	R	W	w	nb	9	196 (10)	115 (9)	53 (9)	
C.A.Newhall	52	28	67	5	-	-		18	9	29	3	-	-	10	196 (11)	150 (10)	53 (10)	
Meade	26	12	36	1	2	-		7	4	16	1	-	-					
Comfort	3	0	7	0	-	-												
Caldwell	2	0	3	0	1	-												
D.S.Newhall	26.1	14	34	3	-	-	(3)	10	5	10	0	-	-					

Umpires: H.W.Brown and H.F.J.Freeman

Toss: Philadelphia.

4 balls per over. Hits to the boundary scored 3 runs, not 4.

Close of play: 1st day – Philadelphia (1) 196 all out; 2nd day – Australians (1) 150 all out.

John Hargrave and T.Hargrave are also known as John Hargreave and T.Hargreave.

C.Haines (Philadelphia) field substitute for A.C.Bannerman on the third day.

Frustrated by grubs

In July 1890, an Irish side travelled to Scotland for a match at the Grange Cricket Club in Edinburgh. Scotland fielded a strong team even though, for reasons which were never made clear, those responsible for the selection omitted Leslie Balfour-Melville, Scotland's leading cricketer of the day and the captain of the host club. Typical of the time, the Scottish side was amateur, but made up of professional people. It contained three solicitors, two stockbrokers, two teachers, a university administrator and a doctor. The latter, George Thornton, became the head of the Government Hospital in Pretoria, after serving in the Boer War. He played for South Africa in 1902/03 before migrating to Ceylon, for which he also played, touring India in 1909/10.

The team also included Malcolm Jardine, the father of Douglas Jardine. There were three who had represented Scotland in rugby union, Henry Stevenson, Andrew Don Wauchope and Gus Asher, who was also the Scottish pole vault champion in 1885 and 1886. The Irish side included three barristers and two solicitors, as well as William Vint, who had played first-class cricket for Victoria (1884/85), and Clement Johnson, who later represented South Africa (1895/96) where he settled on medical advice.

Don Wauchope won the toss for Scotland and, in fine weather, chose to bat. A very leisurely approach to playing hours was taken, so that the match did not get under way until 12.18pm. Scotland lost two early wickets but Stevenson and Asher took the score to 70 when lunch was taken. After the interval, Stevenson was caught at cover, having batted for an hour and a half for his 12 runs, and Asher was run out, his 70 being made without giving a chance. Johnston and Mannes supported Macgregor in partnerships of 81 and 45, before MacGregor missed a straight ball from Synott. Mannes and Don Wauchope engaged in some long hitting, the former driving one ball out of the ground on the northern side. Both fell to the bowling of Booth, who picked up five wickets, as Ireland tried seven bowlers in an attempt to regain control. Facing a large total, Ireland began badly against hostile bowling from Thornton, but Meldon and Nunn batted well and took the total to 65 by the close of play at 7pm.

Despite the second day being scheduled to begin at 11.30am, it was just before midday when the match resumed. The overnight pair extended their partnership until, with the score on 117, Trotter took a splendid return catch to remove Nunn. None of the other batsmen lasted long and Ireland were forced to follow on. Initially, they responded strongly with Meldon and Nunn putting on 115. Browning combined with Meldon to take the score to 154, but Ireland were unable to maintain the momentum and from 183/2, they lost eight wickets for the addition of another 40 runs.

A drawn game looked inevitable as Scotland needed 96 runs to win with an uncertain amount of time in which to make them. Play was initially fixed to end at 6pm, but the visitors agreed to change this to add an extra half an hour and then extend to 6.40pm if there was a chance of a result, even though they then risked missing their train for the journey home.

Opening with Johnston and Mannes, Scotland attacked from the outset, resulting in much applause and cheering from the good-sized crowd. The first 30 runs were made in 12 minutes and the 50 was reached in 18. Nunn, the Irish captain, turned to Vint and asked him to bowl 'grubs' in order to prevent the Scottish batsmen from scoring. Many of the spectators considered this an unfair tactic. Vint bowled eight overs of the stuff. After Johnston and MacGregor were both run out, Asher and Mannes added 30, but in much excitement, Scotland finished two runs short with six wickets in hand. It is likely that one more over would have been sufficient to secure a home victory. While Ireland were heavily criticised, their captain had agreed to the extension of time, without which even a chance of victory would not have been possible.

SCOTLAND v IRELAND

Grange Cricket Club, Raeburn Place, Edinburgh, 11 and 12 July 1890

Match drawn

SCOTLAND		R	B	M	4s	6s		R	B	M	4s	6s
J.A.Allan	c Fleming b Hughes	11		1	-		(4) b Vint	1			-	-
M.R.Jardine	b Johnson	1			-	-	(5) b Johnson	4			1	-
H.J.Stevenson	c Thompson b Hughes	12	90	1	-							
A.G.G.Asher	run out	70			4	-	(6) not out	17			3	-
+G.MacGregor	b Booth	68			7	-	(3) run out	5			1	-
R.H.Johnston	b Synott	37			3	-	(1) run out	24			2	-
C.T.Mannes	c Vint b Booth	31			1	1	(2) not out	42			5	-
*A.R.Don Wauchope	b Booth	37			5	-						
J.J.Trotter	c Johnson b Booth	0			-	-						
G.Thornton	not out	12			2	-						
F.K.Weir	c Johnson b Booth	0			-	-						
	b23 lb2	25					lb1	1				
		304					(4 wickets)	**94**				

IRELAND		R	B	M	4s	6s		R	B	M	4s	6s
F.H.Browning	c MacGregor b Thornton	1			-	-	(3) b Trotter	10			-	-
M.W.Gavin	b Thornton	12			2	-	(4) c MacGregor b Trotter	15			-	-
J.M.Meldon	b Trotter	59			8	-	(2) run out	92			7	-
W.F.Thompson	c Don Wauchope b Weir	8			-	-	(5) b Thornton	6			-	-
*J.H.Nunn	c&b Trotter	33			3	-	(1) c Stevenson b Mannes	60			8	-
+W.Vint	b Mannes	4			-	-	(7) b Weir	4			1	-
W.J.Synott	st MacGregor b Stevenson	14			-	-	(6) c Jardine b Weir	20			2	-
J.L.Fleming	b Mannes	3			-	-	(9) b Stevenson	1			-	-
C.L.Johnson	b Stevenson	20			-	-	(8) c Stevenson b Weir	7			1	-
W.Booth	b Stevenson	9			-	-	b Weir	0			-	-
T.Hughes	not out	1			-	-	not out	0			-	-
	b2 lb7 nb1 w2	12			-	-	b4 lb3 nb1	8				
		176						**223**				

Ireland	O	M	R	W	nb	w		O	M	R	W	nb	w	fow	Sco (1)	Ire (1)	Ire (2)	Sco (2)
Hughes	28	8	62	2	-	-	(2)	2	0	20	0	-	-	1	12 (2)	10 (1)	115 (1)	50 (1)
Johnson	35	16	60	1	-	-	(1)	11	0	42	1	-	-	2	12 (1)	18 (2)	154 (3)	57 (3)
Booth	16.3	6	44	5	-	-								3	80 (3)	41 (4)	183 (2)	59 (4)
Fleming	22	6	56	0	-	-	(3)	8	0	10	0	-	-	4	112 (4)	117 (5)	183 (4)	64 (5)
Nunn	9	4	26	0	-	-								5	193 (6)	126 (6)	209 (5)	
Meldon	1	0	7	0	-	-								6	238 (5)	126 (3)	209 (6)	
Synott	8	3	24	1	-	-								7	249 (7)	129 (8)	214 (7)	
Vint					(4)			8	4	21	1	-	-	8	253 (9)	160 (9)	223 (8)	
														9	292 (8)	173 (7)	223 (9)	
Scotland	O	M	R	W	nb	w		O	M	R	W	nb	w	10	304 (11)	176 (10)	223 (10)	
Weir	24	11	34	1	-	2		30.1	11	54	4	-	-					
Thornton	24	11	47	2	-	-	(3)	10	3	28	1	-	-					
Mannes	16	6	33	2	1	-	(5)	6	0	20	1	1	-					
Trotter	21	9	33	2	-	-	(2)	14	2	47	2	-	-					
Stevenson	5.3	0	17	3	-	-	(4)	21	3	66	1	-	-					

Umpires: [unknown]

Toss: Scotland.

5 balls per over.

Close of play: 1st day – Ireland (1) 65-2 (Nunn 10*, Meldon 32*).

The SS *Bokhara* tragedy

After the second Interport match in 1867, no more matches were played between Hong Kong and Shanghai until 1889. The long sea journey and the resulting time away from home clearly inhibited further contacts. However, new steamships were reducing the travel time to three days and Hong Kong's players were more inclined to travel again in search of opportunities to meet teams from overseas.

By the time Hong Kong visited Shanghai in October 1892, the Interport series was becoming well-established. Even so, several of Hong Kong's top players declined to go, citing business reasons, and the team had to be reinforced from the military. The party of 13 included nine from the Army. The problem for both sides was still one of limited resources. In the early 1890s there were only some 1,700 men in Hong Kong classed as European or American and only a small proportion of these would have been interested in playing cricket. Not that Shanghai had any greater riches; there were only 3,821 foreigners in the International Settlement in 1890. Hong Kong were captained by John Dunn, an Army officer posted to the Territory in 1889, the year he made 107, the first century in Interport matches, which led to him being affectionately known as 'The Grace of the East'. Born in Tasmania, he moved to England at the age of nine and after education at Harrow School and the Royal Military College, Sandhurst, joined the Liverpool Regiment. While serving in Dublin, he played cricket for Ireland, being a member of that country's North American touring party in 1888.

The 1892 fixture was played on a Monday and a Tuesday. These were the most convenient days in relation to the steamship timetables. The Hong Kong team arrived in Shanghai on board the SS *Brindisi* on the morning of 1 October. A report in the local press states that they were greeted by a large crowd, but one suspects that this was not necessarily extraordinary; it is likely that the arrival of any ship in the port with a reasonable number of disembarking passengers was met by friends, relatives and local officials. In the evening the visitors were entertained to dinner by Shanghai Cricket Club. The following morning, they practised at the Shanghai Cricket Club ground before being given tiffin by the Shanghai Recreation Club. An informal practice match was played in the afternoon.

Whether one day was sufficient to acclimatise was always less than certain. Not only was there the need to get used to being on land again, after days at sea, but many cricketers who played at Shanghai referred to the rather special light conditions which took some time to get used to and often led to missed catches and misfields. The Hong Kong team were certainly short of match practice, since the fixture was scheduled before the Hong Kong cricket season had started. On Sunday 3 October, the Shanghai Tandem Club arranged for the players to take a long-distance carriage ride to Unkaza.

The 1892 contest began at 11am the following day, with Shanghai winning the toss and choosing to bat. There was what the local press described as a large crowd, though given the number of Europeans resident in Shanghai with an interest in cricket, it seems unlikely that it could have been more than 1,000. In Lowson's first over, William Moule hit two runs and was then bowled by a yorker. In the next over, bowled by Donegan, Wood might have been caught by the wicketkeeper, but the appeal was rejected. Lowson worked up a good pace and bowled Abbott with a ball of full length and then disposed of Wallace.

Hong Kong bowled few bad balls and runs came slowly, particularly against Mumford's underarm lobs, most of which were trundlers that the batsmen could only block. Neverthless, after 50 minutes of play, the score reached 40. On 45, Arthur Moule was caught by Donegan in the slips and Barff immediately followed, caught by Jeffkins at point. Mann brought up the 50 with a four off Lowson but the bowler soon took his revenge with another good delivery. Bruce-Robertson raised Shanghai's spirits before lunch by taking nine in one over from Lowson. Tiffin was taken with the score on 64/6, all six falling to Lowson, who bowled unchanged throughout the session.

Play restarted at 2pm. The home side soon lost Bruce-Robertson and Crawford. Carruthers, who had learnt his cricket at Fettes College, set about the visitors' bowling with dash and freedom. He and Wood, who remained circumspect, engaged in some fast running between the wickets, so that the score went up in boundaries and singles. By 2.30pm, Shanghai had increased their total to 82. Donegan returned to the attack in place of Mumford, who had bowled 11 maidens in his 18 overs and conceded only 18 runs. In Donegan's first over, Carruthers was badly missed by Dunn, who dropped an easy catch at mid-off. It seems that Dunn's vision was not very good and that he had been suffering from astigmatism. Carruthers was then missed in turn by Jeffkins, Donegan and Jeffkins, again. Perhaps all were struggling with Shanghai's special light. The breakthrough came on 109 when Wood was caught at the wicket to end a patient innings of two and a half hours. By mid-afternoon, the home side were all out for a mere 112. Lowson bowled throughout the innings, a spell of 37 overs, and well deserved his eight wickets.

The visitors commenced their reply at 3.15pm against the pace of Barff and the spin of Carruthers. After some positive strokes, Lowson was struck by a fast ball from Barff and considerably discomforted by his injury. Not surprisingly, he succumbed to another fast delivery which not only hit the stumps; it then continued unhindered past the wicketkeeper and into the pavilion. Dunn joined Jeffkins, but against good bowling and clean fielding, they were able to score few runs. On 33, Jeffkins was bowled and Donegan played on, both wickets falling to Carruthers. Dunn and Markham kept the score moving until Carruthers produced a virtually unplayable ball, which broke wildly off the pitch to remove Dunn.

Thereafter, the visitors offered little and Dunn's 16 proved to be their highest individual score. Boyle brought up the 50, but without further addition to the score, Abbott pulled off a magnificent left-handed catch at short leg to dismiss Markham. Soon after, Mann made another great catch at long slip to account for Boyle, securing the ball a short distance from the ground and holding on to it, despite rolling over. Taverner should have been run out straight away but the wicketkeeper failed to take a splendid throw by Crawford. Nichol had Dawson caught by Arthur Moule at point. In the next over, Wallace was let off by Barff who was unable to hang on to the ball in what would have been the best catch of the match. The miss was not expensive as the innings did not last much longer. The visitors were all out just before the close of play with a deficit of 34 runs. Like Hong Kong, Shanghai used only three bowlers.

Play began on the second day at 11.15am. The home team did not take advantage of their first-innings lead. On the contrary, despite the absence of Lowson from the bowling attack, they began badly. William Moule skied the ball to the wicketkeeper, Wood was given out leg before, Abbott was bowled by one of Mumford's grubs and Wallace fell to Donegan. With four wickets down for only 24 runs, Carruthers was promoted in the order to join Arthur Moule. Following his display in the first innings, Hong Kong placed fielders in the outfield and bowled to induce catches. The plan would have worked, only Markham misjudged a skier and Carruthers survived.

While Moule had difficulty with Mumford's underarm and was forced to block most balls, Carruthers made runs, including an all-run five after hitting Jeffkins to the outfield on the leg side. After he fell to Mumford for a well-played 30, Barff partnered Moule in an excellent stand. The score rose from 75 to 110 before a chance was offered, Moule surviving after T. Wallace, a Shanghai player fielding as substitute for Lowson, was unable to take a far from easy catch. In the absence of Lowson, the Shanghai pair mastered the bowling. Hong Kong did not help themselves by failing to run out Barff, when the score was 140, and missing a chance offered by Moule to Taverner in the slips. When tiffin was taken, the score was 165/5.

Hong Kong's fielding was no better after the break. Wallace missed a somewhat easier catch offered by Barff and Burnett dropped Moule in the long field. Barff was eventually bowled, after which Shanghai's innings fell apart. Mann was run out when Moule refused to take a perfectly safe single, Bruce-Robertson became another casualty of Mumford and Crawford was caught first ball.

Nichol, the last man, opted to hit out and struck Dunn over the pavilion for six. He tried to repeat the stroke next ball and should have been caught on the boundary by Burnett, but the fielder let the ball slip through his hands. The last-wicket partnership was fast and furious and amounted to 27 before Moule was bowled. Shanghai's lead of 236 was largely due to a superb display by Arthur Moule and Barff, who, between them, amassed 65 per cent of their side's runs. The rest never came to grips with Mumford's grubs and failed to take advantage of Hong Kong's inept catching.

A target of 237 to win always seemed an unlikely prospect but a draw should have been a possibility, even though the wicket was deteriorating to Carruthers's advantage. Donegan quickly became Carruthers's first victim, followed immediately by Dunn who was bowled first ball. Markham and Jeffkins played with care and the score rose from 2/2 to 38 before Markham was leg before to Nichol. Lowson then came to the crease, accompanied by Dunn as a runner. Jeffkins fell to a smart catch by Mann at mid-on, Boyle failed to last long and Dawson was caught at the wicket by Bruce-Robertson, who gave a fine display behind the stumps throughout the match. Taverner and Lowson defended well to give the visitors hope, but Lowson, handicapped by his injury, mistimed a ball from Carruthers and skied another catch to Mann. Taverner continued to resist, but to no avail. Carruthers finished off the innings to take eight wickets and get a match return of 13-70. Overall, Hong Kong gave a poor display in a match dominated by bowlers. Shanghai's seemingly easy victory, however, owed much to one important partnership and an injury to Hong Kong's leading bowler.

The visitors were given dinner on the Wednesday evening at Shanghai Cricket Club, an event attended by some 130 hosts and guests. Entertainment was provided by the Town Band. On the Thursday, they were entertained at a Smoking Concert at the Lyceum Theatre, organised by the Shanghai Literary and Debating Society. The cricketers left Shanghai on 8 October, on the SS *Bokhara*, and were due in Hong Kong three days later. By 14 October there were grave fears about the fate of the ship. The presence of a typhoon in the South China Sea had been noted in the Hong Kong press soon after the team's departure from Shanghai. The SS *Bokhara* foundered against a reef on Sand Island in the Pescadores, off Taiwan, and sank in less than two minutes.

Of the 143 crew and 25 passengers, 125 people drowned. Only two passengers survived, John Lowson and Lieutenant Frank Markham. Lowson was severely affected by the experience and had to have a lung removed. Despite this, he continued in his post at the Government Hospital where he was promoted to Medical Superintendent in 1894 at the age of only 28. In the same year, he received notoriety as the person who identified the outbreak of bubonic plague in the Colony and worked with Japanese medical experts to bring it under control. He also became Hong Kong's golf champion in 1895, 1896 and 1899. He returned to the United Kingdom and died in Scotland in 1935. Markham stayed in the Army and was promoted to captain; he died in London in 1909.

SHANGHAI v HONG KONG

Shanghai Cricket Club, Nanjing Lu, Shanghai, 3 and 4 October 1892

Shanghai won by 157 runs

SHANGHAI		R	B	M	4s	6s		R	B	M	4s	6s
W.H.Moule	b Lowson	2					c Dawson b Mumford	9				
A.P.Wood	c Dawson b Lowson	25	150				lbw b Donegan	0				
F.J.Abbott	b Lowson	16					b Mumford	13				
P.Wallace	b Lowson	4					b Donegan	0				
A.J.H.Moule	c Donegan b Lowson	10					b Dunn	78				
C.S.Barff	c Jeffkins b Lowson	0					(7) b Mumford	53				
J.Mann	b Lowson	7					(8) run out	0				
*+W.Bruce-Robertson	b Mumford	11					(9) b Mumford	1				
D.W.Crawford	b Lowson	2					(10) c Burnett b Mumford	0				
A.G.H.Carruthers	not out	30					(6) b Mumford	30				
A.P.Nichol	c Lowson b Donegan	2					not out	12				
	b1 lb2	3					b6	6				
		112						**202**				

HONG KONG		R	B	M	4s	6s		R	B	M	4s	6s
J.A.Lowson	b Barff	10					(5) c Mann b Carruthers	15				
QMS F.G.Jeffkins	b Carruthers	13					(1) c Mann b Carruthers	12				
*Capt J.Dunn	b Carruthers	16					b Carruthers	0				
Sgt T.W.Donegan	b Carruthers	0					(2) b Carruthers	2				
Capt F.D.Markham	c Abbott b Barff	6					(4) lbw b Nichol	19				
Lt G.G.Boyle	c Mann b Barff	5					b Carruthers	4				
+Capt R.H.Dawson	c A.J.H.Moule b Nichol	7					c Bruce-Robertson b Barff	2				
G.E.Taverner	b Carruthers	7					b Carruthers	16				
C.Wallace	lbw b Carruthers	9					b Carruthers	2				
Lt F.A.Burnett	b Barff	0					(11) not out	0				
Sgt G.Mumford	not out	0					(10) b Carruthers	2				
	lb5	5					lb4 nb1	5				
		78						**79**				

Hong Kong	O	M	R	W	nb	w	O	M	R	W	nb	w	fow	Sh (1)	HK (1)	Sh (2)	HK (2)
Lowson	37	19	66	8	-	-							1	2 (1)	16 (1)	9 (1)	2 (2)
Donegan	21	8	25	1	-	- (1)	12	2	34	2	-	-	2	20 (3)	33 (2)	9 (2)	2 (3)
Mumford	18	11	18	1	-	- (2)	23	5	68	6	-	-	3	26 (4)	33 (4)	23 (3)	38 (4)
Taverner							2	0	14	0	-	-	4	45 (5)	42 (3)	25 (4)	40 (1)
Jeffkins							7	2	22	0	-	-	5	45 (6)	50 (5)	75 (6)	?? (6)
Wallace							2	1	4	0	-	-	6	53 (7)	?? (6)	??? (7)	?? (7)
Dunn							11.3	0	45	1	-	-	7	66 (8)	65 (7)	??? (8)	67 (5)
Boyle							2	0	9	0	-	-	8	68 (9)	73 (8)	??? (9)	68 (9)
													9	109 (2)	78 (9)	175 (10)	77 (8)
Shanghai	O	M	R	W	nb	w	O	M	R	W	nb	w	10	112 (11)	78 (10)	202 (5)	79 (10)
Barff	19	7	33	4	-	-	18	10	26	1	1	-					
Carruthers	21	7	29	5	-	-	21.1	6	41	8	-	-					
Nichol	3	0	11	1	-	-	4	1	7	1	-	-					

Umpires: J.L.Scott (Shanghai) and J.T.Turner (Hong Kong)

Toss: Shanghai

Five balls per over

Close of play: 1st day – Hong Kong (1) – 78 all out.

3

The Golden Age 1890–1914

THE PERIOD from 1890 to 1914 is often described as 'The Golden Age' of cricket. Rowland Bowen in his *Cricket: A History Of Its Growth And Development Throughout The World* considers it the age when cricket reached a degree of perfection which has not been attained either before or since. David Frith, in his *Golden Age Of Cricket*, refers to the 'seductive charm' of the late-Victorian and Edwardian periods. It was a time when cricket was seemingly played in a sportsmanlike manner with much friendliness and respect between the players. Although some of this idealism can be put down to hindsight's ability to concentrate on the good times past in comparison to the worst of the present day and its appeal is perhaps heightened by the contrast with what followed when it was ended so abruptly by the horrors of the First World War, there is certainly much to be appreciated. For the countries which are now Associate or Affiliate Members of the ICC, it was the period at which six were accorded first-class status, a number not repeated until the 2000s. It was the peak of cricket in Philadelphia, where it was increasingly the preserve of the leisured class and took on many of the characteristics of country house matches in England.

The Golden Age saw players, who had previously appeared in first-class cricket in England, Australia, South Africa, the West Indies, New Zealand and India, turning out in matches in the Associate and Affiliate countries, whence they had migrated to pursue their non-cricketing careers. Many went on to represent their new countries of residence and perform important roles in developing cricket in their adopted country. This movement contrasts with that of today, when the first-class teams of the Full Member countries frequently poach the best players from the Associates and Affiliates and either prevent them from playing for their country of origin or, at least, restrict their appearances.

By the start of The Golden Age, Philadelphia was already recognised as first-class. In mid-February 1895, they were joined in that status by Fiji. Cricket had taken hold in Fiji between 1878 and 1886 under the governorship of Sir George des Voeux, who was a keen cricketer and took pains to appoint like-minded spirits as his private secretaries. These actively coached the Fijians, gaining the support of the local chiefs, who became very enthusiastic and ensured that cricket was spread throughout the islands. With its predominantly rural population, Fiji failed to follow the trend of cricket becoming an essentially urban activity and, in a throwback to the origins of the game in south-east England, cricket became a sport of the countryside.

By the late 1880s, cricket had declined in the capital, Suva, where the European population preferred tennis to cricket as their sport of relaxation. Its revival was due almost entirely to the efforts of John Symons Udal. A barrister by training, he was appointed Attorney General in 1890. He set about renovating the facilities in the capital, at Albert Park, and promoted competitive matches between the islands and against the crews of visiting ships, as a means of raising the standard. By 1893, he considered cricket in Suva to be strong enough for more serious opposition. He invited the Australian tourists on their way to England via the Pacific Ocean and North America, to play a one-day match against a Suva XVI. The Australians were to be given lunch with the Governor, Sir John Bates Thurston, who was also the president of Suva Cricket Club. Thurston was an amateur botanist and a specialist in the plants of the South Pacific. He established the Suva Botanical Gardens, later renamed Thurston Gardens. Thurston's palm (*Pritchardia thurstonii*) was named in his honour. Unfortunately, the cricket match never happened. Some of the passengers on the ship, RMS *Warrimoo*, contracted measles, and the Australians found themselves quarantined and not allowed to land.

Undaunted, Udal decided on a more ambitious venture, a tour of New Zealand. While visiting that country in 1893, he approached the various cricketing associations with a proposal, which was very well received. Arrangements were made for a tour in early 1895. He wanted Fiji to be represented by its best possible side, but had to overcome the opposition of the Governor in order to include some Fijians, alongside the European players. Fortunately, he had William Allardyce, the native commissioner, on his side and, together, they finally persuaded the Governor to agree to the release of six Fijians from their government posts, for a period of seven weeks, entrusting them to the care of Udal and Allardyce to protect them from any 'unsettling or corrupting influences'.

Responsibility fell, in the end, solely on Udal's shoulders because Allardyce had to remain behind to oversee relief efforts following a hurricane which swept the country two weeks before the team's departure. Philip Snow, in his *Cricket in the Fiji Islands*, considers the chosen touring party to be the strongest available. The selection of Udal as captain was viewed as logical and inevitable, despite his 47 years of age. Only one other member of the team, Alex Joske, was born in England. He was the manager of the merchants, Brown and Joske. Four of the other white cricketers, Reginald Caldwell, John Collins, Islay McOwan and Warner Groom, were Australian. The willingness of Australians like these to further their professional careers in Fiji, represent the country internationally and help develop Fijian cricket was in marked contrast to the attitude of the Australian government some 15 years later, when serious objections were raised to the prospect of a Fijian tour of Australia. The sixth white cricketer in the touring part was Henry Scott, the acting attorney general, who was born in Fiji; he later became Sir Henry Milne Scott.

The most important of the six Fijians in the party was Ratu Penaia Kadavulevu. At the time he was the head of the principal hereditary family in Fiji, being the grandson of Ratu Ebenezer Cakobau, who was the paramount chief or 'king' of Fiji when the islands were ceded to Queen Victoria in 1874. All the Fijians were chiefs, four, including Kadavulevu, hailing from Bau and two from Rewa. During the Golden Age, Bau became the focal point of Fijian rather than European cricket in the country, a quite remarkable achievement for an eight-hectare island with a population of no more than 4,000, off the east coast of the main island of Viti Levu, to which it is connected by a causeway. Kadavulevu had the *rara*, the equivalent of the village green, enlarged by pulling down several houses and he converted the local temple into a cricket pavilion. All the Fijians played in white shirts and white *sulus*, preferring the latter, traditional, kilt-like skirt to trousers. Although they wore pads and gloves when batting, they played in bare feet instead of cricket boots. This contrast in clothing created considerable interest at all the venues they played in New Zealand.

Perhaps the most surprising aspect of the tour was that six of the eight matches were rated first-class. These were the ones against the provinces that, at the time, were accorded first-class status by the New Zealand Cricket Association. Given that, by comparison with cricket in England and Australia, the first-class status of New Zealand teams was certainly debatable, the decision to award that status to matches against even weaker opposition was questionable, particularly as all the games were only of two days' duration. However, there is no record of the decision being criticised. Matches between Scotland and Ireland were recognised as first-class in 1909 and, in 1912, Argentina became the fifth Associate country to achieve that status. Britain was a major investor in agriculture and railways in the country and the British population comprised mainly farmers, plantation owners, bankers, industrialists, civil engineers and railway engineers. Although in the early 1900s, a quarter of the 7.9 million population of Argentina were immigrants, these were largely Italians and Spaniards. The British formed a very small minority. Nevertheless, this was the largest British community outside the Commonwealth.

The British replicated their way of life, setting up their own sporting clubs and schools. Harrods opened a branch in Buenos Aires in 1912, their only representation outside of London and which was not closed until 1996. With the British population being essentially middle-class and a high proportion of the men coming from public schools, it was not surprising that cricket was an important social activity. Indeed, many were prepared to travel considerable distances just to play. Those involved in running the sugar plantations in Tucumán attracted cricketers from Córdoba, some 600km to the south, for occasional weekend matches. In 1868, a team from Buenos Aires travelled across the Plata estuary, an overnight sea journey, to meet their counterparts in Montevideo, and thereby initiate a series which was played intermittently up to the start of the Second World War. In 1893, some players journeyed for three and a half days by mule over the Andes, through the Uspallata Pass, to play the Santiago club in Chile.

Cricket was certainly of good club or close to Minor County standard. In order to promote the game the Argentine Cricket Championships Committee was formed. In the early 1910s, the committee members were impressed by the high standards of many of the new British immigrants, men like Harold Garnett, who had played first-class for Lancashire and been selected for the 1901/02 tour of Australia, Evelyn Toulmin, who had played for Essex, and Sydney Cowper, who had represented Western Province in South Africa. The committee felt that Argentine cricket was strong enough to meet English opposition so, perhaps somewhat audaciously, they invited MCC to send a touring party. Not only did MCC accept, they chose a strong amateur team under the captaincy of Lord Martin Hawke, which included four other Test players, Archie McLaren, Morice Bird, Arthur Hill and Neville Tufnell. The tour was a considerable adventure. The party of 12 left Southampton on the SS *Asturias* on 26 January 1912, and did not arrive back in England until 6 April. While in Argentina, they played nine matches, including three three-day 'Tests' against a representative Argentine side. It was these three matches that MCC designated first-class. With five countries – Argentina, Fiji, Ireland, Scotland and the United States (Philadelphia) – involved in first-class cricket, the Golden Age had laid the basis for the game's international development outside of what became the Test-playing countries. There was great enthusiasm for cricket and a standard of play at Minor County or good club level in Bermuda, Canada, Hong Kong, Federated Malay States, Shanghai and the Straits Settlements.

Cricket of a good standard was also found in Burma and Siam. Burma lost to Ceylon in 1894, but beat Malaya in 1906 and won their second match against Ceylon in 1912. Siam won two matches against the Straits Settlements in 1909 and 1910, but lost in 1911. Neither Burma nor Siam, however, had the number of players required to put the game on a permanent footing. International matches also began in the 1900s between the Gold Coast and Nigeria. As in Hong Kong and Malaya, these were organised by the British settlers, but in 1907, well-educated, middle-class Africans arranged their own internationals, independent of the expatriates. Egypt's international fixtures began in 1907 with a match at Lord's against the MCC. The latter then toured Egypt in 1909, winning a three-match series 2-1. The Egyptian team was selected from the military, the civil service and other settlers. Within Europe, next to Scotland and Ireland, cricket was strongest in The Netherlands where the game was played and administered by the Dutch. Dutch sides toured England in 1901 and 1906. Cricket also featured in the Brussels Exhibition in 1910, when The Netherlands, France, Belgium and MCC were all involved in matches.

Philadelphia surprise

Philadelphia's 1878 match against the Australians turned out to be a one-off in terms of standard. For the next few years, matches against touring sides from both England and Australia were played with odds and resulted in heavy defeats. A Philadelphia XV lost to R. Daft's side by 145 runs in 1879 and a Philadelphia XII were beaten by an innings and 104 runs by J. Lillywhite's XI in 1881. The Australians won by nine wickets over a Philadelphian XVIII in 1882. Despite these setbacks, the Philadelphians were determined to further the sport and compete effectively on the world stage with, at least, the best of the amateur players. They managed to raise some US$8,000 to fund a tour of the British Isles in 1884. Not only did they benefit from the experience, they impressed the English sufficiently to encourage E.J. Sanders to take parties of amateur players to North America in September of 1885 and 1886. Matches between the tourists and Philadelphia were played on equal terms and are now considered as first-class. Further improvements in standard resulted from a second tour of Britain in 1889 after which Lord M.B. Hawke organised a tour to the United States and Canada in 1891. Again the matches with Philadelphia were first-class. Within ten years, the cricketers of Philadelphia had achieved their ambition of moving from a reasonable club standard to being recognised as on a par with the English counties. When the Australians, returning home via North America following a tour of Britain, went to Philadelphia in 1893, two first-class matches were arranged.

Exactly why the Australians agreed to the arrangements before the first game, beginning on 29 September, will, perhaps, never be known. After finishing their last match in England on 9 September, the tourists had ten days of rest before boarding the SS *Germanic* for the crossing to New York. The journey took just over nine days, which was the norm for the time, so the Australians docked in New York on the morning of the scheduled first day's play. A tug was used to take the visitors and their luggage off the ship for transfer to a private train at Jersey City, specially-commissioned from Colonel John Green's private railroad, and onward transport to Belmont Cricket Club's new ground at Chestnut Avenue in Elmwood, a suburb to the south of Philadelphia, near the 49th Street Railroad Station.

Within only a few hours of coming from a rolling ship, the Australians were in Belmont's new club and reception house, a three-storey building in Gothic style, built of wood, stone and brick. On arrival, they practised for an hour and then had lunch. At 1pm, Patterson, the Philadelphian captain, won the toss and elected to bat. The attendance was a tad disappointing at just over 2,000; it might have been more if the arrival of the Australians had been more certain and the prospect of play more definite. Compared to previous Philadelphian home matches, there was only one four-in-hand coach at the ground. There were a few carriages of lighter build, but with the new railroad, most spectators had come by train. There was a service from the town every few minutes. In cold weather, with many of the crowd in heavy wraps, Philadelphia began well but cautiously, as Patterson and Reynolds Brown made 46 in the opening stand, before Brown fell to a good catch behind the wicket off the bowling of Trumble. Patterson entertained the crowd by hitting three consecutive boundaries, but then let himself down by misjudging a run, causing Scott to be run out. Patterson and Wood consolidated the home side's position until, with the score on 124, Patterson made another misjudgement and ran himself out. When Wood was bowled by Bruce soon after, the match was evenly poised. However, by mid-afternoon, the exertions of the journey from England were beginning to tell and the Australians, who had looked stiff in the field, were becoming increasingly tired.

Bohlen and Noble were allowed to score freely, but their efforts were not error free. What chances were offered, however, were put down; Bohlen was dropped twice. By the close of play, he was on 83 and Noble on 73, with Philadelphia having made an impressive 297/4. As the batsmen made their way to the pavilion at the 5.15pm close, the crowd came on to the field to cheer them. Bohlen and Noble acknowledged the gesture by raising their caps. In the evening, the Australians were entertained by a visit to the Broad Street Theater though, by then, many were probably too exhausted to appreciate the programme. Play on the second day, a Saturday, began at 11.30am, with a crowd of some 15,000, proving, without doubt, that cricket in Philadelphia was still popular. The visitors' bowling showed a marked improvement on that of the first day and 15 runs were added slowly before Noble was bowled by Trumble after adding only six to his overnight score. The partnership had been worth 180 which is still the American record for the sixth wicket. The fielding, however, remained vulnerable and Coates was dropped in the slips by Trumble after making only a single. He took a long time to settle and narrowly escaped being bowled several times. Bruce put down Bohlen in the deep, but this was a hard chance, the fielder having to run some distance to reach the ball. Reprieved, Bohlen passed his century with a four off Trumble, but when he had made 118, he was well caught by Trott at point.

After a dull period, when maiden after maiden was bowled, Coates and Muir fell quickly and a Philadelphian total of under 400 seemed likely. But the Australians were tiring again and, with Henry Brown defending resolutely at one end, Ralston struck the bowling all round the ground. What had been 374/8 was 438/8 at lunch, with Brown on 28 and Ralston 37. Some 90 runs were added for the eighth wicket before Ralston was run out. King, on his debut match, quickly showed that his batting talent was far superior to a number 11, as he compiled 36 valuable runs in, for the Australians, a frustrating last-wicket stand of 61. When, with the score on 499, he snicked Gregory to the boundary for four to bring up the 500, the crowd went wild with excitement. The innings closed on 525.

When the Australians batted, King, opening the attack with Patterson, demonstrated his bowling ability by disposing of Bannerman, who could only fend off a bouncer into the hands of Henry Brown in the slips. The catch was possibly a grounder, so it was a close decision. When Lyons was caught by Bohlen at third man and Trott bowled by King without scoring, the visitors were in serious trouble at 31/3. George Giffen went on the offensive, hitting Henry Brown for six, four and six in consecutive balls. King continued to cause problems, however, picking up a third wicket when Bruce fell to a smart slip catch by Wood. Graham then provided some stability and stayed with Giffen to the close. Australia were then 125/4, Giffen on 50 and Graham on 15, a mere 400 runs adrift. At the end of play, the crowd again surged on to the field, but not, this time, in celebration. They were simply making a rush for the trains that were waiting at the station. For the evening, the Australians were the guests of Colonel Edward Morrell at the Morelton Inn. They were taken by steamer up the Delaware River to Torresdale where he met them and drove them to his abode on his tally-ho. Some 7,000 were present on the third morning as play began at 11.30am. Giffen added 12 to his overnight score, but after his dismissal by King, the Australians resisted no longer. Perhaps they were still recovering from the previous evening's social activity. King acquired his fifth wicket and Brown accounted for the rest of the tail.

Trailing by 326 runs, at 12.45pm the visitors followed on with two and a half sessions to survive to save the match. Bannerman and Lyons responded well with a partnership of 40. Giffen, unable to repeat his first-innings performance, fell quickly, but Trott stayed with Bannerman while 94 runs were added. Patterson rotated his bowlers, making it difficult for the Australians to settle. Only Bannerman had the patience to defend indefinitely, the others succumbing in the end by choosing the wrong ball to hit.

Wickets fell regularly and at 5pm, the scheduled close, Coningham was caught by Coates and the Australians were on 249/9. With dusk falling quickly, the match was destined for a draw, since it was unlikely it could be completed before dark. Several people in the crowd shouted 'play it out' and, sportingly, Blackham did just that. After nine runs were added, he fell to a run-out and the Australians were defeated by an innings and 68 runs. The wickets were shared by six of the seven bowlers used.

To their credit, the visitors offered no excuses, despite their obvious lack of preparation and acclimatisation, and commented favourably on the standard of Philadelphian cricket. The Australians won the second match, a more evenly-contested affair, by six wickets.

PHILADELPHIA v AUSTRALIANS

First-class

Belmont Cricket Club, Belmont PA, 29 and 30 September and 2 October 1893

Philadelphia won by an innings and 68 runs

PHILADELPHIA

		R	B	M	4s	6s
*G.S.Patterson	run out	56				
R.D.Brown	c Blackham b Trumble	23				
W.Scott	run out	8				
A.M.Wood	b Bruce	40				
F.H.Bohlen	c Trott b Bruce	118				
W.W.Noble	b Trumble	77				
H.C.Coates	lbw b Bruce	15				
J.W.Muir	b Coningham	9				
H.I.Brown	not out	59				
+F.W.Ralston	run out	47				
J.B.King	c Lyons b Bannerman	36				
	b17 lb12 nb4 w4	37				
		525				

AUSTRALIANS

		R	B	M	4s	6s			R	B	M	4s	6s
A.C.Bannerman	c H.I.Brown b King	16					(2) not out		79				
J.J.Lyons	c Bohlen b Patterson	12					(1) c Ralston b Patterson		30				
G.Giffen	c Wood b King	62					c Bohlen b H.I.Brown		1				
G.H.S.Trott	b King	0					c Scott b Muir		58				
W.Bruce	c Wood b King	11					c Bohlen b Muir		0				
H.Graham	run out	25					c Muir b King		2				
S.E.Gregory	c King b H.I.Brown	12					c Coates b Scott		32				
H.Trumble	c Wood b H.I.Brown	1					b King		0				
W.F.Giffen	not out	18					c Ralston b Scott		2				
A.Coningham	b King	9					c Coates b Scott		30				
*+J.M.Blackham	b H.I.Brown	22					run out		6				
	b6 lb3 nb2	11					b9 lb5 nb3 w1		18				
		199							**258**				

Australians	O	M	R	W	nb	w		fow	Ph (1)	Aus (1)	Aus (2)
G.Giffen	33	7	114	0	-	-		1	46 (2)	24 (1)	40 (1)
Trumble	55	20	104	2	4	-		2	62 (3)	29 (2)	41 (3)
Trott	15	3	45	0	-	-		3	124 (1)	31 (4)	135 (4)
Coningham	20	5	63	1	-	1		4	131 (4)	67 (5)	139 (5)
Lyons	11	4	34	0	-	-		5	311 (6)	125 (3)	146 (6)
Bruce	20	3	100	3	-	3		6	344 (5)	146 (6)	201 (7)
Gregory	12	5	27	0	-	-		7	353 (7)	146 (7)	201 (8)
Bannerman	3.1	2	1	1	-	-		8	374 (8)	149 (8)	208 (9)
								9	464 (10)	160 (10)	249 (10)

Philadelphia	O	M	R	W	nb	w		O	M	R	W	nb	w
King	25	6	78	5	1	-		32.3	5	90	2	2	-
Patterson	6	0	31	1	-	-	(3)	17	4	48	1	1	-
H.I.Brown	12.4	3	41	3	-	-	(2)	19	6	28	1	-	-
Scott	2	0	20	0	-	-		11	1	41	3	-	-
R.D.Brown	4	0	18	0	-	-	(7)	1	0	10	0	-	1
Noble							(5)	5	2	9	0	-	-
Muir							(6)	9	4	14	2	-	-

(fow row 10: Ph (1) 525 (11) | Aus (1) 199 (11) | Aus (2) 258 (11))

Umpires: G.Bromhead and J.Powderley

Toss: Philadelphia.

5 balls per over.

Close of play: 1st day – Philadelphia (1) 297-4 (Bohlen 83*, Noble 73*); 2nd day – Australians (1) 125-4 (G.Giffen 60*, Graham 15*).

Umpire upended

By the time the Fijians met Wellington at the Basin Reserve on 15 and 16 February 1895, they were still adjusting to the slower wickets than those found in Fiji and to the problems posed by spin bowling. The Fijians arrived in Wellington on 14 February, having travelled from Nelson on the SS *Grafton*. They stayed at the Pier Hotel. In order to allow the visitors to recover from their journey, the match did not start until 2pm on the first day, a Friday. The local press described the attendance as fair, but commented that a far larger crowd watched the match from outside the fence.

Wellington batted first and the opening attack of Caldwell, a solicitor from Australia, and Tuivanuavou, a Fijian chief from the island of Bau, proved too much for the Wellington top order. Having struggled to 20, they lost four wickets for three runs and a fifth with the addition of only a further 15. Tuivanuavou was distinctly quick and the local batsmen were quite uncomfortable facing him. In his first 12 overs, he bowled eight maidens and took four of the first seven wickets to fall. The Fijians impressed with their athletic fielding and their ability to pick the ball up one-handed. The catching was less good and several chances were missed. Nevertheless, some keen fielding helped to keep the run rate down until late in the day. By the close, Wellington had reached 184/7 with Warren on 39 and Benbow on 26.

Arguably the most exciting event of the day was when Warren struck a ball firmly to square leg and hit the umpire, Alfred Ashbolt, on the left arm. Although only 46 years old, Ashbolt used a chair to sit on, but this made him somewhat immobile and he was completely upended as a result, much to the amusement of the spectators. Ashbolt, a foreman printer with the *New Zealand Times*, was a highly regarded umpire locally, having been a founder member of the Wellington Umpires' Association. His fellow umpire, Sydney Deane, worked for Williamson & Musgrave's Comic Opera Company; he had previously played first-class cricket for New South Wales in 1889/90.

The game resumed at 11am on the Saturday but Wellington's innings did not last long. The home side lost three wickets for the addition of a mere six runs. Caldwell and Tuivanuavou shared the spoils for the visitors with five wickets each. Fiji lost five wickets by lunch for only 46. The medium pace of Upham did for both openers and the middle order, the off spin of Frank Ashbolt, son of the umpire, took out the rest of the recognised batting, and Holdship finished off the tail. Holdship, despite a pedigree of Cheltenham College and Cambridge University, failed to notice that the deficit on the first innings meant that Fiji could have been asked to follow on. Instead, Wellington went for quick runs.

The scoring rate of just over three an over was not rapid but Fiji's over rate was such that 60 was up in just over the hour. Holdship declared, leaving Fiji less than two hours to make 187 runs or play for a draw. Generally, defensive batting was not part of Fiji's repertoire, but Caldwell played well until falling to a good catch by Burton. Joske also showed sound defence, but it was the captain, Udal, who did what was required. His half-century, containing nine fours, was a mixture of solid defence interspersed with punishing drives, executed all along the ground, and some well-timed square cuts. He was dismissed just before the close which, with the last pair together, came early. The umpires called a halt with a minute and a half still to go and Benbow, Wellington's most successful bowler, ready to bowl the final over. Neither Wellington's players nor the spectators, who numbered 2,000 by the afternoon, found fault with the decision to stop play. Both gave the visitors a well-deserved reception for managing to avoid defeat by one of New Zealand's top provincial sides.

WELLINGTON v FIJI

Basin Reserve, Wellington, 15 and 16 February 1895

Match drawn

WELLINGTON

		R	B	M	4s	6s		R	B	M	4s	6s
C.S.Gore	b Tuivanuavou	7					(3) not out	8				
C.S.Cross	lbw b Caldwell	13					(1) b Caldwell	28				
*A.R.Holdship	c Joske b Caldwell	0					(2) c McOwan b Tuivanuavou	21				
H.G.E.L.Burton	b Tuivanuavou	49					not out	4				
R.V.Blacklock	b Tuivanuavou	0										
D.M.Fuller	b Caldwell	3										
+R.C.Niven	b Tuivanuavou	42										
W.F.Warren	b Caldwell	39										
C.A.Benbow	c McOwan b Caldwell	30										
E.F.Upham	b Tuivanuavou	0										
F.L.Ashbolt	not out	2										
	b1 lb3 w1	5					b1 nb1	2				
		190					(2 wickets declared)	**63**				

FIJI

		R	B	M	4s	6s		R	B	M	4s	6s
J.C.Collins	c Niven b Upham	24					b Upham	2				
R.Caldwell	b Upham	3					c Burton b Upham	5				
A.B.Joske	c Gore b Ashbolt	6					b Upham	17				
Ratu P.Kadavulevu	c Holdship b Ashbolt	3					b Upham	0				
*J.S.Udal	b Upham	8					b Benbow	50				
+I.McOwan	b Upham	0					c&b Benbow	2				
Ratu R.Nailovolovo	c Warren b Upham	11					st Niven b Ashbolt	2				
W.O.Groom	b Holdship	0					b Benbow	1				
H.M.Scott	c Warren b Holdship	21					not out	2				
V.Epeli	not out	5					c Upham b Benbow	0				
Ratu W.Tuivanuavou	b Holdship	0					not out	0				
	b1 lb2 nb3	6					b5 lb2 nb1	8				
		87					(9 wickets)	**89**				

Fiji	O	M	R	W	nb	w	O	M	R	W	nb	w	fow	Wel (1)	Fij (1)	Wel (2)	Fij (2)
Caldwell	25.4	2	61	5	-	-	10	1	33	1	1	-	1	20 (2)	5 (2)	51 (1)	2 (1)
Tuivanuavou	33	13	65	5	-	-	10	1	28	1	-	-	2	20 (1)	34 (1)	51 (2)	11 (2)
Scott	11	4	24	0	-	1							3	20 (3)	34 (3)		11 (4)
Collins	5	1	13	0	-	-							4	23 (5)	44 (4)		40 (3)
McOwan	2	0	9	0	-	-							5	38 (6)	46 (6)		43 (6)
Kadavulevu	4	1	7	0	-	-							6	98 (4)	55 (5)		64 (7)
Groom	3	1	6	0	-	-							7	146 (7)	58 (7)		81 (8)
													8	184 (8)	63 (8)		87 (5)
Wellington	O	M	R	W	nb	w	O	M	R	W	nb	w					
Upham	20	8	43	5	2	-	15	7	26	4	1	-	9	184 (10)	85 (9)		88 (10)
Ashbolt	19	7	32	2	-	-	4	0	27	1	-	-	10	190 (9)	87 (11)		
Holdship	3.2	0	6	3	1	-	3	1	11	0	-	-					
Benbow							12	7	9	4	-	-					
Warren							1	0	8	0	-	-					

Umpires: A.Ashbolt and S.L.Deane

Toss: Wellington

Close of play: 1st day – Wellington (1) 184-7 (Warren 39*, Benbow 26*).

Laing versus King

The match between the United States and Canada, played at Germantown Cricket Club, Philadelphia, in September 1896 was the 28th in the International Series and the 16th since the fixture became an almost annual event in 1879. Up to that time, the United States had won 15 matches to Canada's nine with three being drawn. The superiority of the United States was perhaps surprising because they were regularly unable to field their strongest team. For this match, the position was reversed. The Canadian team was of moderate strength with six of their players being experienced internationals, whereas the American side was extremely strong with all their players having previously appeared in the International Series. All were from Philadelphia, a situation rather pointedly remarked upon by the *New York Times* – it was supposed to be an All-United States team.

Henry won the toss for Canada and chose to bat, but his side performed poorly. Steady but somewhat unattractive batting by Cooper and Goldingham took the visitors to 57/2. Eight wickets then fell for an additional 20 runs. The pace of King and Patterson was decisive as they shared all ten wickets. There was one incident when the Americans thought that Laing had been bowled, but the umpire was unsighted and, for reasons that were not entirely clear, the other umpire declined to come to a decision. Fortunately, there was no effect on the outcome of the match as Laing was dismissed two balls later.

By the time the United States batted, rain had softened the pitch. Against Laing, with his left-arm fast, and McGiverin, who made the ball break both ways, the home side gave a surprisingly inept display. They lost nine wickets for 26 before Clark and Ralston salvaged some pride and doubled the score. Canada lost McGiverin, a strange choice as opener since he had just completed a bowling spell of 12 overs, but Cooper and Goldingham played carefully and were unbeaten at the close when the visitors had a lead of 67.

The damp weather continued on the second day. Facing difficult bowling and keen fielding, Canada batted slowly, adding a mere 17 runs in the first hour. In one 15-minute period, only one run was scored. The spectators must have been very stiff with both the chill and the boredom. Wickets fell regularly, however, and by lunch, Canada had reached a miserable 117/9. King was particularly hard to handle, Goldingham falling to one of the bowler's specials, a fast late in-swinging yorker, known as the 'hellbender'. Rain prevented any play after lunch and the planned two-day fixture should therefore have been a draw. Both sides, however, agreed to return for a third day on the Monday to see if a result could be obtained. King ended the Canadian innings very quickly on the third morning, without addition to the score. This gave him a match analysis of 10-76. Patterson, the American captain, returned 9-62. The Americans required 153 to win, but with two wickets down for 17 and four for 37, any hope of victory soon disappeared.

So well did Laing bowl and so poorly did the home side bat, that there was no chance of even holding out for a draw. Laing was every bit as devastating as King. Although he did not swing the ball as much, his left-arm delivery created different problems. The Americans were dismissed for 112 with Laing taking eight wickets for 37 runs, his career-best performance. His match analysis of 14-54 was also a career best. The Canadians finished easy and surprising victors by 40 runs.

The magnitude of this achievement was recognised on the players' return to Toronto. A crowd of several hundred greeted them, they were welcomed by Alderman Scott, on behalf of the mayor, and given a civic reception. Socially, little had changed since the 1840s. Toronto still dominated the organisation of Canadian cricket and opportunistically took credit for the team's performance, even though only six of the side came from that city.

UNITED STATES OF AMERICA v CANADA

Germantown Cricket Club, Manheim PA, 4, 5 and 7 September 1896

Canada won by 40 runs

CANADA

Batsman	Dismissal	R	B	M	4s	6s	Dismissal	R	B	M	4s	6s
W.H.Cooper	b Patterson	22					(2) c Wood b King	20				
J.T.McIntosh	b King	0					(7) c Clark b Patterson	13				
P.C.Goldingham	c Brown b King	10					b King	14				
G.S.Lyon	c Wood b Patterson	23					b King	1				
J.M.Laing	c Wood b King	1					b Patterson	23				
*W.A.Henry	b Patterson	3					(8) c Clark b King	6				
H.Ackland	c Wood b King	3					(6) c Patterson b King	12				
E.G.Rykert	c&b Patterson	2					(9) not out	12				
W.C.Little	b Patterson	3					(10) run out	0				
W.E.Deane	c Clark b Patterson	5					(11) b King	1				
H.B.McGiverin	not out	3					(1) c Biddle b Patterson	1				
	b8 lb2 w2	12					b12 lb2	14				
		87						**117**				

USA

Batsman	Dismissal	R	B	M	4s	6s	Dismissal	R	B	M	4s	6s
*G.S.Patterson	b McGiverin	3					b Laing	8				
J.W.Muir	b Laing	3					(5) c Cooper b Laing	10				
W.W.Noble	b Laing	0					(7) b Laing	1				
A.M.Wood	c&b McGiverin	5					(3) b Laing	6				
F.H.Bohlen	b McGiverin	6					(4) b Laing	13				
L.Biddle	b Laing	0					c Cooper b Lyon	23				
E.M.Cregar	b Laing	0					(8) b Laing	4				
J.B.King	b Laing	0					(2) c Lyon b Laing	8				
H.I.Brown	c&b Laing	1					(11) b McGiverin	3				
E.W.Clark	b McGiverin	9					not out	18				
+F.W.Ralston	not out	14					(9) b Laing	7				
	b9 lb1 w1	11					b4 lb6 w1	11				
		52						**112**				

USA bowling

	O	M	R	W	nb	w	O	M	R	W	nb	w
King	24	9	35	4	-	1	37	19	41	6	-	-
Clark	5	1	8	0	-	-	4	1	15	0	-	-
Patterson	23	13	24	6	-	1	35	16	38	3	-	-
Brown	4	0	8	0	-	-	3	0	7	0	-	-
Cregar							1	0	2	0	-	-

Canada bowling

	O	M	R	W	nb	w	O	M	R	W	nb	w
Laing	12	4	17	6	-	1	27	12	37	8	-	-
McGiverin	12	4	24	4	-	-	23	6	50	1	-	-
Lyon							3	1	3	1	-	-
Goldingham							3	1	11	0	-	-

Fall of wickets

fow	Can (1)	USA (1)	Can (2)	USA (2)
1	7	7	1	17
2	27	7	40	17
3	57	7	41	32
4	64	19	42	37
5	68	20	62	71
6	68	22	79	72
7	74	22	91	76
8	76	23	109	88
9	80	26	110	95
10	87	52	117	112

Umpires: [unknown]

Toss: Canada.

Five balls per over.

Close of play: 1st day – Canada (2) 32-1 (Cooper 16*, Goldingham 11*); 2nd day – Canada (2) 117-9 (Rykert 12*, Deane 1*).

The match was originally scheduled for two days, but after most of the second day was lost to rain, the two teams agreed to continue into a third day.

Interport resumes

It took five years following the loss of ten of Hong Kong's cricketers in the SS *Bokhara* disaster before cricketing contacts with Shanghai were renewed. In November 1897, Shanghai travelled to the Colony for a three-way competition with the Straits Settlements. The latter proved much too strong, defeating Hong Kong by an innings and 79 runs and Shanghai by an innings and 11 runs. When Hong Kong and Shanghai met on 11 and 12 November, the contest not only renewed the Interport Series, but also decided second place in the triangular tournament. Neither side was particularly strong, Robert Farbridge, Shanghai's captain, being the only player with a known cricket pedigree, having represented Cheshire in 1889. As in earlier matches, both teams comprised professional people, mainly merchants, administrators, lawyers, teachers and bankers. Although Hong Kong had included three from the military in the match against the Straits Settlements, none was selected for the Shanghai match.

Three of Hong Kong's players later followed more illustrious careers. Percy Cox moved to Yokohama with P&O and then to Canada, where he became general manager of the Canadian Pacific Railway. John Hastings was a solicitor who, in 1904, set up his own practice; he was a founder member of the Law Society of Hong Kong. Thomas Sercombe Smith, having been called to the bar at the Middle Temple in November 1893, served in Hong Kong as acting registrar general and acting police magistrate in 1895, acting colonial treasurer in 1897 and financial secretary and police magistrate in 1897 and 1898. He became a Puisne Judge in 1904. He later served in the judiciary of Federated Malay States where he presided over the Proudlock murder trial in 1911.

Smith and two assessors sentenced Ethel Proudlock to death for the murder of William Steward, a mine manager, who visited her while she was alone in her bungalow at the Victoria Institute, Kuala Lumpur. Her husband, a teacher at the Institute, was out having dinner with a colleague. She claimed she was molested and acted in self-defence, but Sercombe Smith found inconsistencies in her testimony. She appealed and was later pardoned by the Sultan of Selangor. The incident created a scandal at the time and formed the basis of *The Letter*, a play by Somerset Maugham.

Sercombe Smith was Hong Kong's most successful bowler, taking three of the first four Shanghai wickets as they struggled to 43/4, after winning the toss. Overall the play on both sides was lamentable. When the match began at 10.50am, the first runs were byes, after which Mann should have been run out but Cox at mid-off produced a poor throw which the wicketkeeper muffed. Mann took advantage of the reprieve by striking Wood for six before Sercombe Smith gained his first victim, bowling Albert Lanning with the score on 19. Vallings took an impressive catch at square leg to dismiss T. Wallace, running a considerable distance and clasping the ball in his outstretched right hand. Campbell made another good catch, also at square leg, to remove Mann, but Tyack showed good form, executing some skilful cuts and hits to the leg side. He also gave several chances. He should have been caught off Sercombe Smith, but the ball fell between Vallings and the wicketkeeper, neither of whom made any attempt to catch it. He might also have been run out.

Campbell took a second catch in the long field to remove S. Wallace. Cumming gave Tyack support, after being missed at slip soon after he came to the crease. The pair put on 48 runs, defying several bowling changes. When Vallings came on to bowl, Tyack struck his first two balls for boundaries, the second one bringing up his half-century. He tried to repeat this success on the third ball, but missed and was bowled. His entertaining innings included one six and nine fours. The hundred was reached after one hour and a quarter's batting. After Cumming was bowled by Howard on 109, Farbridge and Oswald Lanning scored freely.

It was somewhat of a surprise when Farbridge opened his shoulders to an enticing ball from Howard and was bowled. The pair had added 19, but with better choice of shots, it could have been so many more. Bell chanced his arm and played several uppish strokes against Sercombe Smith before missing a straight ball. Stewart played in the same risky vein and benefited by being dropped first by the wicketkeeper and then by Cox in what would have been a fine caught-and-bowled.

In an attempt to control the run rate, Sercombe Smith resorted to underarm lobs, but his first over in this style resulted in eight runs and a bye. Stewart finally gave a catch to Wood. The innings ended with only one more run added, when Lanning got an edge to a ball from Cox which hit the wicketkeeper and rebounded to Howard at slip. Shanghai had batted for only two hours and five minutes, but they had scored their runs at a rate of 83 per hour and Hong Kong had bowled their overs at 28 per hour.

A leisurely luncheon was taken and play did not resume until 2.05pm. The home side began cautiously, but lost Campbell on 18, the result of a smart catch at slip by S. Wallace. Wood and Maitland added 10 before the latter lost patience, hit out at a ball from Lanning and was bowled. Wood scored most of the runs in a partnership with Ward, which ended when Wood attempted a run after playing a late cut off Lanning. Despite a smart return to the wicketkeeper who removed the bails, many thought that Ward, the non-striker, had made his ground. Shanghai's umpire thought otherwise, however.

Hong Kong were fortunate when Howard hit his first ball straight into the hands of Mann at point, only for the fielder to promptly drop it. Runs came mainly in singles, but after an addition of 25, the partnership ended when Howard was bowled by Mann. Wood lifted Moller's first ball over the rails and into the road where it hit a lady. Before any enquiries could be made about a possible injury, she was quickly escorted away by two gentlemen. Wood was receiving good support from Anton, both batsmen being unafraid to hit the ball hard. Wood dispatched a ball from T. Wallace high over square leg into Connaught Road, where it landed in a rickshaw. After Anton had an escape when T. Wallace dropped a well struck caught-and-bowled, he pulled a ball from the bowler over the trees and into the barracks. Not surprisingly, Wallace was removed from the attack after two overs.

The stand was worth 55 when Wood played a tame stroke and hit the ball to the wicketkeeper; his 53 runs had included two sixes and eight fours. Sercombe Smith fell quickly, but Cox kept the scoring rate moving until he was bowled by Lanning. Vallings departed first ball, followed soon after by Hastings. Anton then took charge of the last-wicket partnership which put on 14 before Stewart held a good soaring catch to bring the innings to a close, 11 runs short of Shanghai's total. Anton had struck four sixes and seven fours in his 64. Both teams maintained the fast and furious pace which had characterised the morning session. Hong Kong scored at 81 runs per hour and Shanghai bowled at 24 overs per hour. With light deteriorating, Shanghai began their second innings at 4.25pm. Despite some fast bowling, particularly from Sercombe Smith and Vallings, who made the ball rise awkwardly from the pitch, the openers survived until the close 20 minutes later.

Cricket on the second day began at 10.35am, a different time from that of the first day. The friendly nature of these Interport matches clearly meant that times of start and finish and lunch and tea intervals were no more than approximate. In the second over of the morning, T. Wallace gloved the ball to Smith at short slip, who took the catch right-handed. Ten runs later Oswald Lanning fell to a good catch by the wicketkeeper. Farbridge and Albert Lanning added 30 before the promising partnership was ended when Lanning offered a return catch to the bowler. Tyack, unable to repeat his first-innings exploits, was given out leg before. Mann and Farbridge took the total above 100, with Mann being particularly strong on the leg side. Good fielding by Wood and Campbell, however, saved several boundaries.

After a stand of 41, Arthur took another good catch behind the stumps to remove Farbridge; the latter had hit six fours in his innings of 32 runs. Three runs later, Mann was out leg before. Stewart did not stay long either, edging the ball into slip's hands. Cumming and S. Wallace kept the score moving, taking a liking to the bowling of Howard, but after seeing up the 150, Cumming misjudged a single and was run out. Bell fell to a catch at slip. Moller produced a tail-end slog during which he was missed in the slips and dropped in the outfield. He eventually fell to a stumping, advancing down the pitch to Smith. His somewhat fortunate 14 runs helped add 20 for the last wicket. S. Wallace was undefeated, having hit six fours. Shanghai were again dismissed before lunch, the innings ending at 12.45pm, but, in the session, they had scored at 73 runs per hour. Smith was again the home side's best bowler, gaining match figures of 11-115.

After an hour for lunch, Hong Kong began the task of scoring 201 runs to win. Gloom soon prevailed when two wickets went down for only 12 runs. Anton and Wood played with the same spirit as in the first innings, scoring mainly in fours and singles. Anton was lucky to escape when, on 15, he hit the ball high, but Mann, the bowler, let it slip through his hands. Rather unsportingly, Anton showed his delight by jumping over the wickets. He then drove Oswald Lanning out of the ground.

Under the onslaught, Shanghai's fielding faltered. Farbridge dropped Anton at long-on, Bell missed Wood at mid-on and Anton hit Mann into the hands of Tyack at mid-off, but he grounded it. After a stand of 85, Anton drove Tyack into the air on the off side and S. Wallace took a good catch. Ward failed and Wood departed to a return catch to Stewart. Howard played positively, but lost Sercombe Smith to a good catch at short square leg, before himself being caught by the wicketkeeper. With seven wickets down for 148, run scoring slowed and Shanghai looked like easy winners. When Albert Lanning took the chances offered by Vallings and Hastings, 21 runs were still needed with only one wicket left.

In an unexpected display of batsmanship, Cox contrived ways to make runs and Arthur managed to hold up one end. Despite their best efforts, Shanghai's bowlers could not obtain the necessary wicket. As the target grew nearer, excitement mounted, especially as there was the prospect that either of Hong Kong's batsmen could make an error at any time. One was not forthcoming, however, and when Cox drove the ball to the boundary for the winning hit, the spectators cheered and Smith, Hong Kong's captain, came bounding on to the field in celebration. Cox was carried shoulder high by his team-mates to the pavilion.

Despite the excitement of the finish, the fact remained that the match was between two very mediocre teams. This was illustrated in the next game in the tournament, when a combined Hong Kong/Shanghai XI were beaten by the Straits Settlements by an innings and 231 runs.

HONG KONG v SHANGHAI

Hong Kong Cricket Club, Chater Road, Hong Kong, 11 and 12 November 1897

Hong Kong won by one wicket

SHANGHAI

Batsman	First innings	R	B	M	4s	6s	Second innings	R	B	M	4s	6s
+A.E.Lanning	b Sercombe Smith	2					(3) c&b Howard	12				
J.Mann	c Campbell b Hastings	17					(6) lbw b Vallings	25				
T.Wallace	c Vallings b S'be Smith	0					(2) c S'be Smith b Howard	14				
W.J.Tyack	b Vallings	51			9	1	(5) lbw b Sercombe Smith	1				
S.Wallace	c Campbell b S'be Smith	6					(9) not out	32				6
E.O.Cumming	b Howard	10					(7) run out	11				
*R.C.Farbridge	b Howard	20					(4) c Arthur b Vallings	32				6
O.V.Lanning	c Howard b Cox	22					(1) c Arthur b Se'be Smith	14				
H.F.Bell	b Sercombe Smith	10					(10) c Wood b S'be Smith	5				
A.E.Stewart	c Wood b S'be Smith	16					(8) c Anton b Vallings	6				
N.E.Moller	not out	0					st Arthur b Sercombe Smith	14				
Extras		19						23				
		173						**189**				

HONG KONG

Batsman	First innings	R	B	M	4s	6s	Second innings	R	B	M	4s	6s
G.D.Campbell	c S.Wallace b Mann	11					b Mann	6				
F.Maitland	b O.V.Lanning	6					b O.V.Lanning	5				
D.M.Wood	c A.E.Lanning b Mann	53			8	2	c&b Stewart	42				
A.G.Ward	run out	2					(5) c A.E.Lanning b Mann	0				
T.N.Howard	b Mann	4					(6) c A.E.Lanning b Stewart	31				
A.S.Anton	c Stewart b Mann	64			7	4	(4) c S.Wallace b Tyack	48				
*T.Sercombe Smith	b Mann	0					c Bell b Stewart	8				
P.A.Cox	b O.V.Lanning	9					not out	38				
Rev G.R.Vallings	b O.V.Lanning	0					c A.E.Lanning b O.V.Lanning	8				
J.F.A.Hastings	c Stewart b O.V.Lanning	2					c A.E.Lanning b O.V.Lanning	1				
+H.Arthur	not out	0					not out	9				
Extras		11						5				
		162					(9 wickets)	**201**				

Hong Kong bowling

	O	M	R	W	nb	w		O	M	R	W	nb	w
Wood	4	1	11	0	-	-	(6)	10	3	25	0	1	-
Sercombe Smith	20	3	64	5	-	-	(3)	19	5	51	4	-	-
Hastings	9	3	17	1	-	-	(2)	5	1	22	0	-	-
Howard	15	5	32	2	-	-	(5)	14	4	41	2	-	-
Vallings	10	3	30	1	-	-	(4)	15	9	19	3	-	-
Cox	1.2	1	0	1	-	1	(1)	4	2	8	0	-	-

Shanghai bowling

	O	M	R	W	nb	w		O	M	R	W	nb	w
Mann	22.4	4	76	5	-	-		28.4	6	97	2	-	-
O.V.Lanning	20	6	41	4	-	-		21	3	64	3	-	-
Moller	4	0	16	0	-	-							
T.Wallace	2	0	18	0	-	-							
Tyack							(3)	6	1	20	1	-	-
Stewart							(4)	9	2	15	3	-	-

Fall of wickets

fow	Sh (1)	HK (1)	Sh (2)	HK (2)
1	19 (1)	18 (1)	30 (2)	10 (2)
2	23 (3)	28 (2)	40 (3)	12 (1)
3	33 (2)	41 (4)	70 (1)	97 (4)
4	43 (5)	66 (5)	73 (5)	98 (5)
5	91 (4)	121 (3)	114 (4)	115 (3)
6	109 (6)	121 (7)	117 (6)	141 (7)
7	128 (7)	146 (8)	126 (8)	148 (6)
8	141 (9)	146 (9)	152 (7)	171 (9)
9	172 (10)	148 (10)	169 (10)	180 (10)
10	173 (8)	162 (6)	189 (11)	

Umpires: [unknown]

Toss: Shanghai

Close of play: 1st day – Shanghai (2) 29-0 (O.V.Lanning 9*, T.Wallace 13*).

Breakdown of extras is not known

Barrett batters the Colony

The 1905 fixture between the Colony (Straits Settlements) and the Federated Malay States was arranged to coincide with the public holidays associated with the Chinese New Year. Although Kuala Lumpur can receive considerable amounts of rainfall at any time of year, early February often coincides with a relatively dry spell and the match was not seriously affected by the weather. The team for the Colony was selected from cricketers in Singapore (eight players) and Penang (three). The Singapore contingent left on the SS *Penang* at 4pm on 31 January and arrived at Port Swettenham (now Port Klang) on the morning of 1 February, allowing two days for rest and practice. Those from Penang arrived, also by sea, the same day.

The match started promptly in dry, sunny conditions, on what looked like a good, true pitch. Voules won the toss for the home side and chose to bat. Runs were initially hard to make against some accurate bowling from Reid and Noon. Hubback did most of the scoring while his captain played a defensive role. After half an hour Voules played a poor stroke to one of Carver's leg breaks and was caught by Dunman at point. Hubback also fell to Carver, a fine caught-and-bowled, having made 55, an innings which contained seven fours. Barrett, who had been troubled by Reid's awkward bounce and been twice hit on the knuckles, took 85 minutes to score 34 runs but after settling he hit Francis Mugliston for 17 in two overs and made 45 in only a quarter of an hour. He and Grenier were unbeaten at tiffin with the score on 183/2.

The match resumed at 2.15pm and the 200 was soon posted before Grenier gloved the ball to the wicketkeeper to end a partnership of 136 made in one hour and 46 minutes. Barrett continued his masterly display, reaching his century in two and a quarter hours and lifting Bradbery twice for six on to the club house roof. His innings ended when he skied a ball to Carver at mid-off. His 153 came in two hours and 33 minutes and contained four sixes and 21 fours. A minor collapse followed before, in some tail-end resistance, Fox reached his fifty. The innings closed in late afternoon for 364. A 20-minute interval was taken, but between the resumption of play and the tea interval, the Colony lost three wickets. There was no respite after tea when two more wickets fell. Mugliston and Reid then played sensibly to take the Colony to 67/5 when played stopped for the day at 5.45pm.

With no chance of victory, the Colony decided to defend for a draw when play resumed at 9.37am on the Monday. Mugliston and Reid took their partnership to 83. Following Mugliston's dismissal, Reid, supported by the lower order, fought his way to a century, a mammoth effort of four and a quarter hours, but it was not enough to save the follow-on. The Colony then gave a totally inept display of batting. Even so, with 35 minutes remaining and five wickets in hand, a draw should have been achieved. Whitley took the wickets of Bradbery and Noon, and McKenzie produced a virtually unplayable ball to account for Reid. There were now eight wickets down and 14 minutes left. Treadgold was caught behind off McKenzie, first ball. Hannaford saved the hat-trick, but was leg before to Whitley soon after. The Colony were dismissed in less than two hours for 81, giving the Federated Malay States an easy victory by an innings and 40 runs.

The somewhat disappointed cricketers left for Singapore and Penang two days later, on 8 February. Their performance showed that the standard of play in the Straits Settlements was, at that time, inferior to that of the FMS, whose players included many employed by the Malay Civil Service. It was another two years before there was sufficient improvement to allow the Colony to beat the Federated Malay States, in what was the fourth match in the series, in 1907.

FEDERATED MALAY STATES v STRAITS SETTLEMENTS

The Padang, Kuala Lumpur, 4 and 6 February 1905

Federated Malay States won by an innings and 40 runs

FMS

		R	B	M	4s	6s
A.B.Hubback	c&b Carver	55		7		
*+A.B.Voules	c Dunman b Carver	6	30			
E.I.M.Barrett	c Carver b Bradbery	153	173	21	4	
N.Grenier	c Hannaford b Reid	41				
S.C.G.Fox	c Bradbery b F.H.Mugliston	54				
R.M.McKenzie	b Reid	0				
E.W.N.Wyatt	b Reid	3				
M.H.Whitley	c Cater b Reid	4				
E.W.Birch	c&b F.H.Mugliston	2				
C.W.H.Cochrane	not out	20				
G.C.Valpy	c G.R.K.Mugliston b Reid	11				
	b11 lb2 nb2	15				
		364				

STRAITS

		R	B	M	4s	6s			R	B	M	4s	6s
G.H.Cater	b Wyatt	0					(3) lbw b McKenzie		15				
*W.Dunman	c Voules b McKenzie	7					(1) st Voules b McKenzie		1				
G.R.K.Mugliston	b Wyatt	16					(4) c&b Wyatt		12				
W.E.Cleaver	st Voules b Wyatt	4					(5) lbw b Birch		23				
L.B.Hannaford	b Wyatt	5					(11) lbw b Whitley		2				
R.T.Reid	c Grenier b McKenzie	107	255				(7) b McKenzie		7				
F.H.Mugliston	c Barrett b Birch	37					(2) c Voules b Fox		0				
C.I.Carver	b Wyatt	8					(9) not out		1				
H.W.Noon	c Grenier b McKenzie	13					(8) b Whitley		0				
C.Bradbery	b Fox	20					(6) c&b Whitley		9				
T.G.Treadgold	not out	0					(10) c Voules b McKenzie		0				
	Extras	26							11				
		243							**81**				

Straits	O	M	R	W	nb	w
Reid	38	7	109	5		
Noon	12	0	59	0		
Carver	16	4	50	2		
Bradbery	11	0	57	1		
F.H.Mugliston	15	2	74	2		

FMS	O	M	R	W	nb	w		O	M	R	W	nb	w
Birch	4	1	12	1				3	2	2	1		
Wyatt	28	6	74	5			(5)	3	1	14	1		
Fox	11	4	15	1			(4)	12	8	11	1		
McKenzie	22.2	5	51	3			(3)	13	3	27	4		
Cochrane	5	2	8	0									
Whitley	14	6	22	0			(2)	5.2	1	8	3		
Valpy	11	2	24	0			(6)	3	0	8	0		
Barrett	2	0	11	0									

fow	FMS (1)	SS (1)	SS (2)
1	37 (2)	0 (1)	? (1)
2	72 (1)	?? (2)	7 (2)
3	208 (4)	?? (4)	25 (3)
4	274 (3)	35 (3)	48 (4)
5	274 (6)	38 (5)	?? (5)
6	288 (7)	121 (7)	74 (6)
7	??? (8)	149 (8)	78 (8)
8	??? (9)	195 (9)	?? (7)
9	??? (5)	241 (10)	?? (10)
10	364 (11)	243 (6)	81 (11)

Umpires: H.B.Helbert and Col. R.S.F.Walker

Toss: Federated Malay States

Close of play: 1st day – Straits Settlements (1) 67-5 (Reid 12*, F.H.Mugliston 13*).

Breakdown of extras in first and second innings of Straits Settlements is not known.

On the morning of the second day G.H.Cater fielded substitute for C.W.H.Cochrane, who had a strained muscle; H.L.Talbot substituted after lunch.

The two 'Graces'

Since their previous meeting in 1890, Scotland and Ireland had become recognised as being first-class in standard. When the two teams met in July 1909 for a three-day fixture at the North Inch Ground, Perth, the match was the first of what became an annual first-class fixture, lasting through to 2000, with breaks only for the First and Second World Wars. Whether the teams in this fixture were, indeed, first-class is certainly debatable, since neither side was at full strength. Nevertheless, the two teams were expected to be well-matched and there was some interest in seeing how the competition between Leslie Balfour-Melville, known as 'the W.G. Grace of Scotland' and Robert Lambert, 'the W.G. Grace of Ireland', would fare.

Balfour-Melville, who was inexplicably not selected when the two sides had last met in 1890, was captaining Scotland at the age of 55. An outstanding sportsman, he also represented his country at rugby union and amateur golf, and was the Scottish champion in lawn tennis, billiards and the long jump. Robert Lambert, then aged 35, was recognised as the greatest-ever Irish all-rounder. He so impressed W.G. Grace when playing for Ireland against London County that Grace invited him to play for his London side. Lambert was also an all-round sportsman who represented Ireland at badminton.

Balfour-Melville won the toss for Scotland and elected to bat, a decision which was more than justified when he and Anderson put on 50 in the first 25 minutes. Balfour-Melville passed his own half-century in only 45 minutes. The Irish bowling and fielding were surprisingly poor under the cloudy and damp conditions. Scotland did not lose a wicket in the morning session. After lunch, the spectators, numbering nearly 1,000, saw the opening partnership extended to 111 before Anderson edged a ball from Lambert to the wicketkeeper. Tait helped maintain the scoring rate, but just after 3.00pm, Scotland lost their second wicket when Balfour-Melville was stumped, nine runs short of his century. Duncan came in but, almost immediately, heavy rain caused play to be suspended.

There was a two-hour delay in proceedings and when play did resume, the bowlers and fielders were handicapped by a wet ball and strong gusty winds. In extremely unpleasant conditions, Scotland lost two wickets before, shortly after 5pm, the rain returned and play was abandoned for the day. The second morning saw a continuation of the wet and windy weather and only ten minutes' play was possible before lunch. Although the Irish fielding improved, the bowling did not, and Scotland continued to prosper. Webster and Thorburn added 88 in quick time. There was more frustration for Ireland, as Chapel and Thorburn added 86 for the last wicket. The innings ended finally on 485. Ireland were undoubtedly demoralised, but this was hardly an excuse for their loss of four wickets for 81 runs by the close, since the pitch had not suddenly changed its character.

Ireland showed no more application on the morning of the third day, a Saturday, when the attendance reached 3,000. Uncertain whether to score runs or defend for a draw, they lost wickets regularly. Most of the batsmen were guilty of ill-judged shots rather than Scotland's bowling being especially difficult. Chapel was the main beneficiary, picking up five wickets, and Gardiner gained three victims in a competent display of wicketkeeping. Witnessed by a crowd of some 4,000, the follow-on began poorly with two wickets down for 29, but George Meldon batted well before offering a catch to Chapel. Pollock and Lambert produced Ireland's best batting of the match, scoring 77 runs while attempting to bat out time. Lambert occupied the crease for two and a half hours and Pollock for just over three hours.

The rest of the side were unable to follow their example and from 131/3, Ireland lost seven wickets for 53 runs. Although outplayed, it was a match that Ireland should have drawn. Instead, Scotland triumphed by an innings and 132 runs.

SCOTLAND v IRELAND

First-class

North Inch, Perth, 22, 23 and 24 July 1909

Scotland won by an innings and 132 runs

SCOTLAND

		R	B	M	4s	6s
*L.M.Balfour-Melville	st Browning b Murphy	91		14	-	
J.Anderson	c Browning b Lambert	31		3	-	
R.G.W.Tait	st Browning b Lambert	47		5	-	
A.W.Duncan	b Lambert	31		2	-	
G.W.Jupp	c L.A.Meldon b Murphy	14		3	-	
J.C.Murray	run out	34		4	-	
W.Webster	c Lambert b Napper	65		6	-	
W.H.Thorburn	not out	90		11	-	
W.L.Fraser	c Lambert b Napper	0		-	-	
+R.P.Gardiner	c Browning b Napper	28		4	-	
D.Chapel	c Corley b L.A.Meldon	36		4	-	
	b12 lb5 nb1	18				
		485				

IRELAND

		R	B	M	4s	6s		R	B	M	4s	6s
G.J.Meldon	b Chapel	14		2	-		c Chapel b Jupp	41			4	-
W.L.Bourchier	b Jupp	5		1	-		c Gardiner b Chapel	2			-	-
W.Pollock	c Gardiner b Chapel	4		4	-		(4) b Fraser	47	180		4	-
L.A.Meldon	c Gardiner b Webster	31		-	-		(3) c Tait b Chapel	2			-	-
R.J.H.Lambert	c B'r-Melville b Chapel	36		3	-		c B'r-Melville b Fraser	42	150		6	-
H.C.Corley	b Chapel	3		-	-		b Chapel	2			-	-
*+F.H.Browning	c Tait b Fraser	15		-	-		b Fraser	8			2	-
W.Harrington	c Gardiner b Fraser	28		2	-		c Gardiner b Fraser	1			-	-
W.H.Napper	b Fraser	3		-	-		(11) c Fraser b Webster	10			1	-
J.W.Flood	b Chapel	16		2	-		(9) b Fraser	9			2	-
P.Murphy	not out	4		1	-		(10) not out	8			-	-
	b4 lb3 nb3	10					b10 lb1 nb1	12				
		169						**184**				

Ireland	O	M	R	W	nb	w
Harrington	27	2	107	0		
Murphy	21	1	92	2		
Napper	14	1	79	3		
Lambert	50	11	137	3		
Flood	5	0	27	0		
L.A.Meldon	1.4	0	4	1		
Pollock	4	0	21	0		

fow	Sc (1)	Ir (1)	Ir (2)
1	111 (2)	6 (2)	15 (2)
2	153 (1)	22 (1)	29 (3)
3	195 (3)	32 (3)	54 (1)
4	216 (4)	81 (4)	131 (5)
5	241 (5)	94	144 (6)
6	271 (6)	109	155 (7)
7	359 (7)	126	157 (8)
8	359 (9)	131	158 (4)
9	399 (10)	163	167 (9)
10	485 (11)	169	184 (11)

Scotland	O	M	R	W	nb	w	O	M	R	W	nb	w
Chapel	18	4	59	5			21	5	60	3		
Fraser	16.5	4	26	3			23	5	50	5		
Jupp	19	3	45	1			12	3	23	1		
Webster	11	1	29	1			9.3	2	17	1		
Duncan							4	1	22	0		

Umpires: W.R.Gregson and P.Higgins

Toss: Scotland

Close of play: 1st day – Scotland (1) 239-4 (Duncan 30*, Murray 13*); 2nd day – Ireland (1) 81-4 (Lambert 18*)

All ten for Bart King

In September 1909, Ireland's cricketers made their fourth journey across the Atlantic Ocean, but the first where a reasonably representative side was chosen. The first two tours, in 1879 and 1888, were largely private affairs organised by Phoenix Cricket Club and students and graduates from Trinity College, Dublin, respectively. The squad in 1892 was theoretically selected by the Irish Cricket Union, but disputes between various Dublin clubs over procedures meant that a somewhat weak side was chosen. In 1909, the touring party was selected by the Committee Controlling Cricket in Ireland, but all they did was to name 12 players. The players themselves elected their captain, Francis Browning, on the voyage out. By today's standards, a party of 12 for a month's tour involving seven matches seems rather slight, but it was typical of the time, when no allowance seemed to be made for the likelihood of illness or injury.

The decisions of the selection committee are criticised today for being biased towards cricketers from Dublin and Cork. The only player from Ulster was Oscar Andrews who, apparently, felt somewhat bitter about the treatment of cricketers from the north, such that, on other occasions, he often rejected invitations to represent Ireland. Some of the other top Irish players were unavailable for other reasons, which meant that the party was not the strongest. For example, Bob Lambert and William Pollock didn't go and none of the Meldon family were able to travel.

The Irishmen played two matches in Canada, drawing one and winning one, followed by a fixture against All New York which resulted in an easy victory, the home side being dismissed in the first innings for 29. The focus of the tour, however, was Philadelphia. Not only were they the best team in North America, but they were covering all the expenses. The original intention after the match in New York was to have three days of practice in Philadelphia to get used to the conditions. Whether the Irish had become overconfident because of the limited strength of the opposition they had encountered, or whether they were being good-hearted by responding to local demand, they agreed to a fixture against Baltimore. This was also won but it meant that the tourists had only one day in Philadelphia before their first game at the Haverford ground.

The Philadelphians fielded a strong side, eight having played first-class cricket on tours of the British Isles. Christy Morris, Francis White, Bart King, Arthur Wood, Herbert Hordern and Charles Winter were on the 1908 tour and all six had been in the Philadelphian team which had defeated the Irish in Dublin by an innings and seven runs. Morris, King and Wood toured in 1903, along with Percy Clark and Huck Haines, and King, Wood and Clark were members of the 1897 touring party. King was rated among the best bowlers in the world. He took 237 wickets in first-class matches on his three tours, including 87 in 1908, when he topped the English averages for the season with 11.01.

Hordern was an Australian who came to the University of Pennsylvania to study dentistry. He was one of the leading exponents of the googly and, on returning home after completing his degree, was good enough to be selected to play Test cricket for Australia. He retired from cricket in 1913 to avoid any injury to his fingers so as not to affect his dental career. While the Philadelphian side was very experienced, ominously, for the future, they were ageing. Wood was 48 at the time of the fixture and both King and Clark were 36. Winter was the sole representative of youth, being only 19.

On the first morning, Browning won the toss and decided to bat in far from ideal conditions. The weather was cool and cloudy, with much moisture in the atmosphere, and the pitch was green. It was 12.05pm when proceedings got under way in front of a disappointingly small crowd. Ireland lost two quick wickets before Morrow and Magee put on 40. They began cautiously, scoring only 18 in half an hour, with Magee playing to his reputation as a stonewaller. As the scoring rate increased, Morrow made most of the runs, but when the total had reached 37, King bowled him with an almost unplayable delivery, only to find that the umpire had called a no-ball.

As the day progressed the sun was beginning to appear between the clouds and the visibility had become rather hazy. Nevertheless, the onset of sunshine attracted more spectators and, as the morning and early afternoon progressed, a sizeable crowd materialised. The partnership continued to prosper and Clark, the home captain, effected a bowling change, bringing himself on in place of Hordern, who had surprisingly opened with his leg breaks and googlies, but found the wicket too soft to obtain any response. With the score on 56, Magee departed, a result of a one-handed diving catch at slip by Haines. That he held on to the ball quite surprised the spectators, and probably himself, but it was considered one of the finest catches ever witnessed at Haverford. Lunch was taken at 1.35pm with the score on 75/5.

After play resumed, apart from Morrow, Ireland offered little resistance. In a superb display of swing bowling, King bowled a full length, interspersed with well-directed swinging yorkers. He removed Browning, Aston, Read, Hone (first ball), Harrington and Napper (also first ball). As a result, all interest for the, by now, enthusiastic and quite vocal spectators focused on whether he could acquire all ten wickets. Despite twice taking two wickets in two balls, he had both times been denied a hat-trick. In order to increase his chances, Clark gave the ball to Graham, who was less likely to take a wicket than either Hordern or himself. Morrow reached his fifty, but soon afterwards, King appealed successfully for leg before to remove Lynch and become the first, and still the only, cricketer from an Associate or Affiliate country to take ten wickets in an innings in a first-class match. He had bowled 109 balls for a return of 10-53 and Ireland's total of 111 had taken 165 minutes. He received a splendid ovation on his return to the pavilion.

Morrow, who carried his bat, was also keenly applauded, having made almost half of his side's runs that were scored from the bat, without giving a chance, a truly magnificent innings. Not only was he the only Irish player to look comfortable, he was also the only one who regularly placed his strokes between the fielders, particularly on the off side.

Philadelphia fared little better than Ireland when their innings began at 3.50pm. Morris fell to a good catch by Hone at square leg. A partnership between White and Patton took the score past 50, but Browning continually rotated his bowlers to prevent the batsmen from settling. Nevertheless, Patton batted with great confidence, effecting many attractive strokes on the off side which were greatly appreciated by the crowd. With the score on 57, however, he fell to another fine catch, this time by Andrews at mid-off. Browning took a good catch behind the wicket to account for Evans. Hone then muffed a chance offered by King, but this had no long-term effect as Harrington bowled him soon after. Wood played on to Harrington, trying to cut a ball and in the last over of the day, just before 5.15pm, Andrews bowled Graham. Philadelphia finished the day on 109/6, still two runs behind.

The weather was much improved when play resumed at 11.30am on the Saturday. The bright sunshine quickly attracted a crowd anxious to see some good play from the Philadelphians. They were not disappointed. On a pitch which was now perfect for batting, White and Hordern added 79 runs in entertaining fashion, Hordern moving across his stumps to pull balls from outside the off over to the leg side to thwart the Irish field placings.

After Hordern played on to Morrow, Clark continued the run feast so that, within 50 minutes of the start, 91 had been added, for the loss of only one wicket. White reached his century with a boundary, having batted for 160 minutes which, for him, represented a rather fast rate of scoring. Clark was dismissed with the score on 265 and White fell 11 runs later. He was warmly applauded as he returned to the pavilion. Instead of the last wicket falling quickly for a total under 300, Winter batted sensibly while Haines hit boundaries all round the ground. Ireland's bowlers were unable to control the situation and the partnership reached 77 before Haines was caught in the outfield. Morrow followed up his batting display by being Ireland's most successful bowler, capturing four wickets.

Ireland began their second innings with a deficit of 242 runs in conditions which seemed to be getting progressively easier for batting. They inexplicably collapsed against the combined pace and spin of King and Hordern respectively. Hordern found the harder and faster pitch much more to his liking. The visitors lost two wickets for three runs and then, with the score on 24, King dismissed Morrow, Browning and Aston with successive balls for an all-bowled hat-trick. Hordern took the wickets of Magee and Read and when Hone was run out, eight wickets had fallen for 35. All the Irish batsmen were at a loss to counter the late in-swing of King and the googlies of Hordern. It was left to Harrington, Napper and Lynch to ignore reputations and the state of play with a combination of good shots and slogs. Between them they added 39 for the last two wickets before Hordern finished the innings to give Philadelphia victory by an innings and 168 runs inside two days. Ireland's consolation was to receive some excellent Philadelphian hospitality in the evening in the form of a dinner and dance in the club house.

Ireland did no better in the second match against Philadelphia, losing by an innings and 66 runs. Again they had no answer to King and Hordern who had match returns of 11-60 and 6-24 respectively. These results showed that even though Ireland were rated first-class, they were a long way behind the standard that the best of the Americans could offer.

PHILADELPHIA v IRELAND

First-class

Merion Cricket Club, Haverford PA, 17, 18 and 19 September 1909

Philadelphia won by an innings and 168 runs

IRELAND		R	B	M	4s	6s		R	B	M	4s	6s
W.M.J.Mooney	b King	1					b King	0				
G.A.Morrow	not out	50					b King	15				
O.Andrews	b King	5					b Hordern	0				
J.M.Magee	c Haines b King	16					b Hordern	4				
*+F.H.Browning	b King	1					b King	0				
J.G.Aston	b King	0					b King	0				
H.M.Read	b King	16					b Hordern	0				
W.P.Hone	b King	0					run out	9				
W.Harrington	b King	11					not out	27				
W.H.Napper	lbw b King	0					b Hordern	2				
J.E.Lynch	lbw b King	1					c Wood b Hordern	11				
	b6 lb1 nb1 w2	10					b1 lb4 nb1	6				
		111						**74**				

PHILADELPHIA		R	B	M	4s	6s
C.C.Morris	c Hone b Harrington	2				
F.S.White	c Browning b Morrow	118		180	14	
R.H.Patton	c Andrews b Aston	31				
J.L.Evans	c Browning b Andrews	8				
J.B.King	b Harrington	1				
A.M.Wood	b Harrington	5				
W.Graham	b Andrews	12				
H.V.Hordern	b Morrow	32				
*P.H.Clark	b Morrow	41				
H.A.Haines	c Read b Morrow	58				
+C.H.Winter	not out	18				
	b18 lb3 w6	27				
		353				

Philadelphia	O	M	R	W	nb	w		O	M	R	W	nb	w	fow	Ir (1)	Ph (1)	Ir (2)
King	18.1	7	53	10	1	-		11	2	38	4	1	-	1	2 (1)	15 (1)	0 (1)
Hordern	11	2	38	0	-	-		10.1	0	30	5	-	-	2	16 (3)	57 (3)	3 (3)
Clark	5	1	8	0	-	2								3	56 (4)	73 (4)	24 (2)
Graham	2	0	2	0	-	-								4	61 (5)	74 (5)	24 (5)
														5	61 (6)	86 (6)	24 (6)
Ireland	O	M	R	W	nb	w								6	85 (7)	109 (7)	25 (4)
Napper	15	0	70	0	-	2								7	85 (8)	188 (8)	34 (7)
Harrington	34	7	108	3	-	-								8	109 (9)	265 (9)	35 (8)
Lynch	6	0	29	0	-	4								9	109 (10)	276 (2)	58 (10)
Aston	8	0	19	1	-	-								10	111 (11)	353 (10)	74 (11)
Andrews	15	2	58	2	-	-											
Morrow	12.2	2	42	4	-	-											

Umpires: [unknown]

Toss: Ireland.

Close of play: 1st day – Philadelphia (1) 109-6 (White 44*); match finished in two days.

In Ireland's first innings, in addition to taking all ten wickets, J.B.King bowled G.A.Morrow with a no-ball.

In Ireland's second innings J.B.King did the hat-trick when dismissing G.A.Morrow, F.H.Browning and J.G.Aston.

Conyers causes consternation

By the time Bermuda sent a team for a short tour of Philadelphia in July 1911, cricket in Philadelphia was showing signs of decline. Many of the best players had decided to retire and the newer players were clearly not of the same calibre, whereas Bermuda had bowlers who could match the best that Philadelphia could produce. For international matches the island side was known as All-Bermuda, a description which included civilians and players from the Garrison. The title was a misrepresentation of inclusivity, however, since it did not included any black players.

Cricket, along with other social activities, was, at the time, subject to considerable racial discrimination, as the country was controlled by a small group of wealthy white men, mainly merchants and bankers, based in Hamilton. Thus, the cricketers visiting Philadelphia were all white. The tourists met Philadelphia at Haverford on 14 and 15 July 1911. The Philadelphian team was of moderate strength, but it did include Bart King, who, despite his 37 years of age, was still clearly the best American cricketer by far.

Philadelphia was in the grip of a heatwave, the worst for ten years, which had lasted a fortnight and had already claimed 216 lives. At 11.30am when Bermuda's innings began, the temperature was already 28°C. The visitors gave a very mediocre batting display. They quickly lost Reggie Conyers, Harrower and, after a short period of stubborn defence, Fisher. They relied on a half-century from Gaye and some valuable late order contributions from Johnson and Martin to accumulate a rather moderate total. Philadelphia's five bowlers shared the wickets.

King was surprisingly expensive. He performed far better with the bat. He was the only one of the home side not to struggle against the accuracy of Gerald Conyers, who benefited from the increasingly overcast conditions. King needed some luck, however, being missed four times as the visitors gave a rather sorry display in the field. Only four other batsmen reached double figures. With Gerald Conyers taking six wickets for 69, Bermuda had a lead of 35. The temperature was now falling rapidly as the clouds moved in to bring the hot spell to an end. Bermuda began their second innings in very poor light and, after one over, bowled by King, it became so dark that play had to be abandoned.

By 6pm the temperature had fallen to 21°C and torrential rain and thunderstorms had started. The storms were worse elsewhere in the State of Pennsylvania, where they damaged crops, destroyed culverts and caused landslips along the railroad lines. Hailstones the size of walnuts were reported in some areas.

Despite the overnight rain, the second day began on time. Bermuda soon looked to have lost control of the match as their batsmen failed against the pace of King and Pearce. The score of 130 was very disappointing. Philadelphia needed 166 runs to win and looked to be approaching this with ease when King and Evans put on 87 for the first wicket. Conyers then found his nagging length and dismissed both openers. A home victory still looked feasible on 140/5, with only 26 more runs required.

Conyers then took out Philadelphia's middle order. In three consecutive balls, he dismissed Anderson, Valentine and Harned. Pearce helped Graham take the score to within six runs of victory, only for Conyers to retaliate with yet another hat-trick. This time he removed Graham, Dornan and Fellows to achieve a return of 9-69 and match figures of 15-138. Philadelphia's last six wickets thus fell to two hat-tricks, Conyers taking all six while conceding only two runs in one of the most remarkable bowling feats of all time. Spectators had never seen a performance like it and were full of excitement as Conyers was borne shoulder-high to the pavilion by his colleagues.

As an indicator of changing times regarding the support for cricket in America, the report on the match in the local press occupied one third of a column. Reports on baseball took up 14 columns spread across two complete pages.

PHILADELPHIA v BERMUDA

Merion Cricket Club, Haverford PA, 14 and 15 July 1911

Bermuda won by six runs

BERMUDA

Batsman	Dismissal	R	B	M	4s	6s	Dismissal	R	B	M	4s	6s
J.R.Conyers	c Dornan b Fellows	1					(5) b Pearce	36				
S.D.Harrower	c Pearce b Fellows	8					(1) c Anderson b King	2				
+G.W.Fisher	c Vetterlein b Fellows	8					c Evans b King	1				
A.D.Gaye	c Valentine b King	59					b Vetterlein	36				
G.C.Conyers	b King	4					(6) c Dornan b Pearce	1				
T.S.Gilbert	b Vetterlein	9					(7) b Pearce	36				
*H.J.Tucker	b Vetterlein	10					(8) b Pearce	1				
W.B.T.Johnson	c Anderson b Pearce	26					(2) b King	6				
F.H.Martin	c Vetterlein b Henry	21					c Pearce b King	0				
A.W.West	not out	0					c Pearce b King	0				
C.Conyers	c Evans b King	5					not out	0				
Extras		13						11				
		164						**130**				

PHILADELPHIA

Batsman	Dismissal	R	B	M	4s	6s	Dismissal	R	B	M	4s	6s
J.B.King	c Gaye b G.C.Conyers	62					b G.C.Conyers	35				
J.L.Evans	b Gilbert	13					c West b G.C.Conyers	44				
C.M.Graham	b G.C.Conyers	14					(5) b G.C.Conyers	13				
A.J.Henry	b G.C.Conyers	7					(3) lbw b West	11				
H.S.Harned	lbw b C.Conyers	3					(8) c&b G.C.Conyers	0				
J.R.Vetterlein	b C.Conyers	11					(4) b G.C.Conyers	20				
R.P.Anderson	c Fisher b C.Conyers	14					(6) b G.C.Conyers	6				
A.S.Valentine	b G.C.Conyers	1					(7) b G.C.Conyers	0				
+J.P.Dornan	not out	0					(10) lbw b G.C.Conyers	0				
H.G.Pearce	b G.C.Conyers	0					(9) not out	10				
W.M.Fellows	b G.C.Conyers	0					b G.C.Conyers	0				
Extras		4						20				
		129						**159**				

Philadelphia	O	M	R	W	nb	w	O	M	R	W	nb	w
King	15.3	2	62	3			18	4	43	5		
Fellows	11	3	31	3			9	1	24	0		
Vetterlein	5	1	32	2			2	0	8	1		
Pearce	4	1	15	1			12.2	4	34	4		
Henry	2	0	11	1			2	0	10	0		

Bermuda	O	M	R	W	nb	w	O	M	R	W	nb	w
G.C.Conyers	19	2	69	6			20	1	69	9		
Gilbert	13	2	33	1			3	0	19	0		
C.Conyers	7	1	23	3			12	0	46	0		
West							2	1	5	1		

fow	Ber (1)	Ph (1)	Ber (2)	Ph (2)
1	5 (1)	48 (2)	2 (1)	87
2	14 (2)	63 (3)	6 (3)	90
3	19 (3)	83 (4)	9 (2)	116
4	34 (5)	100 (5)	70	130
5	63 (6)	102 (1)	71	140 (6)
6	85 (7)	128 (6)	111	140 (7)
7	122 (4)	129 (7)	121	140 (8)
8	158 (8)	129 (8)	130	159 (5)
9	158 (9)	129 (10)	130	159 (10)
10	164 (11)	129 (11)	130	159 (11)

Umpires: [unknown]

Toss: Bermuda

Close of play: 1st day – Bermuda (2) 1-0 (Harrower 1*, Johnson 0*).

Breakdown of extras is not known.

In Philadelphia's second innings G.C.Conyers did the hat-trick when dismissing R.P.Anderson, A.S.Valentine and H.S.Harned and achieved a second hat-trick when dismissing C.M.Graham, J.P.Dornan and W.M.Fellows.

In some sources W.M.Fellows (Philadelphia) appears as W.M.Fellowes.

The third 'Grace'

For the first 'Test' match between Argentina and the MCC tourists, played at the Hurlingham Cricket Club ground in January 1912, the Pacific Railway Company ran a special train from Retiro Station in the centre of Buenos Aires to Hurlingham, leaving at 10am and stopping only once, at Palermo. In order to encourage an attendance, there was no admission charge.

Lord Hawke won the toss and elected to bat, perhaps unaware of the strength of the bowling in the unexpectedly hot and humid conditions. The pace combination of left-armer Dorning and right-armer Foy exploited the morning humidity and MCC were soon reduced to 33/7. Hawke, in respective partnerships with Hill and Wilson, added 29 and 18, when the opening bowlers were rested. By the time the pace bowlers returned, the conditions had eased and Wilson and Hatfeild frustrated the home side with a last-wicket partnership of 106.

Under the circumstances, the first-innings total of 186 was quite reasonable. Argentina responded with an opening stand of 57, Jackson and Toulmin playing the visitors' bowling, which turned out to be somewhat weak, with ease. However, there was a 'wobble' before the close with four wickets falling to rather careless shots.

Showery, damp conditions characterised the whole of the second day and it was 5.05pm before play was possible. Argentina added 26 runs and lost two more wickets. The match therefore seemed destined for a draw with only one day remaining. Under still-cloudy conditions on the last day, Whaley and Garnett made useful contributions to secure a small lead of 23 for the home side. With all their experience, MCC should have batted out the remaining time. Again, on a deteriorating pitch, they struggled against Dorning and Foy. Troughton and Hill took advantage of the support bowlers to add 66, but once Hill had surprisingly holed out off the bowling of Toulmin, Troughton was left with the tail.

Tufnell, Hawke and Hatfeild all gave defensive support but it was only enough to raise the total to 157, with Troughton remaining undefeated on 59. Overall, the visitors' batting was very ordinary.

Argentina made rapid progress towards their target of 135 with Jackson and Toulmin in another useful opening partnership of 75. The batsmen contrasted in style, with Jackson hitting vigorously and Toulmin being rather cautious. The middle order found the slow left-arm spin of Hatfeild difficult. Hatfeild also impressed with some brilliant fielding. The scoring rate slowed so much that a win looked unlikely. Garnett livened proceedings, however, and amid much excitement among the 500 or so spectators, took Argentina to victory with only four minutes to spare.

Argentina deserved to win their inaugural first-class match but they were aided by bowling when conditions were most favourable. Dorning and Foy had match returns of 10-125 and 9-114 respectively. The victory gave the home side much satisfaction. The *Buenos Aires Herald* noted that while cricket was entirely a British affair and had never received any support from the Argentine government, the newspaper would claim the team's achievement on behalf of the whole of Argentina.

MCC recovered from this surprise defeat by winning the other two 'Tests' to take the series by two matches to one. The third encounter was closely fought, however, and the visitors struggled before winning it by two wickets. The tour showed that, certainly under home conditions, Argentine cricket was equal in standard to much of English county cricket. The outstanding player was Herbert Dorning. In a career of 55 matches in internationals and the annual North-versus-South domestic fixture, he took 308 wickets, including five or more wickets in an innings 22 times. No wonder he acquired the accolade of the 'W.G. Grace of Argentine cricket'.

ARGENTINA v MARYLEBONE CRICKET CLUB

First-class

Hurlingham Club, Buenos Aires, 18, 19 and 20 February 1912

Argentina won by four wickets

MCC

		R	B	M	4s	6s			R	B	M	4s	6s
W.Findlay	b Dorning	0					(3) c Watson-Hutton b Foy		6				
C.E.de Trafford	c&b Foy	16					lbw b Dorning		2				
M.C.Bird	b Dorning	3					(4) c Biedermann b Foy		29				
H.H.C.Baird	c Garnett b Dorning	1					(5) b Dorning		0				
L.H.W.Troughton	b Dorning	5					(6) not out		59				
A.C.MacLaren	b Dorning	0					(7) b Foy		7				
+N.C.Tufnell	c Dorning b Foy	5					(9) c Garnett b Dorning		2				
A.J.L.Hill	c Watson-Hutton b Dorning	17					c Biedermann b Toulmin		34				
*Lord M.B.Hawke	lbw b Foy	27					(10) b Foy		7				
E.R.Wilson	not out	67					(1) lbw b Foy		1				
C.E.Hatfeild	c Biedermann b Foy	39					b Dorning		0				
	b1 lb3 nb2	6					b6 lb3 nb1		10				
		186							**157**				

ARGENTINA

		R	B	M	4s	6s			R	B	M	4s	6s
N.W.Jackson	c Wilson b Baird	31					(2) c Bird b Hill		49				
E.M.O.Toulmin	c Tufnell b Hatfeild	59					(1) c&b Hatfeild		27				
S.A.Cowper	c Hatfeild b Hill	8											
J.A.Campbell	c MacLaren b Baird	0					st Tufnell b Hatfeild		4				
G.A.Simpson	c&b Wilson	26					(3) run out		10				
H.Dorning	b Hatfeild	16					(5) b Hatfeild		14				
H.E.C.Biedermann	c Hill b Wilson	2					(8) not out		8				
C.H.Whaley	not out	21					(7) c Troughton b Hatfeild		0				
P.A.Foy	b Baird	15											
*+H.G.Garnett	c Troughton b Baird	20					(6) not out		19				
A.P.Watson-Hutton	b Bird	0											
	lb8 nb3	11					b5		5				
		209					(6 wickets)		**136**				

Argentina	O	M	R	W	nb	w		O	M	R	W	nb	w	fow	MCC(1)	Ar (1)	MCC(2)	Ar (2)
Dorning	17	1	65	6	-	-		18.1	3	60	4	-	-	1	7	57	3	75
Foy	17.1	3	65	4	-	-		17	2	49	5	-	-	2	19	75	3	85
Whaley	4	0	25	0	2	0		6	1	17	0	1	-	3	19	78	18	91
Toulmin	4	0	24	0	-	-		6	1	18	1	-	-	4	22	133	21	97
Cowper	1	0	1	0	-	-		2	1	3	0	-	-	5	22	139	42	119
														6	27	147	52	119
MCC	O	M	R	W	nb	w		O	M	R	W	nb	w	7	33	162	118	
Bird	13.1	1	48	1	-	-		3	1	17	0	-	-	8	62	179	139	
Wilson	16	4	32	2	1	-		3	0	12	0	-	-	9	80	209	150	
Baird	24	10	47	4	-	-		4	0	16	0	-	-	10	186	209	157	
Hill	9	0	27	1	2	-		10	2	37	1	-	-					
Hatfeild	16	3	44	2	-	-		12.2	2	49	4	-	-					

Umpires: J.R.Garrod and C.St Clair

Toss: M.C.C.

Close of play: 1st day – Argentina (1) 135-4 (Simpson 29*, Dorning 2*); 2nd day – Argentina (1) 161-6 (Dorning 15*, Whaley 9*).

Nairobi's cricketers reach Uganda

International cricket came to east Africa much later than it did to the Americas and south and east Asia. The East African Protectorate, which became Kenya in 1920, was not established until 1895 and Uganda was not peaceful until 1899. Travel between Nairobi and Entebbe was time-consuming and tedious until the railway line was completed from Mombasa, through Nairobi, to Port Florence, now Kisumu, on the shores of Lake Victoria, in 1910.

After this date there was a weekly service between Nairobi and Port Florence. Even so, the journey was not for the faint-hearted. One passenger described it as '48 hours of continuous jolting'. The train travelled at just under 20kph and every 30km or so it would stop for the engine to take on water.

The changes in temperature while travelling presented a problem of what luggage to take. Part of the time, temperatures were a comfortable 25–30°C, but when the train reached Mau Summit, at 2,530 metres, they were close to freezing at night and warm clothing was a must. On reaching Port Florence, passengers changed on to a lake steamer for a 12-hour journey to Port Bell, the entry point for Kampala. After a stop to load and unload passengers and freight, the boat departed for Entebbe, a further two-hour journey. A round trip of at least two weeks was required for cricketers from Nairobi to play their counterparts in Entebbe.

There were certain risks involved in cricketers being away from their administrative and business activities for so long. With only around 1,000 Europeans in Nairobi at the time it was not easy to find substitutes to act in one's absence, let alone find sufficient players from which to select an international cricket team. The situation was similar in Entebbe, with about 1,000 Europeans, of whom 75 per cent were male. Most, however, were young, enthusiastic, with a public-school education in which cricket was ingrained in their psyche.

There was considerable enthusiasm for cricket in both countries, particularly among the officials attached to the Colonial Service. Uganda's side included Sir William Morris Carter, the chief justice, E.W. Leakey, Uganda's director of customs, the Reverend Herbert Thomas Candy Weatherhead, a member of the Church Missionary Society who became firstly a bishop and later a canon, and Dr G.C. Strathairn, who later served as senior sanitary medical officer in Jamaica in the 1920s and became director of medical services in Cyprus in 1944. The East African Protectorate team included George Hunter Pickering, who later became the chief justice of Zanzibar, and Thomas Shenton Whitelegge Thomas, in his first appointment with the Colonial Service after graduating from Cambridge University. He later served in Nigeria before becoming, in turn, the governor of Nyasaland, the Gold Coast and the Straits Settlements and the high commissioner for the Federated Malay States.

Uganda batted first and quickly lost Vetter, the first of the six victims of Thomas. Carter and Richter took control in a second-wicket partnership of 103, before falling, respectively, to Pickering and Thomas. None of Uganda's remaining batsmen possessed the same degree of confidence and application. They found the bowling of Thomas particularly difficult. Strathairn and Lilley battled to reach double figures, but a few lusty blows from McClure helped to take the home side to a moderate total. Kenya's top order also struggled. Strathairn, one of Entebbe's leading players, and McClure accounted for four batsmen, but when they had to be rested, Thomas and Vidal took control. They added 94 to take East Africa close to victory before Thomas fell to a sharp stumping by van der Velde from one of Weatherhead's flighted off breaks. Ford accompanied Vidal to secure victory, after which East Africa batted on, allowing Vidal to complete the first international hundred on Ugandan soil. Not surprisingly, given the limited talent from which to select, both teams relied on two or three quality players. Thomas was easily the most accomplished player in the match.

UGANDA v EAST AFRICAN PROTECTORATE

Entebbe Sports Club, Entebbe, 11 and 12 April 1914

East African Protectorate won by five wickets

UGANDA

		R	B	M	4s	6s
*W.M.Carter	b Pickering	69				
Vetter	lbw b Thomas	8				
J.E.S.Richter	b Thomas	52				
H.T.C.Weatherhead	c Vidal b Thomas	0				
C.Willmot	b Thomas	4				
Dr G.C.Strathairn	b Thomas	10				
Capt H.A.Lilley	c Vidal b Smith	10				
Gowdy	b Smith	0				
+M.van der Velde	b Thomas	0				
A.McClure	not out	18				
E.W.Leakey	b Pickering	2				
	Extras	20				
		197				

EAST AFRICAN PROTECTORATE

		R	B	M	4s	6s
R.A.Pelham-Burn	b Strathairn	12				
T.S.Muirhead	b Strathairn	10				
Smith	c Weatherhead b Strathairn	7				
W.S.Jackson	b McClure	3				
*T.S.W.Thomas	st van der Velde b Weatherhead	47				
M.R.Vidal	not out	104				
R.Ford	c Lilley b McClure	31				
Weston	not out	2				
G.H.Pickering						
H.H.Brassey-Edwards						
A.C.Kirby						
	Extras	14				
	(6 wickets)	**231**				

East African Protectorate	O	M	R	W	nb	wd		fow
Pickering			2					1
Thomas			6					2
Smith			2					3
								4
Uganda	O	M	R	W	nb	wd		5
Strathairn			65	3				6
McClure			70	2				7
Weatherhead				1				8
								9
								10

Umpires: [unknown]

Toss: [unknown]

In Uganda's innings batting is four runs under.

East African Protectorate won by five wickets and batted on.

Complete bowling analyses have not been published.

The breakdown of extras is not known.

4

Consolidation versus decline
1915–1939

THE FIRST World War marked the end of the Golden Age of cricket in the minor countries, just as it did in the leading Test-playing nations, particularly England and Australia. There were fewer cricketers around in 1918 than in 1913. At least 32 of those who had played internationally for an Associate country prior to the war are known to have either been killed in action or died from wounds sustained while on active service. Scotland, Ireland, Canada and Argentina were the worst affected with the loss of ten, seven, four and four cricketers respectively. In addition, Ireland lost Francis Browning from wounds sustained during the Easter Rising in 1916.

Cricket in the Associate and Affiliate countries during the inter-war period largely followed one of four patterns. In Scotland, Ireland and also Wales, who played representative matches at this time, cricket was well-organised and taken seriously.

In addition to the Scotland–Ireland series which was first-class, first-class matches were arranged against English counties and overseas touring teams. The players were amateurs, but with only two or three matches per year, they could spare the time from work to represent their country. Matches adhered to the first-class format of the English county championship as far as playing hours and time-keeping were concerned. A good standard at international level was reached, with several players going on to play for English counties, or, in the case of Wales, Glamorgan. The disappointment was that attendances at the home games were generally low, fewer than 1,000 per day.

In Hong Kong, Shanghai, Malaya, Singapore and west Africa, cricket was also of a good standard, probably equal to Minor Counties in level. Regular international matches were played, but the atmosphere was somewhat between that of an English county fixture and a country house game. Playing hours were laid down and were kept to the nearest quarter-hour or 20 minutes. Extensions to the lunch interval were common. As in club cricket, either the home side provided the umpires or there was one from each side. Opportunities to play at international level were widened to include the best of the local players, as well as the military and expatriates. Selection was on merit, but was often hampered by availability, as some of the better players found it difficult to cover the expenses of away fixtures.

As in matches before the war, considerable emphasis was placed on the social side. It was important to host the visiting team with receptions, dances and other entertainment. Bands were often present at the matches and visitors were generally greeted at some stage by the governor-general or his representative. Much of the same applied to cricket in South America. The main difference was that there, little attempt was made to involve the local population, so that the game remained very much English public-school based. As a result, playing times were more strictly adhered to. In North America, Bermuda and Fiji, where cricket had reached high standards before 1914, the game declined. The worst situation was in the United States. The effects of the Wall Street crash and the Great Depression meant that those who had supported the country house style cricket in Philadelphia could no longer do so, and many clubs folded. Elsewhere, particularly in New York, California and around Chicago, the game survived as a minority sport, played at a low standard. No attempt was made to turn it into a sport for the mass of the population and create something with an American atmosphere. In Canada, fewer people were taking up the game because of its reputation as an elite English activity. Many Canadian-born, second- and third-generation Europeans wanted to show their allegiance to Canada rather than the British crown and opted to follow ice hockey and baseball as their first-choice sports. Nevertheless, North America continued to attract touring parties from overseas.

In the summer of 1932 an Australian team including Don Bradman, Victor Richardson, Alan Kippax, Arthur Mailey, Stan McCabe, Hanson Carter and Leslie Fleetwood-Smith crossed the continent from Vancouver to New York and back again to Los Angeles, playing 51 matches between mid-June and the end of August. They found the playing standard low and won 43, drew seven and lost only one of their matches, which were mostly one-day affairs against odds.

The other visitors to North America were Sir Julien Cahn's side in 1933. Throughout eastern Canada, the east of the United States and the Chicago area, they won all their games, mostly with ease. Stronger opposition was found in Bermuda, where they scraped a draw against the national side. Unfortunately, Bermuda was not part of the touring party circuit so it was not possible to judge how strong its cricket was. The country's leading player, Alma Hunt, was selected by the West Indies for a trial before their 1933 tour of England. Despite performing well, it was decided not to include him in the touring party because it was argued that Bermuda was not a geographical component of the West Indies. Hunt moved to Aberdeen, where he played league cricket and represented Scotland internationally.

Fiji too suffered geographically as neither Australia nor New Zealand chose the Pacific route via North America for their journeys to and from England. The Australians did visit Suva on their way to Canada in 1932 and MCC planned to meet Fiji on their return home from Australia, via North America, in 1933, but both matches had to be abandoned because of rain. A short tour of Fiji was made by a New Zealand side in 1924 and a New Zealand Universities team visited in 1936. Although neither of these sides represented the best of New Zealand cricket, they were too good for the Fijians.

Cricket remained organised on racial lines and little effort was made to involve any of the Indian community, even though they made up a higher proportion of the population than either the Europeans or the Fijians. The game had become concentrated on Suva Cricket Club, where it was an all-European activity, and the very small island of Bau, where the Fijian chiefs still played. Fiji produced one first-class cricketer at this time. Ratu Etuate Cakobau played for Auckland in 1930/31. Elsewhere cricket prevailed in many countries as a minority interest, but in The Netherlands, Denmark and Greece, local players outnumbered expatriates. MCC made three short tours to Denmark and three to The Netherlands to encourage the game. The Free Foresters were also regular visitors to The Netherlands and Sir Julien Cahn's side made one visit to Denmark.

The last international involving Associate countries before the outbreak of the First World War was Ireland versus Scotland in July 1914. The first match after the war was played in April 1919 when the Straits Settlements met the Federated Malay States. In 1920, Scotland played Ireland and Hong Kong met Shanghai, which meant that within two years of the war ending, three of the regular match series had restarted. The Hong Kong–Shanghai meeting was part of a triangular tournament with All-Malaya, a team chosen from the Straits Settlements and the Malay States.

Towards the end of 1920, Argentina toured Chile and in early 1921, Brazil visited Argentina, thereby establishing the basis of international cricket in South America. On the negative side, cricket in Philadelphia continued its decline. The annual series between the United States and Canada was not resumed and Philadelphia played their last international fixtures against Bermuda in 1923. The Canadians sent a touring side to England in 1922, but it was of poor quality. They played mainly club sides and failed to win a match.

By the time Hong Kong travelled to Shanghai in May 1923, cricket in both territories had regained its strength of the pre-war days. Potentially Shanghai was stronger throughout the 1920s and 1930s because it had an international community of some 60,000 people, most of whom were British. This was the time when Shanghai was at its most colourful, its cabaret, nightclubs and top-class hotels attracting all who wanted to experience a touch of luxury and glitz. In complete contrast to the 1890s and 1900s, Hong Kong was now overshadowed by Shanghai; its population in 1921 was 625,166, with probably no more than 20,000 being British. Assuming that similar proportions of the two populations had an interest in cricket, Shanghai had a much larger player base from which to choose. Hong Kong, however, continued to have the advantage of cricketers from the military stationed there. Both territories also had increasing numbers of migrants from the Indian subcontinent who were forming their own cricket clubs. The Parsi club, founded in Shanghai in 1890, was the first Indian expatriate club in the world. The Hong Kong Parsi club was started in 1897. Neither club exists today. There were clubs of non-Parsi Indians in both territories and clubs for the Chinese, although the latter had few players of a high standard. Hong Kong also had a club for cricketers of Portuguese origin.

Three Associate and Affiliate countries were accorded first-class status between 1918 and 1939. These were Scotland, Ireland and Argentina. Wales also played 15 first-class matches in this period. Argentina retained their pre-1914 first-class position when MCC undertook their second tour of the country in 1926/27. Matches against Sir Julien Cahn's tourists in 1929/30 and Sir T.E.W. Brinckman's side in 1937/38 were also rated first-class. Thus all of Argentina's first-class fixtures were played at home. Cricket in the country remained an expatriate activity, but an increasing number of the players were Argentinian-born of British parents. Many retained their ties with Britain by being educated at boarding schools in England.

Argentina was not the only country in South America with a British population keen on cricket. MCC recognised this on their 1926/27 tour which included visits to Chile, Peru and Uruguay. Surprisingly, Brazil was not on the itinerary. Cricket reached a reasonable standard in Chile and Brazil at this time and the players of both countries made arrangements for matches against Argentina, home and away. Distance and the resultant time and difficulty of travel precluded Chile and Brazil playing each other. Surprisingly, no one came up with the idea of a triangular tournament between the countries to be played in Buenos Aires. Thus there was no South American equivalent of the Hong Kong–Shanghai–Malaya Interports.

Nevertheless, the inter-war period proved the high point for cricket in South America. Many of the players were able to use their professional work to spend the Argentinian summer in Argentina and the British summer in England. While a few played first-class matches for the English counties, those of a lesser standard played for an Anglo-Argentine side organised by Ernest Thomson, the honorary secretary and treasurer of the Argentine Cricket Association. He made arrangements for a South American tour of Britain in 1932 and managed to secure first-class status for six of the 18 matches played. He tried to get two more first-class fixtures, against Cambridge University and Wales, but was unable to obtain convenient dates.

However, it was an ambitious tour lasting from the middle of May to the middle of July. Invitations were sent to 15 players, ten from Argentina, four from Brazil and one from Chile. The team was weakened when two of Brazil's better players, Harold Morrissy and

Oliver (Boy) Cunningham, were unable to spare the time. John Naumann, a Cambridge blue and former Sussex all-rounder, and Richard Latham were selected as replacements. When Naumann later withdrew, Alfred Jackson of Chile was drafted in. He joined the party two weeks late. One surprise omission was Cecil Ayling, brother of Cyril and Dennet, who had already proved a valuable all-rounder in the annual North–South match, Argentina's top domestic fixture. Thomson acted as manager.

The South Americans were led by Clement Gibson, a former Cambridge blue and Sussex player, who was good enough to be selected by MCC for the 1922/23 tour of Australia. Despite being a team of expatriates, the South Americans had a strong commitment to their side. Of the 11 players in the match against Scotland, only Arthur Grass was not born on the continent. Seven were born in Argentina, Latham in Brazil, Jackson in Chile, and Henry Marshal in Colombia. The match against Scotland was the 16th of the tour and the last of the first-class fixtures. By this time, there was no doubt that many of the tourists were tiring of six-day-a-week cricket, even though many were benefitting from the experience of playing better opposition than they were accustomed to.

The 1920s and 1930s witnessed the rise of international cricket in west Africa. The first important fixture had been back in May 1904, when Lagos met the Gold Coast, the latter winning by 22 runs in Lagos. Lagos won the return fixture the following year in Accra. In both territories, as in most British Commonwealth countries at the time, cricket, at the club level, was segregated, but there was much cooperation and interaction between the European and African clubs. In 1904, 1905 and 1906, the international teams were multiracial, but in 1907, the Africans organised their own fixture and from then until 1956, separate series took place between the two countries for European and African teams.

Nigeria did not come into existence until 1 January 1914, when it was formed by merging the two colonial territories of northern and southern Nigeria. It was several years, however, before Nigeria fielded a European international team. When matches between the territories resumed in 1925, it was the Lagos Athletic Club which played the Gold Coast. The first true international fixtures did not take place until 1926. In April that year, the African teams drew a match in Lagos, and, in December, the Gold Coast won the European fixture in Accra.

Cricket in both countries depended on wealthy patrons in both European and African communities and the encouragement provided by public servants like Sir Shenton Thomas, Sir Selwyn Grier and Sir Charles Arden-Clarke in Nigeria and Sir Frederick Guggisberg in Ghana. It is perhaps surprising that the Europeans managed to sustain a regular series of international matches and that the cricket reached a good standard, probably close to Minor Counties level.

The number of Europeans in both countries was small. In 1931, they probably formed no more than three per cent of the population in Lagos or Accra, which at the time, had about 126,100 and 60,700 people respectively. After allowing for women, children, people who were too old and those with no interest, the number of potential players was clearly very limited. These were even more restricted for away fixtures, since only those who could afford to be absent from work for about two weeks were available for selection. It was not surprising, therefore, that both countries relied on the military stationed there to supplement players from the civil service and business communities.

The internationals between Gold Coast and Nigeria were usually played in April each year. Although there is no truly dry season in either Accra or Lagos, April marks either the end of the drier season or the start of the wetter one, depending on one's point of view. By May and June, rainfall levels are too high for cricket to be feasible. April, however, is often the hottest month of the year with daily temperatures rising to 31–32°C by mid-afternoon, whereas during the wet season, they generally remain below 30°. Choosing to play cricket in April seems strange, when the months of November to February were climatically more suitable. Having chosen to play in April, the playing hours were then designed for maximum discomfort, with matches spread over five days, each day starting at 2.30pm and continuing until 6.15pm, by which time it was too dark to continue. A tea interval was taken between 4.15pm and 4.30pm. Play therefore coincided with the hottest and, sometimes, the wettest part of the day.

Unusually for the 1930s, the fixtures included play on a Sunday. Perhaps because it did not start until the afternoon, allowing those who wanted to do so to attend church in the morning, religious objections were minimised. Travel between Lagos and Accra was still by boat, a journey of some three days, with one full day at sea. The visitors were hosted by players and officials of the home side, one host per visitor. Often, one or two players travelled with their wives.

In contrast to the situation in South America, cricket in what is now Malaysia and Singapore was being taken up by the local population. Outside of Singapore, the Europeans had been forced to encourage locals to play in order to provide sufficient numbers to organise matches. These people, particularly the Indian community, but to a lesser extent the Chinese and Malays, set up their own clubs. In the 1920s and 1930s the locals were not granted entry to bodies like the Selangor Club and the Singapore Cricket Club, which were still exclusive to white expatriates. The different communities in Singapore established their own clubs as early as the 1880s. The Singapore Recreation Club for Eurasians was founded in 1883 and the Straits Chinese Recreation Club in 1885. With the growth of a middle class among all the different communities, the European dominance of local sport was brought into question and multiracial representative teams became increasingly accepted.

Against the Australians in 1927, Theo Leijssius, a Eurasian, represented All-Malaya and Lall Singh played for the Federated Malay States. Indeed, Lall Singh became Malaya's outstanding cricketer of his generation and a superior player to any of the Europeans. He found sponsorship from a Kuala Lumpur businessman to gain employment with the Maharajah of Patiala, in whose state he rose to be an assistant district commissioner. He was invited to Test trials and then selected by India for their tour of England in 1932, where he played in one Test match. In the mid 1930s, he played first-class cricket for Patiala, Southern Punjab and the Hindus, but also found time to return frequently to Malaya, where he was a regular choice for the Federated Malay States in their annual fixture against the Straits Settlements. After he returned to Malaya full-time, he was appointed head groundsman and coach to the Royal Selangor Club, even though he could not become a member.

By the 1930s, cricket in Malaysia and Singapore had changed from being the preserve of civil servants with public school and university backgrounds to an activity which, while retaining a public school element, included a wider population of the middle class, both locals and Europeans, as well as the military. This created a problem when selecting teams for the annual Straits–FMS fixture, since all players were expected to pay their own expenses. The hosts usually provided accommodation for the visitors, in the houses of local players and officials, but the transport costs were an issue for people of only modest means, in addition to the loss of income from being away from work. Wherever the fixture was played, travel costs affected both the away and home teams.

When the Federated Malay States hosted, the match was usually held in Kuala Lumpur, but the home team included players from Perak, Negeri Sembilan and, sometimes, other states, all of whom had to travel. By the 1930s, the Straits were alternating their home matches between Singapore and Penang and including players from both areas, so that there were always some 'home' players who had to travel. The outcome was that, often, both sides fielded teams that were weaker than optimum.

Overall, the inter-war period was marked by two general trends. Where efforts were made to promote cricket more widely within the community, to either the growing numbers of middle class or the local rather than expatriate population, it became well-established as an important amateur sport. Where it remained the preserve of an elite, normally expatriate, group, it declined, particularly where, as in South America and China, the British influence on the economy also lessened and, as a result, there were fewer resident expatriates to organise and participate in matches.

Quick hundred, quick victory and quick getaway

Shanghai were confident of beating Hong Kong on their home ground in May 1923, having won the two previous encounters of the Interport Series. The strength of Shanghai can be gauged by the players who were not selected. These included Albert Lanning (8), M.J.Divecha (8), W.G.C.Clifford (4), George Billings (4) and E.G.Barnes (7), the figures in parentheses indicating the number of times each represented Shanghai in other Interport matches. Hong Kong included two Asians; Arthur Rumjahn, who had become the first Asian to represent Hong Kong when he played against Shanghai in 1921, and U.M. Omar, who was five times Hong Kong's national lawn bowls champion. There was only one person from the military, Captain E.R.S. Dodds.

Hong Kong's strengths lay in Tam Pearce, a merchant with J.D. Hutchison & Co. and the father of Alec Pearce, who played for Kent between 1930 and 1946; Geoffrey Sayer, who went to Hong Kong in 1910 as a cadet officer and later became director of education and authored several books on the history of the Territory; and Harold Owen-Hughes, a middle-order batsman and accurate slow left-arm bowler.

Shanghai batted first and scored runs freely and attractively. Their side was strengthened by the arrival of Ivo Barrett, who had left Malaya to join the Shanghai Municipal Police. He, Ollerdessen and Muriel all made half-centuries and, by mid-afternoon, a sizeable total was in prospect. The middle order then inexplicably collapsed against the left-arm spin of Owen-Hughes. Only an aggressive tail-end slog by Peck enabled the home side to post a competitive score. Hong Kong lost Pearce and Rumjahn before the close to finish on 72/2.

On the second day Sayer batted well for his 57, but Quick and Owen-Hughes both got out when well set. Wild, who later moved to Japan and represented Yokohama, frustrated the home side and, with the help of Dodds and 40 extras, took Hong Kong to within 19 runs of Shanghai's first-innings total. The late-order onslaught spoiled the figures of Quayle, another member of the Shanghai Municipal Police, who otherwise bowled well. Owen-Hughes was again in top form as Shanghai lost their top four batsmen for low scores in their second innings. Quayle, Hayward and Leach led the recovery on the third day, the trio of half-centuries taking their side to a winning position. Leach benefitted from some good sportsmanship when the visitors allowed him to continue after he was given out, apparently wrongly, by the umpire. He and Quayle added 132 for the sixth wicket. Owen-Hughes then removed the tail to secure 6-74 and ten wickets in the match.

Requiring 275 to win, Hong Kong lost Sayer, Quick and Owen-Hughes to the bowling of Quayle. Pearce survived to extend the match into the fourth day and went on to give an immaculate performance, scoring from the loose balls and never giving a chance. When Wild was caught by Barrett and Dodds became Quayle's 11th victim of the match, 52 runs were still needed and Shanghai were still favourites to win. Omar, however, defended well, while Pearce went on to an undefeated 145, containing 20 fours, to take Hong Kong to victory just after tea.

The crowd gave Pearce a generous ovation as he was carried shoulder high to the pavilion by his fellow players. To everyone's surprise, he left the ground immediately. He had planned to return to England as soon as the match ended and had to catch the MS *Empress of Asia* before its departure for Canada. It was rumoured that the captain purposely delayed the ship's sailing so that Pearce could finish his innings. Pearce sent a telegram from on board, expressing thanks for the excellent hospitality afforded to Hong Kong's cricketers. The visitors also commented on the sporting attitude of the crowd, despite Shanghai losing the match. With 1,214 runs scored in an even contest, the Shanghai press considered it to be one of the most interesting games for many years.

SHANGHAI v HONG KONG

Shanghai Cricket Club, Nanjing Lu, Shanghai, 16, 17 and 18 May 1923

Hong Kong won by three wickets

SHANGHAI		R B M 4s 6s		R B M 4s 6s
H.B.Ollerdessen	b Young	96	st Davies b Quick	1
A.A.Claxton	c Owen-Hughes b Quick	29	c Quick b Owen-Hughes	12
E.I.M.Barrett	c Wood b Owen-Hughes	60	run out	2
H.E.Muriel	run out	89	b Owen-Hughes	1
J.A.Quayle	b Owen-Hughes	0	c Dodds b Sayer	84
A.W.Hayward	b Omar	3	c&b Owen-Hughes	51
D.W.Leach	b Omar	3	c Davies b Sayer	68
W.N.Hansell	c&b Owen-Hughes	17	not out	18
H.W.Allison	b Young	0	st Davies b Owen-Hughes	10
H.C.B.Peck	c Rumjahn b Owen-Hughes	42	b Owen-Hughes	0
J.A.Isaacs	not out	2	c Young b Owen-Hughes	2
	Extras	10		6
		351		**255**

HONG KONG		R B M 4s 6s		R B M 4s 6s
T.E.Pearce	b Quayle	5	not out	145 20
G.R.Sayer	c Claxton b Quayle	57	lbw b Quayle	7
A.A.Rumjahn	b Isaacs	21	c Quayle b Peck	38
Rev E.K.Quick	b Quayle	21	b Quayle	6
H.Owen-Hughes	b Isaacs	30	b Quayle	0
A.E.Wood	run out	0	c Claxton b Peck	28
R.H.Wild	run out	83	c Barrett b Quayle	34
Capt E.R.S.Dodds	b Quayle	43	c Claxton b Quayle	0
U.M.Omar	not out	14	not out	13
+L.J.Davies	b Quayle	16		
F.N.Young	b Quayle	2		
	Extras	40		5
		332	(7 wickets)	**276**

Hong Kong	O	M	R	W	nb	w		O	M	R	W	nb	w	fow
Young	24	3	83	2				17	1	61	0			1
Owen-Hughes	21	2	92	4				26	3	74	6			2
Quick	18	1	74	1				25	4	84	1			3
Omar	19	1	74	2				2	0	70	0			4
Sayer	5	0	18	0				7	1	23	2			5
														6

Shanghai	O	M	R	W	nb	w		O	M	R	W	nb	w	7
Quayle	17.5	1	70	6			(2)	27.4	3	97	5			8
Allison	23	3	39	0			(1)	26	6	63	0			9
Peck	5	0	24	0			(5)	11	3	30	2			10
Leach	17	2	55	0			(3)	35	9	53	0			
Isaacs	23	5	59	2			(4)	9	0	19	0			
Hansell	8	0	30	0				4	2	9	0			
Barrett	3	0	15	0										

Umpires: [unknown]

Toss: not known.

The breakdown of extras is not known.

Close of play: 1st day – Hong Kong (1) 72-2; 2nd day – Shanghai (2) 133-5; 3rd day – not known.

Hennessy harasses the Australians

Several members of the Australian touring party to England in 1926 wanted to spend some time in Malaya and Singapore on their way home. Nothing could be arranged at short notice, however, so some of the players, notably Charles Macartney and Bill Oldfield, decided to arrange a separate, private visit. Contacts were made with Maurice Phillips and Percy Penman, two Australians working in Malaya as engineers. Penman had played first-class cricket for New South Wales between 1904 and 1906, before moving to Malaya after graduating from Sydney University.

Oldfield managed to get the tour sanctioned by the Australian Cricket Board of Control at its meeting in Melbourne on 25 March 1927. He did this by raising the proposal with Harry Gregory, the board's chairman, after the official meeting had finished. Gregory, a relative newcomer to the politics of Australian cricket, readily gave the board's approval. The decision was not revoked, but it was not popular among the board's members. At the next meeting in September the constitution was amended so that the chairman alone could not authorise any future tours. The tour was underwritten by the Singapore Cricket Union. The Federated Malay States Railways made transport available for the whole tour, including a sleeping car and a dining car when required. The tourists played nine matches between 27 May and 26 June and, in between, were taken on sightseeing tours and entertained at numerous dinners. Unfortunately, the party contained only 11 players, so, when illness or injury occurred, Australians living in Malaya were asked to substitute.

For the first of two Tests against All-Malaya, the Australians travelled on the night train from Singapore and they initially arrived in Kuala Lumpur at 6.50am on 2 June. They were met by the acting British resident in Selangor, the Hon. James Lornie. They had a tour of the Kuala Lumpur Museum and were then taken to the rubber estate of Mr W.R. Shelton-Agar, where they had tiffin. Shelton-Agar became an expert on pests and diseases in plantation agriculture. He later moved to Ceylon, where he managed tea plantations. The rest of the day was free. Heavy rain late in the day and again on the Friday morning meant that there were puddles on the ground before the match was due to start. However, the weather cleared and, after several inspections, play began at 12.15pm. Macartney won the toss and invited the home side to bat.

The Malayan side was very experienced with six of the starting 11 having played first-class cricket in either England or Australia. However, the average age of the side was nearly 40. Their leading player was Dr Patrick Hennessy, a physician and ophthalmologist based at Ipoh in Perak. He was born Patrick Howard Hennessy Pereira in Bengaluru, India, in 1879, but changed his name to Hennessy, his mother's maiden name, in 1907. He studied medicine at Madras Medical College, graduating in 1905. He then became a house-surgeon at the General Hospital, Singapore, before taking postgraduate studies in London. After a short period as an assistant medical officer at Shoreditch Infirmary in east London, he joined the Colonial Medical Service and spent his working life in Malaya. He retired to southern England and served in the Emergency Medical Service during the Second World War, based at Friern Hospital in north London.

Malaya began circumspectly and, in Everett's second over, Congdon was well caught in the slips by Sullivan. Bostock-Hill scored two elegant boundaries off Everett, one to the off and one to leg, but was then bowled by Macartney. Hussey gave a catch to Oldfield behind the wicket, so that, after half an hour, three wickets were down for 21 runs. With the arrival of Leijssius at the crease, the scoring rate slowed. When he fell to Andrews at 1.05pm, only seven more runs had been added. Rhodes and Foster forced the pace and when lunch was taken at 1.20pm, Malaya had reached 58/4. Tiffin was clearly a leisurely affair since play did not resume until 2.40pm. Rhodes and Foster then scored freely, increasing the total to 71 before Foster was leg before. His 30 was the highest individual score of the innings and was made in 73 minutes off 74 balls. Rhodes was dismissed soon after, followed quickly by Braddell, splendidly caught by Adams, and Penman, also caught, both falling to the bowling of Andrews.

An unfortunate accident then took place. Oldfield was hit on the nose by one of Macartney's deliveries and had to retire. Woodfull took over wicketkeeping duties and Green, a local, fielded as substitute. Brand miscued an attempted pull to a ball from Andrews and was caught at long-on by Adams. The tail managed to raise the total to 100 at 3.40pm, but five minutes later, the innings ended on 108. Andrews had figures of 7-44 with his leg spin.

The Australians began their innings at 4pm and soon lost Mayne, caught by the wicketkeeper in Hennessy's second over. Tea was taken 15 minutes later with the score on 10/1. After an interval of only 15 minutes, play resumed and the visitors lost five wickets very quickly for the addition of only 19 runs. Hennessy took four of these, finding a consistently awkward line and length. At one point, his analysis was 5-7 off 49 balls. There were two splendid catches, one by Rhodes at cover point to remove Bardsley and one an excellent caught-and-bowled by Bostock-Hill to dismiss Macartney. Everett attacked the bowling, scoring 26 runs in 14 minutes, including ten (a four and a six) in each of two overs by Hennessy. Bostock-Hill took another excellent catch, this time in the slips, to remove Rofe, but Adams made a useful 20 to give support to Everett. In spite of these efforts, the innings folded for 85, Oldfield being unable to bat because of his injury.

Hennessy was easily the most dangerous of the attack, troubling all the Australians with a superb display of off spin to take 7-42. He managed to get the match ball and have it autographed and mounted as a memento of the occasion. Congdon and Hansell built on the Malayan lead of 23 on the first innings, adding nine runs in ten minutes before poor light stopped play for the day.

On Saturday morning the weather was wet and gloomy and there were concerns that there would be no play. At 9am all the players attended the Sultan of Selangor's birthday parade during which time the clouds began to thin and by 10am the sun was shining. Pitch inspections were carried out at 11.40am and 12.30pm and it was decided that, if there was no further rain, the match would restart at 2.30pm.

Oldfield had recovered sufficiently to take up his wicketkeeping duties but both sides were hampered by illness and injury. For the Australians, Mayne had a stomach upset, C.H. Miller substituting in the field, and Gamble was unable to bowl because of a strained back. For Malaya, Foster had injured his right hand while fielding on the first day and did not bat until number ten; Penman was unable to field because of a bad leg and Green acted as substitute. He therefore fielded for both sides at various times during the match.

Almost immediately after play began, Macartney narrowly missed bowling Congdon and very nearly held a fine caught-and-bowled off Hansell. The latter miss was not expensive as Hansell was soon dismissed. Congdon and Leijssius accumulated runs at a good rate, Congdon reaching his fifty with two consecutive fours off Andrews, who then bowled Leijssius. Hussey hit a four off his first ball, but was caught by Woodfull in the slips off the next ball. Bostock-Hill batted soundly, but with the score on 110, Congdon fell to a smart catch by Everett in the slips. He received a hearty ovation from the crowd for his 71, made in 80 minutes off 99 balls and including one six and eight fours. The visitors then removed Rhodes, smartly stumped by Oldfield, and Bostock-Hill, well caught at cover.

Brand and Braddell proceeded to bat sensibly, defending well and scoring off almost every loose ball. Just before tea, Macartney bowled Brand to leave the score on 152/7 at the break. Two wickets fell at the same score after the interval before Foster and Hennessy frustrated the tourists. They prolonged the innings until 5.15pm, but without scoring many runs. Hennessy faced four overs from Adams without scoring. Malaya were finally dismissed for 158. The Australians required 182 to win. Surprisingly, they made a start at 5.30pm, despite dusk approaching. Twenty minutes of play was possible before the light failed completely with the score at 10/0.

On the Sunday, a rest day, six of the visitors went on a rafting picnic on the River Batang Kali, in the mountains of Upper Selangor to the north of Kuala Lumpur. Today, the area is an even bigger tourist attraction, being part of the Genting Highlands resort. Batang Kali also has a tragic place in Malaysian history as the site of a massacre during the Malayan Emergency in 1948, when 24 unarmed villagers were killed by British troops. After their exertions of the morning, the Australians were entertained at the Sungai Gapi Estate by Mr H.H. Bell, who provided a curry tiffin.

The Monday morning was dry and fine and a prompt start was made at noon. Rofe was soon caught in the slips by Hennessy but Bostock-Hill missed a caught-and-bowled chance offered by Macartney. Woodfull and Macartney played cautiously and were looking dangerous until Penman, fit again, caught and bowled Macartney. The half-century came up with Woodfull and Andrews playing well. Woodfull was run out with the score on 65. Bardsley continued the free scoring, but in the last over before lunch, Penman had Andrews superbly caught by Hennessy in the slips and then trapped Oldfield leg before without scoring. With the score on 98/5, tiffin was taken, hosted by the Selangor Club.

After lunch, Bardsley and Mayne played fine cricket, but some excellent fielding kept the scoring shots down to ones and twos. Bardsley fell to an excellent catch by Foster at mid-on and Mayne was bowled by an almost unplayable delivery from Hennessy. The visitors counter-attacked with Everett hitting Bostock-Hill for six to bring the total to 120 and Sullivan striking the same bowler for ten runs in one over. Hennessy meanwhile accounted for Everett and Gamble and the innings ended on 142, with Adams unable to bat because of sciatica. The spectators gave the home side a tremendous ovation for a splendid victory by 39 runs. Although the Australian side was not the strongest, nine of the 11 had played at first-class level and four had represented their country in Test matches. It was therefore a considerable achievement by Malaya to beat them.

A post-match reception and dinner were held for the teams at the Station Hotel, Kuala Lumpur, during which the Selangor Club Band provided music. This was followed by a dance at The Selangor Club. The following day was free before the team left in the evening by train for Seremban for their next match against Southern Malaya. The Australians gained their revenge in the second Test later in the tour, winning in Singapore by an innings and 136 runs, which was probably a fairer reflection of the difference between the two sides.

ALL-MALAYA v AUSTRALIANS

The Selangor Club Padang, Kuala Lumpur, 3, 4 and 6 June 1927

All-Malaya won by 39 runs

ALL-MALAYA		R	B	M	4s	6s		R	B	M	4s	6s
C.H.Congdon	c Sullivan b Everett	2					c Everett b Andrews	71	99	80	8	1
J.A.Hussey	c Oldfield b Sullivan	5					(4) c Woodfull b Adams	4				
A.J.Bostock-Hill	b Macartney	8					(5) c Andrews b Everett	16				
*N.J.A.Foster	lbw b Andrews	30	74	73			(10) c Bardsley b Macartney	6				
T.J.Leijssius	b Andrews	7					(3) b Adams	19				
V.E.H.Rhodes	c Adams b Andrews	16					st Oldfield b Andrews	8				
R.L.L.Braddell	c Adams b Andrews	7					b Adams	14				
+G.M.Brand	c Adams b Andrews	9					b Macartney	13				
A.P.Penman	c Everett b Andrews	3					b Macartney	0				
W.N.Hansell	not out	3					(2) b Macartney	5				
P.H.Hennessy	c Gamble b Andrews	9					not out	0				
	b2 lb3 nb4	9					lb2	2				
		108						**158**				

AUSTRALIANS		R	B	M	4s	6s		R	B	M	4s	6s
W.M.Woodfull	c Foster b Hennessy	7					run out	37				
E.R.Mayne	c Brand b Hennessy	2					(7) b Hennessy	12				
R.Bardsley	c Rhodes b Hennessy	3					(5) c Foster b Bostock-Hill	11				
T.J.E.Andrews	lbw b Hennessy	8					c Hennessy b Penman	34				
E.F.Rofe	c B'ck-Hill b Hennessy	11					(2) c Hennessy b Bostock-Hill	1				
*C.G.Macartney	c&b Bostock-Hill	2					(3) c&b Penman	16				
J.P.Sullivan	b Hennessy	1					(9) not out	11				
C.S.Everett	c Foster b Hennessy	26	14				b Hennessy	12				
E.W.Adams	c Foster b Bostock-Hill	20					absent ill					
H.S.Gamble	not out	4					(10) b Hennessy	3				
+W.A.S.Oldfield	absent injured						(6) lbw b Penman	0				
	w1	1					b1 lb3 nb1	5				
		85						**142**				

Australians	O	M	R	W	nb	w		O	M	R	W	nb	w	fow	Mal (1)	Aus (1)	Mal (2)	Aus (2)
Everett	8	1	18	1	3	-		11	1	39	1	-	-	1	2 (1)	3 (2)	32 (2)	14 (2)
Macartney	14	7	14	1	-	-		14.2	5	31	4	-	-	2	11 (3)	12 (1)	79 (3)	37 (3)
Sullivan	8	2	23	1	-	-								3	21 (2)	13 (3)	83 (4)	65 (1)
Andrews	15.3	3	44	7	1	-	(4)	12	2	51	2	-	-	4	28 (5)	21 (4)	110 (1)	98 (4)
Adams							(3)	16	6	35	3	-	-	5	71 (4)	28 (6)	122 (6)	98 (6)
														6	72 (6)	29 (7)	125 (5)	113 (5)
All-Malaya	O	M	R	W	nb	w		O	M	R	W	nb	w					
Hennessy	14	4	42	7	-	-		14.5	5	30	3	-	-	7	80 (7)	59 (8)	152 (8)	117 (7)
Braddell	3	0	6	0	-	1	(4)	1	0	11	0	-	-	8	90 (9)	65 (5)	152 (9)	128 (8)
Bostock-Hill	11.1	2	36	2	-	-	(2)	20	1	60	2	1	-	9	91 (8)	85 (9)	152 (7)	142 (10)
Penman							(3)	7	0	25	3	-	-	10	108 (11)		158 (10)	
Hansell							(5)	2	0	11	0	-	-					

Umpires: R.T.Foster and M.L.Phillips

Toss: Australians

Close of play: 1st day – All-Malaya (2) 9-0; 2nd day – Australians (2) 10-0.

In All-Malaya's first innings W.M.Woodfull took over wicketkeeping duties after W.A.S.Oldfield was injured, T.C.Green substituted in the field; Oldfield recovered and kept wicket in All-Malaya's second innings.

On the second day, C.H.Miller substituted in the field for E.R.Mayne, who had a stomach upset, and Green substituted for A.P.Penman who had a bad leg. H.S.Gamble was unable to bowl because of a bad back.

Dour cricket, dire weather

The annual three-day first-class fixture between Scotland and Ireland in 1928 began on 7 July. This was the eighth since the series restarted in 1920 after a break for the First World War. Scotland had won two of these matches to Ireland's one, with the remainder ending in draws. The overall standings in the series since 1909 were very much in Scotland's favour, having won five matches to Ireland's two. The 1928 match was hosted by the Grange Cricket Club at Raeburn Place, Edinburgh.

For once, in an away fixture, Ireland were able to put out a relatively strong side, whereas Scotland were weakened by the unavailability of two of their best bowlers, William Anderson (right-arm fast) and Robert Sievwright (slow left-arm). The Irish team were multi-talented with James Ganly and Arthur Douglas having represented their country internationally in rugby union, James McDonald and Trevor McVeagh in hockey and William Pemberton in table tennis. McVeagh had also played for Ireland at lawn tennis and squash. He eventually gave up his cricket to concentrate on tennis, aside from his professional career as a solicitor. In contrast, James Tennent was the only Scottish dual international, in rugby union. Tennent had previously played cricket for Rangoon against Ceylon in 1913.

Other players in the match who had wider cricket experience were Gilbert Alexander, an Army officer who later represented Gibraltar against a touring side led by G.O.B. Allen in April 1935; Alexander Stevenson, who joined the Colonial Civil Service and went to Kenya, where he played two matches for the Officials in their annual series against the Settlers; and Thomas Dixon, who was born in India and, after graduating from Trinity College Dublin, returned there, where he played four matches for Delhi between 1934/35 and 1936/37. He later went with his brother Patrick to Kenya to work as missionaries.

Despite heavy rain over the previous few days, the match began on time and the day turned out bright and sunny. The attendance, which reached around 2,000 by the afternoon, was viewed as somewhat poor considering the weather, particularly for a Saturday of an international fixture. Ganly won the toss for Ireland and elected to bat on a pitch which proved slow and gave little assistance to the bowlers. Thomas MacDonald and Robinson, perhaps mindful of Ireland's limited success in the series to date, began carefully and only 75 runs were on the board when, just before lunch, Robinson played the first bad stroke of the morning and was caught at cover.

After the interval, James MacDonald and Ganly were dismissed quickly, but Thomas MacDonald passed his half-century and McVeagh gave splendid support in a partnership of 144. Kerr, the Scottish captain, rotated his bowlers, but no combination was able to make the breakthrough. With runs coming more freely, he called in desperation on Stevenson to try his lobs, but these were dispatched for three fours, a two and a single in one over, and he was immediately replaced. Shortly after MacDonald had reached his hundred, McVeagh was caught behind off the bowling of Melville. Douglas, the new batsman, gave the bowlers no respite, hitting any loose balls to the boundary.

With the tea interval approaching, Kerr brought on Alexander as the seventh bowler to be tried, and he was quickly successful in having MacDonald stumped. His 132 had taken four and a half hours during which time he never made a false stroke, but neither did he provide much excitement for the spectators. He hit 11 fours and was never once seen to strike the ball in the air. Alexander soon accounted for Thornton, after which Groves and Watson worked their way through the Irish tail. Ireland were all out for 346 which was a good performance by Scotland, given that, at one time, it looked as though the visitors would bat all day and get over 400.

Scotland were aided by some fine fielding with Kerr and Tennent outstanding. Craig also kept wicket well with two catches and a stumping, but his performance was marred by conceding 22 byes; these came off seven balls, some of which he failed to take because he thought they were going to hit the wicket only for them to narrowly miss the stumps.

Craig went on to lead a charmed life in the three overs that were possible in Scotland's innings before the day's end. Instead of defending, he struck two fours, one of which went in the air close to but just between two fielders.

The second day was cold and windy and decidedly unpleasant for spectators and players alike. The wind was so strong in the afternoon that it was necessary to dispense with the bails. It was barely surprising that the attendance at no time got above about 500. With no noticeable change in the pitch, Scotland gave a surprisingly tame display of batting. The visitors bowled and fielded well, but too many batsmen got out to ill-judged strokes. Scotland made very slow progress. Thirteeen of the first 26 overs were maidens. Craig mis-hit Dixon to cover point with the score on 37 and Ireland should have had another wicket very quickly, but Kelly failed to gather the ball properly from James MacDonald's bowling and Stevenson escaped being stumped. Stevenson eventually fell to a good catch at short square leg, hitting a full toss firmly to Thomas MacDonald, who parried the ball one-handedly and then took the catch safely in both hands. Mackay tried to put some life into Scotland's innings and proved a contrast to the rather dour Kerr, who took no risks, waiting for the bad balls to hit, which were few and far between.

Lunch was taken with the score on 121/3 then, with only one run added after the break, the Irish gained the upper hand when Mackay and Kerr were both dismissed. The Scottish captain had batted for two and a quarter hours and hit seven fours. He gave only one chance when, having made 48, he should have been stumped after advancing down the wicket and missing a full toss. Useful contributions from Alexander and Melville followed. Alexander's effort lasted an hour and a half; his first scoring stroke was a six to which he added six fours in his half-century. After Melville gave a return catch to Pemberton to end a seventh-wicket partnership of 59, the tail succumbed rapidly. The last three wickets fell for the addition of a solitary run.

It was expected that Ireland would endeavour to make quick runs to add to their commanding lead of 135 on the first innings with a view to declaring as early as possible on the last day with sufficient time to bowl the opposition out and win the match. Perhaps the loss of Robinson before a run was scored had an effect, but Ireland proceeded with extreme caution. Six maidens were bowled and the first run from the bat came from a misfield off the fourth ball of the seventh over. After 40 minutes Ireland had reached a mere 13/1. The MacDonald brothers put on 85 for the second wicket but both fell at that score, followed soon after by Ganly. McVeagh and Douglas survived to the close, though the former was lucky to escape being run out, the throw to the bowler's end being poor, and also being caught-and-bowled, Groves failing to hold on to a sharp chance, one-handed.

The weather on the final day was, if anything, worse. The wind remained strong and, again, for a short time it was necessary to dispense with the bails. For much of the day there was continuous drizzle, which seemed to alternate with heavy showers. To their credit, the players and umpires stayed on the field for all but ten minutes early in the day. McVeagh and Douglas at last showed some urgency and scored off almost every ball, adding 104 in only 50 minutes. Douglas was bowled after the partnership reached 120, but, surprisingly, Ireland prolonged their innings while six more runs were added. When the declaration came, Scotland were set a target of 357 runs in about four and a half hours.

Kerr and Alexander opened with a partnership of 50 in 87 minutes before the latter was well caught by Douglas on the boundary. Stevenson and Groves accompanied Kerr in partnerships of 89 and 78 respectively and a victory for Scotland looked a possibility. Ireland's bowling resources were depleted when, after Seymour had bowled two balls, the umpires consulted; Seymour's fourth ball was no-balled as a throw following a decision by Deyes at square leg.

Ganly was forced to retire Seymour from the attack after one over, even though his five overs in the first innings had passed without intervention, despite some criticism from the press. The bowler never appeared for Ireland again.

With 200 on the scoreboard the Irish captain took the new ball and Scotland's innings, on 217/2, surprisingly fell apart, as first Groves, and then Kerr, Mackay, Tennent and Melville were all dismissed for the addition of only 21 runs. Dixon had an inspired spell during which he took 4-9 in six overs. Meanwhile, Kerr played splendidly for his 137, made in three and a half hours, before being brilliantly stumped by Kelly. With 23 fours, 67 per cent of his runs came in boundaries. Kelly also took a good catch to dismiss Mackay and, following an indifferent performance in Scotland's first innings, gave an excellent display of wicketkeeping, standing up to the stumps to the fast-medium bowlers.

Forty minutes remained when Scotland's ninth wicket fell and Watson joined Drinnan. Both had some luck, but, in what was arguably the most exciting period of the match they defended resolutely and despatched the bad balls to the boundary. The pair not only frustrated the Irish by playing out time, they did so with increasing confidence in a partnership of 44. The last quarter of an hour was particularly tense as Scotland got closer and closer to saving the match and eventually succeeded. It was a pity that there were only a few hundred people in the ground to witness the events. The Irishmen were so impressed by Scotland's efforts that they joined the spectators in applauding the batsmen back to the pavilion.

SCOTLAND v IRELAND

First-class

Grange Cricket Club, Raeburn Place, Edinburgh, 7, 9 and 10 July 1928

Match drawn

IRELAND		R	B	M	4s	6s		R	B	M	4s	6s
T.J.MacDonald	st Craig b Alexander	132	270		11	-	b Drinnan	35			3	-
A.J.H.Robinson	c Tennent b Drinnan	32			2	-	lbw b Watson	0			-	-
J.MacDonald	c Craig b Watson	2			-	-	b Groves	38			3	-
*J.B.Ganly	lbw b Melville	4			1	-	lbw b Groves	3			-	-
T.G.B.McVeagh	c Craig b Melville	65			4	-	not out	56			5	-
A.C.Douglas	lbw b Watson	57	50		5	-	b Drinnan	63			8	-
P.A.Thornton	c Tennent b Alexander	1			-	-	not out	3			-	-
+A.P.Kelly	c Kerr b Groves	15			1	-						
T.H.Dixon	b Watson	5			1	-						
E.N.Seymour	b Groves	0			-	-						
W.C.Pemberton	not out	3			-	-						
	b22 lb6 w2	30					b19 lb3 w1	23				
		346					(5 wickets declared)	**221**				

SCOTLAND		R	B	M	4s	6s		R	B	M	4s	6s
*J.Kerr	lbw b Dixon	52	115		7	-	st Kelly b Pemberton	137	210		23	-
+L.Craig	c Douglas b Dixon	17			2	-	(8) b Douglas	13			2	-
A.J.Stevenson	c T.J.MacD'd b J.MacDonald	16			2	-	lbw b J.MacDonald	28			4	-
C.Groves	c Thornton b J.MacDonald	0			-	-	b Dixon	31			4	-
D.A.Mackay	c Thornton b Pemberton	29	30		4	1	c Kelly b Dixon	4			1	-
G.W.A.Alexander	b Dixon	52	90		6	1	(2) c Douglas b Pemberton	19			1	-
J.M.Tennent	b Pemberton	9			-	-	(6) b Dixon	1			-	-
C.Melville	c&b Pemberton	24			4	-	(7) b Dixon	7			1	-
C.S.Scobie	c T.J.MacDonald b Dixon	1			-	-	c McVeagh b Douglas	5			-	-
W.M.R.Drinnan	not out	0			-	-	not out	24			4	-
T.Watson	b Dixon	0			-	-	not out	25	40		4	-
	b9 lb1 nb1	11					b3 lb3 nb1 w1	8				
		211					(9 wickets)	**302**				

Scotland	O	M	R	W	nb	w	O	M	R	W	nb	w
Watson	29	3	74	3	-	- (2)	15	6	34	1	-	-
Drinnan	16	3	59	1	-	- (6)	12	3	43	2	-	1
Melville	24	4	72	2	-	-	5	2	14	0	-	-
Scobie	12	1	35	0	-	2 (5)	4	0	12	0	-	-
Groves	13	3	31	2	-	- (1)	21	5	53	2	-	-
Stevenson	1	0	15	0	-	-						
Alexander	9	1	30	2	-	- (4)	8	1	42	0	-	-

fow	Ir (1)	Sc (1)	Ir (2)	Sc (2)
1	75 (2)	37 (2)	0 (2)	50 (2)
2	92 (1)	79 (3)	85	139 (3)
3	101 (4)	79 (4)	85	217 (4)
4	245 (5)	122 (5)	95 (4)	225 (1)
5	296 (3)	122 (1)	215 (6)	225 (5)
6	304 (7)	151 (7)		233 (6)
7	322	210 (8)		238 (7)
8	332	210 (6)		253 (8)
9	339	211 (9)		258 (9)
10	346	211 (11)		

Ireland	O	M	R	W	nb	w	O	M	R	W	nb	w
Dixon	26.4	10	52	5	-	-	34	11	97	4	-	1
Pemberton	24	9	40	3	-	-	34	8	97	2	-	-
J.MacDonald	22	8	54	2	1	-	35	7	47	1	-	-
Seymour	5	1	17	0	-	-	1	0	4	0	1	-
Douglas	7	1	22	0	-	-	9	4	24	2	-	-
Thornton	4	0	15	0	-	-	2	0	17	0	-	-
Ganly							2	0	8	0	-	-

Umpires: G.Deyes and Fozzard

Toss: Ireland

Close of play: 1st day – Scotland (1) 11-0 (Kerr 1*, Craig 9*); 2nd day – Ireland (2) 111-4 (McVeagh 6*, Douglas 11*).

Nigeria defeat the locusts and the Gold Coast

The Nigerian team was weaker than usual for the 1931 European fixture against the Gold Coast at the Accra Oval. William Shirley, author of *A History of the Nigerian Police* (Lagos, 1950), Arthur Judd, Douglas Sewell, James Outram and Thomas Welch, all civil servants or political officers, had been forced to stay behind to deal with the effects of an invasion of locusts. For these people, work had to come before sport. They were further weakened when Hugh Stockwell seriously damaged his knee in the nets on the day of their arrival. They were fortunate to obtain the services of F.J. Duffy, who happened to be on business in Accra, as a replacement. One player on each side had previous experience of first-class cricket.

For Nigeria, it was Lieutenant-Commander Arthur Webb, who had represented the Royal Navy in 1919 and later went on to play for Leicestershire between 1933 and 1938. For the Gold Coast, it was Captain Michael Green, who had represented Gloucestershire between 1912 and 1928, the Europeans in India in 1922/23 and Essex in 1930. He later rose to the rank of brigadier before becoming better known as the manager of the MCC tour to South Africa in 1948/49 and joint manager of the tour to Australia and New Zealand in 1950/51.

The visitors were entertained on their first evening at a dance held at the Accra Club. Perhaps the evening's social gatherings was one reason why cricket did not start until 2.30pm the next day, after McLaren won the toss for the visitors and elected to bat. Butler and McLaren produced the best batting of the match, putting on 134 runs in an almost faultless display. Butler scored at a good pace and rarely hit the ball in the air. His first real mistake was his last, when he was dismissed leg before. Wickets fell regularly for the rest of the day until the batsmen appealed successfully against the light. Nigeria were then 245/5. In the evening, the teams attended a dinner at Government House.

Rain fell heavily for most of the second morning. The umpires and players agreed to resume play at 5.15pm but conditions were far from ideal. The fielders and the batsmen fell over several times on the slippery surface. Nigeria did their best to increase the scoring rate and at the close they were 316/7. Much against expectations, McLaren did not declare the next day. Rix set about the bowling in earnest in a stand of 74 before Bethem polished off the tail with his medium-paced off breaks, leaving McLaren to become the first player to carry his bat in Nigeria–Gold Coast matches. He received a tremendous ovation for his five hours at the crease.

The Gold Coast's reply was a poor effort. Either their players were jaded after nearly three days in the field or the efforts of entertaining their visitors were taking their toll. McLaren followed his batting with a fine display of bowling, taking five wickets in 17 overs with his right-arm fast-medium pace. Steventon, also right-arm fast medium, tied the batsmen to defence and Rix, with his leg breaks and googlies, removed the lower middle order with a hat-trick. Following on, Gold Coast lost four wickets before the close. On the Saturday evening the players were entertained to a dance at the Accra Tennis Club.

A ninth-wicket stand between Steemson and Gruchy almost secured the Gold Coast a draw. They resisted for nearly two hours while the visitors tried eight bowlers in an attempt to break the partnership. When they were within ten runs of making Nigeria bat again, Gruchy gave a catch to Webb, who kept wicket throughout the innings despite a damaged finger. Cust survived long enough to prevent an innings defeat, but Nigeria required only 19 runs to win with 20 minutes in which to make them. In indifferent light, as the street lamps were turned on, Nigeria secured a clear-cut victory. At 9.30pm, the staff of the Posts and Telegraph Department staged an At Home for the visitors at the Accra Oval.

GOLD COAST (EUROPEANS) v NIGERIA (EUROPEANS)

Accra Oval, Kinbu Road, Accra, 16, 17, 18, 19 and 20 April, 1931

Nigeria won by 9 wickets

NIGERIA		R	B	M	4s	6s		R	B	M	4s	6s
*F.J.McLaren	not out	152	300									
H.W.McCowan	c Bethem b Fitzgerald	1										
F.K.Butler	lbw b Gruchy	74					(1) not out	2				
E.O.Pretheroe	lbw b Bethem	6										
+A.G.G.Webb	b Gruchy	5										
F.R.King	c&b Fraser	19					(3) not out	14				
D.G.Stewart	c Cust b Gruchy	22										
F.J.Duffy	c Green b Gruchy	15										
B.W.Rix	b Bethem	47					(2) b Gruchy	0				
L.E.Steventon	b Bethem	5										
G.M.Cornish	b Bethem	5										
	b14 lb10 w4	28					b4	4				
		379					(1 wicket)	**20**				

GOLD COAST		R	B	M	4s	6s		R	B	M	4s	6s
W.Brian-Smith	c Steventon b Stewart	2					(4) lbw b Steventon	17				
P.H.Fitzgerald	c McLaren b Stewart	21					st Webb b Cornish	53				
W.R.Gosling	c McCowan b McLaren	34					b Steventon	13				
C.P.Woodhouse	not out	10					(1) lbw b Stewart	0				
*+M.A.Green	c Pretheroe b McLaren	19					b Stewart	46				
J.S.Reynolds	c Steventon b Rix	10					b Stewart	20				
R.J.A.Bethem	lbw b Rix	1					c Rix b Stewart	4				
A.R.B.Fraser	c McLaren b Rix	0					b Stewart	7				
B.T.Steemson	c Steventon b McLaren	6					not out	54				
L.S.Gruchy	b McLaren	0					c Webb b Butler	41				
A.D.Cust	lbw b McLaren	4					c McCowan b McLaren	13				
	b1 lb6	7					b10 lb5	15				
		114						**283**				

Gold Coast	O	M	R	W	nb	w		O	M	R	W	nb	w	fow	Nig (1)	GC (1)	GC (2)	Nig (2)
Fitzgerald	8	0	32	1										1	8 (2)	3	6 (1)	0 (2)
Bethem	31.4	7	108	4				1	0	8	0			2	142 (3)	62	29 (3)	
Gruchy	38	7	94	4	(1)			1.3	0	8	1			3	159 (4)	62	64	
Fraser	7	0	31	1										4	172 (5)	84	111	
Cust	5	0	35	0										5	201 (6)	97	146	
Woodhouse	8	0	31	0										6	249 (7)	99	154	
Reynolds	7	2	20	0										7	279 (8)	99	171	
														8	353 (9)	108	172	
Nigeria	O	M	R	W	nb	w		O	M	R	W	nb	w	9	361 (10)	108	255 (10)	
McLaren	16.4	7	28	5				21.3	10	36	1			10	379 (11)	114	283 (11)	
Steventon	9	1	31	0	(7)			26	8	52	2							
Stewart	15	9	17	2				29	9	52	5							
Rix	10	3	31	3				13	0	43	0							
Cornish					(2)			17	2	49	1							
McCowan					(5)			7	2	14	0							
Duffy					(6)			2	0	9	0							
Butler					(8)			3	1	13	1							

Umpires: A.C.Hands and Major C.R.Turner

Toss: Nigeria

Close of play: 1st day – Nigeria (1) 245-5 (McLaren 95*, Stewart 21*); 2nd day – Nigeria (1) 316-7 (McLaren 126*, Rix 24*); 3rd day – not known; 4th day – not known.

In Gold Coast's first innings B.W.Rix completed a hat-trick when dismissing J.S.Reynolds, R.J.A.Bethem and A.R.B.Fraser.

Scotland confirm South America's decline

The match played by the South Americans against Scotland was the 16th of their tour of Great Britain in 1932 and the last of their first-class fixtures. Scotland fielded two rugby union internationals, Ben Tod and William Logan. The encounter began on Thursday 7 July with the South Americans choosing to bat after Gibson had won the toss on a fine and bright day, but despite the good weather fewer than 1,000 attended.

The South Americans began steadily against some very ordinary bowling. There was little to entertain the spectators. The most exciting event was the superb run-out of Paul, who was batting confidently when Baxter ran from mid-on to behind the bowler, picked up the ball with his left hand, transferred it to his right and then threw down the wicket with a direct hit. Jackson put some spirit into the proceedings, displaying a wide range of strokes, including some well-placed cover drives. His 56, made in 75 minutes, included nine fours.

After Ferguson and Dennet Ayling added 69 for the fifth wicket, Scotland's bowling improved and, by mid-afternoon, runs were more difficult to make. Ferguson battled to survive, being missed by the wicketkeeper off Baxter when he had made 32 and getting a favourable decision from the umpire when Jones thought he had made a good low catch at square leg. The lower-order batsmen offered little resistance and the total of 220 was a shade disappointing. Scotland bowled and fielded well and Baxter deserved his five-wicket haul. In the hour and a half before the close, Scotland lost four wickets. The South Americans fielded especially well in this session. Nicholson fell to an excellent catch at square leg by Latham and Knox took an even better catch to remove Tod.

The second day was much cooler than the first, with heavy cloud and strong winds. Although rain threatened, none fell, but for much of the time it was necessary to dispense with the bails. Not surprisingly, the attendance was again below 1,000. The weather seemed to affect the South Americans whose fielding deteriorated throughout the day, with several catches either missed or dropped. McTavish took advantage of the lapses to score a valuable 109, with one six and 11 fours. His partnership with Spowart for the sixth wicket yielded 116 runs and placed Scotland in a strong position, which was enhanced by Mortimer and Baxter in an entertaining last-wicket stand of 44 in 20 minutes.

Facing a deficit of 125, the South Americans responded poorly, losing four wickets for 54 before Latham and Knox offered some resistance. They made little attempt to score runs, waiting for the bad balls of which there were very few. In the last over of the day, Knox edged a ball from Baxter to the wicketkeeper, ending a partnership of 51 and leaving Latham undefeated after a stay of two and a quarter hours.

The cloud was higher on the last day and there were some sunny spells, but the strong cross-wind continued to prove a nuisance. Despite it being a Saturday and with the prospect of victory for the home team, the attendance again remained below 1,000. Dennet Ayling ensured that Scotland would need to bat a second time. In useful partnerships with Latham, Gibson and Grass he batted for an hour and a half, hitting six fours. Baxter gave an impressive display of fast bowling. His match return of 11-175 was his best performance in a career which marked him as one of Scotland's most successful pace bowlers of all time. His work as director of Spicers Ltd meant that he could not find the time to play more than a few matches each season.

Scotland made the 84 runs to win with ease. The match gave a very fair reflection of the relative strength of cricket of the two teams. Scotland were superior in all departments. The South Americans had strength in batting, but not all of their team was of first-class standard. No attempt was made to build on the achievements of the tour and South America never fielded another representative side.

SCOTLAND v SOUTH AMERICA

First-class

Grange Cricket Club, Raeburn Place, Edinburgh, 7, 8 and 9 July 1932

Scotland won by eight wickets

SOUTH AMERICA

Batsman	Dismissal	R	B	M	4s	6s	Dismissal (2)	R	B	M	4s	6s
+H.W.Marshal	lbw b Anderson	11			2	-	b Anderson	11			1	-
A.L.S.Jackson	b Baxter	56	75		9	-	c Logan b Baxter	6			-	-
J.Knox	b Baxter	8			1	-	(6) c Logan b Baxter	27			1	-
J.H.Paul	run out (Baxter)	16			1	-	b Anderson	0			-	-
G.W.Ferguson	b Mortimer	60	120		7	-	c Logan b Mortimer	11			-	-
E.N.D.Ayling	b Mortimer	25			2	-	(7) b Baxter	53	90		6	-
R.L.Latham	c Mortimer b Baxter	6			-	-	(3) c Logan b Mortimer	58	150		4	-
C.E.Ayling	not out	14			1	-	c Mortimer b Baxter	1			-	-
F.F.Keen	lbw b Mortimer	0			-	-	b Baxter	4			1	-
A.C.Grass	b Baxter	1			-	-	(11) not out	16			2	-
*C.H.Gibson	b Baxter	15			1	-	(10) c Logan b Baxter	3			-	-
Extras	b2 lb3 nb3	8					b7 lb7 nb3 w1	18				
Total		**220**						**208**				

SCOTLAND

Batsman	Dismissal	R	B	M	4s	6s	Dismissal (2)	R	B	M	4s	6s
J.Kerr	lbw b Keen	10			1	-	not out	39			5	-
J.F.Jones	lbw b Knox	54	120		3	-	b E.N.D.Ayling	33			5	-
H.L.Stewart	run out	8			-	-	b E.N.D.Ayling	5			1	-
W.Nicholson	c Latham b Paul	27			4	-	not out	3			-	-
B.R.Tod	c Knox b C.E.Ayling	0			-	-						
A.K.McTavish	c&b Gibson	109	150		11	1						
T.Spowart	lbw b Keen	66	130		8	-						
+W.R.Logan	c C.E.Ayling b Gibson	1			-	-						
*W.W.Anderson	b Keen	0			-	-						
J.Mortimer	b Paul	18			2	-						
A.D.Baxter	not out	26	20		3	1						
Extras	b20 lb3 nb2 w1	26					b1 lb2 nb1	4				
Total		**345**					(2 wickets)	**84**				

Scotland

	O	M	R	W	nb	w	O	M	R	W	nb	w	fow	SA (1)	Sc (1)	SA (2)	Sc (2)
Baxter	28.1	4	88	5	2	-	25.4	3	87	6	1	1	1	14 (1)	17 (1)	15 (2)	53 (2)
Anderson	11	2	32	1	-	-	23	5	56	2	1	-	2	38 (3)	28 (3)	29 (1)	71 (3)
Mortimer	24	4	67	3	1	- (4)	15	4	30	2	1	-	3	87 (4)	85 (4)	29 (4)	
Stewart	7	1	25	0	-	- (3)	8	3	11	0	-	-	4	99 (2)	88 (5)	54 (5)	
Tod							3	0	6	0	-	-	5	168 (6)	159 (2)	105 (6)	
													6	181 (7)	275 (6)	139 (3)	

South America

	O	M	R	W	nb	w	O	M	R	W	nb	w	fow	SA (1)	Sc (1)	SA (2)	Sc (2)
Gibson	21	5	72	2	2	1	4	0	18	0	1	-	7	199 (5)	277 (8)	140 (8)	
Keen	32	9	92	3	-	-	11	1	40	0	-	-	8	199 (9)	284 (9)	149 (9)	
C.E.Ayling	16	2	48	1	-	-							9	200 (10)	301 (7)	183 (10)	
E.N.D.Ayling	7	1	22	0	-	- (3)	9	3	22	2	-	-	10	220 (11)	345 (10)	208 (7)	
Paul	9.3	1	38	2	-	-											
Knox	13	3	46	1	-	-											
Ferguson	1	0	1	0	-	-											

Umpires: G.Deyes and C.S.Scobie

Toss: South America

Close of play: 1st day – Scotland (1) 91-4 (Jones 36*, McTavish 3*); 2nd day – South America (2) 105-5 (Latham 38*).

Reed outstanding

For the 1933 fixture, held at the Penang Cricket Club, the Colony (Straits Settlements) and the Federated Malay States had difficulty raising sides. For reasons of work or injury, the Straits had three players withdraw from the original selection and FMS had five. Of the team that eventually played for the Straits, four were from Penang and the remainder had to travel from Singapore two days before the match was due to start. The FMS team comprised eight players from Selangor, two from Perak and one from Negeri Sembilan.

Herbert Hopkins, an Australian doctor who had played first-class cricket for Oxford University and Worcestershire, won the toss for the Straits and decided to bat. He must quickly have regretted that decision when his side were reduced to 24/5, largely through poor choice of shots. Eu Cheow Teik, considered at the time the best batsman of Chinese origin to come from Malaya, commandeered the strike in a stand of 36, which ended when Croome, who had defended stoutly for his four runs, was bowled. Valuable contributions were made by all the remaining players, allowing the Straits to recover to 225 all out.

The FMS lost two early wickets but Lall Singh and Cyril Reed showed just how good both they and the pitch were, playing attractive cricket to leave the visitors on 104/2 at the close. Reed was originally the 12th man and only came into the side at the last minute. He had played for Bedfordshire between 1924 and 1927, making his debut while still a boy at Bedford School, and again in 1932, when in England on leave. He had also played first-class cricket for the Europeans in the Quadrangular Tournament in Bombay in 1928/29. He later returned to India, the country of his birth, where he represented the Europeans in the Presidency Tournament in Madras.

The second day, with seemingly no concerns about playing on a Sunday, was dominated by Reed who outplayed Lall Singh. They extended their third-wicket partnership to 214 but Reed did have some luck. When he had made 140 he was caught by the wicketkeeper, but the umpire had called a no-ball. Lall Singh, in contrast, did not give a chance, until, on 84, he missed a straight ball from Leijssius and was hit on the pads. He walked immediately for a leg before, not waiting for the umpire's confirmation. Not many players, if any, would do that today in any form of cricket.

The fielding side suffered in the heat of the afternoon against continued excellent batting. Reed revelled in the conditions but was unable to find another partner. With Vanderholt unable to bat after injuring his thumb in the field on the first day, Reed was the last person out, splendidly caught by McNeill. His 218 was the highest individual score in the match series and the only double century. He struck two sixes and 24 fours. The Straits used nine bowlers without being able to control the flow of runs. They started their second innings 168 runs in arrears. No risks were taken and Noon and Carpenter were undefeated at stumps.

The overnight batsmen continued to play carefully on the following morning and, with the pitch still good for batting, a draw seemed the most likely outcome. Noon passed his half-century but, when he had made 56, was given out leg before to end a faultless innings. Carr and Carpenter continued the resistance, but not without some alarms, as Carr survived several close calls for run-outs. Two wickets fell just before lunch, with the Straits still 29 runs behind. After the interval, the tenor of the match changed as Lall Singh showed his ability as a bowler, finding a consistent, awkward length and troubling all the batsmen. He took seven wickets in an innings for the only time in his career. He was perhaps underused as a bowler, being better known for stylish batting and his superb cover fielding. The FMS required 71 to win when their innings started at 4.50pm, a target they easily achieved.

STRAITS SETTLEMENTS v FEDERATED MALAY STATES

Penang Cricket Club, The Esplanade, Georgetown, Penang, 5, 6 and 7 August 1933

Federated Malay States won by seven wickets

STRAITS

		R	B	M	4s	6s		R	B	M	4s	6s
H.B.Noon	c Cooper b Jonklaas	5					lbw b Lall Singh	56				
A.J.Carpenter	run out	7					b LaBrooy	57				
J.G.Carr	b Jonklaas	0					c D'sn-Smith b Lall Singh	67				
*H.O.Hopkins	b Denison-Smith	6					lbw b LaBrooy	1				
Eu Cheow Teik	b de Silva	31					b Lall Singh	1				
+V.Croome	b LaBrooy	4					(10) b Lall Singh	2				
D.R.A.Hoblyn	c Low Ah Lum b D'n-Smith	79					st Cooper b Gurdial Singh	26				
T.J.Leijssius	c Cooper b Denison-Smith	41					st Cooper b Lall Singh	14				
H.W.Brady	c Lall Singh b D'n-Smith	20					b Lall Singh	0				
W.H.McNeill	not out	15					(6) c de Silva b Lall Singh	0				
D.H.Palmer	b LaBrooy	12					not out	3				
Extras		5						11				
		225						**238**				

FMS

		R	B	M	4s	6s		R	B	M	4s	6s
G.Denison-Smith	c&b Carpenter	12					not out	38				
Gurdial Singh	b Palmer	1										
Lall Singh	lbw b Leijssius	84					b Hopkins	3				
C.N.Reed	c McNeill b Leijssius	218			24	2	c&b Carpenter	24				
*J.D.Hussey	c Eu Cheow Teik b Noon	38			4							
W.O.Jonklaas	run out (Carr)	1					(5) not out	1				
Low Ah Lum	b Hopkins	4										
L.de Silva	c Brady b Eu Cheow Teik	15					(2) b Hopkins	2				
+T.G.D.A.Cooper	b Eu Cheow Teik	0										
F.C.D.LaBrooy	not out	3										
D.M.Vanderholt	absent hurt											
Extras		17						3				
		393					(3 wickets)	**71**				

FMS

	O	M	R	W	nb	w		O	M	R	W	nb	w	fow	SS (1)	FMS (1)	SS (2)	FMS (2)
Jonklaas			51	2				18	5	34	0			1	8 (1)	12 (2)	56 (1)	?? (2)
Denison-Smith			33	4				17	1	43	0			2	8 (3)	26 (1)	138 (2)	?? (3)
LaBrooy			34	2	(4)			35	10	55	2			3	17 (2)	240 (3)	139 (4)	64 (4)
de Silva			36	1	(3)			13	4	21	0			4	24 (4)	329 (5)	140 (5)	
Lall Singh								21.2	5	52	7			5	24 (6)	332 (6)	143 (6)	
Gurdial Singh								10	3	22	1			6	60 (5)	336 (7)	??? (7)	
														7	135 (8)	381 (8)	223 (8)	
Straits	O	M	R	W	nb	w		O	M	R	W	nb	w	8	181 (9)	391 (9)	223 (9)	
Leijssius			39	2	(3)			2	0	14	0			9	204 (7)	393 (4)	??? (10)	
Palmer			91	1				5	0	15	0			10	225 (11)		238 (4)	
Hopkins			43	1	(1)			8	1	24	2							
Carpenter			72	1	(5)			2	0	6	1							
McNeill			29	0	(4)			2	0	8	0							
Carr			27	0														
Brady			39	0														
Noon			26	1														
Eu Cheow Teik			15	2	(6)			0.1	0	1	0							

Umpires: [unknown]

Toss: Straits Settlements

The breakdown of extras is not known.

Close of play: 1st day – Federated Malay States (1) 104-2 (Lall Singh 31*, Reed 55*); 2nd day – Straits Settlements (2) 54-0 (Noon 33*, Carpenter 20*).

Bowling in Straits Settlements' first innings is 66 runs short – analyses for those who did not take a wicket is not known.

Bowling in Federated Malay States first innings is five runs over.

Defiant Gold Coast

The fixtures between so-called African teams from the Gold Coast and Nigeria were often non-European rather than strictly African. In 1927 and 1931, for example, the Gold Coast selected A.R. Joseph, who was born in Ceylon, but was employed as the games master at Achimota School. Generally the African cricketers were weaker in batting than the Europeans, but equal to, if not stronger, in bowling. The African contests alternated with the European ones for venue, so that, when the Europeans met in Lagos, the African match was played in Accra. The Africans followed the same playing hours as the Europeans, not starting each day until after 2pm and continuing through until stumps at about 6.15pm. Thus, they too chose to play during the hottest part of the day when the probability of rain was also higher. As a result the 1935 fixture extended over five days, even though only 449 runs were scored.

McGregor won the toss for Nigeria and decided to bat, but the innings lasted only 32 overs and one ball. Soares was the top scorer with 18 as all the batsmen struggled against the pace of Bannerman-Hesse and Nortey. The Gold Coast fared little better. At the start of their innings, the bowling of Nuha was almost unplayable. On the second day, conditions eased. Though no one made 20, the visitors, aided partly by some poor fielding, managed to secure a first-innings lead of 16.

Nigeria did slightly better in their second innings, thanks to the partnership between Nuha and McGregor. After Nuha gave a catch to Augustt, Esisi provided useful support. When the innings ended, with McGregor undefeated on 38, Nigeria were able to set the visitors a target of 134 to win. Apart from Nuha, the Nigerians bowled poorly. Fleischer got the Gold Coast off to a good start but they then lost eight wickets for 109 runs. Augustt batted well and reached his half-century before being bowled by Nuha, bringing the last pair together with 13 runs still needed, which was two more than the average partnership throughout the match to that point.

Bannerman-Hesse, who had been the not-out batsman in the first innings, correctly chose the bad balls to hit while Heward-Mills successfully kept out all balls on the wicket. The Nigerians got more and more frustrated, their bowling worsened and their fielding deteriorated. With the task thereby getting easier, the Gold Coast last pair scraped the runs required to secure a one-wicket victory in, arguably, the most exciting match in the history of the fixture.

The European series between the two countries continued up to 1939, when it was interrupted by the Second World War. The African series lapsed after 1937, probably because the majority of the players were of moderate means and could not afford the expenses involved. Many of the European players were keen to test their skills against wider opposition, but West Africa was an unattractive venue for tourists, when compared to Hong Kong, Singapore or Buenos Aires.

An invitation to MCC to send a touring party in 1938 was declined. Contacts were then made with Sir Julien Cahn who had organised private tours to Jamaica in 1929, Argentina in 1930, North America and Bermuda in 1933 and Ceylon and Malaya in 1937. An itinerary for a tour in 1938 was agreed, including what was potentially a first-class fixture against a multiracial West African side, comprising cricketers from Nigeria, the Gold Coast and Sierra Leone. A West African squad was selected, captained by F.K. Butler (Nigeria). It included W.R. Shirley, A.K. Judd, E.H. Cadogan and N.D. Nuha (all from Nigeria), R.C. Parker, C.D.A. Pullan and J.B. Fleischer (Gold Coast) and L.H. Bean, W.F.H. Kempster and R. Whyte (Sierra Leone). Nuha, Fleischer and Whyte, a wicketkeeper, were African. Unfortunately, the arrangements fell through over problems with hosting the visitors' accommodation and West Africa missed out on becoming a major cricketing region, just at the time when their playing standards were at their peak.

NIGERIA (AFRICANS) v GOLD COAST (AFRICANS)

Racecourse Ground, Lagos, 27, 28, 29 and 30 April and 1 May 1935

Gold Coast won by one wicket

NIGERIA

		R	B	M	4s	6s		R	B	M	4s	6s
G.B.A.Egbe	b Bannerman-Hesse	9					(3) c Martinson b Fleischer	5				
H.A.Sowunmi	c Fleischer b Nortey	14					lbw b Bannerman-Hesse	4				
*J.S.McGregor	b Bannerman-Hesse	1					(6) not out	38				
N.D.Nuha	c Okine b Nortey	0					(5) c Augustt b B'man-Hesse	30				
O.Soares	b Bannerman-Hesse	18					(7) b Mills	6				
E.Esisi	c Quaye b Bannerman-Hesse	14					(8) b Mills	21				
A.B.Phillips	c Okine b Nortey	6					(4) c Augustt b Nettey	12				
C.B.Silva	c Bannerman-Hesse b Nortey	0					(9) run out	1				
A.A.Dawodu	b Nortey	5					(11) lbw b Nortey	8				
+E.George	b Bannerman-Hesse	0					(1) b Mills	9				
Y.Olojo	not out	0					(10) c Martinson b B'man-Hesse	2				
Extras		7						13				
		75						**149**				

GOLD COAST

		R	B	M	4s	6s		R	B	M	4s	6s
F.D.Martinson	b Nuha	0					(3) b Nuha	4				
J.M.Quaye	b Esisi	17					b Nuha	4				
J.B.Fleischer	b Nuha	2					(1) b Nuha	23				
A.K.Okine	b Nuha	5					b Esisi	5				
P.D.Quartey	b Egbe	9					(7) lbw b Olojo	9				
M.L.Augustt	b McGregor	11					(5) b Nuha	51				
R.A.Mills	c George b Olojo	15					(8) c Phillips b Nuha	5				
J.W.Nortey	c Silva b Nuha	14					(9) run out	1				
C.B.Nettey	run out	0					(6) lbw b Esisi	2				
*A.G.Heward-Mills	lbw b Nuha	0					not out	1				
R.Bannerman-Hesse	not out	12					not out	18				
Extras		9						11				
		91					(9 wickets)	**134**				

Gold Coast	O	M	R	W	nb	w		O	M	R	W	nb	w	fow
Bannerman-Hesse	16.1	2	34	5			(2)	14	3	29	3			1
Nortey	16	4	34	5			(4)	23	4	42	1			2
Mills							(1)	19	4	34	3			3
Fleischer							(3)	2	0	9	1			4
Nettey								8	0	22	1			5
														6
Nigeria	O	M	R	W	nb	w		O	M	R	W	nb	w	7
Olojo	14	2	19	1				11	3	23	1			8
Nuha	19.1	5	28	5				32.3	7	61	5			9
Esisi	5	0	13	1				20	6	27	2			10
McGregor	3	0	16	1										
Egbe	2	0	5	1			(4)	2	0	7	0			
Silva							(5)	4	2	3	0			

Umpires: [not known]

Toss: Nigeria

The breakdown of extras is not known.

In Nigeria's first innings batting is one run short.

In Gold Coast's first innings batting is three runs over and bowling is one run short.

In Gold Coast's second innings bowling is two runs short.

5

The shoots of recovery
1941–1959

THE SECOND World War was less severe on the lives of cricketers from the Associate and Affiliate countries than the First World War had been. It has been possible to document the deaths of only 14 cricketers. Although there are almost certain to have been more, the differences are in keeping with those found for the Full Member countries. Unlike the situation from 1914–18, international cricket did not stop entirely, but the number of matches was much reduced. In August 1940 the Federated Malay States met the Straits Settlements in what proved to be the last of the series. In April 1942, Fiji played a team from the New Zealand Forces and in July 1944, a somewhat scratch Canadian XI met a Lord's XI, at Lord's. Perhaps most surprising were the games played in Singapore in March 1943 under the Japanese occupation.

Singapore surrendered to the Japanese on 15 February 1942. The immediate effect was that all sport ceased and the Japanese seized all the facilities. The pavilion of the Singapore Cricket Club, which had been badly damaged by bombs in Japanese air raids, effectively became a military hospital, while the Padang was used to assemble members of the European population before marching them off to internment. Once the Japanese had taken over the country and established their military administration, they turned their attention to the restoration of sport, which was seen as a way of increasing social power over the local population.

In April 1942, the occupying authorities approved the setting up of the Syonan Sport Association. The organisation was established in June and by September of that year, it controlled all sport. Sports administration was totally centralised and the old, informal, club structure was ignored. Singapore Cricket Club was transformed into a high-class restaurant for high-ranking military and their geishas, but the clientele generally got so drunk and made so much noise that, in July 1942, it had to be closed because of excessive rowdiness. The Japanese organised a number of festivals with the aim of using sport to promote the ideals of imperialism, strength and loyalty. Some sports historians have likened this to the Japanese equivalent of the Victorian-era muscular Christianity. Such activity was short-lived, however. As soon as the Japanese realised that they were losing the war, military and administrative affairs took precedence over organising local sports. By the time cricket resumed after hostilities had ended, the geography of the area had changed. Penang and Malacca had been incorporated into the Federation of Malaya. In 1958, a new series of matches began between the Federation and Singapore.

Interport matches between Hong Kong and Shanghai ceased after the match in 1948. Political unrest in China led to a decline in the size of the British community and it soon became obvious that there were not enough players to make a team. Although the Civil War ended with the Communist takeover in 1949, the emphasis of the government under Mao Zedong was to restore the infrastructure of roads, railways and bridges, restart industrial production and establish agricultural communes in the rural areas. There was little finance available for or government encouragement of sport, least of all for games which were seen as a preserve of an expatriate elite. Interport fixtures continued, however, between Hong Kong and Malaya.

The most surprising revival of cricket in this period was in Fiji. Thanks to the work of Philip Snow, the organisation and standard of Fijian cricket rose remarkably. A graduate of Cambridge University, he went to Fiji in 1938 as a district commissioner and a magistrate. Although he did not play cricket for the university, he represented it at chess and table tennis. He also played cricket for Leicestershire Seconds in 1937 and 1938. In addition to his duties in the Colonial Civil Service and pursuing an interest in the archaeology and anthropology of the Pacific Islands, on which he wrote many articles, he set about encouraging the various cricket centres in Fiji to play each other on a regular basis.

His enthusiasm led, in 1946, to the formation of the Fiji Cricket Association. One of its first activities was to arrange a cricket tour of New Zealand in 1948, a remarkably ambitious project considering that there were fewer than 500 active cricketers in the country. Not only was it 53 years since the previous Fijian tour, it was probably the most extensive tour of New Zealand undertaken by any side up to that time. Between 6 February and 6 April they played 17 matches. They began at Whangarei in the north and journeyed as far south as Invercargill, before making their way back to Auckland.

Throughout this time the Fijians, along with the local population, had to deal with the effects of post-war rationing. Butter, sugar, tea, meat and petrol were particularly affected. Almost all the food produced in New Zealand at this time was exported to the United Kingdom. The Fijian members of the touring party again played in their *sulus* (calf length split skirts) instead of shirt and trousers, often with a sweater over the top, and in bare feet, even when batting. They willingly gave displays of harmony singing before matches and at evening social events. Before each game they would prepare *kava* or *yaqona*, the national drink, derived from the root of *Piper methysticum*, which is mixed with water and drunk in ceremony from cups made of half-coconut shells. This herbal mixture has a psychological effect, working as an antidepressant and, some authorities suggest, combatting fatigue. Other people have found that it causes drowsiness, but perhaps that depends on how much is consumed.

Canadian cricket underwent a revival after the Second World War. The Canadian Cricket Association set out to restart activity as soon as possible. The Inter-Provincial Tournament resumed in August 1947. MCC were invited to tour in August and September 1951, giving players the chance to compare their strength against first-class opposition. The playing strength was also enhanced by immigrants from the Caribbean and Great Britain. MCC were surprised by the standard of the locals, particularly their fielding, and, in hindsight, awarded first-class status to the match against Canada, played in November of that year.

When Canada reciprocated with a tour to Britain in the summer of 1954, their four three-day matches were classified as first-class in advance. The touring party featured 16 players, six of whom were born in the United Kingdom, two in Australia, two in Barbados, one each in Jamaica and Trinidad, and only three in Canada. It seemed that little change had occurred since the 1880s with respect to spreading the game among the Canadian population.

Ireland and Scotland renewed their annual first-class fixture in 1946. In 1955 the first international match in continental Europe not involving expatriate players took place. The Netherlands met Denmark in what developed into a series known as the 'Continental Tests'. With cricket, particularly in The Netherlands, still recovering from the effects of the Second World War, both teams were no more than moderate club standard. The Danes had first proposed such a fixture in 1930, but the Dutch were unable to comply. With the matches against MCC and the Free Foresters and an annual game against Belgium, there was no room in the Dutch calendar for an additional fixture. Also, the Dutch had little knowledge of the standard of Danish cricket and were therefore unable to judge whether a fixture would be beneficial to their players.

Matches between the Gold Coast and Nigeria resumed in 1947 for the Europeans and 1948 for the Africans. There were, however, fewer Europeans in both countries compared to the inter-war period. The local British Colonial Service was being scaled back and the military presence was much reduced, being limited to personnel on short stays rather than the more permanent presence that characterised the 1920s and 1930s. Not surprisingly, with fewer people available, the standard of local European cricket declined. In contrast, the quality of the African game improved, but against competition from football, cricket remained an activity of an elite minority. By the mid-1950s, it was apparent that, if international matches were to continue, separate European and African fixtures were no longer viable. From 1956, the series was contested by multiracial teams.

The multiracial series continued until 1964 but it was played against a background of cricketing decline. After independence, neither government showed much interest in the game, which was viewed as a colonial import. Nevertheless, an enthusiastic few managed to keep it alive so that, when the ICC invested in cricket worldwide in the 2000s, there was something to revive. Efforts were made in 1975 to support cricket in west Africa by combining the resources of Ghana, Nigeria, The Gambia and Sierra Leone within the West African Cricket Conference. Starved of sufficient supporting finance by the governments of the respective countries, the conference struggled and proved unable to coordinate activities across its members. The WACC was disbanded in 2002. The idea that West Africa might become a regional cricket authority along the lines of the West Indies was never a likely proposition.

In contrast, Kenya, Uganda and Tanganyika combined to form the East African Cricket Association in 1951. The association aimed to promote international matches between the three countries and to organise matches between representative east African sides and touring teams. Cricket was largely the preserve of European and Asian expatriates but, throughout the 1950s and 1960s, the standard was high. East Africa was regarded as an attractive place to visit with its game parks, superb scenery and excellent beaches, so it was relatively easy to persuade overseas teams to come.

The 1950s saw strong teams from Pakistan, under the title of the Pakistan Cricket Writers, and India, under the name of Sunder Cricket Club, tour the region, playing the individual countries, as well as a combined East African side. Both touring teams included a number of Test players in their parties. MCC visited in late December 1957 and January 1958, but they did not meet a combined East Africa side. In August and September 1958, the South African Cricket Board of Control, a coordinating body for multiracial non-white cricket, arranged a tour. They played 16 matches in all, including one match against East Africa.

Syonan sports festival

The main sports festival organised by the Japanese during their occupation of Singapore was always scheduled for 15 February, the anniversary of the country's surrender. On that day in 1943, among the many sports was a cricket match between a combined team of Indians and Malays and a combined side of Chinese and Eurasians. The former were the winners by 126 runs to 86. A few weeks later, on 11 March, a fixture was played between Evan Wong's XI and Lall Singh's XI, which some historians have seen as a Japanese attempt to replicate the annual Federated Malay States versus Colony (Straits Settlements) contest, but without the Europeans, who had either managed to evacuate before the Japanese invasion or had been interred.

There were, however, some important differences between this match and the earlier contests, which make the comparison somewhat dubious. The match was a one-innings affair played over one day. The teams were selected by the Syonan Sports Association to produce two, hopefully, well-matched sides which did not have any geographical or political association. The players were drawn from the Singapore Recreation Club, the Singapore Chinese Recreation Club, the Ceylonese Sports Club, the Sinhalese Association and the Indian Association.

The coverage of cricket in the *Syonan Simbun*, the newspaper that replaced the *Straits Times* during the Occupation, suffered from uncertainty by the editors over local names. Based on the printed text, the best interpretation of the composition of the two sides is as follows. Evan Wong's XI consisted of Gerry Clarke, Ladislaus Outschoorn, Seah Keng Siew, M.A.K. Hamid, Fred van Rooyan, R. Manicam, R.V.S. Sundram, D. Dharmaraj, V.R. Sabapathy and Chellaram Thuraisingam. Lall Singh's side comprised J. Anchant, S. Ayadurai, Eu Cheow Chye, K. Leembruggen, E. Doraisamy, S.K. Sundram, Carl Schubert, K. Muthucumaru, Cecil Wong and Magan Lall.

Cecil Wong was the son of Evan Wong. Eu Cheow Chye was the brother of Eu Cheow Teik, who came from Penang and played regularly for the Straits Settlements in the 1930s. Ladislaus Outschoorn was a Ceylonese who went to Malaya to work. He was later interred by the Japanese and suffered badly. After the war he moved to England to recuperate and was spotted by Worcestershire when playing club cricket for Kidderminster. He became a regular member of Worcestershire's side between 1946 and 1959. Doraisamy and Leembruggen were better known as hockey players than cricketers, a sport in which Doraisamy went on to represent Singapore.

Although nearly all the players were regular members of their pre-war clubs' first teams, only six had previously taken part in the annual FMS–Colony fixture. These were Evan Wong, Sabapathy, Outschoorn, R.V.S. Sundram and Thuraisingam, who had played for the Straits Settlements, and Lall Singh, for the Federated Malay States. After the Second World War, Thuraisingam and Schubert both represented Singapore. Overall, the standard was much lower than that of the previous international series.

The fixture was played at Hong Lim Green, the former home of the Singapore Chinese Recreation Club. The local press stated that it was a good game with some bright cricket. This may have been true but, equally, it could be a report written either by or in support of the Japanese administration. Evan Wong's side batted first and made 166, Clarke scoring 53 and Eu Cheow Chye taking 5-53. In reply, Lall Singh's team were dismissed for 87, Leembruggen scoring 38 and Manicam taking 6-9.

Two weeks later, apparently at the request of the cricketers to which the Japanese acquiesced, Philip d'Almeida's XI played K. Muthucumaru's XI. The Japanese enthusiasm for cricket, however, was short-lived, as athletics, football and boxing were promoted as the main sports before, from mid-1944, all sport ceased as the Japanese military situation worsened.

EVAN WONG'S XI v LALL SINGH'S XI

Hong Lim Green, Jalan Besar, Singapore, 11 March 1943

Evan Wong's XI won by 79 runs

EVAN WONG'S XI	R	B	M	4s	6s
*E.Wong					
G.Clarke	53				
L.F.Outschoorn					
Seah Keng Siew					
M.A.K.Hamid					
F.van Rooyan					
R.Manicam					
R.V.S.Sundram					
D.Dharmaraj					
V.R.Sabapathy					
C.Thuraisingam					

166

LALL SINGH'S XI	R	B	M	4s	6s
*Lall Singh					
J.Anchant					
S.Ayadurai					
Eu Cheow Chye					
K.Leembruggen	38				
E.Doraisamy					
S.K.Sundram					
M.C.Schubert					
K.Muthucumaru					
C.Wong					
Magan Lall					

87

Lall Singh's XI	O	M	R	W	nb	wd		fow
Eu Cheow Chye			53	5				1
								2
Evan Wong's XI	O	M	R	W	nb	wd		3
Manicam			9	6				4
								5
								6
								7
								8
								9
								10

Umpires: [unknown]

Toss: not known.

The full scorecard for this match is not available.

The match was played on what was formerly the ground of the Singapore Chinese Recreation Club.

Viliame victorious

The Fijians' match against Wellington at the Basin Reserve in 1949 was the seventh of their New Zealand tour. Wellington batted first, but after a promising opening partnership of 44 they found Viliame Mataika almost unplayable. He caused the ball to rise awkwardly at great pace off the pitch and, while most of his deliveries moved into the batsman from the off side, he occasionally made one move the other way with no discernible change in action. The home side went swiftly from 44 without loss to 56/7. Useful contributions from the tail allowed the total to rise to a still mediocre 124.

Fiji's innings followed a similar pattern. Apted and Raddock opened with a stand of 41, but a collapse ensued and, at the close of the first day, the tourists were 138/6, a lead of 14. The second day saw Cakobau produce a highly valuable effort to remain unbeaten on 67 and give Fiji a useful lead of 47. Wellington gave an improved display in their second innings with Phillips, Barber, Wilson and McLean all making runs against an enthusiastic attack, which was supported by keen fielding. The catch by Aisea Turuva to remove Vance was brilliant; he moved quickly backwards at short fine leg and threw himself to his left, catching the ball with arm outstretched only a centimetre or so from the ground. He received a tremendous ovation for what many regular spectators considered the finest ever seen at the Basin Reserve. At the end of day two, however, Wellington were well placed at 215 ahead with three wickets in hand.

The final day saw Viliame remove the tail and Cakobau, keeping wicket in place of Raddock who had a badly bruised finger, take a superb catch on his toes, with one hand fully stretched above his head, to account for McLean. Fiji needed 247 to win. Despite his injury, Raddock opened the batting, but left without scoring with the total on two. Bula played well, combining entertainment with good judgement of which balls to hit. He received support from Apted and Cakobau to take the score to 161/2, at which point the game turned as three wickets were taken.

Snow dug in, seemingly with the intention of playing for a draw. He defended for one and a half hours for his seven. His partners had other ideas, however. Turuva struck the ball hard, including one hit out of the ground, which smashed a car windscreen. The owner, who was not attending the match, was not pleased and claimed compensation.

By the time Viliame, the last man, went to the wicket, 19 runs were still needed. Runs were difficult to make because Viliame had aggravated an injury while bowling, and could only limp between the wickets. Snow sought and obtained permission from Barber to employ a runner and Isoa Logavatu came out to perform the role. All too often the use of a runner causes mix-ups between the batsmen, but in this case it was the fielding side that became confused. An appeal by the wicketkeeper for a run-out after Isoa had just scrambled a short single was turned down by the umpire. Eric Tindall, at short slip, seeing Viliame roaming at square leg, took the ball from the keeper and pulled a stump out, believing he had brought out a win for Wellington. He was surprised when his appeal was turned down as he had completely forgotten that it was Isoa and not Viliame who was the key player involved.

Isoa, for Viliame, and Fenn continued to run furiously between the wickets at every opportunity, including an all-run five. With only a few minutes of the day remaining the target was reached. So excited were the tourists by their victory that Apted ran down the pavilion steps to shower Fenn in kisses in celebration. The crowd of 10,000 gave the tourists a standing ovation.

Unfortunately, the Fijians had little time to savour their victory. They had to change, leave the ground at 6pm, get dinner and, at 7.30pm, board the ferry to the South Island. The attendance, some 10,000 each day, was almost as great as that for the matches against MCC in 1946 and the Australians in 1947. One Wellington player who could be pleased with his performance was the wicketkeeper, Mooney, who made four catches and two stumpings in the match.

WELLINGTON v FIJI

First-class

Basin Reserve, Wellington, 27, 28 and 29 February and 1 March 1948

Fiji won by one wicket

WELLINGTON

		R	B	M	4s	6s		R	B	M	4s	6s
R.Phillips	b Viliame	15					b Fenn	67				
*E.W.T.Tindill	lbw b Isoa	26					b Viliame	10				
R.A.Vance	b Viliame	0					c Turuva b Isoa	12				
R.T.Barber	run out	2					b Cakobau	34				
D.S.Wilson	c Apted b Viliame	2					c Turuva b Snow	54				
E.W.Dempster	b Viliame	0					run out	1				
A.McLean	lbw b Cakobau	21					c Cakobau b Isoa	73				
+F.L.H.Mooney	b Isoa	1					run out	8				
R.M.Murray	b Viliame	23					b Viliame	9				
R.S.Challies	not out	11					lbw b Viliame	4				
R.Allen	lbw b Viliame	13					not out	6				
	b9 lb1	10					b8 lb7	15				
		124						**293**				

FIJI

		R	B	M	4s	6s		R	B	M	4s	6s
H.J.Apted	run out	14					b McLean	32				
+P.T.Raddock	c Tindill b Challies	27					c Allen b Murray	0				
I.L.Bula	b Wilson	1					c Murray b Allen	88				
Ratu J.K.Cakobau	not out	67					c Mooney b Wilson	38				
*P.A.Snow	b Allen	1					c Tindill b Murray	7			90	
B.J.Mosese	c Barber b Murray	18					st Mooney b Allen	0				
A.T.Turuva	b Challies	18					c&b Allen	23				
A.J.Wendt	c Mooney b Wilson	11					c Mooney b Wilson	9				
M.J.Fenn	c Barber b Murray	0					not out	25				
T.L.Isoa	b Murray	1					st Mooney b McLean	8				
S.M.Viliame	c Mooney b Wilson	2					not out	14				
	b7 lb4	11					lb3 nb3	6				
		171					(9 wickets)	**250**				

Fiji	O	M	R	W	nb	w	O	M	R	W	nb	w	fow	We (1)	Fi (1)	We (2)	Fi (2)
Isoa	28	11	39	2			30	12	59	2			1	44	41	18	2
Fenn	10	4	18	0			25	10	47	1			2	48	43	45	76
Viliame	26.3	11	34	6			37.1	17	75	3			3	50	51	125	161
Cakobau	9	2	23	1			18	2	53	1			4	52	59	129	161
Snow							12	1	40	1			5	52	95	206	161
Wendt							3	1	4	0			6	55	132	214	187
													7	56	160	242	198
Wellington	O	M	R	W	nb	w	O	M	R	W	nb	w	8	93	161	275	215
Murray	18	4	51	3			18.4	3	83	2			9	105	168	287	228
McLean	5	1	12	0			10	2	30	2			10	124	171	293	
Challies	17	4	42	2			8	0	47	0							
Wilson	17.3	5	40	3			26	8	41	2							
Allen	7	2	15	1			14	1	43	3							

Umpires: M.Malden and J.B.Watson

Toss: not known.

Close of play: 1st day – Fiji (1) 138-6 (Cakobau 43*); 2nd day – Wellington (2) 262-7 (McLean 62*).

In Wellington's second innings, J.K.Cakobau kept wicket on the third day when P.T.Raddock was injured.

B.J.Mosese, A.T.Turuva and T.L.Isoa are also known as M.J.Bogisa, A.T.Tuidraki and I.T.Longavatu respectively.

The match was awarded first-class status retrospectively by the International Cricket Council in 1987.

Boucher the bamboozler

By the time of the 1950 match, Ireland had won three of the four post-war matches against Scotland, with one drawn. Scotland were clearly finding it hard to produce a settled side of good quality. There were five debutants selected for this game: Walter Allan, Hunter Cosh, Alexander McAllister, David Stewart and George Youngson. Compared to the teams selected pre-war, there was a wider representation of players from middle-class backgrounds. Scotland included a newsagent, a grocer and a sales manager in their team, as well as two schoolteachers, a doctor and a lecturer. Ireland had a journalist, a printer, a doctor and a lecturer.

On the opening day, a reasonable-sized crowd at the North Inch ground in Perth saw 199 runs scored in five and a quarter hours. Play was far from dull, however, because 20 wickets fell and, at the close, Scotland were batting for a second time. After Scotland won the toss, Chisholm and Allan were cautious against the new ball, but as soon as a bowling change was made and Boucher applied his off spin, a wicket was lost. Allan gave the bowler a return catch after batting for 38 minutes. Aitchison and Chisholm raised the score to 43, but after the latter was bowled by Boucher, having batted for 75 minutes, Scotland's batsmen gave an inept display, losing eight wickets for 12 runs.

Although the pitch was taking spin, the ball was not turning sharply. But Boucher was virtually unplayable, as he kept a good length and flighted the ball skilfully. In 16.1 overs, with eight maidens, he took 7-18. The home side were all out just after lunch for 58, a miserable score which did not include a boundary. The Irish gave an even more pathetic display in reply and lost six wickets for 20. Youngson created the most difficulty with his ability to swing the ball late in its flight. The tail effected a recovery, allowing Ireland to obtain a lead of 60 on the first innings. Before the close, Allan and Aitchison made 23 without a semblance of difficulty.

On the second day, in fine weather, batting looked easier. Allan and Aitchison extended their first-wicket partnership to 78 when they were both dismissed. A collapse then ensued and six wickets were lost for 33 runs. Boucher again did the damage before Henderson and Edward produced the best batting of the match in a partnership of 176, still the Scottish record for the seventh wicket. The runs were made in two hours and 20 minutes. Edward saved his most aggressive shots for the bowling of Boucher, twice striking him out of the ground over long-on. In total, he hit two sixes and eight fours but fell one short of his century, Martin spectacularly catching a cover drive one-handed. The innings ended in the evening, leaving Ireland to bat for 40 minutes, as they set out in pursuit of 256 runs to win.

Ireland began slowly on the following morning, Bergin playing a typically dour innings. In a first-wicket partnership of 45 he contributed only 13. The Irish failed to build on this start and, by lunch, five wickets were down for 94. Jacobson, however, remained solid. Martin helped add 58 before falling to an excellent catch down the leg side by Cosh. Rain caused a 24-minute delay, after which Boucher played aggressively, still believing that Ireland could win. He made 32 out of a partnership of 55 in 40 minutes.

Once he was out, Ireland played for the draw. Jacobson remained undefeated, after batting for four hours and 28 minutes. He gave one chance, a difficult one to Allan in the slips when he had made 86. If this had been taken, Scotland might have won. If it had not rained, Ireland might have won. The draw, with two wickets still standing, was a fair result, but one which had seemed most unlikely at the end of the first day. Boucher's performance was typical of a career which lasted from 1929 to 1954, during which he took 307 wickets for Ireland at an average of 15.25. He was the first Irish cricketer to take 300 wickets and took seven wickets in an innings eight times.

SCOTLAND v IRELAND

First-class

North Inch, Perth, 24, 26 and 27 June 1950

Match drawn

SCOTLAND

		R	B	M	4s	6s		R	B	M	4s	6s
R.H.E.Chisholm	b Boucher	23	75	-	-		(3) b Boucher	2	23	-	-	
W.R.Allan	c&b Boucher	7	38	-	-		(1) st Miller b Warke	30	117	1	-	
Rev J.Aitchison	b Boucher	10	50	-	-		(2) c Miller b Gill	42	120	7	-	
W.Nichol	b Hill	3	5	-	-		c Caprani b Boucher	2	9	-	-	
A.E.McAllister	c Caprani b Ingram	9	35	-	-		(6) c Warke b Boucher	4	6	-	-	
+S.H.Cosh	b Boucher	0	3	-	-		(7) b Hill	16	12	3	-	
J.D.Henderson	run out	0	8	-	-		(5) b Hill	83	198	8	-	
*W.A.Edward	b Boucher	0	6	-	-		c Martin b Boucher	99	151	8	2	
I.A.H.Syme	b Boucher	0	2	-	-		c Caprani b Hill	12	10	1	-	
D.Stewart	c Ingram b Boucher	2	7	-	-		not out	5	8	-	-	
G.W.Youngson	not out	0	2	-	-		b Boucher	2	3	-	-	
	b4	4					b15 lb3	18				
		58						**315**				

IRELAND

		R	B	M	4s	6s		R	B	M	4s	6s
S.F.Bergin	c Cosh b Stewart	5	8	-	-		b Youngson	13	92	1	-	
L.C.Jacobson	c Cosh b Henderson	10	32	2	-		not out	101	282	8	-	
J.D.Caprani	b Youngson	0	10	-	-		(5) b Edward	5	15	1	-	
J.S.Pollock	c McAllister b Youngson	4	13	-	-		b Nichol	10	20	1	-	
*E.Ingram	c&b Youngson	1	8	-	-		(3) c Cosh b Youngson	1	9	-	-	
L.Warke	c Cosh b Youngson	0	3	-	-		lbw b Henderson	8	23	1	-	
H.Martin	b Youngson	15	50	1	-		c Cosh b Youngson	21	43	1	-	
J.C.Boucher	b Youngson	21	66	1	-		b Henderson	32	40	1	-	
R.I.Gill	b Stewart	37	99	2	-		b Youngson	6	8	1	-	
J.W.Hill	not out	14	73	-	-		not out	1	18	-	-	
+F.J.Miller	lbw b Youngson	4	15	-	-							
	b5 lb1 nb1	7					b11 lb4	15				
		118					(8 wickets)	**213**				

Ireland	O	M	R	W	nb	w		O	M	R	W	nb	w	fow	Sc (1)	Ir (1)	Sc (2)	Ir (2)
Gill	11	3	22	0			(4)	12	4	27	1			1	26 (2)	6 (1)	78 (1)	45 (1)
Ingram	10	5	7	1			(1)	33	15	56	0			2	43 (1)	11 (3)	78 (2)	49 (3)
Boucher	16.1	8	18	7				43.5	10	130	5			3	46 (4)	19 (2)	83 (4)	64 (4)
Hill	10	4	7	1			(2)	40	14	70	3			4	48 (3)	19 (4)	85 (3)	73 (5)
Warke								6	2	14	1			5	48 (6)	19 (6)	90 (6)	94 (6)
														6	52 (7)	20 (5)	111 (7)	151 (7)
Scotland	O	M	R	W	nb	w		O	M	R	W	nb	w	7	52 (8)	57 (7)	287 (8)	198 (8)
Youngson	24.1	8	42	7				40	7	77	4			8	52 (9)	66 (8)	305 (5)	210 (9)
Stewart	11	5	12	2				6	2	9	0			9	58 (5)	111 (9)	308 (9)	
Henderson	18	3	31	1				25	7	45	2			10	58 (10)	118 (11)	315 (11)	
Syme	2	0	7	0														
Edward	10	2	16	0			(5)	14	3	30	1							
Nichol	3	1	3	0			(4)	21	9	37	1							

Umpires: G.H.Fisher and W.Nelson

Toss: Scotland

Close of play: 1st day – Scotland (2) 23-0 (Allan 6*, Aitchison 11*); 2nd day – Ireland (2) 23-0 (Jacobson 16*, Bergin 3*).

Canadian misery

Canada's tour of England in 1954 coincided with one of the coldest and wettest summers on record. The batsmen had difficulty adjusting to the soft wickets, the bowlers were too inconsistent, though they bowled some good balls, and the fielding fell below the level expected, except for the wicketkeeping of Alec Percival, which was highly regarded.

The tourists were particularly looking forward to their fixture against Pakistan, which would show how they compared with the latest country to be accorded Full Membership of the ICC. The Pakistanis rested their opening batsman, Alimuddin, and their best bowler, Fazal Mahmood. They were replaced by M.E.Z. Ghazali, a middle-order batsman, and Shakoor Ahmed, the reserve wicketkeeper who had previously played for Kenya, although his birthplace was Kampala in Uganda.

Conditions for the first day were miserable. Over 50mm of rain had fallen the previous day, the pitch was drying out slowly and unevenly and the temperature reached a maximum of 17°C. Kardar won the toss and invited Canada to bat. The umpires came to the wicket on time but it immediately started raining and they had to retreat to the pavilion. When play eventually began 23 minutes late, Maqsood Ahmed shared the new ball with Mahmood but they were not kept on long. Kardar decided that the slow left-arm of Shujauddin and the off breaks of Zulfiqar Ahmed would be more effective. Canada lost three wickets for 13, two of them stumpings by Imtiaz Ahmed, a clear indication of the inexperience of the Canadian batsmen in dealing with a turning ball. Canada were indecisive in both batting and running. Their players showed little inclination to score runs, which only allowed the spin bowlers to increase their domination. By lunch, they had struggled to 63/5.

The afternoon session was marred by two stoppages for rain. Although this would have upset the batsmen's concentration, it hardly explained the procession that marked the end of the Canadian innings. By shortly after 3pm Canada were all out for 87. Canada's bowlers, however, found the conditions helpful and soon had Pakistan in difficulty. Hanif Mohammad fell to a catch at leg slip, Imtiaz Ahmed nicked the ball to the wicketkeeper, who made an outstanding catch, stretched at full length, and Waqar Hasan was caught in the slips. Canada did even better after the tea interval, Kardar falling first ball. Ghazali and Wazir Mohammad struggled against the left-arm swing of Christen and gave three chances, all of which were dropped. With three further stoppages for bad light, batting was far from easy, but the Pakistanis survived without further loss to be 92/4 at the close, a total aided by Canada's contribution of 13 no-balls, 12 bowled by Christen.

If the first day was miserable, the second day was diabolical, the temperature reaching a maximum of 13°C. The weather, the timing of the match for midweek, and a contest between two sides in which the majority of the local population had no interest all served to keep spectators away. The not-out batsmen added a further 32 runs but after they were dismissed, Shujauddin, Zulfiqar Ahmed and Mahmood Hussain took Pakistan to a useful 149-run lead.

When Canada batted, the Pakistani bowlers were of a different standard. Mahmood Hussain found line and length, accompanied by late away swing, and Shujauddin and Zulfiqar Ahmed again showed up the lack of experience of the batsmen against good quality spin bowling. Canada were handicapped by the loss of John Lucas, who required stitches in a cut hand and was unable to bat. The only resistance was provided by Brierley, who used his experience of English conditions to give an obdurate display, and Percival, who tried to hit his way out of trouble. The failure of Trestrail and Cameron, two former West Indian Test players, was particularly disappointing. By 5.45pm Canada were bowled out for 82, giving the Pakistanis an easy win by an innings and 67 runs in two days.

CANADA v PAKISTAN

First-class

Lord's, St John's Wood, London, 18, 19 and 20 August 1954

Pakistan won by an innings and 67 runs

CANADA

		R	B	M	4s	6s		R	B	M	4s	6s
T.L.Brierley	c Imtiaz Ahmed b Shujauddin	12					c Ghazali b Zulfiqar Ahmed	28				
R.N.Quintrell	st Imtiaz Ahmed b Shujauddin	1					b Mahmood Hussain	5				
J.H.Lucas	b Zulfiqar Ahmed	3					absent hurt					
K.B.Trestrail	st Imtiaz Ahmed b Z'qar Ahmed	6					(3) b Mahmood Hussain	2				
F.J.Cameron	c Imtiaz Ahmed b M'd Hussain	36					(4) c Zulfiqar Ahmed b M'd Hussain	10				
+W.A.Percival	lbw b Shujauddin	1					(5) c Imtiaz Ahmed b Z'r Ahmed	23				
*H.B.O.Robinson	run out	13					(6) c Ghazali b Zulfiqar Ahmed	0				
A.S.Hendy	b Zulfiqar Ahmed	0					(7) st Imtiaz Ahmed b Z'r Ahmed	8				
H.D.S.Padmore	run out	8					(8) run out	1				
B.Christen	b Zulfiqar Ahmed	1					(9) b Zulfiqar Ahmed	0				
P.Stead	not out	0					(10) not out	4				
	b4 lb2	6					b1	1				
		87						82				

PAKISTAN

		R	B	M	4s	6s
Hanif Mohammad	c Cameron b Stead	1				
+Imtiaz Ahmed	c Percival b Padmore	2				
Waqar Hasan	c Hendy b Christen	17				
M.E.Z.Ghazali	c Cameron b Padmore	62				
*A.H.Kardar	b Christen	0				
Wazir Mohammad	b Christen	59				
Maqsood Ahmed	c Quintrell b Stead	18				
Shujauddin	not out	33				
Shakoor Ahmed	b Hendy	0				
Zulfiqar Ahmed	c Percival b Padmore	13				
Mahmood Hussain	b Stead	11				
	b5 lb2 nb13	20				
		236				

Pakistan	O	M	R	W	nb	w	O	M	R	W	nb	w	fow	Ca (1)	Pk (1)	Ca (2)
Mahmood Hussain	10	6	5	1	-	-	13	3	23	3	-	-	1	2	3	8
Maqsood Ahmed	2	2	0	0	-	-	4	0	14	0	-	-	2	5	5	10
Shujauddin	20	5	46	3	-	-	6	1	19	0	-	-	3	13	33	28
Zulfiqar Ahmed	16	7	25	4	-	-	8	3	14	5	-	-	4	37	33	65
Ghazali	5	1	5	0	-	-	5.3	2	11	0	-	-	5	51	124	65
													6	73	150	72
Canada	O	M	R	W	nb	w							7	76	183	77
Padmore	23	5	54	3	-	-							8	76	185	77
Stead	22.5	7	52	3	-	-							9	78	225	82
Christen	23	9	47	3	12	-							10	87	236	
Cameron	8	2	23	0	-	-										
Hendy	18	5	40	1	-	-										

Umpires: J.S.Buller (England) and P.Corrall (England)

Toss: Pakistan

Close of play: 1st day – Pakistan (1) 92-4 (Ghazali 46*, Wazir Mohammad 19*). Match finished in two days.

Dutch–Danish inaugural

The inaugural 'Continental Test' took place at the Haagsche Cricket Club ground at De Dieput, on 20 and 21 August 1955. The Dutch were captained by Walter van Weelde, one of their outstanding batsmen in domestic competition, who, once set, could demolish an opponent's bowling attack. He was also an excellent fielder at leg slip. The van Weelde family were to play an important role in Dutch cricket. Walter's brother Henk played for The Netherlands, as did his two sons, Robert and Bert. In Robbie Colthoff, they had a highly competent wicketkeeper, who was also a useful middle-order batsman.

The other leading players were Herman Stolk, a very correct batsman of good temperament, Peter van Arkel, a 19-year-old who became a regular choice as an opening bat in the late 1950s and early 1960s, and Ernst Vriens, a right-arm bowler of medium pace who was one of the most successful Dutch bowlers of all time. Danish cricket at the time was dominated by the Morild family, three of whom played in this match. Axel was a fast-scoring batsman who also kept wicket, Svend was probably the best left-arm spin bowler the Danes ever produced and Carsten was the country's leading all-rounder, an attacking batsman and a bowler who could vary his style from right-arm fast to slow and medium-paced off spin.

The Dutch won the toss and batted first. Schuur and van Arkel put on 50 for the first wicket. Both fell at that score, after which the Dutch failed to establish any worthwhile partnerships. Their batsmen concentrated on defending their wickets rather than scoring. The Danish attack was accurate rather than penetrating, but this was enough to keep the run rate down. Stolk was the only batsman to gain any mastery of the bowling. His 59 runs with four fours was largely instrumental in The Netherlands passing 200, although he was dismissed with the score on 199. Altogether, the Dutch innings lasted for four hours. Petersen, with his spin, was the most successful bowler; 11 of his 27 overs were maidens.

Denmark began poorly in reply, losing three wickets for 37 including that of Carsten Morild, who was unnecessarily run out after he had made an attractive 21. Knudsen dominated the fourth-wicket partnership of 56 but he was the victim of a smart stumping when two runs short of his half-century. The Danish middle order was troubled by Vriens, who kept a tight line and length. The Danes batted even more slowly than the Dutch until Jensen struck some lusty blows, hitting anything loose to the boundary. Provis provided back-up in a ninth-wicket partnership of 60 which saw Denmark take first-innings lead of 36, with Jensen undefeated on 60 and Vriens well worth his return of 4-65 from 33 overs.

The Danes maintained the initiative, taking the first three Dutch wickets in their second innings for 28. The home side had, however, changed their batting order in an attempt to score quick runs. Walter van Weelde fulfilled the requirement with a fourth-wicket stand of 103, aided by a more sedate van Manen, who hit only one boundary in his 36. Van Weelde made a superb 72 in 81 minutes, which included ten fours. Van Arkel and Vriens maintained the scoring rate, enabling van Weelde to declare, setting Denmark a target of 157 in 90 minutes.

The Danish captain accepted the challenge and opened with Nielsen and Provis, both known for making quick runs. Both fell quickly, however, and the Danes thereafter opted to play for a draw. The two sides were well-matched. The Danish bowling was generally better than the Dutch, but the Dutch had the more accomplished batting. Overall, the encounter was typical of the series that followed, being well contested with a number of good individual performances. The matches were played in a very friendly atmosphere, but spectators were few, limited largely to members of the host club and friends and family of the players, a typical situation for internationals between countries in which cricket is a minority sport.

NETHERLANDS v DENMARK

Haagsche Cricket Club, De Diepput, The Hague, 20 and 21 August 1955

Match drawn

NETHERLANDS

		R	B	M	4s	6s		R	B	M	4s	6s
A.Schuur	b S.Morild	17			–	–	b Provis	16			2	–
P.van Arkel	b Petersen	32			2	–	(6) not out	29			4	–
W.C.van Manen	b Provis	14			1	–	(5) c&b Provis	36			1	–
H.Stolk	b Petersen	59			4	–	(2) c Søndergaard b C.Morild	12			2	–
*W.van Weelde	b C.Morild	5			–	–	(4) b Provis	72	81		10	–
L.S.Mulder	c S.Morild b Petersen	10			1	–						
+R.G.Colthoff	c A.Morild b S.Morild	12			2	–	(3) c Petersen b Provis	0			–	–
N.H.J.Leeftink	st A.Morild b Søndergaard	21			2	1						
H.J.van Weelde	b Petersen	5			1	–						
E.W.C.Vriens	not out	19			2	–	(7) not out	24			4	–
P.Maas	b Provis	5			1	–						
	b5 lb3	8					b1 lb2	3				
		207					(5 wickets declared)	**192**				

DENMARK

		R	B	M	4s	6s		R	B	M	4s	6s
*E.Knudsen	st Colthoff b H.J.van Weelde	48			4	–	(4) not out	5			–	–
K.B.Rieck	b H.J.van Weelde	0			–	–						
C.Morild	run out	21			3	–	lbw b van Manen	27			5	–
E.Nielsen	b Vriens	0			–	–	(1) c Schuur b Leeftink	2			–	–
B.Lorentzen	run out	19			2	–						
W.Søndergaard	c Mulder b Vriens	12			–	–						
+A.Morild	c Mulder b van Arkel	29			4	–	(5) not out	7			1	–
E.Jensen	not out	60			7	–						
S.Morild	b Vriens	4			–	–						
T.A.J.Provis	b van Arkel	23			3	–	(2) b Leeftink	6			–	–
H.F.Petersen	c Leeftink b Vriens	7			1	–						
	b12 lb3 nb5	20										
		243					(3 wickets)	**47**				

Denmark	O	M	R	W	nb	w	O	M	R	W	nb	w	fow	Ne (1)	De (1)	Ne (2)	De (2)
Søndergaard	9	1	24	1			8	0	49	0			1	50 (2)	4 (2)	24 (1)	2 (1)
Petersen	27	11	41	4			8	2	34	0			2	50 (1)	37 (3)	28 (2)	13 (2)
S.Morild	12	4	27	2			5	1	25	0			3	69 (3)	37 (4)	28 (3)	40 (3)
Provis	14	3	39	2			12	0	55	4			4	79 (5)	93 (1)	131 (5)	
Jensen	4	0	19	0									5	97 (6)	104 (5)	142 (4)	
C.Morild	16	2	49	1	(5)		6	0	26	1			6	114 (7)	130 (6)		
													7	150 (8)	160 (7)		
Netherlands	O	M	R	W	nb	w	O	M	R	W	nb	w	8	154 (9)	168 (9)		
Leeftink	14	3	40	0			6	3	8	2			9	199 (4)	228 (10)		
Maas	11	4	24	0									10	207 (11)	243 (11)		
W.van Weelde	3	1	10	0	(2)		10	2	20	0							
van Arkel	12	4	25	2													
H.J.van Weelde	31	8	59	2													
Vriens	33	13	65	4													
van Manen					(3)		5	2	19	1							

Umpires: W.F.Bok, M.A.V.Slingenberg and L.C.F.Wunder

Toss: Netherlands

West Africa goes multiracial

The first multiracial fixture between Nigeria and the Gold Coast took place in March 1956, somewhat earlier in the year than the previous separate encounters between European or African teams, which were held in either April or May. As normal, it took place over four days, with no play in the mornings. The Lagos and Colony Club in Nigeria were the hosts.

On paper, Nigeria were the stronger team with three of their players having previous first-class experience. Major Victor Troman was stationed in India at the end of the Second World War and played one match for the Europeans in 1945/46. Henry Savory had played one game for Gloucestershire in 1937 and Geoffrey Anson appeared seven times for Kent in 1947. Anson had gone to Cambridge University in 1942, but his university studies were interrupted by the war; he returned to the university in 1947 and played three first-class matches before deciding to leave and join the Colonial Service. The Gold Coast had no players with similar experience. Compared with the inter-war teams, the military representation was small, being limited to Lt Smith for the Gold Coast and Lt B.V. O'Gorman and Troman for Nigeria.

The match followed the pattern of previous African matches, being low-scoring with the bowlers generally having the upper hand. The Gold Coast batted first and lost Dodoo, bowled by Obadan, before a run was scored. Woodroffe and Attoh Okine played soundly, the latter maintaining his reputation, established in the 1930s, as his country's best African batsman. When Woodroffe fell leg before to end a partnership of 64 the visitors were in a strong position, but they were unable to build on this. With the exception of Feaver, the batsmen were troubled by the bowling of Troman and King. The last nine wickets fell for 105 and the innings total of 169 was disappointing.

Nigeria found batting equally difficult against the pace of Janney and the economy of Haizel. Only two players made more than 20 as wickets fell regularly. The Gold Coast had a lead of 41 on first innings and proceeded, albeit slowly, to take command of the match. Although Troman and King were again the most successful bowlers, they were not as threatening second time round. Okine was again outstanding and he received good support from Brookes in a third-wicket partnership of 65 and from Haizel in an unbeaten stand of 34 for the fifth wicket.

With a lead of 207, Feaver declared, but his side was unable to bowl out Nigeria in the time available. The home side's players made no effort to win, but all their batsmen defended stoutly. Even though the top score was only 29, made by Anson, six players reached double figures and, when the end came after 84 overs, only eight wickets were down. Smith took four of them.

The multiracial series continued until 1964 but it was played against a background of cricketing decline. It was not until the early 2000s that a revival occurred, aided by a change in the dominant format from multi-innings matches to one-day internationals.

NIGERIA v GOLD COAST

Lagos and Colony Club, Lagos, 2, 3, 4 and 5 March 1956

Match drawn

GOLD COAST		R	B M 4s 6s		R	B M 4s 6s
D.R.Woodroffe	lbw b Troman	28		c Troman b King	20	
E.O.Dodoo	b Obadan	0				
A.K.Okine	c Anson b King	55		not out	49	
J.E.Brookes	run out	0		st Sagoe b Troman	34	
*W.R.Feaver	b Troman	39		b Troman	14	
B.H.Williams	lbw b King	5				
Lt M.Smith	b Irvine	4		(2) c Sagoe b King	12	
E.A.Haizel	c Irvine b King	11		(6) not out	28	
C.E.Shepherd	c Chambers b Troman	7				
J.J.Janney	not out	5				
+F.Osman	c O'Gorman b King	4				
Extras		11			9	
		169		(4 wickets declared)	**166**	

NIGERIA		R	B M 4s 6s		R	B M 4s 6s
+A.K.Sagoe	b Janney	7		(9) lbw b Smith	8	
Lt B.V.O'Gorman	b Shepherd	0		lbw b Smith	27	
N.Eno	st Osman b Brookes	18		c Smith b Haizel	15	
Maj V.T.W.Troman	b Haizel	17		b Shepherd	25	
H.J.Savory	b Janney	12		c Haizel b Janney	6	
G.F.Anson	c Okine b Haizel	0		c Feaver b Smith	29	
A.Chambers	b Smith	22		c&b Smith	3	
E.A.Hughes	b Janney	2		(1) c Janney b Shepherd	15	
D.H.Irvine	c Williams b Haizel	15		(8) not out	15	
*W.S.King	c Feaver b Smith	23		not out	2	
T.O.Obadan	not out	4				
Extras		8			5	
		128		(8 wickets)	**150**	

Nigeria	O	M	R	W	nb	w	O	M	R	W	nb	w	fow	GC	Nig	GC	Nig
Obadan	17	5	35	1			10	2	30	0			1	0	0	30	44
Troman	23	6	47	3			22	6	58	2			2	64	10	41	63
King	15.5	4	36	4			11	3	32	2			3	69	42	106	67
O'Gorman	7	1	19	0									4	91	44	132	106
Hughes	2	1	2	0									5	93	44		119
Irvine	4	0	19	1		(4)	5	0	13	0			6	114	62		121
Savory						(5)	7	0	24	0			7	119	64		146
													8	152	85		148
Gold Coast	O	M	R	W	nb	w	O	M	R	W	nb	w	9	155	123		
Shepherd	25	16	25	1			19	6	31	2			10	169	128		
Janney	22	5	46	3			20	10	31	1							
Brookes	10	4	12	1		(4)	7	2	16	0							
Haizel	18	7	29	3		(3)	15	2	35	1							
Smith	9.4	3	8	2			23	7	32	4							

Umpires: [unknown]

Toss: not known

The breakdown of extras is not known.

Abed swings SACBOC to victory

In September 1958 the East African Cricket Association chose a representative side to play SACBOC, the coordinating body for multiracial non-white cricket in South Africa, which was touring in the region. The East African side contained ten Asians and one European, Malcolm Ronaldson, who was made captain. East African sides of the 1950s thus followed the pattern set in the West Indies in that they had to be captained by a white person. Ronaldson took over from Denis Dawson, who had captained all of East Africa's previous matches. The team contained three players from Tanganyika, Ronaldson, Ramesh Patel and Mohamed Hussein, and two from Uganda, Zahid Shah and Bhanu Patel; the rest were from Kenya.

The South Africans proved a strong side and were captained by Basil D'Oliveira. Largely unknown at the time, he was described by the *Kenyan Cricketers' Almanack* as being an outstanding batsman who could hold his own in first-class cricket in any country. The strength of the visitors was in their bowling. Eric Petersen, Gesant Abed and John Neethling provided the pace. Owen Williams, slow left-arm chinamen, and George Langa, off-breaks, gave the supporting spin. In Salie Abed, they had an agile and highly reliable wicketkeeper who stood up to the stumps to the pace bowlers; his excellent anticipation resulted in almost flawless performances.

Ronaldson won the toss and chose to bat. East Africa were soon in difficulty, losing two wickets for 31 runs to a splendid spell of pace bowling from Petersen. Mehboob Ali and Gursharan Singh led a recovery with a partnership of 79, before Gursharan received a good ball from Gesant Abed and was only able to edge it to the wicketkeeper. Gesant Abed, in a superb display of fast-medium swing bowling, troubled all the middle-order batsmen, who were not used to facing such a penetrative attack. Four wickets went down while only 44 runs were added, including the fall of Mehboob Ali to Petersen for a well-constructed 88. Zahid Shah and Bhanu Patel put on 30 for the seventh wicket and Ranjit Singh struck some lusty blows in a last-wicket partnership before the home side were dismissed for a somewhat disappointing 213. The South Africans fielded well, holding nine catches, while their speed over the ground and accurate throwing helped to restrict the runs.

The visitors, in reply, lost three wickets for 38 runs, but Deedat and D'Oliveira proved far too good for the home bowling in a partnership of 149. The bowlers persevered and managed to dismiss both batsmen but were unable to prevent another major partnership, this time of 118 runs for the sixth wicket by Neethling and Abrahams. With a lead of 136, D'Oliveira declared in the late afternoon. D'Cunha was the most successful bowler, taking 4-78 with his leg breaks and googlies. He managed to deceive D'Oliveira who advanced down the pitch to a googly, seeking a boundary when four runs short of his hundred, only to misjudge it and be smartly stumped by Ramesh Patel.

East Africa began their second innings in determined fashion as Ghafoor Ahmed and Ramesh Patel reduced the deficit to 102 before the close at 6pm.

The not-out batsmen extended their partnership to 93 on the third morning but just as it looked as though East Africa would fight hard for a draw, both fell victim to D'Oliveira. The home side then collapsed to some excellent pace bowling with Gesant Abed again outstanding. Eight wickets went down at regular intervals for 79 runs, including, at one stage, the loss of four with just five runs scored.

Jhalla and Ranjit Singh put on 32 with some defiant slogs before Petersen brought the innings to a close with two quick wickets. The South Africans required 70 to win and again they began poorly, losing three wickets for 35. Raziet and Abrahams, however, took them to victory shortly after tea.

EAST AFRICA v SOUTH AFRICA (SACBOC)

Sikh Union Club, Nairobi, 13, 14 and 15 September 1958

South Africa (SACBOC) won by seven wickets

EAST AFRICA

		R	B	M	4s	6s		R	B	M	4s	6s
Ghafoor Ahmed	c G.Abed b Petersen	4					c Neethling b D'Oliveira	72				
Mehboob Ali	c Deedat b Petersen	88					(3) lbw b Williams	0				
+R.D.Patel	c Abrahams b Petersen	8					(2) lbw b D'Oliveira	51				
Gursharan Singh	c S.Abed b G.Abed	33					c Raziet b G.Abed	17				
*M.B.Ronaldson	c Neethling b G.Abed	0					b Neethling	9				
B.A.L.D'Cunha	c Williams b G.Abed	6					lbw b G.Abed	1				
Zahid Shah	b G.Abed	16					c Neethling b G.Abed	11				
Bhanu Patel	c Neethling b Williams	34					c S.Abed b G.Abed	0				
G.B.Jhalla	b Neethling	0					b Petersen	19				
Ranjit Singh	c Williams b Abrahams	11					c Neethling b Petersen	23				
Mohamed Hussein	not out	2					not out	0				
	Extras	11						2				
		213						**205**				

SOUTH AFRICA

		R	B	M	4s	6s		R	B	M	4s	6s
S.Raziet	c R.D.Patel b Zahid Shah	11					not out	19				
S.N.Solomon	lbw b D'Cunha	15					c R.D.Patel b Jhalla	8				
+S.Abed	c G'ran Singh b Bhanu Patel	2										
A.I.Deedat	c sub b Zahid Shah	66					(3) c R.D.Patel b Ranjit Singh	13				
*B.L.D'Oliveira	st R.D.Patel b D'Cunha	96					(4) b Ranjit Singh	0				
J.J.Neethling	not out	53					(5) not out	31				
C.J.Abrahams	c Zahid Shah b D'Cunha	77										
E.Petersen	b D'Cunha	2										
G.Abed	not out	16										
O.L.Williams												
G.O.Langa												
	Extras	11						1				
	(7 wickets declared)	**349**					(3 wickets)	**72**				

South Africa	O	M	R	W	nb	w		O	M	R	W	nb	w	fow	EA (1)	SA (1)	EA (2)	SA (2)
Abrahams	16.3	4	31	1				12	3	36	0			1	9	18	93	11
Petersen	17	8	36	3				11.1	3	18	2			2	31	25	100	35
Neethling	18	8	49	1				7	0	24	1			3	110	38	130	35
Langa	3	1	10	0										4	118	187	151	
Williams	9	0	33	1			(4)	11	2	31	1			5	134	198	151	
D'Oliveira	7	2	13	0			(5)	22	7	44	2			6	154	316	154	
G.Abed	20	5	30	4			(6)	25	10	50	4			7	184	318	156	
														8	189		172	
East Africa	O	M	R	W	nb	w		O	M	R	W	nb	w	9	200		204	
Ranjit Singh	21	4	44	0				6	2	10	2			10	213		205	
Jhalla	24	11	53	0				9	4	17	1							
Zahid Shah	19	1	62	2														
Mohamed Hussein	23	5	60	0			(3)	4	1	6	0							
Bhanu Patel	16	3	41	1			(4)	10	2	34	0							
D'Cunha	21	1	78	4														
Gursharan Singh							(5)	0.1	0	4	0							

Umpires: [unknown]

Toss: East Africa

The breakdown of extras is not known.

Close of play: 1st day – not known; 2nd day – East Africa (2) 34-0.

Entertainment from Aitchison

The 1959 contest between Ireland and Scotland was unusual for its high scores, although the match ended in a dull draw. Ireland were without the unavailable Alec O'Riordan while the visitors had one debutant, Mike Denness, who, still a pupil at the Ayr Academy, became the first schoolboy to be selected by Scotland.

Cosh won the toss for Scotland and in warm, sunny conditions, elected to bat. Dudman and Chisholm posted 50 in 70 minutes, which was quite fast going with Chisholm at the crease. The scoring rate slowed with the introduction of Huey to the attack. He bowled nine maidens in his first 16 overs and conceded only seven runs, picking up one wicket, just before the lunch break, when he had Dudman caught at silly mid-off with the score on 70.

Between lunch and tea Scotland scored 122 runs and lost only the wicket of Chisholm, caught at cover off Huey for 51, after a stay of two and a half hours. Aitchison, dropped at leg slip on 46, reached his fifty in 103 minutes. Denness gave an impressive display in partnership, playing some delightful cut strokes. Aitchison batted superbly after tea, scoring his second 50 runs in only 43 minutes to bring up his century. He reached 150 after a further 70 minutes, entertaining the crowd with five huge sixes into the trees.

Denness fell three runs short of his half-century with the score on 237, to end a third-wicket stand of 144, and give Huey his third wicket. With 75 minutes left for play, Allan joined Aitchison and, together, they put on 117. Despite the onslaught of runs, Ireland's bowlers made no attempt to slow the game down and sent down 144 overs at a rate of 24 per hour. Aitchison ended the day on 190 not out, still his country's highest individual first-class score in an international match.

On the Monday, the second day, Cosh declared, thereby depriving Aitchison of a chance of a double hundred. McCloy and Bergin batted through the morning session but more sedately than Scotland had done on the first day, so leaving their lunch score at just 75. After Scotland had tried all of their five main bowlers without success, Cosh turned to Chisholm. His leg breaks produced a result, McCloy pulling a short ball to deep square leg where Aitchison took a good low catch with the score on 94. Martin joined Bergin and the latter had two pieces of luck, either side of reaching his half-century in 136 minutes. In both instances he was surprisingly missed by Brown at the wicket, who was normally the most reliable of keepers. Perhaps he was taken by surprise that on such a batting surface any chance came at all, or, possibly, his senses had been dulled by Bergin's stubborn but rather unexciting batting.

There was no success for Scotland until the new ball was taken, Wilson eventually enticing Martin to give a catch to leg slip. Bergin hit the last ball before tea to the boundary to reach his maiden first-class century, after having batted for 260 minutes. Corry was dismissed soon after the interval, Brown finally holding a catch behind the wicket. Warke and Bergin took the score to 247, by which time Bergin was visibly tiring and he gave a tame catch to Roberts at cover. He had hit 16 fours in his 137 during an innings that had lasted for five hours and 40 minutes. Ireland lost two more wickets before the close when they were still 63 behind with four wickets remaining.

Rain reduced play to four and a half hours on the final day but Ireland lost their remaining wickets for 26 runs. With a lead of 37, Scotland scored at over a run a minute in an attempt to gain a sufficient advantage to declare with. Dudman and Chisholm began well, largely through some smart running between the wickets. The loss of Dudman, followed by Aitchison, proved a setback and although Cosh and Barr tried to force the pace, Chisholm got bogged down and the declaration did not come until 3.40pm. Ireland were set to score 159 in 82 minutes, a task that Bergin and McCloy chose to ignore. Just before the close, Chisholm dismissed McCloy for the second time in the drawn match.

IRELAND v SCOTLAND

First-class

College Park, Dublin, 13, 15 and 16 June 1959

Match drawn

SCOTLAND

		R	B	M	4s	6s		R	B	M	4s	6s
L.C.Dudman	c Warke b Huey	34		2	-		c&b Bodell	22		1	-	
R.H.E.Chisholm	c Corry b Huey	51	150	6	-		not out	54		6	-	
Rev J.Aitchison	not out	190	256	16	5		b Bodell	0		-	-	
M.H.Denness	c Martin b Huey	47		4	-							
D.Barr	st Fawcett b Hope	0		-	-		c Fawcett b Hunter	30		3	-	
J.M.Allan	not out	31		2	-		not out	0		-	-	
*S.H.Cosh							(4) c Hunter b Bodell	12		1	1	
+J.Brown												
J.B.Roberts												
D.Livingstone												
J.S.Wilson												
	b2	2					nb3	3				
	(4 wickets declared)	**355**					(4 wickets declared)	**121**				

IRELAND

		R	B	M	4s	6s		R	B	M	4s	6s
T.McCloy	c Aitchison b Chisholm	37		4	-		(2) st Brown b Chisholm	31	74	4	-	
S.F.Bergin	c Barr b Roberts	137	340	16	-		(1) not out	49	82	3	-	
H.Martin	c Barr b Wilson	39		3	-		not out	1		-	-	
C.V.Corry	c Brown b Wilson	4		-	-							
*L.Warke	b Allan	21		2	-							
W.R.Hunter	c Aitchison b Livingstone	21		2	1							
G.A.A.Duffy	c Denness b Allan	22		1	-							
K.W.Hope	b Wilson	5		-	-							
+G.W.Fawcett	c Denness b Livingstone	13		-	-							
S.S.J.Huey	c Cosh b Livingstone	1		-	-							
E.H.Bodell	not out	0		-	-							
	b5 lb5 nb8	18										
		318					(1 wicket)	**81**				

Ireland	O	M	R	W	nb	w		O	M	R	W	nb	w	fow	Sc (1)	Ir (1)	Sc (2)	Ir (2)
Bodell	25	3	92	0				19	6	54	3			1	70 (1)	94 (1)	36 (1)	78 (2)
Hunter	16	2	46	0				7	3	15	1			2	93 (2)	175 (3)	36 (3)	
Huey	57	25	103	3				9	2	22	0			3	237 (4)	198 (4)	57 (4)	
Hope	27	9	45	1										4	238 (5)	247 (2)	117 (5)	
Duffy	12	4	26	0										5		253 (5)		
Warke	6	0	26	0		(4)		7	1	27	0			6		273 (6)		
McCloy	1	0	15	0										7		296 (8)		
														8		316 (9)		
Scotland	O	M	R	W	nb	w		O	M	R	W	nb	w	9		316 (7)		
Barr	27	8	47	0				5	0	13	0			10		318 (10)		
Wilson	24	9	49	3				7	1	15	0							
Allan	45	20	64	2				6	0	24	0							
Livingstone	28.1	9	66	3				4	0	12	0							
Roberts	23	5	53	1				4	2	12	0							
Chisholm	10	3	21	1				2	0	4	1							
Aitchison								1	0	1	0							

Umpires: J.Connerton, K.Orme and C.Fox

Toss: Scotland

Close of play: 1st day – Scotland (1) 355-4 (Aitchison 190*, Allan 31*); 2nd day – Ireland (1) 292-6 (Duffy 13*, Hope 5*).

Stan Nagaiah's Interport

The Hong Kong side for the Interport in December 1959 was different than that of pre-Second World War matches. Although still largely made up of administrators, businessmen and other professional people, those of South Asian origin formed a larger proportion. The side included George Rowe, father of Charles Rowe (Kent and Glamorgan) and brother of Anthony Rowe (an English rower who had represented Great Britain in the 1948 Olympic Games). George came to Hong Kong on joining the Colonial Secretariat and later became the director of social welfare.

Among those of South Asian origin was Jalu Shroff who was born in Shanghai and whose parents moved to Hong Kong when he was a child. Jalu became the managing director of S. Framjee and Company. Another difference to the 1930s was the smaller presence of the military, Captain J.S. Watts being the only representative.

Malaya were captained by their coach, the Ceylonese cricketer Mahadevan Sathasivam, a flamboyant batsman with one first-class double century and two other centuries to his name. Sathasivam also coached in Singapore and captained them, thereby becoming the only person to captain three different countries at international cricket. Malaya's other leading player was Michael Shepherdson who represented Malaysia at hockey in the Asian Games in 1958 and 1962 and the Olympic Games in Melbourne in 1956.

Pritchard, Hong Kong's captain, won the toss and chose to bat, but his side made a poor showing on what he expected to be a good batting wicket. Pritchard and Shroff were the only players to exceed 20 as Schubert and Cheah Teow Keat bowled splendidly to dismiss the home side in the 56th over. Malaya bowled at a rate of 24 overs per hour.

Malaya's innings followed a similar pattern against the bowling of Carnell and Pritchard. Again only two batsmen exceeded 20, but Rajalingam (34) and Sathasivam (47) made the difference and Malaya led by 38 on the first innings.

Hong Kong gave a more convincing display in their second innings. Pritchard and Stanton added 77 for the second wicket and Souza helped Stanton put on 65 for the fourth. There was a wobble in the middle order, but Lalchandani and Dhabher scored freely. Through their efforts, the tail took the score to 291, a lead of 253. Carnell then removed three of the Malayan top order with only 12 runs scored. By lunch on the final day, the visitors were on 114/6 and Hong Kong looked to be on the way to an easy victory. When three more wickets went down for a further 49 runs, any chance of Malaya saving the match seemed over.

Schubert joined Nagaiah, who was on 11, with 91 runs still to score and 90 minutes left for play. Nagaiah decided to attack the bowling and clearly enjoyed thumping the ball to all parts of the ground. Since many of his shots sent the ball to places other than those intended, the ball frequently eluded the fielders. Schubert preferred to block almost every ball or, at best, send it for a single.

In very little time, 40 runs were added and the pair realised that, if they played sensibly, the target was in reach. A period ensued where runs came mainly in singles, some of which were a shade risky, but Hong Kong's fielders could never quite effect a run-out. Pritchard tried rotating his bowlers but to no avail. Luck was with the visitors. When Carnell produced a full toss, Nagaiah was tempted into the pull; Rowe, fielding at silly mid-on, fell to the ground to avoid being hit, but Nagaiah miscued the shot and the ball lobbed gently over the fielder's head.

With ten needed Nagaiah struck a six and the winning runs came soon after. The last-wicket stand was worth 92, Nagaiah was undefeated on 81 and Malaya had achieved a remarkable victory. The Hong Kong side were devastated. Carnell had bowled well for his ten-wicket return and it would have been remembered as his match, if Hong Kong had won. Instead, it has become known as the 'Stan Nagaiah Interport'.

HONG KONG v MALAYA

Hong Kong Cricket Club, Chater Road, Hong Kong, 12, 13 and 14 December 1959

Malaya won by one wicket

HONG KONG		R	B	M	4s	6s		R	B	M	4s	6s
G.T.Rowe	b Cheah Teow Keat	7					c G'ran Singh b K K Leong	7				
*G.H.P.Pritchard	lbw b Gurucharan Singh	25					c&b Gurucharan Singh	35				
I.L.Stanton	c Nagaiah b Schubert	12					run out	80				
J.S.Shroff	b Schubert	27					c&b Gurucharan Singh	4				
G.A.Souza	b Schubert	4					b Nagaiah	30				
C.J.B.Leader	b Cheah Teow Keat	19					c Shepherdson b Nagaiah	1				
Capt J.S.Watts	c Rajalingam b Cheah Teow Keat	3					c Shepherdson b Nagaiah	13				
+R.Lalchandani	b Cheah Teow Keat	5					lbw b Schubert	29				
D.P.Dhabher	not out	0					c Shepherdson b C T Keat	54				
B.C.N.Carnell	b Schubert	10					c Rajalingam b Schubert	4				
R.W.Bell	c da Silva b Schubert	0					not out	1				
	Extras	20						33				
		132						**291**				

MALAYA		R	B	M	4s	6s		R	B	M	4s	6s
+S.Rajalingam	c&b Pritchard	34					lbw b Carnell	0				
A.Murugesu	b Carnell	0					b Bell	51				
R.A.da Silva	c Carnell b Pritchard	17					(6) b Carnell	2				
*M.Sathasivam	b Pritchard	47					(7) c Watts b Pritchard	32				
M.Shepherdson	c Leader b Carnell	2					c Dhabher b Bell	8				
R.Bowles	c Lalchandani b Dhabher	18					(4) c Dhabher b Carnell	0				
Koay Khoon Leong	not out	18					(8) c Souza b Carnell	16				
Gurucharan Singh	lbw b Bell	5					(9) c Stanton b Carnell	11				
S.Nagaiah	lbw b Bell	0					(10) not out	81			104	
M.C.Schubert	c Leader b Carnell	0					(11) not out	21				
Cheah Teow Keat	b Carnell	5					(3) c Leader b Carnell	4				
	Extras	24						29				
		170						(9 wickets)	**255**				

Malaya	O	M	R	W	nb	w		O	M	R	W	nb	w	fow	HK	Mal	HK	Mal
Nagaiah	5	2	18	0			(6)	9	1	38	3			1	20	2	13	0
Cheah Teow Keat	12	7	12	4			(1)	20.1	5	58	1			2	40	54	90	11
Schubert	17.5	9	35	5			(2)	23	5	57	2			3	70	103	104	12
Koay Khoon Leong	6	1	11	0			(3)	7	7	0	1			4	77	112	169	30
Gurucharan Singh	15	1	36	1			(4)	31	7	100	2			5	92	122	177	38
Murugesu							(5)	1	0	5	0			6	111	143	179	84
														7	116	163	207	131
Hong Kong	O	M	R	W	nb	w		O	M	R	W	nb	w	8	117	163	259	135
Bell	11	1	39	2			(2)	14	3	49	2			9	132	164	271	163
Carnell	17	6	39	4			(1)	22.4	2	97	6			10	132	170	291	
Dhabher	14	3	39	1			(4)	14	3	33	0							
Pritchard	12	1	29	3			(3)	10	1	37	1							
Souza								4	0	10	0							

Umpires: H.F.Mellowes (Hong Kong) and [unknown]

Toss: Hong Kong

The breakdown of extras is not known.

Close of play: 1st day – Malaya (1) 153-6; 2nd day – not known.

6

Touring attractions 1960–1979

THE POST-WAR pattern of international cricket between the Associate and Affiliate countries continued into the 1960s and early 1970s. Denmark met The Netherlands and Ireland played Scotland on an annual basis. The Interport matches involving Hong Kong, Malaya and Singapore took place regularly. Matches between Kenya, Tanganyika and Uganda developed into an annual Triangular Tournament, which became Quadrangular with the inclusion of Zambia in 1968. Argentina exchanged tours with both Brazil and Chile. In West Africa, Sierra Leone, The Gambia, Nigeria and Ghana all played each other, although there was no overall west African competition to rival that in east Africa.

The main feature of the period between 1960 and 1979, however, was the large number of tours made to Associate and Affiliate countries by teams from the Full Member countries. East Africa and south-east Asia (Malaya, Singapore and Hong Kong) were the main beneficiaries, reflecting the attraction of these regions as places to visit, the quality of the local cricket, the presence of suitable grounds, many with grass wickets, and the excellent hospitality. These tours gave an opportunity for local cricketers and spectators to see some of the best players in the world in action and for the tourists to experience cricket in a club-like atmosphere, without the pressure of representing their own country in a Test-match arena.

In addition, the Full Member countries touring England frequently took advantage of side trips to Ireland, Scotland and The Netherlands for short periods of relative relaxation, as a break from the pressure of Test matches and the grind of match after match against the English counties. Similarly, Bermuda benefitted from visits of Full Member countries touring the West Indies.

In February 1962, R.A. Roberts organised a three-month world tour of an international side to Rhodesia, East Africa, Pakistan, Hong Kong and New Zealand, covering a total of 64,000km. The team used 25 players; seven from England, seven from Australia, three from South Africa (two white and one, Basil D'Oliveira, non-white), three from the West Indies, one from India, two from Pakistan, one from Rhodesia, and one, Ramanbhai Patel, from East Africa. Nine of the players had represented their countries at Test level. So successful was the venture that, in September the same year, a Commonwealth side was assembled to tour Rhodesia, east Africa, Malaya and Singapore.

The team arrived in Kuala Lumpur for the start of the Malayan leg on 3 September 1962 where they were met at the airport by officials from the Malayan Cricket Association. Coming from east Africa, the squad were minus Colin Ingleby-Mackenzie, who was delayed in Karachi because he had mislaid his vaccination papers. The following day was free for the players to explore Kuala Lumpur before meeting at the Selangor Club Padang for nets in the late afternoon. In the evening, a buffet party was given to visitors by the acting Prime Minister, Tun Abdul Razak bin Hussein, at the Istana Tetamu.

On Friday 5 September they played a one-day match against Selangor State, winning easily by 311 runs. In the evening, the visitors attended a cocktail party hosted by the UK High Commissioner. Such a sequence of events was typical of these tours. It was probably as well that the local opposition was not always of high quality, as the frequency and level of the hospitality meant that the visitors were often short of sleep and well below the fitness required for serious cricket. The aim was to have a good time, make friends and enjoy the tourist attractions of the country.

As well as the visits of touring teams to the Associate and Affiliate countries, the period was marked by the revival of one international series and the start of another. Both involved multi-innings matches spread over either two or three days. The revival was the series between the United States and Canada, last played in 1912. The idea came from John Marder, the first president of the United States Cricket Association, formed in 1961. He saw it as a way of providing publicity and a focus for immediate activity to his overall plan of reviving and promoting cricket, which had declined in America, slowly throughout the 1930s and more rapidly since the end of the Second World War. He approached Donald King, the secretary of the Canadian Cricket Association, who responded with enthusiasm. A tentative arrangement was made for a match to be played in Chicago in 1962 but this proved impossible to organise. The Canadians then offered to host a fixture in Toronto in 1963.

In the expectation that the series, renewed after a lapse of 51 years, would become a regular event, the two cricket associations offered a trophy to be awarded to the winners. The K.A. Auty Trophy was dedicated to Karl André Auty, who was largely responsible for keeping cricket alive in the 1930s and 1940s and making Chicago a leading cricket centre. Auty was born in England in July 1878, but moved to Vancouver in 1909 to take the post of power and contract manager for the British Columbia Railway Company. In 1918 he became the sales manager for the Commonwealth Edison Company in Chicago. He was president of the Chicago Cricket Club and the Illinois Cricket Association, and died aged 81 in 1959.

Both sides in the inaugural match of the new series comprised largely expatriates from the Caribbean, the Indian subcontinent and the British Isles. Expatriates or locally-born players with expatriate parents continued to form the basis of both sides throughout the series which was played annually from 1963 until 1980, then every alternate year from 1983 to 1991. There were matches in 1994 and 1995 before the series lapsed again until 2011. It was then played annually until 2013. Apart from a short period in the early 1970s, Canada have been the stronger of the two teams, winning the K.A. Auty Trophy 13 times to the USA's six, with seven matches drawn.

The following year saw the inauguration of the series of matches between Malaysia and Singapore, for the Saudara Cup. Throughout the 1950s and 60s, games between the two countries continued the pattern established in 1905 between the Federation of Malaya and the Straits Settlements, with teams comprising a mixture of indigenous players, British administrators, settlers from the United Kingdom and the white Commonwealth, and the military. Anyone who was resident at the time a match was played was eligible for selection.

In June 1970, two such sides met on the Singapore Cricket Club Padang, with Singapore winning by an innings and 22 runs. Des Garnes, a serviceman stationed in Singapore, was key to this victory; he scored an unbeaten 55 in Singapore's innings and took ten wickets for 92 in the match.

The cricket associations of both countries realised that more needed to be done to ensure that cricket remained strong among their nationals. They therefore decided to institute an annual fixture for citizens only, a decision which proved to be farsighted, in that it predated by nine years the regulations of the International Cricket Council, setting qualifying criteria for players to represent their country internationally. The fixture has also remained a two-innings affair, one of the few to survive the onslaught of one-day and

T20 cricket in the international calendar. The choice of title, the Saudara Cup, reflected the long history of close association between the cricket sides of both countries, *saudara* being the Malay word for brother, sister or any collateral relative and therefore often used to denote 'kinship'. This one word provides what today might be called the 'mission statement' of the competition.

Unfortunately the international series between The Netherlands and Denmark ended during this period. After the last match was played in 1980, the Dutch had won five times to Denmark's one, with five games ending in draws.

One-day matches involving what were then or are now Associate or Affiliate countries began in this period. On 25 May 1969 Scotland met the International Cavaliers in a 40-over game, but bowlers were permitted a maximum of nine overs each, whereas eight would be the maximum under current rules for a 40-over innings. In January 1969, Ceylon played two 60-over matches against MCC; on 29 June 1972 Leicestershire met East Africa in a 50-over match, and on 3 July 1974 Canada played Denmark, the first one-day fixture between two Associate sides. The match was scheduled for 50 overs each but it was reduced to 45 overs because of the weather.

May and June 1979 saw the first global competition between Associate and Affiliate countries. A proposal for such a competition was put to a meeting of the ICC in 1966 by Philip Snow, the Fijian representative. It was supported by Gamini Goonesena of Sri Lanka and John Marder of the USA. No action was taken, however, as the ICC gave priority to organising the first World Cup for Full Members, which eventually took place in 1975 and to which two Associate teams, Sri Lanka and East Africa, were invited as a way of increasing numbers.

The Associate countries soon realised that a better way was needed to decide which of their number should play in future World Cups and the International Cricket Council Trophy was born. The tournament did not include all the countries which had Associate status at that time. Hong Kong were unable to raise a side that met the ICC's residential requirements, West Africa failed to submit their application in time and Gibraltar withdrew because the dates coincided with an international hockey tournament in which several of their players were involved. Wales were therefore invited to field a side with the proviso that, should they finish in the top two, they would not be allowed to qualify for the World Cup, since they were not a recognised Associate country.

Fifteen countries took part in the competition, staged at various club grounds in England. Matches were 60 overs per side, the norm at the time for fixtures played in the English summer, benefitting from the long daylight hours. With the spread of one-day internationals across the globe, the regulations had to change to provide uniformity across a wide range of environment conditions; hence the reduction in length to 50 overs per side as standard.

There's a *bomoh* in the basement

The two-day match between All-Malaya and a Commonwealth XI began on Saturday 6 October 1962. With the fixture well-publicised and a large attendance expected, there were always concerns about the weather and how much play would be lost through rain. Whether or not they believed in the supernatural or animistic magic, the Selangor Club, on whose ground the match was played, employed the services of a local shaman or *bomoh*. Inche Labai Abdullah bin Omar, aged 60, was chosen for the role. On both days, he hid himself in the club house and worked his magic by apparently tying up the rain in a knot in a large handkerchief.

Da Silva, Malaya's captain, won the toss. Whether he thought there would be some assistance in the wicket for his bowlers or whether he judged that the spectators would be better entertained by some top-class batting rather than a collapse of his own side, he did not make clear. However, he chose to field.

Initially, Marshall and Willie Watson made sedate progress as Beckett, Malaya's left-arm medium-pace bowler, dropped the ball on a good length and had to be watched. After 25 minutes the score was only 20, but Malaya's bowlers could not maintain the pressure; 50 was reached in 46 minutes and 100 in only 67. With the score on 110, Delilkan, with his leg breaks and googlies, was brought on at the Church End. His first ball spun into Watson, clipped the edge of his bat and was well caught by Rajalingam behind the stumps. Watson's 43 had come in 69 minutes with four fours.

Delilkan bowled a nagging and consistent length and got the ball to turn. With Gurucharan Singh providing spin from the other end, Malaya threatened to get on top. Marshall mis-hit Gurucharan to the long-off boundary, only for Navaratnam to drop the catch with the team score at 126. Four runs later, Baig mis-read the spin of Delilkan and steered the ball to short fine leg where, again, Navaratnam failed to take the catch. What could have been 130/3 went on to become 175/1, then Marshall, trying for his century, attempted to square cut Delilkan, only to hit his stumps. His 97 had taken 100 minutes and contained two sixes and 12 fours. When lunch was taken, after 107 minutes of morning play, the Commonwealth had reached an impressive 190/2.

Following a sunny morning, rain clouds threatened in the afternoon, but after shedding a few drops, they disappeared. The *bomoh*'s magic appeared to be working. Baig and Kanhai scored freely off Malaya's pace attack, the former pulling a short ball from Milner into the verandah of the long bar in the pavilion to bring up the century partnership in 61 minutes. Four runs later, with the spinners recalled, Baig went full stretch to smother the break, but Delilkan's ball curled away and bowled him. There was no respite for the local bowlers, however, as Alley struck Milner for ten in one over and reached 20 in 17 minutes before falling leg-before, another wicket to Delilkan.

When D'Oliveira was beaten playing for a break to a ball that went straight on, the score was 321/5 and Delilkan had taken all five for 56 runs. With the visitors going for very quick as opposed to merely quick runs, Borde went cheaply and Kanhai, attempting to sweep Delilkan, dragged the ball into the stumps. Chester Watson fell to a brilliant catch at silly mid-off by Williams. After an afternoon session of 114 minutes, tea was taken and Willie Watson declared on 369/8.

Malaya began in style. With Hall bowling at half pace and short of a length, seven runs came off the first over. Nine followed from the next, bowled by Chester Watson. Williams and Milner put on 20 in 11 minutes. Watson decided on full pace for his second over and Williams was struck a painful blow on the hip. While still recovering, he edged the next ball to second slip, but Kanhai spilled the catch. In Watson's third over, Williams was hit on his left hand while trying to avoid a bouncer. He was forced to retire hurt and taken to hospital, where a broken finger was diagnosed.

Milner continued to play strokes, hooking Hall to the fine-leg boundary, but was then leg before next ball, which Hall pitched on a fuller length. Beckett was unnerved by

Watson's pace and was, perhaps, only too happy to be bowled by the sixth ball he faced. Mike Shepherdson and da Silva entertained the crowd with good strokeplay and saw off the opening attack, Watson being replaced by Loader after a spell of five overs, and Hall by D'Oliveira, after six. After an hour's play, Malaya were 46/2. With the score on 55, Shepherdson drove D'Oliveira for four wide of mid-off but, trying to repeat the stroke the next ball, he failed to get to the pitch and D'Oliveira took a fine return catch, ankle high, running to his left.

Da Silva took a liking to the spin of Borde and hit him for three consecutive fours. Christie Shepherdson tried to do the same but, after driving one ball to the mid-off boundary, he tried to hit the next one out of the ground, missed and was bowled. This was the first of three wickets which the home side lost through recklessness. Next to go was Delilkan who drove Borde to cover, started to run, but was sent back by da Silva. Loader threw the ball directly at the stumps before the batsman could get back. Gurucharan Singh struck two fours to long-off but, trying for a third, holed out to Kanhai at deep extra cover.

Da Silva took Malaya passed the century mark before Navaratnam completed an unhappy day by being bowled without scoring. Rajalingam stayed with da Silva to the close at which time Malaya were still 246 runs in arrears with only two wickets remaining, assuming Williams would not bat again. The follow-on looked likely. The first day saw 98 overs bowled and 492 runs scored, all of which provided excellent fare for the large crowd. After play, the visitors attended a subscription dinner, hosted by the Selangor club.

Two changes were made to the teams for the second day with the approval of both captains. Daljit Singh replaced the injured Williams and Colin Ingleby-Mackenzie, now arrived in Malaya, took over from Bill Alley. Both players were allowed to bat in their respective team's second innings. It took only 15 minutes to bring the home side's first innings to an end, but, in that time, da Silva completed a well-deserved half-century. A further 26 runs were added in total with Rajalingam the last person out for a valuable 23.

Willie Watson decided not to enforce the follow-on which could so easily have resulted in the match ending around lunchtime. Instead, he opted to give the spectators a full day's cricket to watch. He and Marshall put on 93 for the first wicket in only 44 minutes. Malaya's pace bowlers were quickly removed from duty, but neither Delilkan nor Gurucharan Singh were able to control the flow of runs. They were, however, more likely to take wickets. Delilkan was the first to succeed when da Silva made a brilliant low catch at mid-off to dismiss Marshall. Soon after, Gurucharan took a return catch to remove Watson.

Quick runs were the requirement but increasing the scoring rate beyond what was already more than a run per minute was fraught with risk, particularly as the Malayan spinners were getting the ball to turn. Some dark clouds covered the ground in the early afternoon and a few spots of rain fell. Nothing of significance affected the cricket, however, even though there were storms in the surrounding area. Again the *bomoh*'s magic seemed to be working. Kanhai hit Delilkan high into the deep field where Perera held a head-high catch. Gurucharan took a low, diving, left-hand catch off his own bowling to dismiss Ingleby-Mackenzie, Baig fed Perera another catch and Gurucharan removed Hall, Borde and Chester Watson in a superb spell of bowling.

Delilkan held on to another fine caught-and-bowled to end D'Oliveira's innings, but not before he had made the fastest fifty of the match in 41 minutes with seven fours. Roy Swetman, who, for some reason, was wearing a tie, added 37 for the last wicket with Loader. The stand ended when Gurucharan bowled Loader for his sixth wicket of the innings. The Commonwealth score of 252 was made in 53.3 overs and 147 minutes. Malaya had bowled their overs at nearly 22 per hour.

Malaya required 473 runs to win, but, more importantly, the Commonwealth had two and a half hours to dismiss them a second time. Hall and Chester Watson were effective from the start. Milner waved his bat at a ball from Hall and gave a simple return catch. Daljit Singh failed to lay bat on the first three balls of Watson's first over and was then bowled by the fourth. Mike Shepherdson lasted eight balls before being caught at slip. Christie Shepherdson was dropped by Willie Watson at slip off the third ball he received, only to be caught behind off the third ball of the next over. The edge offered to the wicketkeeper was only the second time he had managed to hit the ball. Malaya thus went into tea with the score on no runs for the loss of four wickets.

After the interval, Willie Watson gave his opening bowlers a rest and the home side some respite by giving the ball to Borde and Loader. Beckett scored Malaya's first runs, sweeping Borde to the fine-leg boundary to take the score to 4/4 after 35 minutes. With the score on 13, Beckett missed a straight ball from Loader. Twelve runs later, da Silva was bowled round his legs by Borde; he had battled for 40 minutes for his one run, being totally unable to reproduce his form of the first innings.

Delilkan made no attempt to play for a draw. Instead he tried to score off every ball. He was successful for a while, but after making 25 in 28 minutes, he mis-hit Borde and gave an easy catch to Swetman. Rajalingam, who had supported Delilkan with defence, went one run later without scoring. Gurucharan Singh made easy runs off Kanhai's donkey drops, but Willie Watson decided that the time had come to secure victory. He gave the ball to Hall with clear instructions to finish off the innings. Gurucharan lifted Hall's first ball to extra cover. Malaya's last man came to the wicket, accompanied by the *bomoh*, who pulled the handkerchief from his pocket and, in bright sunshine, loosened the large knot to release the rain. Perhaps bemused by this ceremony, Perera was bowled first ball, giving victory to the visitors by 406 runs. Hall finished with four wickets without conceding a run.

It was estimated that some 8,000 people watched the match over the two days with the takings exceeding M$12,000. They were fortunate to have cricket uninterrupted by the weather, with no rain at all in the centre of Kuala Lumpur and only 3mm in the surrounding areas. The following day, 8 October, 10.9mm of rain fell.

Although Malaya were outplayed they impressed with some excellent fielding and catching. Their spin attack of Delilkan and Gurucharan Singh was certainly of English Minor County standard. Delilkan was at the peak of his powers. The following year, representing the Malaysian Cricket Association President's XI against E.W. Swanton's XI, he took seven wickets for 79 and then, playing for Malaysia, bowled Garfield Sobers first ball. His performances led to him being invited to play for the International Cavaliers on their tour of the United Kingdom in 1967.

Alex Delilkan followed Dr Stephen Fox and Dr Peter Hennessy as Malayan cricketers with a career in the medical profession. He graduated as a medical doctor from the University of Singapore in 1960 and served as a medical officer and then registrar with the Malayan government. In 1965 he joined the University of Malaya as a lecturer in anaesthesiology, working at the University Hospital in Kuala Lumpur from where he retired as a professor in 2001. He regularly represented Malaysia, was recognised as their greatest all-rounder of the time and became captain of the national side. He was happy to play cricket at any level, one day representing his country internationally, the next day turning out for the University of Malaya staff, leading a team of moderate to very mediocre players against local club sides.

MALAYA v COMMONWEALTH XI

Selangor Club Padang, Kuala Lumpur, 6 and 7 October 1962

Commonwealth XI won by 406 runs

COMMONWEALTH XI

		R	B	M	4s	6s		R	B	M	4s	6s
*W.Watson	c Rajalingam b Delilkan	43	69	4			c&b Gurucharan Singh	60	55		7	1
R.E.Marshall	ht wkt b Delilkan	97	100	12	2		c da Silva b Delilkan	46	44			
A.A.Baig	b Delilkan	68	93	9	1		c Perera b Delilkan	20				
R.B.Kanhai	b Delilkan	97	109	14			c Perera b Delilkan	1				
W.E.Alley	lbw b Delilkan	20	17				A.C.D.Ingleby-M'zie b G'n Singh	0				
B.L.D'Oliveira	b Delilkan	2					(7) c&b Delilkan	53				
C.G.Borde	lbw b Gurucharan Singh	3					(8) b Gurucharan Singh	1	41		7	
C.D.Watson	c Williams b G'n Singh	4					(9) b Gurucharan Singh	3				
W.W.Hall	not out	16					(6) b Gurucharan Singh	24				
+R.Swetman							not out	26				
P.J.Loader							b Gurucharan Singh	16				
	Extras	19						2				
	(8 wickets declared)	**369**						**252**				

MALAYA

		R	B	M	4s	6s		R	B	M	4s	6s
C.Williams	retired hurt	12					(2) Daljit Singh b C.D.Watson	0	4			
R.Milner	lbw b Hall	13	31	2			(1) c&b Hall	0				
D.G.Beckett	b C.D.Watson	0	6				(6) b Loader	8				
M.Shepherdson	c&b D'Oliveira	18	42				c W.Watson b C.D.Watson	0	8			
*R.A.da Silva	c Swetman b Borde	51					b Borde	1	40			
C.Shepherdson	b Borde	4					(3) c Swetman b Hall	0				
A.E.Delilkan	run out	5					c Swetman b Borde	25	28			
Gurucharan Singh	c Kanhai b Borde	8					(9) c Kanhai b Hall	23			3	1
C.Navaratnam	b D'Oliveira	0					(10) not out	5				
+S.Rajalingam	lbw b Loader	23					(8) c Ingleby-M'zie b D'Oliveira	0	1			
F.Perera	not out	3					b Hall	0				
	Extras	12						4				
		149						**66**				

Malaya	O	M	R	W	nb	w		O	M	R	W	nb	w		fow	Co (1)	Ma (1)	Co (2)	Ma (2)
Beckett	15	3	66	0				6	0	23	0				1	110 (1)	29 (2)	93 (2)	0 (1)
Milner	11	2	49	0				3	0	20	0				2	175 (2)	29 (3)	99 (1)	0 (2)
Perera	11	4	60	0				4	0	28	0				3	279 (3)	59 (4)	120 (4)	0 (4)
Gurucharan Singh	14.2	0	75	2	(5)			18.3	6	77	6				4	315 (5)	80 (6)	121 (5)	0 (3)
Delilkan	19	1	79	6	(4)			22	2	101	4				5	321 (6)	86 (7)	143 (3)	13 (6)
C.Shepherdson	3	0	21	0											6	340 (7)	94 (8)	161 (6)	25 (5)
															7	354 (4)	102 (9)	163 (8)	42 (7)
Commonwealth	O	M	R	W	nb	w		O	M	R	W	nb	w		8	369 (8)	141 (5)	193 (9)	43 (8)
Hall	6	0	23	1				3.2	3	0	4				9		149 (10)	215 (7)	66 (9)
C.D.Watson	5	2	8	1				3	3	0	2				10			252 (11)	66 (11)
Loader	5.2	3	8	1	(4)			7	3	12	1								
D'Oliveira	9	3	26	2	(5)			3	1	5	1								
Borde	11	0	72	3	(3)			8	3	26	2								
Kanhai								2	0	19	0								

Umpires: [unknown]

Toss: Malaya

The breakdown of extras is not known.

Close of play: 1st day – Malaya (1) 123-7 (da Silva 43*, Rajalingam 9*).

In Malaya's first innings C.Williams (12*) retired hurt on 25-0.

Daljit Singh was allowed to replace C.Williams as a full substitute for Malaya. A.C.D.Ingleby-Mackenzie replaced W.E.Alley as a full substitute for the Commonwealth XI.

Bowling in the Commonwealth XI second innings is 1 run short.

History revived

In 1963, as a result of initiatives taken by John Marder and Donald King, the International Series between the United States and Canada was revived after a lapse of 51 years. The Canadians hosted the match in Toronto with the winners being awarded the K.A. Auty Trophy. Not unexpectedly, the 1963 encounter was a mismatch. Canadian cricket at the time was approaching Minor County standard. Their team comprised players from Ontario and Quebec.

In contrast, cricket in the United States was played in a large number of cities but was very localised, with no national or inter-state competitions. Five of their team came from Los Angeles, with other players from St Louis, Chicago, Washington DC, New York, Kansas City and Louisville. They included only two American-born players, Winston Severn and Vincent Masterton. When the team assembled in Toronto, it was the first time that the captain, Jim Reid, had met some of the players and he had no idea of their strengths and weaknesses.

On the morning of the first day, Reid won the toss for the United States and, given the easy-paced pitch, he probably made an error in inviting the Canadians to bat. He possibly thought that his side would do better by fielding first, which would give his players the experience of feeling part of a team. Unfortunately, the American bowling was unable to obtain any assistance from the atmosphere or the pitch and was inconsistent in line and length. Walker and Nascimento, both of whom were born in British Guiana, put on 129.

Nascimento gave a chance, after having scored 20, but the catch was dropped, an expensive miss. Although Walker was bowled by Surr, a 42-year-old Yorkshireman who had emigrated to the United States in 1953, the second wicket added 80 and the third a further 89. Of the first six batsmen, only Taylor failed to pass 20.

Nascimento went on to make 176, still the highest individual score in the series. His innings included 17 fours and lasted four and a half hours. The Americans tried eight bowlers without success but were handicapped by an injury to Mitra, a spin bowler. Called upon, almost in desperation, he bowled three balls, taking one wicket, after which – with the Canadian total having passed 400 – Walker declared, to give the Americans an awkward period of batting near the end of the day. His ploy was successful, as Lashkari, a player good enough to be selected as 12th man for India's Test side in 1954, and Nolan, who had played for Middlesex's second XI in 1951, fell to Peters. The umpires ended play early because of bad light. This was somewhat surprising since the match was played in ideal weather conditions throughout. The problem was that the hours of play were such that the end of the day was too close to sunset.

The Americans began well on the second day with Reid, a former Minor Counties cricketer with Lancashire II, and White completing a partnership of 53. The remainder of the batsmen, however, were hapless against the spin bowling of Branker and the visitors were dismissed shortly after lunch for a mere 117. In the follow-on, Lashkari and Reid showed that the pitch was still good for batting with an opening partnership of 68. When both were dismissed after the tea interval, the middle order was again nonplussed by the spinning ball and the innings developed into a procession until the ninth wicket fell with the score on 108. Altogether, nine wickets had fallen for the addition of 40 runs.

White, however, was in stubborn mood and, with the assistance of Surr, set out to achieve a draw. Although there was still an hour's play left, White succeeded in protecting his partner from facing Branker and, with only seven minutes remaining, it looked as though the Americans would succeed. White then attempted a suicidal single in an effort to keep the strike but was run out, giving the Canadians an emphatic victory by an innings and 164 runs. Branker finished with a match return of 12-87 but, surprisingly, he never played for Canada again.

CANADA v UNITED STATES OF AMERICA
K.A.Auty Trophy
Toronto Cricket, Skating and Curling Club, Wilson Avenue, Armour Heights, Toronto, 1 and 2 September 1963
Canada won by an innings and 164 runs

CANADA		R	B	M	4s	6s
*+V.J.Walker	b Surr	68				
R.Nascimento	c Perera b Masterson	176	270	17		
N.Grant	c Verity b White	30				
R.C.Aldridge	c Surr b Masterson	45				
K.A.Branker	not out	41				
V.K.Taylor	st Nolan b White	0				
R.J.Stevens	c Nolan b Mitra	23				
A.G.Duckworth						
D.M.M.Orr						
N.F.Harris						
B.Q.Peters						
	b17 w3	20				
	(6 wickets declared)	**403**				

USA		R	B	M	4s	6s		R	B	M	4s	6s
*J.J.Reid	c Branker b Stevens	35					b Branker	29				
A.H.Lashkari	c Stevens b Peters	5					b Branker	36				
+G.Nolan	b Peters	9					b Harris	17				
R.White	b Branker	32					run out (Nascimento-Taylor)	11				
D.Kaufmann	c Duckworth b Branker	2					lbw b Branker	0				
A.Perera	run out (Duckworth-Walker)	6					b Harris	0				
W.F.M.Severn	b Branker	0					b Branker	7				
V.V.Masterson	b Branker	0					c Taylor b Branker	2				
T.Surr	b Branker	0					(11) not out	5				
M.A.Verity	c Aldridge b Peters	17					(9) c Taylor b Branker	4				
A.K.Mitra	not out	0					(10) c Orr b Branker	0				
	b6 lb1 nb4	11					b6 lb5	11				
		117						**122**				

USA	O	M	R	W	nb	w		fow	Ca (1)	US (1)	US (2)
Perera	10	2	39	0				1	129	8	68
Surr	13	2	46	1				2	209	21	77
Lashkari	17	1	70	0				3	298	74	93
White	29	1	142	2				4	345	89	96
Severn	3	0	21	0				5	346	96	97
Reid	5	0	33	0				6	403	100	104
Masterson	8	0	30	2				7		100	104
Mitra	0.3	0	2	1				8		100	108
								9		117	108

Canada	O	M	R	W	nb	w		O	M	R	W	nb	w						10		117	122

Canada	O	M	R	W	nb	w	O	M	R	W	nb	w
Peters	16	3	35	3			7	1	20	0		
Aldridge	4	1	8	0								
Branker	22.4	5	50	5	(2)		33	11	37	7		
Stevens	11	5	13	1	(3)		7	4	7	0		
Harris					(4)		27	15	38	2		
Taylor					(5)		2	0	9	0		

Umpires: J.Henderson (Canada) and E.A.Wigley (Canada)

Toss: USA

Close of play: 1st day – USA (1) ??-2 (J.J.Reid ??*, R.White ??*)

Australia too relaxed

The visit of the Australians to The Netherlands in August 1964 was typical of those made by tourists to England as a side trip, combining relaxation and cricket away from the pressures of Test matches. The 1964 journey took place after the Australians had completed their programme of five Tests and their matches against the English counties. They rested their captain Bob Simpson, who had an injured finger, the leadership passing to Brian Booth. The Dutch were weakened by the absence of their all-rounder Nico Spits, who was playing hockey for his country against Great Britain, a friendly in preparation for the Olympic Games.

Some 3,000 spectators saw the Australians decide to bat first having won the toss. They took some time to adjust to the matting surface. Compared to grass, the pitch took more spin and the ball rose quickly and more sharply, making it difficult to play forward with confidence. Lawry failed to deal with the bounce and pace of Trijzelaar and gave a hard chance to the slips where van Weelde took a brilliant catch close to the ground.

Grout and O'Neill played comfortably against some undistinguished bowling, but with the score on 36, the former missed a straight ball from Trijzelaar. A change in bowling brought Pierhagen and Vriens together. The scoring rate slowed, good bowling being supported by some excellent fielding. The only lapse was a missed catch offered by O'Neill when he had made 15. Burge found Pierhagen's left-arm medium particularly difficult, being beaten twice in one maiden over, before eventually falling to him after making a somewhat laborious 22. Booth tried to raise the scoring rate, hitting a six and a four in the first over he faced, but was caught by Bouwman in the deep, trying to hit Vriens for six. Although he walked, there was some doubt whether the catch was legal. Some spectators felt that Bouwman had stepped over the boundary.

An unfortunate accident occurred when Potter mis-hit a rising ball from Trijzelaar and was struck on the head. He was taken to hospital where a fractured skull was diagnosed, an injury which was to keep him out of the rest of the tour and the forthcoming visit of the Australians to India and Pakistan. After a ten-minute break for rain, O'Neill advanced the score through hooks and square cuts. Shortly after lunch, he became the fifth wicket to fall, the result of a smart stumping by Schoonheim. The visitors lost their remaining wickets cheaply, the last five falling for only 37 runs, and they were dismissed for a somewhat disappointing 197.

When the Dutch batted, the Australians found the fielding and bowling conditions difficult. Spikes could not be worn on the matting and the visitors had to wear rubber-soled plimsolls, which gave little grip on the grass outfield. The Dutch, in contrast, wore boots with flat studs. Even so, it was a surprise when Marseille and van der Wegt failed by only one run to make a century opening partnership, their stand of 99 taking only an hour and a half. A further break for rain made the conditions worse for the Australians. Van Arkel gave a fine display of strokeplay. When he was out, the third wicket to fall, the Dutch required only 46 to win in just over 40 minutes.

With victory over a Full Member country a possibility, the Dutch were perhaps overwhelmed and lost four wickets quickly. The Australians could have bowled negatively to secure a draw but, instead, endeavoured to win the match. With 17 runs needed, Onstein took the initiative and drove Cowper over the boundary for six. He and Wijkhuizen scampered two singles before the latter played out a maiden against McKenzie. With only one over left, nine runs were required and Onstein on strike. Two further singles were made, very risky or perhaps, since they were successful, well-judged. Onstein then hit the third ball of Cowper's over for another six and hooked the fourth for four to give The Netherlands a remarkable victory by three wickets with two balls to spare.

NETHERLANDS v AUSTRALIANS

Haagsche Cricket Club, De Diepput, The Hague, 29 August 1964

Netherlands won by three wickets

AUSTRALIANS

		R	B	M	4s	6s
W.M.Lawry	c van Weelde b Trijzelaar	6			-	-
+A.W.T.Grout	b Trijzelaar	20			3	-
N.C.L.O'Neill	st Schoonheim b Pierhagen	87		110	12	1
P.J.P.Burge	c Trijzelaar b Pierhagen	22			1	-
*B.C.Booth	c Bouwman b Vriens	13			1	1
J.Potter	retired hurt	7			-	-
R.M.Cowper	c&b Trijzelaar	2			-	-
T.R.Vievers	run out	12			2	-
J.W.Martin	lbw b Pierhagen	12			2	-
G.D.McKenzie	not out	8			-	1
A.N.Connolly	b Vriens	1			-	-
	lb6 nb2	8				
		197				

NETHERLANDS

		R	B	M	4s	6s
P.A.Marseille	lbw b Cowper	77			5	-
W.L.van der Wegt	b McKenzie	33		90	3	-
*P.van Arkel	c&b Cowper	45		30	4	2
W.van Weelde	b McKenzie	8			1	-
P.A.L.Bouwman	c Vievers b Cowper	1			-	-
R.F.Onstein	not out	24			1	2
E.W.C.Vriens	lbw b Cowper	3			-	-
H.B.Trijzelaar	b McKenzie	0			-	-
H.A.G.Wijkuizen	not out	2			-	-
+R.F.Schoonheim						
W.A.Pierhagen						
	b4 lb4	8				
	(7 wickets)	**201**				

Netherlands	O	M	R	W	w	nb
Trijzelaar	11	2	41	3	-	3
van Arkel	4	0	20	0	-	-
Pierhagen	21	6	75	3	-	-
Vriens	14.1	0	53	2	-	-

Australians	O	M	R	W	w	nb
McKenzie	19	4	48	3	-	-
Connolly	4	0	11	0	-	-
Vievers	6	1	13	0	-	1
Martin	10	0	46	0	-	-
O'Neill	6	2	6	0	-	-
Cowper	12.4	1	69	4	-	-

fow	Au (1)	Ne (1)
1	15 (1)	99 (2)
2	36 (2)	129 (1)
3	91 (4)	152 (3)
4	120 (5)	161 (4)
5	160 (3)	174 (5)
6	162 (7)	180 (7)
7	186 (8)	181 (8)
8	186 (9)	
9	197 (11)	
10		

Umpires: W.Amons (Netherlands) and G.Stallmann (Netherlands)

Toss: Australians

When all seems lost, be bold

Until it was among the first group of countries to be elected as Associate Members of the ICC in 1965, Sri Lanka, or Ceylon as the country was known until 22 May, 1972, relied for its international cricket largely on the willingness of India and Pakistan to meet them, both home and away. Unofficial Test matches were played, normally over four days, which were accorded first-class status. The best that Ceylon usually managed was to force a draw. When they lost the first two 'Tests' on their tour of India in 1964/65, there was little expectation that anything would change. For the third 'Test' at Ahmedabad, in early January 1965, India chose a strong but not full-strength side. Their first five batsmen had all played Test cricket, but the remainder consisted of young players who had been doing well domestically in that season's Ranji Trophy.

Rain prevented any play on the first day and most of the second day was lost while the pitch and outfield dried out. It was not until after an early tea interval had been taken that play was possible. India's captain, the Nawab of Pataudi, won the toss and took most of the local pundits by surprise by deciding to bat. Neither side had any top-class fast bowlers but Frederick managed to swing the ball at just above medium pace. He created considerable difficulty. Three wickets were down for 37 before Pataudi and Hanumant Singh defended stoutly to the close.

The pitch continued to favour the bowlers on the third day. Jayasinghe, bowling his off spin and varying his pace and length, troubled all the batsmen with the exception of Saxena, to take six wickets as the hosts crumbled to 189 all out. Saxena was undefeated, having scored one-third of his team's total. India's bowlers were also able to exploit the conditions and soon reduced Ceylon to 18/4. The visitors were handicapped by an injury to Edward, their opening batsman, who suffered a serious injury to his eye while fielding in the slips. The ball hit him in the face and shattered his spectacles, leaving him unable to take any further part in the game. Polonowita and Fernando came to the rescue as conditions eased towards the end of the day, which Ceylon finished 45 runs behind with three wickets in hand.

Instead of batting on and trying to gain a first-innings lead, Tissera took the initiative and declared. He decided that it would be better if his bowlers took advantage of the morning dew rather than let his tail-enders scratch about and achieve little. It was a bold decision which would be almost unthinkable today. However, it worked. India's strong batting line-up failed completely and they were bowled out for 66 with Ceylon's four bowlers sharing the wickets. Despite the swinging and turning ball, wicketkeeper Fernando stood up to the stumps. Although he conceded nine byes, he effected two catches and two stumpings in a superb display, to give him seven victims for the match.

Ceylon's positive attitude continued. With 112 runs needed to win, Fuard and Ponniah paved the way with an opening stand of 41. Jayasinghe and Tissera helped take the score to 98/3, at which point perhaps a lack of self-belief set in. Goel used his left-arm spin with considerable skill and brought about a collapse as three wickets fell for no runs. Tissera held firm, however, and with the help of Polonowita took Ceylon through to victory. Even though Sri Lanka have had many memorable victories since, they still have not won a Test match against India in India. This victory, therefore, stands as a remarkable achievement, as well as being testament to what can be achieved if a captain is prepared to be bold and take a risk.

INDIA v CEYLON

First-class – Unofficial Test Match

Sardar Vallabhbhai Patel Stadium, Ahmedabad, 2, 3, 4 and 5 January 1965

Ceylon won by four wickets

INDIA		R	B M 4s 6s		R	B M 4s 6s
D.N.Sardesai	c Tissera b Frederick	9		b Frederick	0	
+F.M.Engineer	c Polonowita b Frederick	17		(7) c Fernando b Jayasinghe	2	
A.A.Baig	c Fernando b Frederick	10		(2) b Lieversz	4	
Hanumant Singh	lbw b Jayasinghe	30		lbw b Frederick	0	
*Nawab of Pataudi	c Fernando b Frederick	28		c Polonowita b Frederick	8	
R.C.Saxena	not out	63		c Fernando b Polonowita	12	
A.K.Roy	c Polonowita b Jayasinghe	3		(3) lbw b Jayasinghe	16	
S.Venkataraghavan	c&b Jayasinghe	13		st Fernando b Polonowita	4	
U.N.Kulkarni	b Jayasinghe	0		b Jayasinghe	1	
C.K.Bhaskaran	st Fernando b Jayasinghe	8		st Fernando b Polonowita	5	
R.Goel	lbw b Jayasinghe	0		not out	1	
	lb2 nb6	8		b9 lb4	13	
		189			**66**	

CEYLON		R	B M 4s 6s		R	B M 4s 6s
M.A.H.Fuard	lbw b Kulkarni	6		b Goel	40	
C.E.M.Ponniah	b Kulkarni	8		st Engineer b Venkataraghavan	22	
L.N.G.Rodrigo	c Saxena b Kulkarni	0		run out	9	
S.Jayasinghe	b Bhaskaran	3		b Goel	19	
*M.H.Tissera	c Roy b Kulkarni	28		not out	15	
N.Chanmugam	c Hanumant Singh b B'ran	0		c Pataudi b Goel	0	
A.Polonowita	b Venkataraghavan	53		(8) not out	3	
+H.I.K.Fernando	not out	38		(7) b Goel	0	
D.W.L.Lieversz	not out	0				
N.Frederick						
T.C.T.Edward						
	b6 lb2	8		b2 lb4 nb1	7	
	(7 wickets declared)	**144**		(6 wickets)	**115**	

Ceylon	O	M	R	W	nb	wd		O	M	R	W	nb	wd	fow	Ind (1)	Cey (1)	Ind (2)	Cey (2)
Lieversz	18	5	43	0				5	2	8	1			1	24	13	4	41
Frederick	28	8	85	4				11	4	24	3			2	36	13	4	77
Jayasinghe	17.4	6	38	6				7	4	14	3			3	37	16	4	87
Chanmugam	4	0	14	0										4	79	18	20	98
Polonowita	1	0	1	0		(4)		3.4	1	7	3			5	114	25	44	98
														6	122	57	46	98
India	O	M	R	W	nb	wd		O	M	R	W	nb	wd	7	166	142	50	
Kulkarni	13	2	43	4				11	4	18	0			8	178		51	
Bhaskaran	10	1	35	2				8	5	16	0			9	187		55	
Goel	10	3	24	0				13.2	6	33	4			10	189		66	
Venkataraghavan	12	2	34	1				18	5	34	1							
Hanumant Singh								1	0	3	0							
Saxena								1	0	4	0							

Umpires: R.Bose and J.Reuben

Toss: India

Close of play: 1st day – no play; 2nd day – India (1) 51-3 (Hanumant Singh 9*, Pataudi 2*); 3rd day – Ceylon (1) 144-7 (Fernando 38*, Lieversz 0*).

The Nawab of Pataudi was later known as M.A.K.Pataudi.

Perplexed by Parfitt

In the summer of 1969 the Dutch suffered an embarrassing and spectacular defeat. Bermuda were touring Europe and arrived in The Netherlands in early June, having just beaten Denmark in a two-day fixture at Aarhus by an innings and 11 runs. Clarence Parfitt was responsible for this remarkable victory. After Bermuda had made a measly 155 in the only innings they required, he took 11 wickets for 45 in the match with his medium-paced left-arm bowling.

Parfitt had achieved international prominence four years earlier when he took eight New Zealand wickets for 41 at Hamilton, a performance that helped his country to a draw against the tourists who were ending a tour of the West Indies with a short visit to Bermuda. Bermudan cricket was particularly strong at this time. Cricket was still the national sport with youngsters learning the game by playing in alleyways, on the beaches and anywhere else they could find. Parfitt developed into one of Bermuda's best-ever players, before becoming a professional cricketer with Arbroath in Scotland. He went on to represent Scotland internationally and, after retirement, became a development officer for Cricket Scotland.

In the two-innings match against The Netherlands at Haarlem, Bermuda won the toss and batted first. Wainwright and Sheridan Raynor saw off the Dutch opening attack, but with the score on 24 and a change of bowling, Wainwright was bowled by Burki. Raynor and James added 60 for the second wicket to place the visitors in a strong position, but the Dutch hit back with two quick wickets. Several small partnerships followed, but at 158/6, the two sides seemed evenly matched.

Bailey took on the Dutch bowlers, making 55 in a stand of 74, striking six fours and one six. Vriens bowled him in the end, trying to slog a straight ball, after which Wijkhuizen dismissed the tail. Nevertheless, Bermuda's score of 269 was certainly competitive. It looked even more so when Parfitt dismissed van der Bruggen without a run on the board.

The Dutch batsmen had no idea how to deal with Parfitt's left-arm. Not only did he slant the ball awkwardly across the batsman, he was able to make it swing in and pitch on a full to yorker length. Only Anton Bakker and Schoonheim reached double figures as he took 6-34, all bowled. He was virtually unplayable off the matting pitch and bowled 11 maidens in one ball short of 25 overs. The batsmen were not the only ones to struggle. Wainwright conceded 12 byes which, with the addition of four leg byes, made extras the top scorer.

Not surprisingly, the Dutch were asked to follow on. Although they totalled above 100 they were still unable to cope with Parfitt, who took seven wickets this time to finish with a match analysis of 13-75 off 48.4 overs with 21 maidens.

After struggling to 22 in an opening stand, the home side lost wickets regularly. Only some spirited displays by the lower order brought some respite. Dérogée and Wijkhuizen put on 35 for the eighth wicket. Dérogée's 30 was the highest individual Dutch score of the match; he also hit three fours, one more than any other Dutch player. Overall, this was a humiliating performance, with the Dutch batting arguably at its weakest in their cricket history.

NETHERLANDS v BERMUDA

Rood en Wit, Sportpark Koninklijke HFC, Spanjaardslaan, Heemstede, Haarlem, 7 and 8 June 1969

Bermuda won by an innings and 70 runs

BERMUDA		R	B	M	4s	6s
+D.A.Wainwright	b Burki	6			-	-
*S.S.Raynor	c Schoonheim b Burki	40			4	-
L.G.James	c Schoonheim b Vriens	55			3	1
C.A.Daulphin	b Burki	0			-	-
I.R.D.Scotland	c Schoonheim b Wijkhuizen	21			1	-
E.W.Raynor	c A.Bakker b Burki	16			1	-
L.R.Raynor	c Burki b Wijkhuizen	36			1	-
J.L.O.Bailey	b Vriens	55			6	1
S.Ali	b Wijkhuizen	17			1	-
R.Horton	not out	10			-	1
C.L.Parfitt	b Wijkhuizen	0			-	-
	b4 lb5 nb3 w1	13				
		269				

NETHERLANDS		R	B	M	4s	6s		R	B	M	4s	6s
H.A.Rikse	c James b E.W.Raynor	5			-	-	c Daulphin b Horton	10			1	-
M.W.van der Breggen	b Parfitt	0			-	-	c Bailey b Parfitt	16			2	-
H.van der Heijde	b Parfitt	9			-	-	b Parfitt	4			1	-
A.Bakker	b Parfitt	15			2	-	c Bailey b Parfitt	4			1	-
C.D.van Schouwenburg	b Parfitt	8			1	-	(6) b E.W.Raymor	7			1	-
+R.F.Schoonheim	c Horton b E.W.Raynor	12			1	-	(5) b Parfitt	10			2	-
C.R.P.Bakker	b Parfitt	3			-	-	b Parfitt	0			-	-
R.W.Dérogée	b E.W.Raynor	4			-	-	c James b E.W.Raynor	30			3	-
H.A.G.Wijkhuizen	lbw b E.W.Raynor	0			-	-	b Parfitt	18			1	-
*E.W.C.Vriens	not out	4			-	-	not out	12			2	-
C.Burki	b Parfitt	0			-	-	b Parfitt	8			1	-
	b12 lb4	16					b1 lb1 nb2	4				
		76						**123**				

Netherlands	O	M	R	W	nb	w		fow	Ber (1)	Net (1)	Net (2)
Dérogée	11	2	20	0	-	1		1	24 (1)	0 (2)	22 (1)
Rikse	10	2	22	0	-	-		2	84 (2)	12 (3)	31 (3)
Burki	25	4	74	4	3	-		3	84 (4)	17 (1)	32 (2)
Wijkhuizen	26.3	5	52	4	-	-		4	118 (3)	34 (5)	38 (4)
Vriens	29	7	74	2	-	-		5	140 (5)	45 (4)	48 (5)
A.Bakker	1	0	7	0	-	-		6	158 (6)	53 (7)	48 (7)
C.R.P.Bakker	4	1	7	0	-	-		7	232 (8)	66 (8)	67 (6)
								8	254 (7)	66 (9)	102 (8)
Bermuda	O	M	R	W	nb	w		9	269 (9)	67 (6)	103 (9)
L.R.Raynor	13	0	15	0	-	-		10	269 (11)	76 (11)	123 (11)

Bermuda	O	M	R	W	nb	w	O	M	R	W	nb	w
L.R.Raynor	13	0	15	0	-	-	5	2	4	0	-	-
Parfitt	24.5	11	34	6	-	-	23.5	10	41	7	1	-
Ali	6	4	3	0	-	-	3	1	5	0	-	-
E.W.Raynor	9	6	8	4	-	-	17	4	29	2	-	-
S.S.Raynor							5	0	14	0	-	-
Horton							14	7	26	1	1	-

Umpires: L.van Reeven (Netherlands) and J.B.de Wolf (Netherlands)

Toss: Bermuda

Slaughter at Sion Mills

In early July 1969, as a break from their tour of England, the West Indians visited Northern Ireland for two matches, a two-day game in Belfast preceded by a one-day encounter at Sion Mills, a model village of only 1,600 people, founded in 1835 by the Herdman brothers (James, John and George) to provide a mill-workers' community attached to a linen mill on the banks of the River Mourne, south of Londonderry. The visit was a major attraction for the local population. The mill was closed for the day and the owners provided lunch and tea for the players and officials. The visitors were without their main star, Garfield Sobers, who, like the wicketkeeper Jimmy Hendricks, was injured. Neither travelled to Ireland and Basil Butcher took over the captaincy. The Irish were without their star player, Dermott Monteith.

The day started poorly for the visitors when their flight arrived late in Belfast and, after the long drive to Sion Mills from the airport, they had little time to relax before the start of play. Nevertheless, when their captain won the toss, they chose to bat, expecting to do so until just before tea, when they would declare and bowl the Irish side out cheaply before the close. The pitch was green, typical for north-west Ireland, with plenty of grass, and the atmosphere was damp. With conditions ideal for swing bowling, all the Irish bowlers had to do was to produce a consistent line and length. This they did superbly.

Camacho steered the first ball of Goodwin's first over into the hands of midwicket. Carew attempted a similar shot off O'Riordan in the next over and lobbed the ball to square leg. Butcher drove a ball to the left of mid-off and called for a single, only to see his partner Foster amble past him to be easily beaten by Hughes's throw to the wicketkeeper, leaving the visitors at 3/3. Butcher and Lloyd played carefully, without mastering the conditions, until in O'Riordan's sixth over, Butcher offered a low catch to gully which was well taken by Duffy.

Walcott, the West Indies manager, appeared and demonstrated to his colleagues how to deal with the conditions by playing on the back foot and watching the ball off the pitch. His partners ignored the lesson.

Lloyd was caught at mid-off, miscuing a front-foot drive, and John Shepherd mis-hit a cut shot, giving Duffy another catch at gully, meaning the visitors were in serious trouble at 8/6. Findlay gave support for six overs before being dismissed without scoring. Eventually, even Walcott lost patience, hitting wildly at a ball from O'Riordan and skying it to mid-off. He had scored all six runs made from the bat since he came to the crease. When Roberts fell first ball, the West Indies were an incredible 12/9.

Perhaps Shillingford and Blair were luckier than their colleagues as their big hits went into the gaps between the fielders. Their partnership more than doubled the score before Blair was bowled. In an innings that lasted only 86 minutes, no batsman made double figures and four failed to score. Goodwin had the remarkable analysis of 12.3-8-6-5. He and O'Riordan bowled unchanged.

When Ireland began their reply, Shillingford and Blair bowled fast and short, thereby mitigating the chance of getting the ball to swing. Ireland's openers took advantage and put on 19 in 25 minutes before Waters edged a back-foot shot to the wicketkeeper. Lunch was then taken. After the interval, Pigot and Reith took Ireland past the West Indies' total in the 11th over to give the home side victory by nine wickets.

The two sides agreed to continue play, a decision which undoubtedly pleased the spectators. Ireland were able to declare shortly after tea with a lead of 100. Carew and Butcher ensured that there would be no embarrassing innings defeat.

IRELAND v WEST INDIANS

Holm Field, Sion Mills, 2 July 1969

Ireland won by nine wickets

WEST INDIANS		R	B	M	4s	6s		R	B	M	4s	6s
G.S.Camacho	c Dineen b Goodwin	1					c Dineen b Goodwin	1				
M.C.Carew	c Hughes b O'Riordan	0					c Pigot b Duffy	25				
M.L.C.Foster	run out (Hughes-Colhoun)	2					c Pigot b Goodwin	0				
*B.F.H.Butcher	c Duffy b O'Riordan	2					c Waters b Duffy	50			73	
C.H.Lloyd	c Waters b Goodwin	1					not out	0				
C.L.Walcott	c Anderson b O'Riordan	6					not out	0				
J.N.Shepherd	c Duffy b Goodwin	0										
+T.M.Findlay	c Waters b Goodwin	0										
P.Roberts	c Colhoun b O'Riordan	0										
G.C.Shillingford	not out	9										
P.D.Blair	b Goodwin	3										
	b1	1										
		25					(4 wickets)	**76**				

IRELAND		R	B	M	4s	6s
D.R.Pigot jr	c Camacho b Shillingford	37	120			
R.H.C.Waters	c Findlay b Blair	2				
M.S.Reith	lbw b Shepherd	10				
J.Harrison	lbw b Shepherd	0				
I.J.Anderson	c Shepherd b Roberts	7				
P.J.Dineen	b Shepherd	0				
A.J.O'Riordan	c&b Carew	35	51			
G.A.A.Duffy	not out	15				
L.P.Hughes	c sub (V.A.Holder) b Carew	13	8			
*D.E.Goodwin						
+O.D.Colhoun						
	lb2 nb4	6				
	(8 wickets declared)	**125**				

Ireland	O	M	R	W	nb	w		O	M	R	W	nb	w
O'Riordan	13	8	18	4				6	1	21	0		
Goodwin	12.5	8	6	5				2	1	1	2		
Hughes								7	4	10	0		
Duffy								12	8	12	2		
Anderson								7	1	32	0		

West Indians	O	M	R	W	nb	w
Blair	8	4	14	1		
Shillingford	7	2	19	1		
Shepherd	13	4	20	3		
Roberts	16	3	43	1		
Carew	3.2	0	23	2		

fow	WI (1)	Ir (1)	WI (2)
1	1 (1)	19 (2)	1 (1)
2	1 (2)	30 (3)	1 (3)
3	3 (3)	34 (4)	73 (4)
4	6 (4)	51 (5)	78 (2)
5	6 (5)	55 (6)	
6	8 (7)	69 (1)	
7	12 (8)	103 (7)	
8	12 (6)	125 (8)	
9	12 (9)		
10	25 (11)		

Umpires: A.Titchett (Ireland) and M.Stott (Ireland)

Toss: West Indies

Ireland won the match on the first innings by nine wickets. Play continued in order to entertain the crowd and because there was the possibility of a result over two innings in the one day.

In Ireland's innings V.A.Holder fielded substitute for P.D.Blair who retired with a muscle strain. In West Indians' second innings R.H.C.Waters took over the captaincy when D.E.Goodwin retired with a leg strain.

Saudara inaugurated

Saudara, the Malay word often used to denote 'kinship', was chosen as the title of the trophy, the Saudara Cup, for a new contest between the cricketers of Malaysia and Singapore. As befits the spirit of the word, the competition is for teams of citizens only. The first match took place in September 1970 on the Selangor Club Padang in Kuala Lumpur.

On a cloudy, humid morning, Malaysia won the toss and Delilkan elected to bat. The pitch was expected to favour the spin bowlers as the match progressed and it was thought a good idea to avoid being the side taking the fourth innings. Ranjit Singh and Alwi Zahaman began slowly against the medium pace of Martens and Mehta, but becoming increasingly confident, they put on 50 in 72 minutes. A change to spin with da Silva and Muruthi caused the run rate to slow and gave Singapore more control. Da Silva achieved the breakthrough, bowling Alwi Zahaman. Two runs later, Ranjit sliced a ball from Muruthi to the wicketkeeper. He had batted 105 minutes for his 48, hitting eight fours.

Durairatnam and Zainuddin Meah took the home side through to lunch on 85/2. Heavy rain fell during the interval and the early afternoon and it was not until 4.38pm that a resumption was possible. Da Silva reverted to his medium-pace bowlers. Although Martens accounted for Durairatnam, Zainuddin Meah and Christie found batting relatively easy. Their partnership was worth 71 by the close, with Zainuddin having reached his fifty in only 58 minutes.

After just one over on the second morning, Zainuddin's fine innings came to an end when he sliced a short ball from Mehta on to his pads whence it ricocheted on to the stumps. Christie, with a half-century, Khoo Kim Kuang, Delilkan and Navaratnam all made valuable contributions, enabling Malaysia to declare at the lunch break. After the early loss of Tessensohn, de Silva and Houghton produced an excellent partnership of 64 and seemed completely untroubled, until Houghton misjudged a yorker from Gurucharan Singh and was bowled. Zainon Mat then took three quick wickets as the visitors capitulated to 91/6, including the all-important one of de Silva, three runs short of his fifty. A seventh-wicket stand of 43 between Ishwarlal and Sooceleraj appeared to be the basis of a recovery, but once Ishwarlal was bowled, wickets fell in quick succession to leave Singapore 104 runs behind at the close with only two wickets in hand.

The visitors added only 18 more runs on the last morning, the remaining wickets falling to Gurucharan who finished the innings with an impressive analysis of 4-14 in 21 overs, 13 of which were maidens. Zainon Mat also took four wickets. With a lead of 86, Malaysia set out to score quickly and were not phased by losing wickets regularly. Sooceleraj took six wickets, but was expensive. With nine wickets down, Delilkan declared and set Singapore 229 runs in 180 minutes, a challenging but perfectly feasible target.

Houghton failed to score but Tessensohn and de Silva took the total to 42, albeit somewhat tediously. Christie's seven overs were all maidens and Marimuthu conceded only seven runs in his seven overs. Once de Silva was leg before to Zainon Mat, the home sides's spinners wreaked havoc. Singapore lost their next seven wickets for 47 runs, leaving their side on 89/9. Sooceleraj again came to the rescue and with Mehta managed to defy everything Malaysia's bowlers tried until the close. The first Saudara Cup thus ended excitingly in a draw, even though Malaysia had held the initiative throughout. The home team's spin bowlers were more penetrative than their visitor's counterparts.

PIONEERS

Early cricket in Philadelphia was dominated by the Newhall brothers (left) including, from left to right, George, Charlie, Dan and Bob. (Photo courtesy of the C.C. Morris Cricket Library). Sir Shenton Thomas (bottom left) played for the East African Protectorate, Nigeria and the Gold Coast as he moved from one position to another in the Colonial Service. Brigadier Sir Gordon Guggisberg (bottom middle) played for the Straits Settlements, Gold Coast and Nigeria. Captain Ivo Barrett (bottom right) represented the Straits Settlements and Federated Malay States before moving to Shanghai where he was a regular member of their side in the Interport Series against Hong Kong (Hampshire County Cricket Club).

THREE 'GRACES'

Leslie Melville Balfour-Melville (left) was Scotland's leading cricketer of his generation and was often styled the 'W.G. Grace of Scotland'. Bob Lambert (centre), considered by many as Ireland's greatest all-rounder, was generally known as the 'W.G. Grace of Ireland'; Grace invited him to play for his London County side. Herbert Dorning (right), arguably the best cricketer to come from Argentina, was accorded the moniker of the 'W.G. Grace of Argentina'.

GREATEST ASSOCIATE PLAYER OF ALL TIME

Above: Barton King, a right-arm fast bowler, took 42% of the wickets in the 65 first-class matches he played for Philadelphia between 1893 and 1912, including ten wickets in an innings against Ireland and five or more wickets in an innings 38 times. His total of 415 wickets was obtained at an average of 15.65. He also scored 2,134 runs, average 20.51, including one century. (Photo courtesy of the C.C. Morris Cricket Library).

TWO IRISH ALL-TIME GREATS

Above, left: Jimmy Boucher was one of Ireland's greatest bowlers and, at his peak, was among the top spin bowlers in the world. In 60 matches for his country he took 300 wickets at an average of 15.26, including five or more wickets in an innings 31 times. He headed the English first-class averages in 1931, 1937 and 1948. He never sought to play English county cricket, though some observers rated him as Test-match standard (Cricket Europe)

Above, right: Dermott Monteith, a left-arm spinner, played 76 matches for Ireland, taking 326 wickets at 17.37, including five or more wickets in an innings 27 times. He was also an adventurous and successful captain. His career was cut short by a hit-and-run car accident which left him with a fractured skull and shattered pelvis (Cricket Europe).

DENMARK'S ALL-TIME GREAT

Left: Ole Mortensen, right-arm fast, was a terrifying prospect for most batsmen from Associate countries, unused to a combination of pace and swing. In 33 matches for Denmark, he took 76 wickets at an average of 12.62, including 63 at 10.41 in 26 ICC Trophy matches between 1979 and 1994. He had a successful first-class career with Derbyshire, obtaining 411 wickets at 23.53. In likening him to Bloodaxe, Peter Sellman has captured his ferocity, but retained his characteristic glint in his eyes so indicative of his enjoyment of challenging batsmen with unplayable deliveries (Ole Mortensen).

THE BATTERS

South African-born Ryan ten Doeschate (top left) assisted The Netherlands to great effect until deciding to play county cricket for Essex full-time. He also developed a global career, playing Twenty20 cricket in Australia, New Zealand and Zimbabwe. He is the only Associate player to score two centuries in World Cup matches (Cricket Europe). In contrast David Hemp (top centre) chose to play for Bermuda, the place of his birth, after his first-class career with Warwickshire had ended (Cricket Europe). Pauline te Beest (top right) represented the Netherlands in 70 internationals to become one of the top Dutch women cricketers of all time and the only one to score two centuries (ESPNcricinfo Ltd).

Huang Zhuo (left), a young and improving cricketer from China, is the first woman from that country to make an international hundred (Barry Chambers). Neisha Pratt (right) averaged over 50 in women's internationals for Hong Kong, with a top score of 98 (Asian Cricket Council).

Ed Joyce (right) has scored over 4,000 runs at an average of over 40 for Ireland and is their only player to have scored two double centuries. He has played one-day internationals and Twenty20 for both England and Ireland as well as captaining Sussex during a long career with the county (Barry Chambers).

THE BOWLERS

Hamid Hassan (top left), taker of 281 wickets for Afghanistan at an average of 16.57, was the best of the modern Associate bowlers until he was seriously injured colliding with a boundary board in a match in Sharjah, after which he never recovered his effectiveness (Asian Cricket Council). Mehboob Alam (top right) takes his tenth wicket in an innings for Nepal against Mozambique, the first bowler to do so in one-day internationals and the fourth Associate bowler to do so in all formats (Cricket Europe). Mei Chunhua (left) took 47 wickets in 20 matches for China at an average of 4.83, but retired from cricket in 2011 to become a teacher because there was no career structure for the sport in her country (Asian Cricket Council).

THE ALL-ROUNDERS

Steve Tikolo (left), Kenya's top player of all time and arguably the best of the modern Associate cricketers with over 14,000 runs for his country at an average of 44, including 33 centuries. He also took over 300 wickets in international matches (Cricket Europe). Isobel Joyce (right), the top women's player in Associate cricket with over 2,000 runs, average 20, and over 120 wickets, average 23, for Ireland (Barry Chambers).

Mohammad Nabi (left), taker of over 300 wickets with his off spin and scorer of over 5,000 runs, with three centuries, has been a regular member of Afghanistan's side since their first international matches in 2004 (Asian Cricket Council). Suresh Navaratnam (centre) was Malaysia's leading player of his generation with three centuries and seven times taking five or more wickets in an innings. Sornarin Tippoch (right) has been the inspiration behind Thailand's women's team with over 700 runs, including one century, and 40 wickets in 51 matches (Asian Cricket Council).

THE WICKETKEEPERS

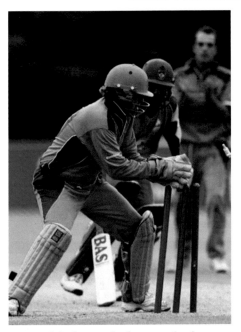 

Many of the best wicketkeepers of today are just one in a long line of excellent keepers who have represented their country. Left: Jeroen Smits of the Netherlands, who was compared favourably with the best in the world during the 2003 World Cup, was the successor to Robbie Colthoff, Reinhout Scholte and René Schoonheim (Cricket Europe). Right: Colin Smith inherited his position as Scotland's keeper from James Brown and Alec Davies (Cricket Scotland).

Left: Gary Wilson, displaying his skills in practice, follows on from Frank Browning and Augustine Kelly and vies with Ossie Calhoun, Paul Jackson and Niall O'Brien as Ireland's top keeper of all time (Barry Chambers). Right: Sultan Ahmed has no predecessors, but has been his country's first-choice keeper in over 100 matches since Oman played their first international in 2004 (Asian Cricket Council).

UNSUNG HEROES

Moosa Kaleem (left), speaking at a welcoming-home ceremony after his country won the Asian Cricket Council Elite Trophy in 2010, in which he scored a double century. The only cricketer from the Maldives to score an international hundred, he made four in his career (Maldives Cricket). Niluka Obris (right), born in Sri Lanka, but resident in Verona and now one of Italy's leading women cricketers, receives her medal after her country won an international tournament in Jersey in 2015. In 15 matches she has already made over 400 runs (Sevil Oktem).

THE SERIES

Left: The series between the United States and Canada began as the first-ever international match in 1844 and has been played intermittently since. Always a multi-innings fixture, the United States have won 32 times, Canada 24 and 12 matches have been drawn. A batsman from the United States faces Canada's close fielders at Toronto, 2011 (Cricket Canada). Right: The Hong Kong–Shanghai Interport series was played between 1866 and 1948. Hong Kong won 20 matches to Shanghai's 16, with only two draws. In 1908 the teams met at Chater Road, Hong Kong.

The inaugural Saudara Cup match in 1970 between Malaysia and Singapore took place on the Padang, Kuala Lumpur (now occupied by Dataran Merdeka or Independence Square). The multi-innings fixture has been played regularly since. At the end of 2015, Malaysia had won 13 matches and Singapore 9, with 22 drawn and one abandoned.

The Inter-Insular series between Jersey and Guernsey began in 1950, since when Jersey have won 29 matches, Guernsey 21 and 14 have been drawn, the latter before the series changed to a limited-overs format in 1978. Guernsey's Jeremy Frith (below) masters the bowling in the 2011 fixture at Castel (Martin Gray).

OUTPOSTS

Cricket has been played on Francis Plain, Jamestown, Saint Helena for over 200 years, but it was not until 2012 that the Islanders competed internationally, when their players made a round trip of 36 days, including ten at sea, to take part in Division 3 of the Africa Twenty20 Championships in South Africa (David George).

The new, specially-developed international cricket ground of Cricket Romania at Moara Vlăsiei, near Bucharest (right), where the facilities include eight turf pitches, the only ones in central and eastern Europe, and one artificial pitch, seen on the right (Cricket Romania).

New Caledonia take the field in the 2011 Pacific Games at their purpose-built facility at Ndu (Pacific Games Council).

Cricket at the Korínn Ground, Reykjavík (left), where Iceland are happy to host visiting teams (CricketIceland).

MALAYSIA v SINGAPORE
Saudara Cup
Selangor Club Padang, Kuala Lumpur, 4, 5 and 6 September 1970
Match drawn

MALAYSIA		R	B	M	4s	6s		R	B	M	4s	6s
Ranjit Singh	c Stevens b Muruthu	48	105	8			b Sooceleraj	26				
Alwi Zahaman	b da Silva	23					b Sooceleraj	29				
H.Durairatnam	lbw b Martens	6					(5) c Ishwarlal b Sooceleraj	20				
Zainuddin Meah	b Mehta	55					c da Silva b Sooceleraj	1				
A.Christie	c da Silva b Muruthi	62					(9) run out	1				
+Khoo Kim Kuang	c Houghton b da Silva	23					run out	10				
*A.E.Delilkan	not out	14					(10) run out	0				
C.Navaratnam	not out	12					(3) c&b Sooceleraj	1				
Gurucharan Singh							(6) not out	44				
S.Marimuthu							(8) b Sooceleraj	3				
Zainon Mat												
Extras		13						7				
(6 wickets declared)		**256**					(9 wickets declared)	**142**				

SINGAPORE		R	B	M	4s	6s		R	B	M	4s	6s
S.N.Houghton	b Gurucharan Singh	29					b Marimuthu	0				
R.Tessensohn	b Marimuthu	0					c K K Kuang b Zainon Mat	30				
A.de Silva	lbw b Zainon Mat	47					lbw b Zainon Mat	23				
J.Martens	b Zainon Mat	3					(5) c Christie b G'ran Singh	8				
*R.A.da Silva	lbw b Zainon Mat	0					(6) b Zainon Mat	0				
P.Ishwarlal	b Christie	29					(4) c M'muthu b G'ran Singh	6				
K.Elloy	lbw b Gurucharan Singh	0					lbw b Gurucharan Singh	3				
S.Sooceleraj	not out	33					not out	14				
+R.Stevens	c K K Kuang b Zainon Mat	7					b Gurucharan Singh	0				
S.Muruthi	c Marimuthu b G'ran Singh	8					lbw b Delilkan	5				
M.K.Mehta	c Z'din Meah b G'ran Singh	0					not out	2				
Extras		14						10				
		170					(9 wickets)	**101**				

Singapore	O	M	R	W	nb	w	O	M	R	W	nb	w
Martens	27	13	53	1			11	2	38	0		
Mehta	12	5	26	1			5	0	14	0		
Elloy	12	5	39	0								
da Silva	29	9	49	2			6	0	25	0		
Muruthi	26	10	41	2								
Sooceleraj	14	3	35	0		(3)	12	0	58	6		

Malaysia	O	M	R	W	nb	w	O	M	R	W	nb	w
Marimuthu	17	10	21	1		(2)	7	4	7	1		
Christie	10	7	10	1		(1)	7	7	0	0		
Ranjit Singh	4	1	8	0			3	1	10	0		
Delilkan	24	8	46	0		(5)	11	4	11	1		
Zainon Mat	29	8	52	4		(4)	24	11	32	3		
Gurucharan Singh	21	13	14	4			21	8	33	4		
Navaratnam	3	2	4	0								
Durairatnam	1	0	1	0								

fow	Ma (1)	Si (1)	Ma (2)	Si (2)
1	75 (2)	1 (2)	55	5 (1)
2	77 (1)	65 (1)	59	42 (3)
3	93 (3)	85 (4)	62	49
4	171 (4)	85 (5)	69	61
5	228 (5)	88 (3)	106	61
6	239 (6)	91 (7)	126	70
7		134 (6)	137	72
8		148 (9)	139	73
9		170 (10)	142	89
10		170 (11)		

Umpires: [unknown]

Toss: Malaysia

The breakdown of extras is not known.

Close of play: 1st day – Malaysia (1) 164-3 (Zainuddin Meah 51*, Christie 24*); 2nd day – Singapore (1) 152-8 (Sooceleraj 23*, Muruthi 0*).

Success at last

By the time Denmark and The Netherlands met in 1972, seven matches of the 'Continental Tests' had taken place. The first two had ended in draws but the remainder had resulted in wins for The Netherlands, even though, save the one in 1969, which the Dutch won by an innings, they were closely contested. Thus, there was no reason to expect anything other than a very competitive fixture when the two countries met at Bagsvaerd, the ground of the Akademisk Boldklub, 12km north of Copenhagen. The Danes had the advantage of home conditions and their team contained at least three strong players, opening batsman Hardy Sørensen, and the all-rounders, Carsten Morild and Henrik Mortensen. The Dutch were a side in transition, with a few highly experienced players, like Ernst Vriens and Rudi Schoonheim, towards the end of their careers, and some promising youngsters, like Steve Lubbers and Rob van Weelde, making their debuts.

Rijkens won the toss and chose to bat, but must have regretted it as all the batsmen struggled against the Danish attack of Mortensen, Isaksson and Morild. The early batsmen tried to play their strokes when the conditions merited a stronger, defensive approach. Isaksson dismissed both openers and Schoonheim soon followed, caught behind off Mortensen. The visitors lost four wickets for only 53 and their last six wickets went down for only 25 more runs. None had an answer to the bowling of Mortensen and Morild who made the ball behave awkwardly off the matting pitch. Overall, it was a spiritless effort. The Danes fielded well and Fausbøll held three good catches behind the stumps without conceding a bye.

The Dutch reply began well with van Weelde also extracting life from the mat to remove Luther and Nistrup. Sørensen, however, was untroubled and with careful defence and dispatch of the loose balls to the boundary, he provided an example to his colleagues. The Danish middle order played well with Buus, Morild and Mortensen providing good support. Mortensen reached his half-century before becoming too confident, advancing down the wicket to Oostra, only to miss the ball. The resultant stumping ended a fifth-wicket partnership of 86. Surprisingly, for all his experience, Vriens found the mat unresponsive; perhaps his bowling was just a shade too slow.

Isaksson helped take the total to 226 before falling victim to van Weelde, who then quickly removed the tail, leaving Sørensen to carry his bat for a well-made 92, the highest individual score made by a Dane in international cricket at that point. Van Weelde bowled well for his five wickets, but with his colleagues unable to find much help from the conditions, could not prevent the Danes from obtaining a first-innings lead of 173.

The Dutch quickly lost van Laer and van Schouwenburg to Mortensen in the second innings before Trijzelaar and Schoonheim at last mastered the conditions in a partnership of 74. Once Trijzelaar was bowled, four runs short of his half-century, the innings fell apart. Schoonheim went on to reach his fifty, but the middle order gave him little support and when he was out with the score on 128, an innings defeat looked a possibility. Oostra and van Osch, with some lusty hitting, ensured that Denmark had to bat again. The Dutch had managed to bat for 108 overs, well over twice as long as in their first innings and 18 overs more than Denmark had achieved. Mortensen took seven wickets in the innings to give him a match analysis of 10-115. Morild's match return was 7-59.

With the target a mere eight runs, Sørensen and Luther took only 11 balls and two boundaries to secure Denmark's first series victory. The win marked the start of a period in the 1970s when Danish cricket was, arguably, at its peak, culminating in 1979 when they reached the semi-finals of the ICC Trophy.

DENMARK v NETHERLANDS

Akademisk Boldklub Ground, Bagsvaerd, Copenhagen, 21, 22 and 23 July 1972

Denmark won by ten wickets

NETHERLANDS

		R	B	M	4s	6s		R	B	M	4s	6s
C.D.van Schouwenburg	c Olesen b Isaksson	9		2	-		(3) b Mortensen	4			-	-
G.W.A.van Laer	b Isaksson	11		2	-		c Fausbøll b Mortensen	7			1	-
P.J.Trijzelaar	lbw b Morild	21		1	-		(1) b Mortensen	46			4	-
+R.F.Schoonheim	c Fausbøll b Mortensen	0		-	-		c Kristensen b Morild	53			4	1
S.W.Lubbers	c Mortensen b Morild	13		1	-		b Mortensen	6			-	-
*H.A.Rijkens	c Buus b Larsen	2		-	-		c Fausbøll b Mortensen	1			-	-
D.E.Oostra	lbw b Morild	0		-	-		c Nistrup b Morild	17			2	-
E.J.Abendanon	c Fausbøll b Mortensen	10		1	-		(9) ht wkt b Mortensen	12			-	-
R.A.H.van Weelde	not out	4		-	-		(8) c Nistrup b Mortensen	1			-	-
K.van Osch	c Fausbøll b Mortensen	4		-	-		not out	21			2	-
E.W.C.Vriens	b Morild	4		1	-		c Mortensen b Morild	1			-	-
							b5 lb6	11				
		78						**180**				

DENMARK

		R	B	M	4s	6s		R	B	M	4s	6s
H.Sørensen	not out	92		8	-		not out	4			1	-
J.Luther	b van Weelde	0		-	-		not out	4			1	-
F.Nistrup	b van Weelde	16		2	-							
K.Buus	c van Osch b Oostra	26		2	-							
*C.Morild	c van Laer b Vriens	18		2	1							
H.Mortensen	st Schoonheim b Oostra	50		4	1							
E.Olesen	b Oostra	1		-	-							
O.Isaksson	c Oostra b van Weelde	27		1	-							
J.S.Larsen	c Abendanon b van Weelde	0		-	-							
K.Kristensen	c Vriens b van Osch	5		-	-							
+H.Fausbøll	c Abendanon b van Weelde	7		1	-							
	b1 lb5 nb3	9										
		251					(no wicket)	**8**				

DENMARK	O	M	R	W	nb	w		O	M	R	W	nb	w	fow	Ne (1)	De (1)	Ne (2)	De (2)
Mortensen	12	3	25	3	-	-		43	13	90	7	-	-	1	15 (1)	2 (2)	4 (2)	
Isaksson	9	4	24	2	-	-		6	3	3	0	-	-	2	20 (2)	29 (3)	19 (3)	
Morild	11.3	3	25	4	-	-		32	18	34	3	-	-	3	25 (4)	75 (4)	93 (1)	
Larsen	6	3	4	1	-	- (5)		17	8	27	0	-	-	4	53 (5)	95 (5)	117 (5)	
Kristensen					(4)			10	2	15	0			5	56 (3)	181 (6)	123 (6)	
														6	60 (7)	183 (7)	128 (4)	
NETHERLANDS	O	M	R	W	nb	w		O	M	R	W	nb	w	7	60 (6)	226 (8)	141 (8)	
van Weelde	16.5	6	33	5	2	-		1	0	4	0	-	-	8	67 (8)	226 (9)	143 (7)	
Abendanon	9	2	25	0	-	-		0.5	0	4	0	-	-	9	73 (10)	235 (10)	179 (9)	
van Osch	15	3	41	1	-	-								10	78 (11)	251 (11)	180 (11)	
Vriens	29	7	76	1	-	-												
Oostra	14	1	45	3	-	-												
Lubbers	7	2	22	0	1	-												

Umpires: P.Hald (Denmark) and Z.Møller (Denmark)

Toss: Netherlands

Magnificent Monteith

Even if this was a high point of Denmark's cricket history, the Danes were still no match for the Irish, particularly on grass wickets away from home. The match in June 1973, played at Castle Avenue, Dublin, was typical. Scheduled for three days, it was completed in two. The Irish were at full strength, but the Danes had three debutants, Per Sørensen, Lars Hansen and Jørgen Holmen. They also had a new captain, Finn Nistrup taking over from Carsten Morild. The weather was cloudy and cold, a continuation of a poor summer which affected the ability of the groundsman to prepare the pitch. As a result conditions were unpredictable, with uncertain bounce. The chill factor was off-putting to spectators and hardly anybody came to watch.

O'Riordan won the toss for Ireland and elected to bat, a decision which seemed less than wise when their fourth wicket fell with only 37 runs scored. The Danes bowled and fielded excellently. Søegaard was warned by umpire Rodney Smith for running on the pitch during his follow through. This caused him to change to bowling round the wicket and, as a left-armer, enabled him to move the ball away from the batsmen off the seam. Harrison and O'Riordan survived until lunch, taking the score from 37 to 85, but not without some alarms. There were many edges which did not carry and a chance offered by Harrison to the wicketkeeper, who dropped it. In fact, Holmen found the unpredictable bounce very trying and conceded 13 byes during the innings in what turned out to be his only match for Denmark. Not surprisingly, Søegaard began to tire, having bowled a spell of 16 overs, for a return of 3-33.

The Danes were unable to maintain their momentum in the afternoon. Their main bowlers had to be rested and Buus and Hansen, their replacements, were unable to contain the Irish batsmen. O'Riordan and Harrison both reached half-centuries as 64 runs were added in the first hour. O'Riordan went on to score his second century for Ireland, reached in 145 minutes off 150 balls with 15 fours. With the score on 212, Harrison gave a tame return catch which was gratefully taken by Morild to end the fifth-wicket partnership of 175 runs in 155 minutes. Monteith and O'Riordan were undefeated at tea, after an afternoon session which yielded 147 runs in 125 minutes for the loss of only one wicket.

Ireland struggled in the evening session as Morild took the new ball. O'Riordan ended the agony by declaring to give Denmark 45 minutes' batting before the close. The period was a disaster for the visitors who ended the day on 19/3. Hardy Sørenson and Isaksson played well for the first 50 minutes the following morning but once Sørensen was dismissed, the Danes struggled as Elder got the ball to rise unpleasantly off the pitch and O'Riordan maintained a tight line and length. The Irish captain set four slips, three short legs and a point; mid-off was the fielder furthest from the batsman. In an inspired piece of captaincy, O'Riordan replaced himself with Monteith, introducing spin for the first time. He took three wickets for only four runs either side of lunch and Denmark were forced to follow on, 191 runs behind.

Denmark's second innings was a disaster and in one hour and 55 minutes they were dismissed for 61. O'Riordan was unable to bowl because of a strained knee but after Elder and Goodwin had removed Hardy Sørensen and Nistrup respectively, Monteith was brought into the attack. Jannings defended stoutly for 71 minutes for his eight runs but failed to score off the last 30 balls he received. Monteith took the last five wickets in 42 balls, conceding only 11 runs, to finish with a return of 6-13 off 13 overs. Six of these runs came from one hit by Hansen. Given how much the conditions favoured the pace bowlers, it was surprising that the main cause of Denmark's defeat was their inability to deal with some excellent spin bowling.

IRELAND v DENMARK

Clontarf Cricket Club, Castle Avenue, Dublin, 23, 24 and 25 July 1973

Ireland won by an innings and 130 runs

IRELAND		R	B	M	4s	6s
D.R.Pigot jr	c Hansen b Isaksson	3				
B.A.O'Brien	c Nistrup b Søegaard	15				
J.Harrison	c&b Morild	64		209		
I.J.Anderson	c Nistrup b Søegaard	0				
C.C.J.Harte	c H.Sørensen b Søegaard	7				
*A.J.O'Riordan	c Kristensen b Isaksson	119	198	206	17	
J.D.Monteith	b Morild	16				
D.E.Goodwin	c H.Sørensen b Morild	36		55		
G.A.A.Duffy	c Kristensen b Morild	6				
J.W.G.Elder	not out	1				
+O.D.Colhoun						
	b13 lb5	18				
	(9 wickets declared)	**285**				

DENMARK		R	B	M	4s	6s		R	B	M	4s	6s
H.Sørensen	c O'Riordan b Elder	21					c Colhoun b Elder	5				
K.Jannings	c Colhoun b Goodwin	1					b Duffy	8		71		
*F.Nistrup	lbw b Elder	4					c Anderson b Goodwin	8				
K.Buus	b Elder	0					(5) c Pigot b Duffy	6				
O.Isaksson	c Duffy b Goodwin	33					(4) c Duffy b Monteith	6				
C.Morild	c Colhoun b Elder	8					c Harrison b Monteith	9				
P.Sørensen	b Elder	6					(8) b Monteith	5				
L.Hansen	b Monteith	18					(7) b Monteith	13				
+J.Holmen	c O'Brien b Monteith	0					not out	0				
K.Kristensen	not out	0					b Monteith	0				
F.Søegaard	c Colhoun b Monteith	0					c O'Riordan b Monteith	0				
	b2 lb1	3					nb1	1				
		94						**61**				

Denmark	O	M	R	W	nb	w		fow	Ir (1)	De (1)	De (2)
Søegaard	21	7	63	3				1	9 (1)	6 (2)	5 (1)
Isaksson	16	4	41	2				2	29 (2)	19 (3)	14 (3)
Morild	23.1	7	63	4				3	29 (4)	19 (4)	28 (4)
Kristensen	13	2	45	0				4	37 (5)	45 (1)	33 (2)
Buus	9	2	26	0				5	212 (3)	53 (6)	38 (5)
Hansen	6	1	29	0				6	234 (7)	61 (7)	44 (6)
								7	260 (6)	86 (8)	60 (7)

Ireland	O	M	R	W	nb	w		O	M	R	W	nb	w		8	281 (9)	92 (5)	61 (8)
O'Riordan	12	3	34	0											9	285 (8)	92 (9)	61 (10)
Goodwin	29	13	20	2		(1)		10	6	12	1				10		94 (11)	61 (11)
Elder	14	6	33	5		(2)		5	0	19	1							
Monteith	3.3	2	4	3		(3)		13	8	13	6							
Duffy								9	4	16	2							

Umpires: G.T.Doyle (Ireland) and R.Smith (Ireland)

Toss: Ireland

Close of play: 1st day – Denmark (1) 19-3 (H.Sørensen 14*, Isaksson 0*). Match ended in two days.

Battle of the injured

May and June 1979 saw the first global competition between Associate and Affiliate countries. Fifteen teams took part in the ICC Trophy, which was also used as a qualifying competition to determine which two Associates would join the six Full Member countries in the 1979 World Cup. Unfortunately, the tournament, staged at various club grounds in England, was badly affected by the weather. May was the coldest and wettest in England since 1722. Six of the matches were abandoned, four without a ball being bowled.

In the semi-final between Bermuda and Canada, both sides were suffering from injuries. Canada were missing their captain, Garnet Brisbane, leaving Bryan Mauricette to take over the leadership duties. Bermuda's leading bowler, Clarence Parfitt, was also unfit, but the selectors decided to risk playing him. Canada were the more experienced. Three of their team had previously played first-class cricket: Bryan Mauricette for the Windward Islands, Glenroy Sealy for Barbados and Tariq Javed for Karachi. Bermuda had only two such players: Lionel Thomas of the Windward Islands and Colin Blades of Barbados.

The semi-final was played at the Allied Breweries (now Ind Coope) ground at Burton-on-Trent. Bermuda won the toss and chose to bat. Brown and Reid put on 40 runs for the first wicket, but progress was slow for a one-day game. Valentine bowled his left-arm medium pacers very tidily and was difficult to force away. His 12 overs cost only 13 runs but his sole success was to bowl Reid. Patel, with his slow left-arm, also proved hard to score from. Bermuda's top order succumbed to the pressure and went from 40 without loss to 84/4 and 103/5. Two of the wickets were run-outs, the result of simple misjudgements that should have been avoided.

Tucker came to the rescue with a well-constructed 49. He had support from Bailey and James which, although not sufficient to ensure that Bermuda batted for all of their 60 overs, took them to a defendable score of 181, the seventh highest in the competition to date. Perhaps ominously, two of those higher scores had been made by Canada.

When Canada's top order failed with four wickets falling for 36 runs, victory for Bermuda looked likely. The bowlers, however, were unable to maintain their momentum. Parfitt was only able to bowl six overs instead of 12, and Bermuda struggled to find an effective sixth bowler. Also, their attack contained three left-arm and two right-arm bowlers, all of medium to medium-fast pace. There was no spin bowler to add variety.

With Gibbons going for 40 runs off nearly five overs, Canada were able to do more than recover. Mauricette and Javed showed their experience, gradually mastering the bowling and, towards the end of their partnership, virtually scoring at will. They added 111 runs for the sixth wicket before Reid took a brilliant left-handed catch to end Mauricette's innings for 72 runs, which included nine fours.

With only nine more runs needed, Sealy and Javed took Canada to a surprisingly easy victory with 13 balls to spare that qualified them for the 1979 World Cup where they were joined by Sri Lanka, who outplayed Denmark by 208 runs in the other semi-final. Canada and Sri Lanka met in the final of the ICC Trophy at New Road, Worcester, on 21 June when Sri Lanka won by 60 runs in a high-scoring game (324/8 against 264/5).

The tournament showed that one-day matches were the way forward for international cricket for the Associate and Affiliate countries. Instead of one three-day fixture, three separate matches can be played. If these are against three different teams, a tournament of several countries becomes a possibility. Henceforward, one-day cricket would dominate the calendar over multi-innings encounters.

BERMUDA v CANADA

60 overs

ICC Trophy – Semi-final

Allied Breweries Ground, Burton-on-Trent, 6 June 1979

Canada won by four wickets

BERMUDA		R	B	M	4s	6s
*G.A.Brown	run out	34				
W.A.Reid	b Valentine	23				
L.E.Thomas	run out	8				
C.F.Blades	c&b Patel	12				
N.A.Gibbons	c Henry b Sealy	9				
J.A.Tucker	b Vaughan	49				
J.L.O.Bailey	c Valentine b Marshall	17				
+E.B.DeCouto	c Patel b Henry	4				
W.H.Trott	lbw b Vaughan	1				
E.G.James	b Henry	12				
C.L.Parfitt	not out	0				
	lb5 nb3 w4	12				
	(58.1 overs)	**181**				

CANADA		R	B	M	4s	6s
M.P.Stead	b James	4				
C.J.D.Chappell	b Trott	7				
F.A.Dennis	c Trott b Blades	9				
J.C.B.Vaughan	c DeCouto b Parfitt	15				
C.A.Marshall	b Blades	18				
*+B.M.Mauricette	c Reid b Trott	72		9		
T.Javed	not out	47				
G.R.Sealy	not out	5				
J.M.Patel						
C.C.Henry						
J.N.Valentine						
	lb3 nb5 w1	9				
	(6 wickets, 57.5 overs)	**186**				

Canada	O	M	R	W	nb	w		fow	Ber	Can
Valentine	12	4	13	1				1	40	8
Henry	5.1	0	17	2				2	62	14
Vaughan	10	1	35	2				3	74	32
Sealy	12	0	46	1				4	84	36
Marshall	7	1	24	1				5	103	62
Patel	12	3	34	1				6	142	173
								7	164	
Bermuda	O	M	R	W	nb	w		8	168	
James	12	3	29	1				9	175	
Trott	11	2	27	2				10	181	
Parfitt	6	1	24	1						
Blades	12	5	14	2						
Thomas	12	1	43	0						
Gibbons	4.5	0	40	0						

Umpires: P.G.Berry and G.A.Wenman

Toss: Bermuda

Player of the Match: B.M.Mauricette (Canada)

7

Globalisation 1980–1999

THE PERIOD from 1980 to 1999 saw cricket being established and organised in such a large number of countries that it can be truly considered a time of globalisation. In 1979, in addition to the Full Member countries, there were 17 Associate Members of the ICC. By 1999, there were 26 Associate countries and a new category of membership had been created, the Affiliates. Since there were 20 of these, this meant that, in the ICC's eyes, cricket had expanded from 17 to 46 countries outside of the Test-match structure. In reality, cricket was more widespread than that because it was played regularly in many countries which had not yet applied to join the ICC, like Brazil, Chile and New Caledonia.

Compared to 1979, when 15 countries took part in the ICC Trophy, there were 16 in 1982 and 1986, 17 in 1990, 20 in 1994 and 22 in 1997. In addition, a number of regional tournaments were initiated. Cricket was included in the South Pacific Games (now the Pacific Games) held in Fiji in 1979 and again in 1987 and 1991. It was only present, however, when the Games were hosted by a cricket-playing country. Hence, it did not appear again until 2003.

The Asian Cricket Council Trophy was first contested in 1984, with only three countries. Further tournaments were held in 1988, 1992, 1996 and 1998, by which time ten countries were taking part and the competition had become established as a contest staged every two years. In 1991, Hong Kong, Malaysia and Singapore competed for the Tuanku Ja'afar Cup, set up to provide one-day international experience prior to the 1992 ICC Trophy. Thailand joined the competition in 1992 and it was held annually until 2004. By this date, the international calendar was so crowded that it was impossible to fit the tournament in. The South American Championships were first played in 1995, since when they have been held, with some exceptions, every other year.

The European Championships were first staged in 1996, with Ireland, The Netherlands, Scotland, Denmark, Israel, Gibraltar and an English amateur side, drawn mainly from the Minor Counties, as competitors. The growth of cricket in Europe was so rapid at this time, however, that a Second Division of the tournament was established in 1998 and a Third Division in 1999. Europe also started a Women's Championship in 1989 with England, Ireland, The Netherlands and Denmark fielding teams. This and the various divisions of the men's competition are now well established events, taking place every two years.

In 1995, Malaysia and Singapore began the Stan Nagaiah Cup as an annual contest comprising three one-day internationals. This competition continues to this day, but other ventures have been less fortunate. The Triple Crown, inaugurated in 1993 as an annual event involving Ireland, Scotland, Wales and an English Minor Counties side, lasted only until 2001. Bermuda, the United States and Canada contested the Atlantic Cup in 1985 but the tournament was never repeated. An attempt was made to restart in 1996 with a four-country contest, additionally involving Barbados, but again it had only one year of life.

Despite the proliferation of one-day internationals, some multi-innings competitions did continue, notably the Saudara Cup between Malaysia and Singapore, the K.A. Auty Trophy between Canada and the USA and the series between Ireland and Scotland.

The first women's matches between Associate countries took place in 1983. Prior to that the only Associate country to have played women's internationals on a regular basis was The Netherlands, with matches against Australia in 1937, the English Women's Cricket Association in 1952, 1959 and 1967, and South Africa in 1968 and 1969. Ireland was scheduled to play New Zealand at Belfast in 1966, but torrential rain caused the match to be abandoned without a ball being bowled. The 1983 tournament, held in Utrecht to mark the centenary of the Nederlandsche Cricket Bond, involved The Netherlands, Denmark and Ireland.

Further tournaments followed. A quadrangular with these three sides and an England A team was held in Ireland in 1986. In July 1987, The Netherlands met Ireland in what has become the only three-day women's international match ever held between Associates. Ireland's women had previously played a three-day match against Trinidad and Tobago in 1985. The only other three-day women's matches involving Associates are the two Test matches: Ireland against Pakistan in 2000 and The Netherlands against South Africa in 2007.

The 1990s saw the extension of men's international cricket in Europe beyond the well-established countries of Ireland, Scotland, The Netherlands and Denmark. The European Cricket Federation was founded in 1989 to promote continental cricket but, initially, progress was slow because all the members of the ECF thought that organising tournaments would be too difficult and too costly. In the meantime, Ben Brocklehurst and his colleagues at *The Cricketer* showed what could be achieved. They managed to sign up 20 sponsors to support an international tournament for The Cricketer Cup, involving ten countries, held in June 1990 in Guernsey.

Two years later, Worksop College hosted the second tournament, again involving ten countries. These events spurred the ECF into action and they organised their first competition for the ECF Nations Cup in Germany in 1993. Unlike The Cricketer Cup, where there were no restrictions on who could represent a particular country, the ECF stipulated that each team must contain at least seven passport-holders and these must include at least three nationals by birthright; in addition, there could be no more than four players qualified by residence only and each of these must have been resident for a minimum of four years.

In order to reduce costs, the ECF chose venues where the players and officials could be accommodated in one place relatively cheaply, as well as being able to provide suitable grounds. The first tournament was staged in Berlin, courtesy of the British Army. In 1995, the hosts were Radley College, Oxford. The Osnabrück Garrison staged the 1996 tournament and, in 1997, the setting was the Lyceum Alpinum, in the small village of Zuoz, in the Engadine, Switzerland. France won the competition in 1993 and 1996, while Germany were the winners in 1995. Thus, when Germany and France qualified for the final in 1997, the rivalry was considerable and, for a small number of enthusiastic cricketers, matched that of the two countries meeting each other at football. The competition was eventually merged into the ICC structure of European cricket, involving several divisions with promotion and relegation.

By the end of the 1990s, virtually every country in Europe had an international cricket team. With migrants from India, Pakistan, Sri Lanka and Bangladesh there were now large numbers of people familiar with cricket from their homelands and wanting to continue to play. Once they had been resident long enough to satisfy ICC requirements, these people made up a high proportion, if not the whole, of the international teams. Their children and grandchildren are now eligible to represent their countries by right of birth and citizenship.

The diaspora of the Indian subcontinent is not confined to Europe, however. It underpins cricket in a large number of countries in North, Central and South America, to a lesser extent in Africa and, crucially, in most countries of the Middle East. In the USA and Canada, it has combined with an earlier influx of migrants from the Caribbean. In east Africa it is less important because there was already a strong Asian influence from the descendants of migrants from India in the early 1900s.

The most controversial contribution to cricket by migrants from the Indian sub-continent was in the United Arab Emirates. The Emirates Cricket Board was not established until 1989 and, following admission to the ICC the following year, the immediate objective was to select a team for the 1994 ICC Trophy in Kenya. Not surprisingly, the board took advantage of those expatriates in the country who met the ICC's residential requirements. Their squad comprised nine Pakistanis, five Indians and one Sri Lankan, with the sole Emirati chosen as captain. On paper this approach looked reasonable until it became apparent that nine of the squad had previous first-class experience in the country of their birth.

Three players were possibly destined for higher honours since Mazhar Hussain had represented Pakistan B, Johan Samarasekara had appeared for Sri Lanka B and Riaz Poonawala for India under-25s. The result could easily have been interpreted, and was by some, as the Emirates Board having deliberately targeted high-calibre cricketers in the Indian subcontinent to come and settle in the Emirates, with the sole objective of assembling a team for the tournament. After the event, the ICC changed the regulations for citizenship and residence to prevent a similar occurrence.

The period of globalisation was one of hope for Associate and Affiliate cricket. Not only were more countries becoming members of the ICC, there were also more opportunities for the best Associate countries to play Full Members. Following Zimbabwe's election to Full Membership in 1992, the number of Associates allowed to qualify for the World Cup was increased from one to three for 1996. Kenya, The Netherlands and the United Arab Emirates took part. In 1999, the Associates were represented by Kenya, Bangladesh and Scotland, after which Bangladesh and Kenya were granted official one-day international status. Bangladesh became a Full Member in 2000 and the expectations were that Kenya would soon follow. Their application in 2001 was, however, rejected, the first indicator of a change in the ICC's policy.

Fearless Fletcher

Zimbabwe became an Associate Member of the ICC in 1981. They qualified for the 1983 ICC World Cup by winning the ICC Trophy in 1982. They were clearly the best of the Associate countries and were about the standard of a first-class English county side. Against Full Member countries they were not expected to do anything other than perform gallantly. Their first match in the competition was against Australia, at Trent Bridge, Nottingham. Under cool, initially sunny but later cloudy conditions, a typically British June day, Australia won the toss and decided to field. They had a four-pronged pace attack of Lawson, Hogg, Lillee and Thomson and were expected to demolish Zimbabwe very quickly. All Omarshah and Paterson could do was to survive, but this they did.

They had one life when Wessels dropped Omarshah off the bowling of Hogg. This proved to be a precursor of what was to come. The opening partnership tediously reached 55, after which Lillee removed both openers. Worryingly for Australia, they had conceded 12 extras thus far, before Heron and Pycroft put on 31. Yallop proved his worth as Australia's fifth bowler by dismissing Heron and Houghton in successive balls, both caught by the wicketkeeper. With half the side out for 94 off 33 overs at lunch, the match seemed to be going to plan.

After the interval, Fletcher adopted a more attacking approach. Assisted by Curran and Butchart in partnerships of 70 and 75 and aided by some appalling fielding by the Australians, who fluffed five chances, he took Zimbabwe to a respectable total of 239/6. Extras had increased to 31.

By today's standards, Zimbabwe's total was low considering it was made off 60 overs instead of 50. The strike rate was only 66 runs per 100 balls, but these were early days for the one-day format. Players were less adventurous as they adjusted their techniques from multi-innings matches. This was very apparent as Wood and Wessels opened Australia's innings. They put on 61 before Fletcher introduced himself into the attack and soon induced Wood to edge a catch to the wicketkeeper. Wood's 31 had taken 60 balls. Fletcher removed Hughes and then proceeded to destroy Australia's middle order. In contrast to the Australians, Zimbabwe's fielding was first rate and they held some remarkable catches, including those of Traicos at cover, to dismiss Hookes, and Pycroft on the boundary, to remove Yallop.

By this time, Australia were well behind the required run rate and when Heron's direct throw at the stumps led to Wessels's departure, Zimbabwe were clearly on top. With the loss of two more wickets, Australia required 64 runs, but had only three wickets left.

Marsh and Hogg made a valiant effort. With 30 balls remaining, 53 runs were needed, a not impossible target today, but in 1983, it was too many. By the time they ran out of overs Australia were still 14 runs short and Zimbabwe had won their first official international match at the first attempt. Duncan Fletcher was named man of the match for his all-round performance but there were many others whose contributions were vital, particularly Curran and Butchart with the bat, and Vince Hogg and Traicos with their highly economical bowling. It was, however, the fielding that made the greatest difference between the two sides.

After this performance, no Full Member country treated Zimbabwe lightly. As a result they lost all their remaining matches in this tournament, all their matches in the 1987 competition and their first seven in 1992, before beating England by nine runs. Even so, throughout this period, Zimbabwe clearly remained the top country of the Associates and they were promoted to Full Membership of the ICC in 1992. With ICC's policy at the time in favour of supporting cricket worldwide, the path to Full Membership seemed very straightforward in the 1990s.

AUSTRALIA v ZIMBABWE

One-Day International – List A – 60 overs

Prudential World Cup First Round – Group B

Trent Bridge, Nottingham, 9 June 1983

Zimbabwe won by 13 runs

ZIMBABWE		R	B	M	4s	6s
A.H.Omarshah	c Marsh b Lillee	16	57	80	-	-
G.A.Paterson	c Hookes b Lillee	27	59	78	2	-
J.G.Heron	c Marsh b Yallop	14	40	38	1	-
A.J.Pycroft	b Border	21	41	53	1	-
+D.L.Houghton	c Marsh b Yallop	0	1	1	-	-
*D.A.G.Fletcher	not out	69	84	139	5	-
K.M.Curran	c Hookes b Hogg	27	46	59	2	-
I.P.Butchart	not out	34	38	55	2	-
P.W.E.Rawson						
A.J.Traicos						
V.R.Hogg						
	lb18 nb6 w7	31				
	(6 wickets, 60 overs)	**239**				

AUSTRALIA		R	B	M	4s	6s
G.M.Wood	c Houghton b Fletcher	31	60	69	3	-
K.C.Wessels	run out (Heron)	76	130	147	5	-
*K.J.Hughes	c Omarshah b Fletcher	0	4	7	-	-
D.W.Hookes	c Traicos b Fletcher	20	48	45	1	-
G.N.Yallop	c Pycroft b Fletcher	2	17	15	-	-
A.R.Border	c Pycroft b Curran	17	33	34	-	-
+R.W.Marsh	not out	50	42	63	3	2
G.F.Lawson	b Butchart	0	4	4	-	-
R.M.Hogg	not out	19	22	29	1	-
D.K.Lillee						
J.R.Thomson						
	b2 lb7 w2	11				
	(7 wickets, 60 overs)	**226**				

Zimbabwe	O	M	R	W	nb	wd
Lawson	11	2	33	0		
Hogg	12	3	43	1		
Lillee	12	1	47	2		
Thomson	11	1	46	0		
Yallop	9	0	28	2		
Border	5	0	11	1		

Australia	O	M	R	W	nb	wd
Hogg	6	2	15	0		
Rawson	12	1	54	0		
Butchart	10	0	39	1		
Fletcher	11	1	42	4		
Traicos	12	2	27	0		
Curran	9	0	38	1		

fow	Zim	Aus
1	55 (2)	61 (1)
2	55 (1)	63 (3)
3	86 (3)	114 (4)
4	86 (5)	133 (5)
5	94 (4)	138 (2)
6	164 (7)	168 (6)
7		176 (8)
8		
9		
10		

Umpires: D.J.Constant (England) and M.J.Kitchen (England)

Toss: Australia

Player of the Match: D.A.G.Fletcher (Zimbabwe)

In Australia's innings G.E.Peckover fielded as substitute for V.R.Hogg who retired after pulling a back muscle.

Super Saker

The 1983 Saudara Cup match was originally scheduled for 23, 24 and 25 September but on 16 September, the Malaysian Cricket Association announced its postponement because of wet weather. Daljit Singh of the MCA explained that the rain had hindered preparation of the pitch on the Kuala Lumpur Padang and, that with the wet spell likely to continue, it would be futile to attempt to stage the match.

The secretary of the Singapore Cricket Association, R. Sivasubramaniam, was less than impressed. He argued that you could schedule a match for any date and it could rain and that 'rain and [sun]shine are part and parcel of cricket'. In hindsight, the weather records were in his favour. On the day the announcement was made, 44mm of rain fell in Kuala Lumpur, following 111mm over the previous four days, but, ironically, the day after the announcement was completely dry, as were the four days prior to the original start date. The match could probably have gone ahead.

The fixture was eventually played in December and, with the Padang required for other activities, it was held at the Kilat Club. This was the first time the fixture had been staged at a ground other than that of the Selangor and Singapore Cricket Clubs. The ground is now the Tenaga Nasional Sports Kompleks with much improved facilities, but in 1983 it was an ordinary club venue, albeit with a normally very true turf pitch. Again, ironically, the weather on the first day was appalling. Nearly 8mm of rain fell and play was very restricted.

Singapore were asked to bat first and Saker and Amarjit Singh exploited the conditions. Singapore's early batsmen had no answer to the swinging ball and were quickly reduced to 6/3 and 18/4, with Saker picking up all the wickets in a spectacular spell of bowling. When the opening bowlers were rested, Imran Hamid and Sathivail effected a small recovery, but rain prevented it getting very far. Singapore ended the first day on 49/4 and Saker with the analysis of 9-4-15-4. With four and a half hours lost to the weather, the captains agreed to limit the first innings of each side to 70 overs.

Though Sathivail survived on the second day, his colleagues found Saker almost unplayable. Harkrishnan Singh provided some support in an eighth-wicket stand of 21, but the resistance was short-lived and Singapore's innings ended on 80. Saker's second-day analysis was 8-5-10-6, giving him all ten wickets, the third player from an Associate country to achieve this feat in international matches, equalling T.S. Gilbert's 10-17 for Bermuda against Philadelphia in 1907 and J.B. King's 10-54 for Philadelphia against Ireland in 1909.

After a first-wicket stand of 36, no Malaysian batsman was secure against the pace of Mehta, Rajalingam and Harkrishnan Singh. Only some lusty blows from Amarjit Singh took the hosts into a first-innings lead. So much for the limit of 70 overs on the first innings – Singapore's had lasted a mere 45 overs and Malaysia's only five balls more.

Saker again bowled well in Singapore's second innings, but this time, without success. Amarjit Singh and Banerji took the wickets which left the visitors in trouble at the close, despite some sound defence fron Goh Swee Heng, promoted as a nightwatchman.

On the last day, Goh continued in good form, but his colleagues were unable to counter an inspired spell of bowling from Stevens. In just over ten overs he took 6-15 and Singapore were dismissed for 84. Goh remained undefeated, three runs short of what would have been a well-deserved half-century. Malaysia required 55 runs to win and were expected to struggle. Balakrishnan had other ideas, however, and, with the support of Chan Yow Choy, the target was reached without loss in 45 minutes.

MALAYSIA v SINGAPORE

Saudara Cup

Kelab Kilat, Jalan Pantai, Kuala Lumpur, 2, 3 and 4 December 1983

Malaysia won by ten wickets

SINGAPORE

		R	B	M	4s	6s			R	B	M	4s	6s
+M.Neethianathan	b Saker	3					c Harris bin Abu Bakar b A Singh	2					
S.T.Rajah	c Harris bin Abu Bakar b Saker	1					c Harris bin Abu Bakar b Banerji	6					
Imran Hamid Khwaja	c sub (M.Sham Jalil) b Saker	21					b Banerji	7					
*S.Muruthi	c Harris bin Abu Bakar b Saker	0					(8) b Stevens	4					
R.C.K.da Silva	c Bell b Saker	7					c Balakrishnan b Durairatnam	3					
S.Sathivail	not out	33					c Harris bin Abu Bakar b Stevens	1					
M.Rajalingam	c Banerji b Saker	5					(9) lbw b Stevens	1					
Goh Swee Heng	lbw b Saker	0					(4) not out	47					
M.K.Mehta	b Saker	0					(7) c&b Stevens	5					
Harkrishnan Singh	c Amarjit Singh b Saker	6					(11) b Stevens	0					
S.Sivalingam	b Saker	0					(10) b Stevens	0					
Extras		4						8					
		80						**84**					

MALAYSIA

		R	B	M	4s	6s			R	B	M	4s	6s
P.Balakrishnan	c Sathivail b Rajalingam	21					(2) not out	43	45				
Chan Yow Choy	c Neethianathan b H'nan Singh	19					(1) not out	11	45				
P.Banerji	c Neethianathan b da Silva	3											
A.Stevens	c Sathivail b da Silva	6											
S.Bell	c Goh Swee Heng b Mehta	9											
H.Durairatnam	c Rajah b Harkrishnan Singh	9											
K.Kamalanathan	c Rajalingam b H'nan Singh	0											
Zainon Mat	c Goh Swee Heng b Mehta	4											
+M.Harris bin Abu Bakar	c Muruthi b Harkrishnan Singh	6											
*Amarjit Singh Gill	not out	19											
K.Saker	lbw b Sivalingam	1											
Extras		13						2					
		110					(no wicket)	**56**					

Malaysia	O	M	R	W	nb	w		O	M	R	W	nb	w	fow	Sin (1)	Mal (1)	Sin (2)	Mal (2)
Saker	17	7	25	10				9	4	16	0			1	5	36	8	
Amarjit Singh Gill	13	8	21	0				7	1	11	1			2	6	39	16	
Durairatnam	5	1	9	0	(6)			5	2	7	1			3	6	47	39	
Banerji	4	1	5	0	(3)			16	6	19	2			4	18	63	48	
Kamalanathan	2	0	8	0										5	50	65	50	
Zainon Mat	3	0	8	0	(5)			6	1	8	0			6	58	67	64	
Stevens	1	1	0	0	(4)			10.4	4	15	6			7	58	76	72	
Singapore	O	M	R	W	nb	w		O	M	R	W	nb	w	8	58	76	80	
Mehta	14	4	24	2				5	1	23	0			9	79	94	82	
Sathivail	3	0	12	0				3	1	5	0			10	80	110	84	
Rajalingam	9	3	20	1	(4)			6	3	8	0							
Harkrishnan Singh	13	6	19	4	(3)			2	1	8	0							
da Silva	5	2	18	2														
Sivalingam	1.5	1	4	1	(5)			3	0	10	0							
Imran Hamid Khwaja								0.1	0	1	0							

Umpires: [unknown]

Toss: Malaysia. The breakdown of extras is not known.

Close of play: 1st day – Singapore (1) 49-4 (Imran Hamid Khwaja 21*, Sathivail 16*); 2nd day – Singapore (2) 54-5 (Goh Swee Heng 29*, Imran Hamid Khwaja ??*). Bowling in Malaysia's second innings is one run over.

After losing 4½ hours to rain on the first day, the captains agreed to limit the first innings of each side to 70 overs.

Bray bothers the Dutch

In July 1987, The Netherlands met Ireland in what has become the only three-day women's international match ever staged between Associates. Such was the difficulty that the Nederlandse Dames Cricket Bond were having in the 1980s in getting access to facilities, the fixture had to be played at the ground of the Klein Zwitserland Hockey Club in The Hague, instead of at a dedicated cricket ground of one of the leading men's clubs. The Dutch won the toss and chose to bat in very pleasant conditions, dry and sunny with temperatures rising to above 20°C by the middle of the afternoon. They struggled to score runs against the Irish attack of Stella Owens and Bray.

The opening partnership lasted 15 minutes but produced only four runs. Wesenhagen and van der Flier made a defiant middle-order stand lasting just over an hour but it produced a mere 20 runs. Bray was virtually unplayable, bowling faster than the Dutch were accustomed to and getting lift off the matting pitch. Only Wesenhagen reached double figures, no player hit a boundary and the Dutch were bowled out for 54 in two hours and 13 minutes. Bray finished with 7-21 from 18 overs and two balls.

The Irish did not experience the same problems when they batted. They were a side with recent match practice, having played three one-day fixtures against Australia earlier in the month. Also, the Dutch had no bowlers with the speed of Bray and Owens. The opening partnership lasted 77 minutes and yielded 46 runs. All of the Irish middle order made contributions. Owens and Walsh both made half-centuries and were undefeated in a sixth-wicket stand of 110, when Moore decided to declare with a first-innings lead of 184. Veltman, with her left-arm medium pace, was the most successful Dutch bowler, taking three of the five wickets to fall. The Dutch were handicapped by an injury to van der Flier after she had bowled six overs of her off-breaks, the only bowler of spin used in the match.

The Dutch changed their batting order in the second innings, promoting Wesenhagen to open, but this was not a success. She became the first wicket to fall, after 33 minutes, with the score on 12. For the first time in the match, the home side offered some real resistance. Vernout and van Lier put on 92 runs, but more importantly, defied the Irish for four hours and six minutes. Vernout was given out leg before to Moore, having made 43 runs including one four, in 279 minutes. Van Teunenbroek continued the defence, lasting one hour and 43 minutes, during which time she made the grand score of six from 105 balls.

The partnership was worth 44 but van Lier was caught at the wicket off Bray, one run later. Three more wickets fell at the same score and the eighth wicket only four runs further on. The ninth wicket added 12 runs in 26 minutes, largely due to extras; only two runs came from the bat. The Irish seemed to have some difficulty with direction during the Dutch second innings and contributed 25 wides. With van der Flier unable to bat, the visitors were victorious by an innings and 19 runs.

Bray took another five wickets to give her a match analysis of 12-56. Nearly half of her 45 overs in the Dutch second innings were maidens, a reflection of the home side's scoring rate of 1.2 runs per over. The Irish, by contrast, managed 2.1 runs per over.

It was probably as well that few people were interested enough in women's cricket to watch the game. The players may have enjoyed themselves but there was little of interest to excite spectators. Apart from the bowling of Bray, a feature of the match and typical of the period, was that both sides selected wicketkeepers for their efficiency behind the stumps, rather than any ability with the bat. Both batted last, but both had good matches, Kay Bergin taking three catches, all induced by Bray, and Isabelle Koppe having a hand in two of the five wickets that Ireland lost.

NETHERLANDS WOMEN v IRELAND WOMEN

Klein Zwitserland Hockey Club, Klatteweg, The Hague, 10, 11 and 12 July 1987

Ireland won by an innings and 19 runs

NETHERLANDS

Batter	Dismissal	R	B	M	4s	6s	Dismissal	R	B	M	4s	6s
L.Vernout	c Reamsbottom b Bray	5	24	32	-	-	lbw b Moore	43	282	279	1	-
H.Dinnissen	b S.A.Owens	1	16	15	-	-	(5) b Bray	0	11	14	-	-
*A.van Lier	c Bergin b Bray	4	10	12	-	-	c Bergin b Bray	61	339	350	4	-
B.van Teunenbroek	b S.A.Owens	2	10	11	-	-	c Clancy b Moore	6	105	103	-	-
V.Wesenhagen	c Stanton b Bray	12	74	79	-	-	(2) c Clancy b S.A.Owens	8	34	33	-	-
C.Z.van der Flier	c Walsh b Bray	8	50	61	-	-	absent hurt					
I.Dulfer	c Bergin b Bray	2	14	11	-	-	(6) c Clancy b Moore	1	4	5	-	-
C.Grevers	not out	8	27	24	-	-	(7) b Bray	11	63	48	-	-
E.Veltman	c Armstrong b Bray	0	2	5	-	-	(8) c Murray b Bray	0	14	8	-	-
D.L.Loman	b S.A.Owens	3	8	13	-	-	(9) b Bray	2	7	7	-	-
+I.Koppe	b Bray	0	3	3	-	-	(10) not out	0	6	26		
	b1 nb4 w4	9					b3 lb1 nb4 w25	33				
		54						**165**				

IRELAND

Batter	Dismissal	R	B	M	4s	6s
S.E.Reamsbottom	c van Lier b Veltman	23	75	83	2	-
A.B.Murray	c Koppe b Veltman	26	81	77	1	-
A.V.Stanton	c Koppe b van der Flier	8	28	30	-	-
*M.P.Moore	c sub (M.L.Loman) b Dulfer	32	112	106	-	-
D.K.Armstrong	c Vernout b Veltman	20	133	164	-	-
S.A.Owens	not out	64	103		4	-
J.Walsh	not out	50	99		1	-
E.Owens						
G.M.Clancy						
S.Bray						
+K.Bergin						
	b4 lb5 w6	15				
	(5 wickets declared)	**238**				

Ireland

	O	M	R	W	nb	w	O	M	R	W	nb	w
S.A.Owens	18	7	23	3	2	3	19	7	27	1	-	7
Bray	18.2	8	21	7	1	-	45	22	35	5	1	1
Clancy	4	1	6	0	-	1 (4)	21	8	24	0	-	2
E.Owens	3	1	3	0	1	- (3)	13	7	9	0	1	1
Moore							25	9	24	3	1	3
Stanton							14	4	34	0	1	8
Armstrong							3	0	8	0	-	-

fow	Ne (1)	Ire (1)	Ne (2)
1	4 (2)	46 (2)	12 (2)
2	8 (1)	49 (1)	104 (1)
3	14 (4)	63 (3)	148 (4)
4	18 (3)	107 (4)	149 (3)
5	38 (6)	128 (5)	149 (6)
6	41 (5)		149 (5)
7	44 (7)		149 (8)
8	44 (9)		153 (7)
9	52 (10)		165 (9)
10	54 (11)		

Netherlands

	O	M	R	W	nb	w
Dulfer	28	8	50	1	-	-
Loman	17	8	34	0	-	-
Veltman	23	7	42	3	-	4
van Lier	17	3	35	0	-	-
Grevers	9	0	24	0	-	-
van der Flier	6	0	20	1	-	-
Vernout	12	3	24	0	-	1

Umpires: J.P.A.W.Molenaar (Netherlands) and L.W.van Vugt (Netherlands)

Toss: Netherlands

In Ireland's innings M.L.Loman fielded as substitute for C.Z.van der Flier.

A.van Lier became A.Becheno after marriage. I.Dulfer and I.Koppe were known as I.Keijzer and I.van Dishoek before marriage.

Myth or not, let's party anyway

Cricketers representing MCC and France gathered at the ground of the Standard Athletic Club, Meudon, on 24 September 1989 to celebrate the bicentenary of a match that never happened, namely that between the Duke of Dorset's side and what would have been a team drawn from British residents in Paris, representing France.

If some cricket historians are to be believed, the celebration was for a myth put about to discredit the Duke of Dorset, rather than for a match called off because of the French Revolution. Regardless of the truth, the opportunity for a cricket match and a party was too good to miss and certainly did not dampen the enthusiasm of the players taking part. The French team was slightly, but only slightly, more French than that which would have played in 1789. The nearest to true French players were the Brumant half-brothers, Guy and Valentin, who hailed from the West Indian island of Guadeloupe, which is administratively part of Metropolitan France. Otherwise, like their counterparts a century earlier would have been, the players were all expatriates residing and working in France.

The side was captained by a former Irish international, John Short, who had moved to Paris in 1984 to work for the OECD. Their other player of note was Simon Hewitt, who had played first-class cricket for Oxford University in 1984, but was living in France. Later, he would become the director of cricket in the country.

MCC selected a strong side. There was one former Test-match player, John Jameson, and seven others with previous first-class experience. The batting was, however, considerably stronger than the bowling.

As would have been the case in 1789, the fixture was played as a one-day game under standard, rather than one-day, rules. MCC, captained by Knight, won the toss and opted to bat. The French bowling was steady but the visitors batted well and there was a good contest between bat and ball. No one reached 50, Cooke being the highest scorer at four runs short. Most of the batsmen got starts, however, so, as in a typical club game, the score mounted along quite happily at just over three runs per over.

Hewitt was the most successful bowler, with three wickets, and he was well supported by his opening partner, Shahzada, who picked up two. By mid-afternoon the score was beyond 150 and, in order to keep the match competitive, it was time to declare.

In reply, Short and Hafiz made light work of MCC's bowlers in an opening stand of 66. After the loss of Hafiz and Hellawell, Hewitt accompanied Short in a partnership of 56 to put France in a dominating position. With Hewitt's dismissal, Drummond was content to let Short take the leading role as, together, they took the home side to a seven-wicket victory in just over 41 overs. The French scoring rate was nearly four runs per over.

The loss to France followed defeats earlier in the season by England against Australia, losing the Ashes by four matches to none with two drawn, and by an England XI against The Netherlands, though the series of two one-day matches finished one each. Overall, it was not a good summer for English representative XIs.

FRANCE v MARYLEBONE CRICKET CLUB

Standard Athletic Club Ground, Meudon, Paris, 24 September 1989

France won by seven wickets

MCC		R	B	M	4s	6s
J.A.Jameson	c Payne b Shahzada	21				
R.P.Hodson	lbw b Hewitt	17				
S.P.Henderson	b Hewitt	26				
R.M.O.Cooke	b Hewitt	46				
A.Needham	c Barclay b Shahzada	9				
*R.D.V.Knight	c Barclay b G.L.Brumant	10				
C.D.Hitchcock	st Payne b Hellawell	15				
+J.I.McDowall	not out	4				
W.G.Merry						
A.J.Colbeck						
C.W.Farrell						
	b5 lb8 nb3	16				
	(7 wickets declared)	**164**				

FRANCE		R	B	M	4s	6s
*J.F.Short	not out	73				
M.Hafiz	b Needham	26				
I.Hellawell	lbw b Needham	8				
S.M.Hewitt	c McDowall b Knight	35				
N.Drummond	not out	9				
S.W.Shahzada						
J.Barclay						
+J.V.N.Payne						
F.Wasserman						
V.Brumant						
G.L.Brumant						
	b10 lb2 nb1 w1	14				
	(3 wickets)	**165**				

France	O	M	R	W	nb	w
Shahzada	15	3	45	2		
Hewitt	13	2	45	3		
V.Brumant	9	1	20	0		
G.T.Brumant	12	1	34	1		
Short	2	0	4	0		
Hellawell	1.1	0	3	1		

MCC	O	M	R	W	nb	w
Merry	12	2	34	0		
Farrell	5	2	15	0		
Knight	7.2	1	25	1		
Needham	13	2	48	2		
Colbeck	4	0	31	0		

fow	MCC	Fr
1	28	66 (2)
2	64	80 (3)
3	69	136 (4)
4	84	
5	107	
6	160	
7	164	
8		
9		
10		

Umpires: [unknown]

Toss: MCC

Multi-innings *déjà vu*

Although cricket in east and south-east Asia in the 1990s was a more cosmopolitan activity than in its early days in Hong Kong, when it relied heavily on expatriate businessmen, administrators and the military, these people still played an important role. One such person was Ronald Endley who worked for Volvo in Bangkok and later became chairman of the South African-Thai Chamber of Commerce.

In the late 1980s he persuaded Volvo to sponsor the Volvo Cup for what was intended to be a series of matches between Thailand and Hong Kong. The first match was played at the Royal Bangkok Sports Club Polo Ground in January 1990. There was still some enthusiasm then for two-innings matches and the inaugural game was played over two days. In atmosphere and team composition, the fixture was like a hangover from the 1930s.

The Hong Kong side included Pat Fordham, an investment manager with Matheson plc. He spent ten years in Hong Kong before returning to the UK in 1998. Glyn Davies was a policeman who made his career in the territory, eventually becoming superintendent of the Hong Kong Police Force. Rod Eddington, an Australian, had played first-class cricket for Oxford University in 1975 and 1976, while he was studying for a DPhil in Engineering Science. He joined Cathay Pacific in 1979, working his way through the company to become managing director in 1992, before leaving Hong Kong in 1997 to take up the post of chairman of Ansett, which lasted until the airline folded in 2001. He was chief executive of British Airways from 2000 to 2005, when he was knighted for his services to the aviation industry.

Though largely expatriate, Thailand's team included two Thais, the Thongyai brothers, Larn Kathatong and Luke Buathong. They had, however, learnt their cricket in Australia, where their father had lived and worked as the Thai trade commissioner from 1984 to 1986.

The match was played in hot weather during Bangkok's dry season. Under the cloudless skies the sun was relentless, the temperatures reaching 31°C by mid-afternoon. In order to keep the game moving and encourage the captains to seek a result, the first innings of each side was limited to 50 overs. Thailand batted first and owed much to Larn Thongyai who contributed a well-crafted 77. Four others reached double figures. At the end of their 50 overs, the home side had lost seven wickets but had scored a very competitive 179 runs.

Kumar and Farouq batted superbly in a second-wicket stand of 117 to put Hong Kong in a dominant position. Following their dismissal though, it was left to Graham and Vachha to ensure a first-innings lead. When their 50 overs were up, Hong Kong were 27 ahead.

Davies prevented a rout of Thailand in their second innings, as their early batsmen failed to master the off-spin of Vachha, who obtained considerable turn from the mat. Wickets fell at regular intervals as the home side reached 159/7, a lead of only 132. Davies's 90 was invaluable. Endley attacked the bowling with some fierce shots all round the wicket. His fast half-century helped to set Hong Kong the challenging task of making 213 runs for victory.

Kumar and Farouq made another excellent partnership. Vachha followed up his bowling performance of 4-86 with a rapid 39, but when the close came the visitors were still 26 runs short. Hong Kong took the Volvo Cup on the basis of their first-innings lead.

The following year, the trophy was contested in Hong Kong as a one-day international, Thailand gaining revenge and winning by three wickets. In 1992, the tournament became three-way, with the inclusion of Malaysia, Hong Kong regaining the trophy by beating both their opponents, but that was the last time the trophy was contested.

THAILAND v HONG KONG
Volvo Cup

Royal Bangkok Sports Club Polo Ground, Soi Polo, Pathum Wan, Bangkok, 26 and 27 January 1990

Match drawn

THAILAND

		R	B	M	4s	6s			R	B	M	4s	6s
*M.L.K.Thongyai	c Davies b Cox	77					c Graham b Vachha		10				
P.Davies	lbw b Davies	6					c Kumar b Vachha		90				
A.Zakhariya	c Gelding b Eddington	20					c Fordham b Davies		1				
C.Price	st Fordham b Davies	13					c Kumar b Vachha		5				
N.White	c Gelding b Cox	28					(7) c Fordham b Vachha		16				
M.L.B.Thongyai	c Fordham b Davies	10					(9) c Gelding b Fordham		8				
D.Dance	run out	13					(5) run out		5				
N.Hassan	not out	3					(6) st Fordham b Farouq		16				
R.I.C.Endley							(8) c Gelding b Cox		55				
S.Mathews							b Fordham		5				
N.Malik							not out		16				
	Extras	9							12				
	(7 wickets, 50 overs)	**179**							**239**				

HONG KONG

		R	B	M	4s	6s			R	B	M	4s	6s
S.N.K.Kumar	c Malik b Dance	75					c M.L.K.Thongyai b Hassan		36				
A.Ebrahim	c&b M.L.B.Thongyai	16					c Davies b Zakhariya		8				
R.Farouq	c Price b Malik	52					c Hassan b Zakhariya		70				
+J.P.Fordham	c&b Malik	13					c Mathews b Malik		8				
*G.H.Davies	b Malik	8					(7) not out		8				
M.Graham	not out	12											
Y.J.Vachha	not out	18					(5) b White		39				
D.Gelding							(6) not out		3				
R.Nissim													
J.Cox													
R.I.Eddington													
	Extras	12							15				
	(4 wickets, 50 overs)	**206**					(5 wickets)		**187**				

Hong Kong	O	M	R	W	nb	w		O	M	R	W	nb	w	fow	Th (1)	HK (1)	Th (2)	HK (2)
Davies	20	3	63	3				15	2	45	1			1	7	31	31	14
Cox	10	7	52	2				12.3	2	53	1			2	66	148	37	94
Vachha	8	1	20	0			(4)	20	3	86	4			3	100	153	57	111
Eddington	12	2	39	1			(6)	5	1	20	0			4	141	169	78	?
Fordham							(3)	9	3	22	2			5	153	177	120	173
Farouq							(5)	3	1	8	1			6	173		144	
														7	179		159	
Thailand	O	M	R	W	nb	w		O	M	R	W	nb	w	8			203	
White	6	1	15	0				11	1	35	1			9			211	
Zakhariya	4	2	8	0				8	0	41	2			10			239	
M.L.B.Thongyai	5	0	18	1														
Malik	19	2	65	3				9	0	48	1							
M.L.K.Thongyai	3	0	11	0														
Hassan	4	0	22	0			(5)	7	0	38	1							
Dance	9	1	63	1			(3)	4	0	16	0							

Umpires: S.Gale and J.Verwoed

Toss:

The breakdown of extras is not known.

The first innings of each side was restricted to 50 overs.

Don't be silly! The second day of a match is really the first

With the ICC Trophy in 1994 being staged in Nairobi during the shorter of the region's two rainy seasons, it was surprising that more attention was not given to problems likely to arise in the event of wet weather. The only regulations were that, if necessary, play could be extended into a second day and that, in a rain-affected match, a result could be awarded on run rate, if the innings of the side batting second lasted a minimum of 30 overs.

With the tournament being held for the first time outside northern Europe, play into the evening was not possible so, with dusk just after 5.30pm and darkness half an hour later, the organisers put a limit on the time of closure at 5.40pm but for some reason, applied this only to the second day. Play on the first day could be extended beyond this time, if the umpires thought there was a chance of a result and it was safe to do so.

The first problem came in the match between Canada and Singapore, when rain prevented play on the first day. Most people expected the next day to be treated as the second day of the match, but Paddy O'Hara, the Irish umpire, decided that if there was no play on the first day, then the second day must, by default, be the first day. As it happened, further rain put a stop to Singapore's innings after 20 overs and the match was abandoned.

A day later, Ireland played Papua New Guinea. There was no play on the first day and, again, the umpires ruled that the following day was, therefore, the first day. Papua New Guinea won the toss and asked the Irish to bat. Despite taking early wickets, their bowlers failed to maintain the pressure. Benson, Harrison and Lewis placed Ireland in a strong position, with Lewis reaching his half-century off 65 balls. Curry made 18 off 19 balls and Dunlop struck a fine 30 off 34 balls, as Ireland added 117 runs in the last 20 overs, before the innings closed on 230/8.

Surprisingly, Papua New Guinea made little effort to chase the target. They hoped that rain would cause the match to be abandoned before they had batted 30 overs and, therefore, the points would be shared. After ten overs they had scored only 18. The sky was getting ever darker and, in an effort to bowl the 30 overs required as quickly as possible, the pace bowlers gave way to the spin of Hoey and Curry.

After the first ball of the 21st over a thunderstorm soaked the ground. The Irish players and their supporters rushed to help the ground staff place tarpaulins over the wicket but it looked as though their efforts were in vain as the rain continued. Eventually it relented and, with the same group of helpers, the ground staff carefully removed the tarpaulins without causing too much damage. The umpires ignored the wet outfield and ruled that play could begin again after a delay of two and a half hours.

By this time it was 5.53pm and almost dark. With the umpires' ruling that this was the first day of the match, Papua New Guinea were forced to resume their innings in increasing darkness and with no indication of how long play might continue. With the spinners bowling, the umpires decided that there was no danger to the batsmen. In an effort to meet the 30-over regulation the bowlers rushed through their overs and, to their credit, the batsmen did not adopt delaying tactics. The umpires allowed the innings to continue until the end of the 32nd over before deciding it was too dark to continue. Papua New Guinea's innings ended on 88/7, leaving Ireland easy winners on a faster run rate.

Papua New Guinea lodged a protest. They argued that either the match should have been abandoned at 5.40pm or they should have been allowed to complete their 50 overs on a third day, which would, of course, have been the second. It took four days before the organisers ruled that the result should stand, a verdict perhaps recognising that Papua New Guinea had been completely outplayed, made no effort to win and did not deserve to share the points.

IRELAND v PAPUA NEW GUINEA

50 overs

ABN-AMRO ICC Trophy – First Round Group A

Ngara Sports Club, Nairobi, 14 and 15 February 1994

Ireland won on faster run rate

IRELAND		R	B	M	4s	6s
J.D.R.Benson	c Pala b Gaudi	46	83	99	4	-
M.P.Rea	c A.Leka b Arua	9	28	31	1	-
C.McCrum	run out	6	15	25	-	-
*D.A.Lewis	run out	50	65	85	7	-
G.D.Harrison	c A.Leka b Amini	26	37	38	1	1
J.D.Curry	run out	18	19	29	-	1
A.R.Dunlop	c Oala b Arua	30	34	44	2	1
P.McCrum	lbw b Raka	2	8	9	-	-
+P.B.Jackson	not out	14	11	17	-	-
A.N.Nelson	not out	5	4	7	-	-
C.J.Hoey						
	b4 lb6 w14	24				
	(8 wickets, 50 overs)	**230**				

PAPUA NEW GUINEA		R	B	M	4s	6s
L.Oala	c P.McCrum b Hoey	22	56	62	2	-
C.Amini	lbw b Harrison	3	36	34	-	-
T.Raka	c Jackson b Nelson	0	1	2	-	-
L.Leka	b Hoey	9	23	24	1	-
N.Maha	b Hoey	4	11	12	1	-
*A.Leka	st Jackson b Hoey	22	35	32	1	-
V.Pala	c Dunlop b Hoey	2	6	5	-	-
K.Ila	not out	14	17	19	2	-
+N.Alu	not out	1	9	4	-	-
F.Arua						
T.Gaudi						
	b2 lb3 nb2 w4	11				
	(7 wickets, 32 overs)	**88**				

PNG	O	M	R	W	nb	w
Raka	10	1	42	1	1	3
Arua	7	1	27	2	-	9
Pala	8	1	41	0	-	-
Gaudi	10	0	42	1	2	2
A.Leka	8	0	42	0	-	-
Amini	7	0	26	1	1	-

Ireland	O	M	R	W	nb	w
P.McCrum	5	1	11	0	2	2
Harrison	10	2	19	1	1	-
Nelson	1	0	2	1	-	-
Hoey	10	2	29	5	-	-
Curry	6	1	22	0	-	1

fow	Ir	PNG
1	25 (2)	18 (2)
2	57 (3)	19 (3)
3	105 (1)	40 (1)
4	151 (5)	40 (4)
5	156 (4)	47 (5)
6	185 (6)	53 (7)
7	203 (8)	87 (6)
8	215 (7)	
9		
10		

Umpires: G.H.Lever (Hong Kong) and G.Hewitt (Kenya)

Toss: Papua New Guinea

There was no play on the first day.

Player of the Match: C.J.Hoey (Ireland)

Mortensen the Mighty

Since 1979, when Denmark reached the semi-finals of the ICC Trophy, their performances in international cricket had disappointed. The retirement of Carsten Morild and Henrik Mortensen left gaps, particularly in the batting, which had not been possible to fill. Bowling, however, was a different matter because of the emergence of Ole Mortensen, no relation to Henrik.

For a short period, Ole and Henrik overlapped and in the ICC Trophy in 1979, they demolished Fiji for 89 runs in 33.5 overs, taking 4-15 and 3-12 respectively. By the time of the ICC Trophy in 1994, Ole Mortensen had pursued a successful career in English county cricket with Derbyshire, where he had developed into a world-class fast bowler with the ability to move the ball consistently off the pitch away from right-handed batsmen and deliver well-controlled yorkers. At his peak, many county players rated him as Test-match standard.

In addition, Søren Henriksen had played three first-class matches as an all-rounder for Lancashire and Aftab Ahmed was showing promise as a batsman. Much was therefore expected of Denmark this time, but again they disappointed. They failed to qualify for the second round and had to enter the Plate competition. Their first match in the Plate was against Israel, an enthusiastic squad renowned for fair play, but with rather limited ability. In five ICC Trophy competitions up to that time, they had managed to win only two matches.

Overall, the Danish batting was more successful chasing targets than setting them so it was not a surprise when, on winning the toss, their captain decided to field first. The Israelis were outclassed as Mortensen bowled superbly. Their batsmen had never before faced bowling of his pace and difficulty so all they could do was protect their stumps and any runs made were a bonus.

Nichol and Awasker struggled to take the opening partnership into double figures, but both were forced to play at balls close to and moving away from the off stump, finding the outside edge, and were caught behind. This laid the pattern for the innings with Saddique taking six catches to set a Danish record that still stands for the most catches in an innings by a wicketkeeper.

Mortensen was virtually unplayable. In just over eight overs, two of them maidens, he took 7-19, then a Danish record for a one-day international, since beaten by Thomas Hansen who took 7-13 against Bermuda at Svanholm in 2007.

The Israeli players did their best with Ward reaching the heights of double figures, but they kept losing wickets. Their effort lasted only 16.4 overs for which the reward was a total of 45, their lowest innings score in international cricket until they made only 38 against an England NCA side in the European Championships two years later.

Denmark took just under ten overs to win the match without losing a wicket but their form did not last, however, as they lost their next match to the USA and then struggled to beat Malaysia by two wickets.

Despite this poor record, the Danes found themselves contesting the Philip Snow Trophy in the Plate Final where they faced Namibia. The final should have been between the USA and Papua New Guinea but both teams had left Nairobi, having booked flights home not expecting to still be involved in the competition. Denmark again disappointed, losing by 41 runs. Their only consolation was that at least they were not in the group competing for the wooden spoon.

Unfortunately for Denmark, Mortensen never played for them again, age and knee problems forcing him to retire. In 26 matches in the ICC Trophy he took 63 wickets at an average of 10.41. In 145 first-class matches for Derbyshire, he took 411 wickets at 23.53. He was undoubtedly the best player ever to come from Denmark and one of the top Associate cricketers of all time.

DENMARK v ISRAEL

50 overs

ABN-AMRO ICC Trophy – Plate Group H

Impala Sports Club, Nairobi, 24 February 1994

Denmark won by ten wickets

ISRAEL		R	B	M	4s	6s
R.Nichol	c Saddique b Mortensen	5				
H.Awasker	c Saddique b Pedersen	5				
S.Raj	c Saddique b Mortensen	5				
N.Ward	c Pfaff b Mortensen	14				
B.David	c Saddique b Pedersen	1				
*N.Jhirad	c Slebsager b Mortensen	1				
R.Aston	c Saddique b Mortensen	1				
D.Moss	b Henriksen	0				
+G.Talkar	c Saddique b Mortensen	5				
S.Samuel	not out	1				
J.Divekar	b Mortensen	0				
	b1 nb1 w5	7				
	(16.4 overs)	**45**				

DENMARK		R	B	M	4s	6s
M.S.Christiansen	not out	13				
Atif Butt	not out	22				
H.Pfaff						
Aftab Ahmed						
S.Henriksen						
S.Vestergaard						
+M.Saddique						
L.Slebsager						
O.H.Mortensen						
*M.Seider						
P.Pedersen						
	lb3 nb2 w6	11				
	(no wicket, 9.4 overs)	**46**				

Denmark	O	M	R	W	nb	w
Mortensen	8.4	2	19	7	1	-
Pedersen	6	0	20	2	-	4
Henriksen	2	0	5	1	-	1

Israel	O	M	R	W	nb	w
Divekar	3	0	9	0	-	3
Aston	3	0	17	0	2	3
Moss	2	0	9	0	-	-
Awasker	1.4	0	8	0	-	-

fow	Isr	Den
1	11	
2	11	
3	19	
4	25	
5	36	
6	37	
7	38	
8	43	
9	45	
10	45	

Umpires: G.Hewitt (Kenya) and G.C.Scott (Kenya)

Toss: Denmark

Player of the Match: O.H.Mortensen (Denmark)

Emirates' expatriates excel

With Sri Lanka and Zimbabwe promoted from Associate to Full Membership of the ICC, there was no obvious favourite for the 1994 ICC Trophy. The United Arab Emirates, who were competing for the first time, were the surprise of the tournament. They reached the final unbeaten where they met the hosts, Kenya. Not unexpectedly, local interest was high. Spectators began to arrive at the Ruaraka Sports Club Ground at 6am in order to get the best vantage points. By 9am, an hour before the start, the ground was full with an estimated 6,000, a number probably not seen at an Associate international since before the First World War, when Philadelphian cricket was at its peak.

The spectators were hoping to see Kenya produce a great victory. Their opponents had not been popular because of the composition of their team. Only the captain, Sultan Zarawani, was born in the Emirates. The rest were expatriates from the Indian subcontinent, nine with previous experience of first-class cricket in their country of origin. Although the team was strictly legal, there was a strong feeling locally that it amounted to no more than a group of mercenaries that had been specially assembled for the tournament.

Zarawani won the toss and asked Kenya to bat first, intending to take advantage of any early morning dew, which might encourage the ball to swing. Conditions, however, were ideal. The pitch was hard and true, and the temperatures ranged from the low 20s at the start to a maximum of 29°C by mid-afternoon.

Maurice Odumbe and Otieno batted well in a partnership of 98, despite all attempts by the bowlers to put the batsmen under pressure. With Steve Tikolo joining Odumbe, the scoring rate rose to over a run a ball, providing much enjoyment for the spectators who cheered every boundary with great enthusiasm as the pair added 102. With nine overs remaining the scene was set for a massive scoring spree to take the total beyond 300, but it was not to be. Zarawani encouraged his bowlers and fielders while Tim Tikolo attempted to do what was required, making 42 not out from 24 balls. When the innings closed on 281/6, there was a feeling that, though competitive, it was probably 20 runs short.

The Emirates could not have made a better start as Poonawala and Azhar Saeed made light of the bowling in an opening stand of 141 in 28 overs. Just as it looked as though they might reach their target without loss, both fell to Edward Odumbe. With Suji bowling the experienced Mazher Hussain, the Emirates were pegged back, but Mohammad Ishaq played in his typical fashion, trying to score off everything, and looking as though he would fall at any minute. His partner, Mehra, was more circumspect. Nevertheless, 30 runs came in three overs.

Suji returned to the attack in the 41st over and, in an inspired spell, took three wickets. Under pressure to score, two batsmen succumbed to run-outs, both direct hits, but the second of these did not occur until the scores were level. Imtiaz Abbasi made the winning run off the first ball of the last over. The final five overs had given the crowd much excitement and the possibility that the hosts might even win, but in the end, the spectators left the ground in disappointment.

At the closing dinner, the chairman of the Kenyan Cricket Association called for a change in the ICC's rules for eligibility and criticised the make-up of the Emirates' team. Whether his comments were constructive or simply sour grapes because Kenya did not win was open to interpretation. Sultan Zarawani took exception to them and led his squad in a walk-out in protest. The ICC rejected the comments, but later made changes to the residential qualifications for players.

KENYA v UNITED ARAB EMIRATES

50 overs

ABN-AMRO ICC Trophy – Final

Ruaraka Sports Club, Nairobi, 6 March 1994

United Arab Emirates won by two wickets

KENYA		R	B	M	4s	6s
D.N.Chudasama	c Saleem Raza b Sohail Butt	0				
+K.O.Otieno	c&b Azhar Saeed	49				
M.O.Odumbe	b Samarasekara	86	115			
S.O.Tikolo	b Saleem Raza	54	53			
M.S.Kassam Ali	c Imtiaz Abbasi b Saleem Raza	0				
*T.J.Tikolo	not out	42	24			
E.O.Odumbe	run out (Azhar Saeed-Samarasekara)	25				
M.Odumbe	not out	1				
M.A.Suji						
Rajab Ali						
A.Y.Karim						
	b1 lb17 w6	24				
	(6 wickets, 50 overs)	**281**				

UAE		R	B	M	4s	6s
R.H.Poonawala	lbw b E.O.Odumbe	71				
Azhar Saeed	c M.O.Odumbe b E.O.Odumbe	59				
Mazhar Hussain	b Suji	9				
Mohammad Ishaq	c Chudasama b Suji	51	36			
V.Mehra	run out (T.J.Tikolo)	34	34			
Saleem Raza	c T.J.Tikolo b Suji	6				
J.A.Samarasekara	run out (M.O.Odumbe)	4				
Arshad Laeeq	c T.J.Tikolo b Suji	20				
+Imtiaz Abbasi	not out	1				
Sohail Butt	not out	0				
*S.M.Zarawani						
	b1 lb13 nb1 w12	27				
	(8 wickets, 49.1 overs)	**282**				

UAE	O	M	R	W	nb	w		fow	Ken	UAE
Samarasekara	10	1	48	1	-	2		1	1 (1)	141 (1)
Sohail Butt	9	0	48	1	-	3		2	99 (2)	148 (2)
Arshad Laeeq	9	0	50	0	2	1		3	201 (3)	177 (3)
Azhar Saeed	9	0	46	1	-	-		4	202 (5)	233 (4)
Saleem Raza	10	0	48	2	-	-		5	211 (4)	242 (6)
Zarawani	3	0	23	0	-	-		6	268 (7)	254 (7)
								7		276 (8)
Kenya	O	M	R	W	nb	w		8		281 (5)
Suji	10	0	61	4	-	2		9		
Rajab Ali	6	0	27	0	-	4		10		
M.Odumbe	2	0	14	0	3	1				
M.O.Odumbe	10	0	44	0	-	1				
Karim	9	0	56	0	-	-				
S.O.Tikolo	3	0	14	0	-	-				
E.O.Odumbe	9.1	0	52	2	-	4				

Umpires: J.Luther (Denmark) and P.L.O'Hara (Ireland)

Toss: United Arab Emirates

Player of the Match: Mohammad Ishaq (United Arab Emirates)

Note: M.S.Kassam Ali is also known as Sibtain Kassam Ali; M.Odumbe is Martin Orewa Odumbe but is known as M.Odumbe rather than M.O. to distinguish him from his brother Maurice Omondi Odumbe; Rajab Ali is also known as R.W.Ali.

Argentina follow on despite a first-innings lead

Cricket in Italy today owes its origin to some enthusiastic Italians who founded the Associazione Italiana Cricket (now the Federazione Cricket Italiana) in 1980. By 1984 the sport was sufficiently well established to select a squad of 17 players, nine of whom were Italians, to undertake a tour of England, playing against club sides. In 1987, under Simone Gambino, the AIC insisted that clubs in the national championships had to include at least seven Italians, a number which was later increased to nine.

After an embarrassing loss to Denmark in 1989, Italy being dismissed for 30 in reply to the Danish total of 439/6, the requirements were altered to one where all cricketers in the national side and in domestic competitions had to be Italian passport-holders. The AIC was certainly ambitious and, in 1995, sent a squad of 14 on a tour of Argentina, during which Italy played their only two-innings international, which turned out to be memorable for other reasons.

The match was played at the ground of the Belgrano Athletic Club in Buenos Aires under warm, dry conditions. Although torrential rain amounting to just over 40mm fell on 16 February, the following days were sunny with afternoon temperatures reaching around 26°C.

Forrester won the toss and asked the Italians to bat first. There was no obvious reason for this, except that the visitors, playing out of season, were short of match practice. This became only too apparent when the Italian captain, Pezzi, was leg before to Jooris without scoring and Maggio and Akhlaq Qureshi were both bowled by Forrester, so three of Italy's top four failed to make a run between them.

Javed and Zuppiroli put on 46, mostly after the opening bowlers were rested, but both were dismissed with the total on 51. A partnership of 46 followed for the sixth wicket between Razzaq and Khizer but the recovery was ended when the latter offered a catch, five runs short of a half-century. With the first innings of each side being limited to 50 overs the visitors' contribution ended on 160, even though they had two wickets in hand.

Argentina responded strongly with a 57 opening stand. The top four batsmen all made starts but none got beyond 37. Qureshi, who had played first-class cricket for Lahore, bowled particularly well and his medium pace proved difficult to score from. The home side owed their first-innings lead to Alonso, whose 43 held the middle order and tail together. Even so, Argentina underperformed and were unable to bat the full 50 overs. Qureshi finished with 4-33 from his 14 overs.

There was no rain but the morning of the second day found the pitch saturated. The ground staff had been using a computerised sprinkler system and either the software or the hardware had failed and it had irrigated the ground all night. A new pitch was quickly prepared but the Italians refused to bat on it. It was not clear whether they considered it potentially dangerous or because they thought that, once started, it was improper to change pitches during a match.

However, Forrester thought the conditions were fine and offered to bat instead and the side with a first-innings lead effectively followed on. Argentina's batsmen hardly supported the view that the replacement pitch was acceptable. They struggled to score runs against some tight Italian bowling, again led by Qureshi, who took five wickets to finish with a match return of 9-60.

The game was kept alive by Forrester declaring with nine wickets down to set Italy a target of 157 runs. The visitors lost two early wickets, but Pezzi and Zuppiroli put on 49 to give the Italians a sniff of victory, although it was merely an illusion. The visitors lost wickets regularly and had to defend the last few overs for a draw. A remarkable feature of the match was the number of batsmen given out leg before. Twelve, or 35 per cent of the wickets which fell, were dismissed in this way. Eight of these decisions were given in favour of Argentina and only four for the visitors.

ARGENTINA v ITALY

Belgrano Athletic Club, Buenos Aires, 18 and 19 February 1995

Match drawn

ITALY

		R B M 4s 6s		R B M 4s 6s
*A.Pezzi	lbw b Jooris	0	b Jooris	16
M.Javed	lbw b Jooris	16	lbw b Forrester	3
R.Maggio	b Forrester	0	(8) not out	6
Akhlaq Qureshi	b Forrester	0	(6) lbw b Ryan	10
V.Zuppiroli	c Cortabarria b Irigoyen	24	(4) b Ryan	35
M.Razzaq	b Alonso	37	(3) lbw b Alonso	2
M.Khizer	c Shimamoto b Forrester	45	(5) lbw b Jooris	5
+I.K.Kariyawasam	lbw b Alonso	6	(7) lbw b Forrester	6
M.B.M.da Costa	not out	4		
E.P.Ciappina	not out	2	(9) not out	4
M.G.L.Rajapakse				
	b5 lb5 nb2 w14	26	b4 w8	12
	(8 wickets, 50 overs)	**160**	(7 wickets)	**99**

ARGENTINA

		R B M 4s 6s		R B M 4s 6s
G.P.Kirschbaum	c da Costa b Rajapakse	34	run out	7
M.J.Paterlini	run out	33	b Akhlaq Qureshi	0
B.I.Irigoyen	b Akhlaq Qureshi	18	lbw b Zuppiroli	18
*D.Forrester	lbw b Akhlaq Qureshi	37	(5) c Akhlaq Qureshi b da Costa	10
M.D.Morris	run out	3	(6) b Akhlaq Qureshi	30
L.J.Alonso	c da Costa b Khizer	43	(7) c K'asam b Akhlaq Qureshi	3
+M.E.Cortabarria	c Rajapakse b Khizer	8	(11) not out	1
M.E.Ryan	b Rajapakse	3	lbw b Akhlaq Qureshi	1
L.A.Jooris	b Akhlaq Qureshi	0	(10) b Akhlaq Qureshi	15
I.Shimamoto	not out	10	(4) c Kariyawasam b Zuppiroli	15
S.J.Ciaburri	lbw b Akhlaq Qureshi	1	(9) not out	1
	b4 lb7 w4	15	b4 lb3 w3	10
	(49 overs)	**205**	(9 wickets declared)	**111**

Argentina	O	M	R	W	nb	w		O	M	R	W	nb	w	fow	It (1)	Arg (1)	Arg (2)	It (1)
Jooris	8	0	21	2	(4)			20	6	29	2			1	0	57	1	5
Forrester	15	0	51	3	(1)			13	4	24	2			2	5	82	8	11
Alonso	14	2	41	2	(2)			4	1	6	1			3	5	103	28	60
Ryan	6	1	7	0	(5)			14	6	16	2			4	51	127	44	65
Irigoyen	7	0	30	1										5	51	141	79	73
Shimamoto					(3)			4	0	20	0			6	127	172	85	81
														7	149	192	87	91
Italy	O	M	R	W	nb	w		O	M	R	W	nb	w	8	154	192	92	
Akhlaq Qureshi	14	1	33	4				15.5	5	27	5			9		?	92	
Rajapakse	13	0	44	2				9	3	13	0			10		205		
Ciappina	4	1	17	0				8	3	20	0							
Zuppiroli	10	0	48	0	(6)			?	?	19	2							
da Costa	6	2	35	0				6	1	9	1							
Khizer	2	0	17	2														
Maggio					(4)			4	0	16	0							

Umpires: D.R.Ker (Argentina) and C.G.Niño (Argentina)

Toss: Argentina

Close of play: 1st day – Argentina (1) 205 all out

After a failure of the sprinkler system to switch itself off overnight, the pitch was flooded on the second morning. A replacement pitch was hurriedly prepared, but the Italians refused to bat on it. Argentina agreed to bat instead, resulting in an instance of a side with a first-innings lead following on.

The first innings of each side was restricted to 50 overs.

Kenya inspired, the West Indies inept

By finishing in the runners-up spot in the 1994 ICC Trophy, Kenya qualified for the 1996 World Cup, but no one expected much from them when faced with teams like the West Indies. When Maurice Odumbe lost the toss in the encounter at Pune and Richardson, the West Indian captain, asked Kenya to bat, most of the spectators expected they would be dismissed cheaply against the all-pace attack of Ambrose, Walsh, Bishop and Cuffy.

Walsh duly took the first three wickets as the Kenyan batsmen, so strong against fellow Associate sides, struggled against unfamiliar pace. Tariq Iqbal batted for 44 minutes but no one else stayed long until Tikolo showed he could just about cope at this level. His 29 from 50 balls, with three fours and one six, offered some hope. However, he gave a catch to Adams, the West Indian part-time wicketkeeper, to become the fifth wicket to fall with the score on only 77.

Suji departed to the spin of Harper on the fourth ball he received, after which Modi and Odoyo added 44 in Kenya's best partnership of the match. The rate of scoring was too slow, however, Modi taking 74 balls to make 26 and Odoyo 59 balls to score 24. Karim and Rajab Ali managed 11 runs between them for the last wicket but the total of 166 was hardly expected to give the opposition problems.

The only fault that could be found against the West Indies was that they contributed 37 extras, which exceeded anything that any Kenyan batsman made. Their bowlers needed more discipline and should not have been responsible for 13 no-balls and 14 wides.

The West Indians made 18 for the first wicket before Richardson lost his leg stump to Rajab Ali, who managed to get the ball to move in the air and off the pitch. Four runs later, fellow opener Campbell moved across the wicket to a ball from Suji and was bowled behind his pads, meaning Lara and Chanderpaul were at the crease. After only 11 runs had been added, Lara, without moving his feet, waved his bat at a ball outside the off stump, got an outside edge and Tariq Iqbal took the catch behind the stumps. Not only was it a surprise that Lara was dismissed so quickly, it was also unexpected since, although the ball wobbled in his gloves, Iqbal actually held the catch. Up to that point, he had looked no better than an average keeper on the village green.

When Arthurton attempted a short single which was never on and was easily run out, the West Indies did not seem to be taking their task seriously. Maurice Odumbe produced a competent spell of off spin, although he was rather fortunate with his first wicket, that of Chanderpaul, who cut a loose ball straight to Tikolo at point. This effectively ended the West Indian resistance. Chanderpaul's 19, made off 48 balls, turned out to be his team's top score.

With the exception of Bishop, who remained not out with six from 42 balls, their batsmen just continued in a cavalier manner, hoping that if contact between bat and ball was made the runs would come. What came instead were catches. Adams gave a straightforward chance to Modi and Harper fell to an excellent catch by Tariq Iqbal, whose wicketkeeping had been transformed.

Walsh was given out caught by Chudasama although some people questioned the legitimacy of the dismissal; there was some doubt as to whether the ball actually hit Walsh's bat. Ambrose fell to another foolish run-out, then Rajab Ali returned to the attack to bowl Cuffy and bring a dismal display to an end as the West Indies were dismissed for 93 in only 35.2 overs, with neither side managing to complete a full 50-over innings.

Not surprisingly, the Kenyans were delighted; it was the highlight of their cricketing history to date. For the West Indies, it was like a bad dream. The match was over. Once it was clear that an upset was possible, the local crowd wholeheartedly supported the Kenyans and cheered every wicket that fell. The Kenyans showed their appreciation by completing a lap of honour.

KENYA v WEST INDIES

One-Day International – List A – 50 overs

Wills World Cup – First Round Group A

Nehru Stadium, Pune, 29 February 1996

Kenya won by 73 runs

KENYA		R	B	M	4s	6s
D.N.Chudasama	c Lara b Walsh	8	7	8	2	-
+Tariq Iqbal	c Cuffy b Walsh	16	32	44	2	-
K.O.Otieno	c Adams b Walsh	2	5	7	-	-
S.O.Tikolo	c Adams b Harper	29	50	85	3	1
*M.O.Odumbe	ht wkt b Bishop	6	30	48	-	-
H.S.Modi	c Adams b Ambrose	26	74	111	1	-
M.A.Suji	c Lara b Harper	0	4	8	-	-
T.M.Odoyo	st Adams b Harper	24	59	61	3	-
E.O.Odumbe	b Cuffy	1	4	2	-	-
A.Y.Karim	c Adams b Ambrose	11	27	43	1	-
Rajab Ali	not out	6	19	16	-	-
	lb10 nb13 w14	37				
	(49.3 overs)	**166**				

WEST INDIES		R	B	M	4s	6s
S.L.Campbell	b Suji	4	12	19	1	-
*R.B.Richardson	b Rajab Ali	5	11	15	1	-
B.C.Lara	c Tariq Iqbal b Rajab Ali	8	11	19	1	-
S.Chanderpaul	c Tikolo b M.O.Odumbe	19	48	72	3	-
K.L.T.Arthurton	run out	0	6	8	-	-
+J.C.Adams	c Modi b M.O.Odumbe	9	37	57	1	-
R.A.Harper	c Tariq Iqbal b M.O.Odumbe	17	18	26	3	-
I.R.Bishop	not out	6	42	55	-	-
C.E.L.Ambrose	run out	3	13	13	-	-
C.A.Walsh	c Chudasama b Karim	4	8	15	1	-
C.E.Cuffy	b Rajab Ali	1	8	8	-	-
	b5 lb6 nb2 w4	17				
	(35.2 overs)	**93**				

West Indies	O	M	R	W	nb	w
Ambrose	8.3	1	21	2	-	5
Walsh	9	0	46	3	6	3
Bishop	10	2	30	1	2	1
Cuffy	8	0	31	1	7	5
Harper	10	4	15	3	-	-
Arthurton	4	0	13	0	-	-

Kenya	O	M	R	W	nb	w
Suji	7	2	16	1		
Rajab Ali	7.2	2	17	3		
Karim	8	1	19	1		
M.O.Odumbe	10	3	15	3		
Odoyo	3	0	15	0		

fow	Ken	WI
1	15 (1)	18 (2)
2	19 (3)	22 (1)
3	45 (2)	33 (3)
4	72 (5)	35 (5)
5	77 (4)	55 (4)
6	81 (7)	65 (6)
7	125 (8)	78 (7)
8	126 (9)	81 (9)
9	155 (6)	89 (10)
10	166 (10)	93 (11)

Umpires: Khizer Hayat (Pakistan) and V.K.Ramaswamy (India)

TV umpire: S.K.Bansal (India). Referee: M.A.K.Pataudi (India)

Toss: West Indies

Player of the Match: M.O.Odumbe (Kenya)

Rajab Ali is also known as R.W.Ali

Kenya confused by Duckworth-Lewis

Kenya were at their peak in the mid-1990s and it was no surprise, therefore, when they made the final of the ICC Trophy in 1997. Their opponents were Bangladesh, who had never got that far in any previous competition. The match was staged at the upgraded ground of the Kilat Club, in Kuala Lumpur, which had become the Tenaga Nasional Sports Kompleks and the leading cricketing venue in the country. Since then, Malaysia has developed even better facilities at the Bayuemas Oval and, more recently, the Kinrara Oval.

Heavy overnight rain delayed the start. The umpires inspected the ground at 11.45am, and predicted that the outfield would be dry enough for play to commence at 1.45pm. With light becoming a problem soon after 5pm, the decision was made to play only one innings and use the reserve day to finish the match.

Akram Khan won the toss and decided to field. The decision looked justified as Saiful Islam removed Karim, somewhat surprisingly chosen to open the innings, and Otieno, with only 15 runs scored. A rather tedious period followed and it must have been as much relief to Kenya as to Bangladesh when Gupta gave a caught-and-bowled opportunity to Khalid Mahmud. If Gupta had stayed and maintained his scoring rate of 16 runs off 48 balls, Kenya would have got nowhere near a competitive total.

With their two best batsmen together, however, the impetus quickly changed. Steve Tikolo was at his most aggressive and a partnership of 138 ensued, with Odumbe content to play the supporting role. Their effort quietened the crowd, a large proportion of which were highly vocal Bangladeshis, mostly migrant workers employed in the construction industry. Akram Khan resorted to eight bowlers but with little success. When the innings closed at 241/7 the stage was set for a great final day.

Persistent rain during the morning prevented the match from resuming on time. It was 2.30pm before the umpires could even consider an inspection. The outfield dried quickly, however, and play was able to begin at 3.30pm.

With insufficient time to bowl 50 overs, the Duckworth-Lewis method applied and Bangladesh were set a target of 166 runs in 25 overs. While none of the Bangladeshi batsmen played a convincing innings they all scored at around a run a ball or better. With a need for quick runs, Mohammad Rafique opened the batting instead of Athar Ali Khan, who, in the end, did not bat at all. Kenya responded by using the off breaks of Tikolo rather than another pace bowler to accompany Martin Suji. He was not successful but it was the spin of Karim that accounted for Bangladesh's middle order.

With 11 runs needed from the last over, bowled by Martin Suji, Kenya remained favourites, but the odds altered slightly when Khaled Mashud hit the first ball for six. Four more runs were scrambled in singles as Kenya's fielding disintegrated under pressure. With one ball to go, few people could understand what happened next. Odumbe moved his fielders into positions to save two runs, apparently believing that 166 was equivalent to a revised Kenyan total and that Bangladesh needed to score 167 to win. It was early days of using the Duckworth-Lewis method and Odumbe was certainly not the last captain to misunderstand how the system works.

Hasibul Hossain flung his bat at the last delivery and missed, but the ball hit his pads and Khaled Mashud quickly called him for a leg bye. The run was barely on but in the confusion, Kenya's fielders missed the run-out and Bangladesh were victorious by two wickets, much to the joy of the crowd which was estimated to include some 4,000 Bangladeshi supporters.

It was the first time Bangladesh had won an international competition. The following day, the team were met at Dhaka International Airport by the Prime Minister who gave them breakfast at her official residence and then an official reception in the capital, held before large crowds on Manik Mia Avenue.

BANGLADESH v KENYA

50 overs

ICC Trophy – Final

Tenaga Nasional Sports Kompleks, Kuala Lumpur, 12 and 13 April 1997

Bangladesh won by two wickets (Duckworth-Lewis method)

KENYA

		R	B	M	4s	6s
A.Y.Karim	b Saiful Islam	0	5	·	-	-
S.K.Gupta	c&b Khaled Mahmud	16	48		1	-
+K.O.Otieno	lbw b Saiful Islam	2	15		-	-
S.O.Tikolo	c Saiful Islam b Khaled Mahmud	147	152		12	3
*M.O.Odumbe	st Khaled Mashud b M'mad Rafique	43	63		3	-
T.M.Odoyo	b Mohammad Rafique	1	7		-	-
H.S.Modi	not out	12	8		1	-
A.O.Suji	st Khaled Mashud b M'mad Rafique	1	2		-	-
L.O.Tikolo						
M.A.Suji						
B.J.Patel						
	b1 lb9 w9	19				
	(7 wickets, 50 overs)	**241**				

BANGLADESH

		R	B	M	4s	6s
Naimur Rahman	b M.A.Suji	0	1		-	-
Mohammad Rafique	c Odumbe b A.O.Suji	26	15		2	2
Minhajul Abedin	c Patel b Odoyo	26	33		2	-
Aminul Islam	b Karim	37	37		1	1
*Akram Khan	c Odoyo b Odumbe	22	27		1	1
Enamul Hoque	c Gupta b Karim	5	7		-	-
Saiful Islam	c Odumbe b Karim	14	13		-	-
+Khaled Mashud	not out	15	7		-	2
Khaled Mahmud	st Otieno b Odumbe	5	5		1	-
Hasibul Hossain	not out	4	5		-	-
Athar Ali Khan						
	b3 lb4 w5	12				
	(8 wickets, 25 overs)	**166**				

Bangladesh	O	M	R	W	nb	wd
Saiful Islam	9	0	39	2	-	3
Hasibul Hossain	6	0	15	0	-	4
Athar Ali Khan	5	0	22	0	-	-
Khaled Mahmud	7	1	31	2	-	1
Enamul Hoque	10	0	41	0	-	-
Naimur Rahman	4	0	21	0	-	-
Moh'd Rafique	6	1	40	3	-	1
Akram Khan	3	0	22	0	-	-

fow	Ken	Ban
1	0 (1)	0 (1)
2	15 (3)	50 (2)
3	58 (2)	63 (3)
4	196 (5)	116 (4)
5	212 (6)	118 (5)
6	230 (4)	123 (6)
7	241 (8)	139 (7)
8		151 (9)
9		
10		

Kenya	O	M	R	W	nb	wd
M.A.Suji	4	0	28	1	-	1
S.O.Tikolo	4	0	29	0	-	2
Odoyo	5	0	27	1	-	-
A.O.Suji	5	0	26	1	-	2
Karim	4	0	31	3	-	-
Odumbe	3	0	18	2	-	-

Umpires: D.B.Hair (Australia) and S.Venkataraghavan (India)

TV umpire: N.T.Plews (England). Referee: J.R.Reid (New Zealand)

Toss: Bangladesh

Player of the Match: S.O.Tikolo (Kenya)

Close of play: 1st day – Kenya 241-7 (innings closed). Bangladesh were set a target of 166 runs in 25 overs.

France win by a 'head' bye

The 1990s saw the extension of international cricket in Europe beyond the well-established countries of Ireland, Scotland, The Netherlands and Denmark. The European Cricket Federation was founded in 1989 to promote cricket, but progress was initially slow and it was not until 1993 that the Federation started organising tournaments. In the 1997 competition, Germany, who had won in 1995, met France, winners in 1993 and 1996, in the final at the Lyceum Alpinum, in the small village of Zuoz, in the Engadine, Switzerland.

France batted first but both sides struggled with the conditions. Whether it was the altitude, at 1,750m, or the uneven ground, the German bowlers were unable to maintain a consistent line and length. They bowled 33 wides, ten no-balls, and gave away 11 byes. With the ball as often wide of the wicket as on the stumps the batsmen found it difficult to connect and scoring runs was hard.

Palmer and Ash opened with a partnership of 61 but a high proportion of these were extras and when Ash was the first to be dismissed, he had made a mere six runs. Nevertheless, all of the French middle order contributed and the score rose through partnerships of 50, 28, 44 and 52 respectively. Germany looked to be regaining some control when the sixth and seventh wickets fell within two runs, but Shabbir Hussain helped add 25 for the eighth wicket, taking France towards what was promising to be a more than competitive total.

Germany's opening bowler, Saeed, returned to the attack and removed Edwards and Valentin Brumant. With two balls of the innings to go he produced a bouncer which struck Bordes on the head. Unfortunately, because he had only a maximum of two balls to face, he had not bothered to wear a helmet. He courageously responded to his partner's call and ran through for what counted as a leg bye before collapsing at the non-striker's end. He was forced to retire hurt and taken to hospital, where a fractured skull was diagnosed.

The French bowling proved no more accurate than Germany's. Their bowlers contributed fewer wides, 26 as against 33, but they produced far more no-balls, 22 compared to ten. Rathore and Shamsuddin Khan batted confidently, putting on 90 for the first wicket but Germany then lost five wickets for the addition of only 28 runs. This was an all-round effort by the French with the wickets being shared by three bowlers and a run-out.

With France clearly on top, Younis Khan and Dar managed the perfect rescue act with a partnership of 89. Saeed then protected the lower order effectively, so that, despite the loss of wickets, Germany drew ever nearer to the target. With every wicket to fall, the French looked closer to victory, but the next partnership put on just sufficient runs to return the initiative to Germany.

With increasing tension on the field and much excitement off it, Hewitt, France's captain, entrusted himself with the final over. He looked to have made the right decision as, with two balls left, Germany still needed eight runs. Saeed, however, had retained the strike, and he sliced the first of these high in the air towards third man, where the fielder, on the boundary, fumbled it and it went over the rope for six.

Only two runs were then required with one delivery left. Again Saeed hit the ball hard and high and the Germans completed the runs required, only to see the ball land safely in the hands of Valentin Brumant at mid-on, and France were the winners by one run, the all-important and now legendary 'head' bye off the last ball of their innings.

Bordes was in hospital for two weeks and took several months to recover but he was able to resume indoor cricket before Christmas that year. In a match in which 23 per cent of the runs were extras, no batsman reached fifty and no bowler took more than three wickets, Shabbir Hussain impressed with a sound display of wicketkeeping.

FRANCE v GERMANY

50 overs

European Cricket Federation Nations Cup – Final

Lyceum Alpinum, Zuoz, 23 August 1997

France won by one run

FRANCE

FRANCE		R	B	M	4s	6s
S.Palmer	b Rathore	35				
O.Ash	c A.S.Bhatti b Younis Khan	6				
N.Jones	c Shamsuddin Khan b Younis Khan	22				
J.Howe	c Ellerbeck b Patzwald	21				
G.L.Brumant	c A.S.Bhatti b A.H.Bhatti	42				
G.B.James	run out	24				
*S.M.Hewitt	c A.S.Bhatti b Saeed	31				
+Shabbir Hussain	not out	10				
G.Edwards	c A.H.Bhatti b Saeed	8				
V.Brumant	b Saeed	0				
D.L.Bordes	retired hurt	1				
	b11 lb13 nb10 w33	67				
	(49.5 overs)	**267**				

GERMANY

GERMANY		R	B	M	4s	6s
T.Rathore	b G.L.Brumant	32				
Shamsuddin Khan	c Shabbir Hussain b Hewitt	45				
A.S.Bhatti	c James b Howe	8				
*A.H.Bhatti	c Shabbir Hussain b Howe	6				
Younis Khan	c V.Brumant b James	44				
J.Mirza	run out	0				
A.Dar	b Hewitt	45				
Saeed	c V.Brumant b Hewitt	22				
V.Ellerbeck	c Hewitt b V.Brumant	0				
B.Patzwald	st Shabbir Hussain b G.L.Brumant	6				
C.Musfeldt	not out	0				
	b2 lb8 nb22 w26	58				
	(50 overs)	**266**				

Germany	O	M	R	W	nb	w		fow	Fr	Ger
A.H.Bhatti	10	2	42	0				1	61	90
Saeed	9.5	1	61	3				2	62	93
Ellerbeck	3	0	21	0				3	112	108
Younis Khan	10	2	30	2				4	140	118
Rathore	10	0	33	1				5	184	118
A.S.Bhatti	5	0	34	1				6	236	207
Patzwald	2	0	22	1				7	238	241
								8	263	248
France	O	M	R	W	nb	w		9	263	260
Palmer	4	0	30	0				10		266
Jones	8	0	49	0						
Hewitt	10	0	44	3						
V.Brumant	10	0	68	1						
G.L.Brumant	10	5	16	2						
Howe	6	1	37	2						
James	1	0	6	1						
Edwards	1	0	6	0						

Umpires: N.Bahado and P.Guest

Toss: not known.

Danish women's disappearing act

Although not appreciated at the time, the contest between the Danish and the Dutch women in the European Championships on 21 July 1999 proved to be the last match played by Denmark's women's team in 50-over internationals. The Danish women made their international debut in 1983, when they competed in the Dutch Women's Centenary Tournament. Between then and 1999 they took part in two World Cups and four European Championships.

In 1999 they hosted the European competition for the second time, when matches were played at the Nykøbing Mors Cricket Stadium. The fixture against the Dutch was effectively a play-off for third place behind Ireland and an England A squad. It was the 12th time the sides had met in one-day internationals, the record of previous encounters standing at eight wins for The Netherlands to three for the Danes.

On paper the Dutch side was the more experienced, their captain, Pauline te Beest, being recognised as one of Europe's leading women's players. Both sides fielded sisters, Helmien and Caroline Rambaldo for the Dutch and Susanne and Inger Nielsen for the Danes.

Having won the toss the Dutch batted first and, typical of women's matches between Associate countries at the time, gave a very tedious display. Only three players and the extras got into double figures with te Beest and Verheul top-scoring with 17 each. The Danish bowlers were flattered by their analyses, as, on the matting pitch, the Dutch concentrated on survival rather than run-scoring. Gregersen had the best return with four wickets while conceding only six runs in her ten overs, five of which were maidens. The total of 88 from 40 overs and three balls was hardly scintillating cricket, perhaps explaining why hardly anyone came to watch.

The Danes began disastrously in reply, losing four wickets for 17, including their best player Jønsson, who was dismissed without scoring. Mikkelsen came closest to mastering the conditions and Vibeke Nielsen and Susanne Nielsen, in turn, provided stubborn support, though not contributing much in the way of runs. Partnerships of 37, the highest of the match, and 17, not only led a recovery, but placed the home side within sight of victory. They were aided by the waywardness of the Dutch bowling, which produced 13 wides, as well as being largely responsible for the ten byes from balls well outside the wicketkeeper's reach.

When Kottman dismissed Mikkelsen the Dutch were still in with a chance, but aided by further extras, Susanne Nielsen, Eva Christensen and Inger Nielsen managed to scrape together the runs required to give the Danes a victory by three wickets. Reynolds was the most successful bowler with three wickets from her ten overs, half of which were maidens, as she conceded only nine runs.

Within a couple of years, most of the women who had served Denmark so well for a decade retired. The failure of the Dansk Cricket Forbund to invest in women's cricket at junior level, largely a result of lack of finance and the decision to use what limited monies were available to concentrate on men's cricket, meant that no new players were available. Not only was Denmark unable to raise an international team, the game also died out at club level.

The Danish experience shows how fragile women's cricket can be in countries where there are only a few active cricketers and little effort is made to encourage girls in the following generations to develop an interest in the game. Fortunately, after just over a decade, an attempt was made at revival and Denmark's women reappeared in a T20 tournament in 2013.

DENMARK WOMEN v NETHERLANDS WOMEN

50 overs

European Championships

Nykøbing Mors Cricket Stadium, Nykøbing Mors, 21 July 1999

Denmark won by three wickets

NETHERLANDS		R	B	M	4s	6s
M.A.Köster	lbw b I.Nielsen	11				
H.W.Rambaldo	c S.Nielsen b Gregersen	8				
*+P.J.te Beest	lbw b Vilsgaard	17				
J.Howard	lbw b Gregersen	9				
C.A.Salomons	b Gregersen	0				
D.Kooij	c Slebsager b Gregersen	3				
C.M.S.Verheul	c V.G.Nielsen b S.Nielsen	17				
C.H.Rambaldo	c Jønsson b S.Nielsen	2				
C.F.F.Oudolf	c Frost b Jønsson	0				
S.Kottman	not out	2				
E.I.Reynolds	b S.Nielsen	2				
	b6 lb1 nb1 w9	17				
	(40.3 overs)	**88**				

DENMARK		R	B	M	4s	6s
M.Frost	c Verheul b Reynolds	5				
+D.T.Christensen	lbw b Oudolf	0				
M.Gregersen	b Salomons	5				
*J.Jønsson	c Salomons b Kottman	0				
V.G.Nielsen	c H.W.Rambaldo b Reynolds	6				
K.Mikkelsen	c Salomons b Kottman	36				
S.Nielsen	lbw b Reynolds	3				
E.Christensen	not out	2				
I.Nielsen	not out	1				
L.Vilsgaard						
M.Slebsager						
	b10 lb2 nb7 w13	32				
	(7 wickets, 41.3 overs)	**90**				

Denmark	O	M	R	W	nb	w
I.Nielsen	8	2	20	1		
Vilsgaard	9	0	28	1		
Gregersen	10	5	6	4		
Jønsson	10	2	21	1		
S.Nielsen	2.3	1	5	3		
Frost	1	0	1	0		

Netherlands	O	M	R	W	nb	w
Oudolf	10	4	25	1		
Reynolds	10	5	9	3		
Salomons	10	2	18	1		
Kottman	10	3	14	2		
C.H.Rambaldo	1.3	0	12	0		

fow	Neth	Den
1	22 (1)	8 (1)
2	43 (3)	9 (2)
3	55 (2)	17 (3)
4	55 (5)	17 (4)
5	56 (4)	54 (5)
6	80 (6)	71 (6)
7	81 (7)	82 (7)
8	84 (9)	
9	84 (8)	
10	88 (11)	

Umpires: [unknown]

Toss: Netherlands

Suppiah's debut hat-trick

For the 40th Saudara Cup match between Malaysia and Singapore, which took place on the Royal Selangor Club Padang, Kuala Lumpur, in August 1999, both countries gave debuts to young spin bowlers.

Singapore introduced Mainuddin Shabbir, a 16-year-old leg-spinner, and Malaysia selected Arul Suppiah, the younger brother of their off-spinner Rahul Suppiah. Arul, who bowled slow left-arm, was still 15, his 16th birthday being the day after the match was due to finish.

Selvaratnam won the toss for Malaysia and, on a true pitch, opted to bat. A slow start was made against the new ball but in sunny, warm conditions, there was little help for the pace bowlers and Lyles and Thambinayagam were soon replaced by the spinners. Mani and Suresh were economical but hardly penetrative.

Sharani Ahmed settled in and he and Ramadas increased the scoring rate in a third-wicket partnership of 82, aided by Shroff, Singapore's captain, having to give his main bowlers a rest. On their return to the attack the spinners removed both batsmen. Sharani batted particularly well for his 84, displaying many attractive forcing strokes.

With the first innings restricted to 75 overs per side the race was on to achieve as high a total as possible. Risks were taken and two batsmen were run out before the innings closed on 269/9.

In reply, Singapore seemed uncertain whether to defend to the close of play or to score as many runs as possible. The uncertainty level increased when Kapoor was caught behind with only six runs on the board. Shroff never settled and soon fell victim to the off spin of Rahul Suppiah. With the score on 56, Vijay gave a catch to cover point where it was well taken by Sharani. Four more runs were added before the close. Although the initiative was clearly with the home side, Seth had looked untroubled, giving hope for Singapore the following day.

Despite Seth continuing to bat well, Singapore struggled against the spin of Rahul Suppiah and Chew Pok Cheong. Once Prasad was unnecessarily run out, only Suresh and Puri gave any resistance. Singapore failed to bat through their 75 overs, finishing seven short, and were dismissed for 131 when Lyles became another player to prove a poor judge of a run. Rahul Suppiah finished with 4-50 from 22 overs.

With a first-innings lead of 138 Malaysia went for quick runs, with a declaration in mind early on the third day. They lost two quick wickets, Madhavan leg-before to Lyles and Sharani bowled by Suresh. Their intentions were then thwarted when rain ended play two hours early.

Malaysia batted for 100 minutes on the third day before declaring and setting the visitors a target of 281. They batted steadily to reach 58/1 before panic set in against the combined spin of the Suppiah brothers. Six wickets fell for the addition of only 17 runs, three of them, Mani, Suresh and Thambinayagam, in successive balls to give Arul Suppiah the first and, to date, only hat-trick in Saudara Cup matches.

Singapore's only hope was to play for a draw but with the ninth wicket going down on 93, victory for Malaysia seemed assured. Puri and Mainuddin Shabbir, however, had other ideas. In a superb tail-end partnership they frustrated Malaysia for 64 minutes and added 71 runs. Their valiant effort ended when Puri misjudged the turn of a ball from Arul Suppiah and Retinam held on to the catch behind the stumps. Malaysia were relieved to gain the victory for which, despite the margin being 116 runs, they had to work hard. Arul Suppiah finished with the analysis of 21.3-6-48-6 and it looked as though there was a top-class Malaysian cricketer in the making. Unfortunately for his country he played for them only nine more times, deciding to focus instead on a career as a first-class cricketer with Somerset.

MALAYSIA v SINGAPORE
Saudara Cup
Royal Selangor Club Padang, Kuala Lumpur, 27, 28 and 29 August 1999
Malaysia won by 116 runs

MALAYSIA

		R	B	M	4s	6s		R	B	M	4s	6s
N.Durairatnam	c Puri b Mani	28					run out	22				
R.Madhavan	c Puri b Thambinayagam	12					lbw b Lyles	10				
Sharani Ahmed	b Suresh	84					b Suresh	1				
K.Ramadas	b Suresh	43					c Puri b Lyles	11				
*R.M.Selvaratnam	c Lyles b Mainuddin Shabbir	27					(7) not out	33				
M.A.Muniandy	run out	12					(5) c Kapoor b Lyles	0				
A.V.Suppiah	b Mani	18					(6) b Mani	24				
+S.Retinam	run out	10					(9) not out	21				
R.V.Suppiah	not out	11					(8) b Suresh	2				
V.Ramadass	c Puri b Mani	2										
Chew Pok Cheong	not out	0										
	b4 lb9 nb5 w4	22					b6 lb4 nb3 w5	18				
	(9 wickets, 75 overs)	**269**					(7 wickets declared)	**142**				

SINGAPORE

		R	B	M	4s	6s		R	B	M	4s	6s
A.V.Vijay	c Sharani Ahmed b Ch Pk C'g	27					run out	16				
R.Kapoor	c Retinam b Ramadass	3					c Ramadas b Ch Pk Cheong	19				
*Z.A.Shroff	b R.V.Suppiah	10					c Retinam b A.V.Suppiah	24				
S.Seth	c Retinam b R.V.Suppiah	33					b R.V.Suppiah	0				
S.S.Prasad	run out	13					c&b A.V.Suppiah	7				
S.Mani	b R.V.Suppiah	6					c Muniandy b A.V.Suppiah	5				
R.C.Thambinayagam	c Durairatnam b R.V.Suppiah	0					(8) lbw b A.V.Suppiah	0				
K.R.Suresh	lbw b Madhavan	14					(7) c Ramadas b A.V.Suppiah	0				
+S.Puri	c Ramadas b Chew Pok Cheong	14					c Retinam b A.V.Suppiah	59				
M.Lyles	run out	0					run out	0				
Mainuddin Shabbir	not out	0					not out	15				
	b4 lb1 nb3 w3	11					b7 lb2 nb8 w2	19				
	(68 overs)	**131**						**164**				

Singapore	O	M	R	W	nb	w		O	M	R	W	nb	w
Lyles	5	1	7	0			(2)	11	2	56	3		
Thambinayagam	5	1	14	1									
Suresh	16	2	69	2			(1)	17	3	46	2		
Seth	9	3	19	0									
Mani	23	2	78	3			(3)	10	1	30	1		
Prasad	7	1	26	0									
Mainuddin Shabbir	7	0	28	1									
Kapoor	3	0	15	0									

fow	Mal (1)	Sin (1)	Mal (2)	Sin (2)
1	16	6	23	31
2	87	28	26	58
3	169	56	41	65
4	192	84	45	67
5	212	93	73	75
6	244	95	68	75
7	247	101	101	75
8	260	126		88
9	268	131		93
10		131		164

Malaysia	O	M	R	W	nb	w		O	M	R	W	nb	w
Muniandy	8	1	15	0				9	5	9	0		
Ramadass	6	3	17	1				5	0	25	0		
R.V.Suppiah	22	2	50	4			(4)	18	4	45	1		
A.V.Suppiah	18	3	31	0			(3)	21.3	6	48	6		
Chew Pok Cheong	11	7	10	2				10	3	28	1		
Madhavan	3	1	3	1									

Umpires: [unknown]

Toss: Malaysia

Close of play: 1st day – Singapore (1) 60-3 (Seth 15*, Prasad 1*); 2nd day – Malaysia (2) 37-2.

In Singapore's second innings A.V.Suppiah completed a hat-trick when dismissing S.Mani, K.R.Suresh and R.C.Thambinayagam.

The first innings of each side was restricted to 75 overs.

R.C.Thambinayagam is also known as R.T.Chandran.

8

The struggle for multi-innings cricket

THE 1990s were marked by an increase in the number of one-day internationals played by the Associate and Affiliate countries. With matches confined to one day rather than the two or three days required for two-innings contests, the players were able to take part in more of them, while devoting the same number of days to cricket each year or each season. Matches could be played on Saturdays and Sundays whereas, to fulfil a three-day fixture the players would need to take time away from work for either a Friday or a Monday as well.

The introduction of one-day competitions in the domestic calendars of the Full Member countries meant that there was less room for matches between, for example, the English counties and Scotland or Ireland. The period leading into the 2000s also saw the demise of the short tours by English county sides to South America, East Africa and south-east Asia. Their players no longer had the time and, with more matches to play, there was little room in the calendars of the Associates and Affiliates to host them.

By the mid-1990s the only multi-innings cricket left in Associate countries on a regular basis was the annual contest between Scotland and Ireland, and the Saudara Cup match between Malaysia and Singapore. The East African Quadrangulars, involving Kenya, Uganda, Tanzania and Zambia, stopped in 1980. Two-innings fixtures between Denmark and The Netherlands ended in 1981. The Interport matches involving Hong Kong, Malaysia and Singapore ceased in 1987 and the contest between Canada and the United States for the K.A. Auty Trophy, which was revived in 1963, stopped in 1995 and was not played again until 2011.

The situation was even worse for women cricketers. The admission of Ireland and The Netherlands to the International Women's Cricket Council gave them Test-match status, but it coincided with a decline in the number of women's Test matches played. Thus, when the Irish women met Pakistan at College Park, Dublin, in July 2000 to play their first Test match, they found, as history unfolded, that it was also to be their last.

There is a penalty to be paid if multi-innings cricket is lost entirely. Players in Associate and Affiliate countries would no longer be exposed to the need to build an innings over time, bowl a consistent line and length for long periods, and adapt to the demands for changes in tactics between attacking and defensive play as a match evolves over several days. In response to these concerns, the ICC established the Intercontinental Cup, a multi-innings competition for the top Associates and Affiliates. It gave recognition to the tournament's importance by awarding it first-class status.

Despite its success, enthusiasm for multi-innings cricket is far from universal among the Associates and Affiliates. Countries are often forced to field weakened sides because their top players, with commitments to English first-class counties or Australian state sides, do not make themselves available. It is these professional cricketers who decide when and if they are prepared to represent their country, whereas the amateurs are still generally happy to do so, taking holidays if they cannot negotiate leave from work.

In contrast, the professionals are frequently, though not always, available for their country's one-day and T20 matches, particularly where they are in qualifying tournaments for the respective World Cups. Participation at the top level in these competitions seems to have a far higher priority than multi-innings cricket, a situation that is reinforced by the ICC which states that professional cricketers must be released to play for their country in these tournaments, but not for the Intercontinental Cup. As long as this attitude prevails, multi-innings cricket will continue to struggle for existence.

Ireland unbeaten

Ireland were perhaps fortunate to meet Pakistan when women's cricket in that country was in its infancy. It had developed largely as a result of initiatives taken by Shaiza and Sharmeen Khan, sisters who both played in the match in Dublin. They had been introduced to cricket by their brothers in Karachi, developed their skills further at boarding school and university in England, and had founded the Pakistan Women's Cricket Control Association which was recognised by the ICC. Sponsorship was provided by the United Carpets Group of Companies, run by their father.

In the mid-1990s some women cricketers in the Punjab, unhappy with the control exerted from Karachi and the role played by the so-called 'super-rich sisters', established a rival organisation. With two bodies disputing who should run women's cricket in Pakistan, it was not surprising that the country was unable to field its strongest side.

In warm, moist conditions on 30 July 2000, following overnight rain, Pakistan's captain Shaiza Khan probably made an error in choosing to bat after winning the toss. Her team were quickly in trouble, losing four wickets for ten runs, with McDonald taking the first three to fall.

Saibh Young bowled well at the other end but without reward and conceded only one run in her ten overs. Pakistan struggled on for 47.4 overs, spread across four and three quarter hours, and were only able to realise 53 runs for their effort with only two players reaching double figures.

Metcalfe finished with 4-26 but all the bowlers were economical as Pakistan's women proved unable to hit the ball off the square. Twenty-five of the 47 overs completed were maidens.

Ireland lost O'Leary, leg-before without scoring to Sharmeen Khan, but Karen Young and Beggs dominated the proceedings in a second-wicket stand of 112. It was as though they were batting on an entirely different pitch. Pakistan managed to take two more wickets but with a lead of 140 and, perhaps, an eye on the weather forecast, Grealey declared, giving Pakistan a short but awkward period of batting before the close.

The decision was a surprise since the match was scheduled for four days, and, perhaps, reflected a lack of experience with multi-innings cricket. Nevertheless, the result was a success. Pakistan chose to change their batting order, entrusting the responsibility to Deebah Sherazi, the second-highest scorer in the first innings, and Sajida Shah, a 12-year-old. Sajida managed to survive to the close but lost her partner.

Rain prevented any play before lunch on the second day. With the afternoon temperature reaching 23°C, four degrees warmer than the day before, the conditions were again ideal for bowling. The ball was moving both in the air and off the pitch.

Pakistan either lacked any policy or their captain did not know the capabilities of her players because they continued to alter their batting order. Those who came in early found Joyce virtually unplayable. The middle order fell to O'Neill, after which Joyce returned to pick up three more wickets and finish with 6-21 off 11.1 overs, a performance for which she was given the player of the match award.

Pakistan were dismissed for 88, giving Ireland victory by an innings and 54 runs with two days to spare. Overall, it was a highly impressive performance. Ireland scored at a rate of 4.11 runs per over compared to Pakistan's dismal 1.36. Ireland's strike rate was one wicket every 61 balls; Pakistan's was one every 94. If another match was played today, the result is unlikely to be repeated.

Since 2005, when the ICC took over responsibility for women's cricket worldwide, more money has been invested in women's cricket in Full Member countries like Pakistan than in Associate countries. Since and including 2010, Ireland have met Pakistan eight times in one-day and T20 internationals and lost every time. Nevertheless, Ireland remain unbeaten in Test cricket from this, their only, match.

IRELAND WOMEN v PAKISTAN WOMEN

Test Match

College Park, Dublin, 30 and 31 July and 1 and 2 August 2000

Ireland won by an innings and 54 runs

PAKISTAN

		R	B	M	4s	6s		R	B	M	4s	6s
Nazia Nazir	b McDonald	2	32	35			(4) b Joyce	0	3	5		
Zehmurad Afzal	c K.N.Young b Metcalfe	25	134	124			(6) lbw b O'Neill	20	76	54		
Kiran Baluch	lbw b McDonald	0	2	2			(5) c Linehan b Joyce	12	18	13		
*Shaiza Khan	c Shillington b McDonald	2	12	9			(8) b O'Neill	3	19	17		
Sajida Shah	c McDonald b Metcalfe	2	25	28			(2) lbw b Joyce	0	19	18		
Sharmeen Khan	c Joyce b O'Neill	2	12	11			(7) lbw b O'Neill	0	6	7		
Deebah Sherazi	b O'Neill	12	39	51			(1) b McDonald	4	7	8		
Khursheed Jabeen	b O'Neill	2	16	15			(3) b Joyce	13	182	156		
Mahewish Khan	b Metcalfe	0	6	6			(10) b Joyce	7	23	18		
Sadia Butt	b Metcalfe	0	1	1			(9) b Joyce	10	28	23		
+Uzma Gondal	not out	0	3	4			not out	0	13	7		
	b1 lb1 w4	6					b8 lb1 w8	17				
		53						**86**				

IRELAND

		R	B	M	4s	6s
K.N.Young	st Uzma Gondal b Nazia Nazir	58	105	100		
C.M.O'Leary	lbw b Sharmeen Khan	0	10	5		
C.M.Beggs	not out	68	152	128		
*M.E.Grealey	c Shaiza Khan b Nazia Nazir	16	25	23		
+A.M.Linehan	not out	27	28	26		
C.O'Neill						
C.M.A.Shillington						
S.A.Young						
C.J.Metcalfe						
I.M.H.C.Joyce						
B.M.McDonald						
	b17 lb1 w6	24				
	(3 wickets declared)	**193**				

Ireland	O	M	R	W	nb	w	O	M	R	W	nb	w	fow	Pak (1)	Ire (1)	Pak (2)
McDonald	12	6	9	3			14	4	19	1			1	6 (1)	5 (2)	7 (1)
S.A.Young	10	9	1	0		(5)	7	3	10	0			2	6 (3)	117 (1)	8 (2)
O'Neill	13.4	7	15	3			14	7	12	3			3	8 (4)	146 (4)	8 (4)
Metcalfe	12	3	26	4			8	3	16	0			4	10 (5)		22 (5)
Joyce						(2)	11.1	5	21	6			5	21 (6)		56 (6)
													6	50 (7)		58 (7)
Pakistan	O	M	R	W	nb	w							7	50 (2)		62 (8)
Sharmeen Khan	8	1	30	1									8	53 (9)		75 (9)
Mahewish Khan	5	1	10	0									9	53 (10)		77 (3)
Khursheed Jabeen	7	0	24	0									10	53 (8)		86 (10)
Shaiza Khan	9	0	35	0												
Nazia Nazir	11	0	48	2												
Kiran Baluch	7	1	28	0												

Umpires: S.Moore (Ireland) and A.R.Tuffery (Ireland)

Toss: Pakistan

Player of the Match: I.M.H.C.Joyce (Ireland)

Close of play: 1st day – Pakistan (2) 8-1 (Sajida Shah 0*, Khursheed Jabeen 0*). Match finished in two days.

The end of the series

August 2000 witnessed another match that seemingly heralded the demise of multi-innings cricket among Associates and Affiliates. The annual three-day fixture between Scotland and Ireland, played at Ayr, proved to be the last in a series which began in 1888 and was considered first-class since 1909.

McCallan won the toss for Ireland and decided to bat, despite the cool, cloudy conditions. Progress was slow against the pace attack of Brinkley and Asim Butt, right-arm and left-arm respectively. In the eighth over with the score on only 17, Shields struck the ball straight into the hands of short leg and, seven balls later, Haire gave a catch to the wicketkeeper. Dunlop and Joyce took the total to 72/2 at lunch despite two short interruptions for rain.

Scotland continued with their pace attack in the early afternoon and Butt trapped Joyce leg-before to end a partnership of 73. Gillespie was cautious but secure while Dunlop gradually accelerated the scoring rate. He was particularly severe on Tennant when Scotland tried spin, striking him for 16 in one over, including a six. Dunlop reached his century off 141 balls with 14 fours and one six as Scotland failed to take a wicket in the afternoon session.

After tea, play alternated between continued caution and frenetic run-scoring as Ireland seemed uncertain whether to bat to the close or declare and try to get one or two Scottish wickets. Once Dunlop departed for 150, made in 282 minutes of chanceless batting with 20 fours and one six, Patterson played well, but lost partners in an attempt to make runs. McCallan declared at 6.20pm, leaving Scotland to face seven overs before the close. Lockhart was superbly caught by Andy Patterson, diving low to his right, but nightwatchman Smith survived with Bruce Patterson.

On the second morning Scotland adopted the same cautious approach as Ireland had taken on the first day. The score increased to 56 before the nightwatchman's stay ended, Smith falling leg-before to Dwyer. At lunch, the home side were 124/5 after a morning session in which several batsmen made starts, but none was able to counter the inconsistencies in bounce and go on to make a large score. The afternoon was similar, though Wright and Brinkley were more aggressive. Brinkley was the dominant partner in stands with Wright, Maiden, Butt and Tennant.

When the innings closed on 259 to leave the scores tied at the halfway point, 90 minutes remained in the day, during which time 25 overs were bowled. Ireland batted poorly and ended the day on 54/3.

The fine weather continued into the third morning but the Irish batting did not match the conditions, being a mixture of defence and poor choice of shots. Two more wickets were lost before lunch, after which it took Scotland only 19 overs to take the other five. With rain threatening, the players agreed to take tea between the innings, which left Scotland 75 minutes plus 16 overs in the last hour in which to score 122 runs.

Williamson was promoted to open with Patterson and, in ten overs, 60 runs were made. An interruption of 32 minutes for rain had the effect of improving the scoring rate still further, the additional moisture taking some of the bounce out of the pitch, making runs easier to obtain.

Both openers fell to Gillespie's leg spin. Ireland slowed Scotland's progress when Dwyer accounted for Smith and Salmond, the latter falling first ball, but Parsons and Wright struck the final 21 runs required in only three overs, Wright taking Scotland to victory with the second six of the match, a huge hit off Gillespie. Scotland made their runs at just over five per over, but after the dour play earlier in the match, the real excitement was whether this rate would enable them to reach the target before the rain returned.

The win meant that Scotland led the series, as it came to an end, with 20 wins in the 75 first-class matches played to Ireland's 19.

SCOTLAND v IRELAND

First-class

New Cambusdoon Ground, New Alloway, Ayr, 19, 20 and 21 August 2000

Scotland won by six wickets

IRELAND

		R	B	M	4s	6s		R	B	M	4s	6s
I.P.Shields	c Lockhart b Asim Butt	7	20	27	-	-	b Asim Butt	31	102	107	3	-
A.Joyce	lbw b Asim Butt	29	105	131	4	-	c Patterson b Brinkley	2	5	7	-	-
R.S.Haire	c Smith b Asim Butt	0	8	8	-	-	b Brinkley	0	15	13	-	-
A.R.Dunlop	c Brinkley b Tennant	150	230	282	20	1	c Smith b Asim Butt	10	19	35	1	-
M.A.Gillespie	c Brinkley b Maiden	34	97	121	3	-	lbw b Brinkley	22	59	78	4	-
*W.K.McCallan	lbw b Maiden	0	4	6	-	-	b Maiden	17	92	95	-	-
+A.D.Patterson	not out	20	52	79	3	-	c Brinkley b Tennant	10	76	91	-	-
P.J.K.Mooney	run out	2	6	9	-	-	c Lockhart b Tennant	9	19	16	-	-
M.D.Dwyer	b Brinkley	2	9	12	-	-	not out	4	22	30	-	-
G.J.Neely							lbw b Tennant	0	7	8	-	-
A.G.A.M.McCoubrey							b Asim Butt	0	7	13	-	-
	b1 lb9 nb4 w1	15					b3 lb8 nb5	16				
	(8 wickets declared)	259						121				

SCOTLAND

		R	B	M	4s	6s		R	B	M	4s	6s
B.M.W.Patterson	c Patterson b Mooney	31	66	90	6	-	b Gillespie	24	37	60	1	-
D.R.Lockhart	c Patterson b McCoubrey	0	10	13	-	-						
+C.J.O.Smith	lbw b Dwyer	24	49	66	2	-	(4) c Joyce b Dywer	7	15	22	-	-
R.A.Parsons	b Gillespie	20	51	62	3	-	(3) not out	27	35	47	2	-
*G.Salmond	c Joyce b Dwyer	36	82	115	3	-	lbw b Dwyer	0	1	4	-	-
J.G.Williamson	lbw b Gillespie	7	9	5	1	-	(2) b Gillespie	41	45	53	3	-
C.M.Wright	b McCallan	40	122	114	3	-	(6) not out	15	13	12	1	1
J.E.Brinkley	not out	43	132	147	4	-						
G.I.Maiden	b Dwyer	7	37	36	-	-						
Asim Butt	b Neely	10	17	20	1	-						
A.M.Tennant	b Neely	5	12	16	1	-						
	b12 lb15 nb9	36					lb10	10				
		259					(4 wickets)	124				

Scotland	O	M	R	W	nb	w		O	M	R	W	nb	w	fow	Ire (1)	Sco (1)	Ire (2)	Sco (2)
Brinkley	19.5	7	40	1	-	-	(2)	14	6	31	3	-	-	1	17 (1)	8 (2)	2 (2)	67 (2)
Asim Butt	22	6	63	3	-	1	(1)	20.2	8	25	3	-	-	2	17 (3)	56 (3)	4 (3)	70 (1)
Wright	9	2	25	0	1	-	(5)	3	0	6	0	2	-	3	90 (2)	62 (1)	33 (4)	97 (4)
Williamson	9	1	26	0	1	-								4	194 (5)	102 (4)	61 (1)	101 (5)
Tennant	13	5	45	1	-	-	(3)	21	12	20	3	-	-	5	202 (6)	116 (6)	73 (5)	
Maiden	15	1	50	2	2	-	(4)	11	3	28	1	3	-	6	247 (4)	159 (5)	96 (6)	
														7	249 (8)	191 (7)	110 (8)	
Ireland	O	M	R	W	nb	w		O	M	R	W	nb	w	8	259 (9)	216 (9)	115 (7)	
Mooney	6	0	26	1	3	-								9		243 (10)	116 (10)	
McCoubrey	16	2	43	1	4	-	(1)	2	0	16	0	-	-	10	259 (11)	259 (11)	121 (11)	
McCallan	25	6	54	1	-	-	(2)	9	0	39	0	-	-					
Neely	8.2	1	29	2	1	-												
Dwyer	24	7	39	3	-	-	(3)	6	0	25	2	-	-					
Gillespie	17	4	41	2	1	-	(4)	7.2	1	34	2	-	-					

Umpires: J.W.Thallon (Scotland) and D.Walker (Scotland)

Toss: Ireland

Close of play: 1st day – Scotland (1) 24-1 (Patterson 11*, Smith 10*); 2nd day – Ireland (2) 54-3 (Shields 30*, Gillespie 12*)

Devilish Davison

One of the earliest matches in the ICC Intercontinental Cup was between the USA and Canada in May 2004, the first time the two countries had met in a two-innings match since 1995. It was played on a newly-laid turf pitch at the Brian Piccolo Park, in Cooper City, a suburb of Fort Lauderdale, Florida.

Both teams contained players with previous first-class experience. Although born in Canada, John Davison had played most of his cricket in Australia, representing Victoria and South Australia, Ian Billcliff most of his in New Zealand, with Otago, Wellington and Auckland, and Nick de Groot and Sunil Dhaniram had represented Guyana. The USA had Clayton Lambert, who had played Test cricket for the West Indies and three others with first-class experience, Richard Staple for Jamaica, Leon Romero for Trinidad and Tobago and Nasir Javed for Lahore. Of the 22 players, ten hailed from the Caribbean and two each from India, Pakistan and Sri Lanka. With both umpires coming from the West Indies, there was a strong Caribbean feel to the fixture.

Davison won the toss for Canada and elected to bat in hot, sunny conditions. On all three days the temperature rose to as high as 32°C in mid-afternoon. The American opening attack of Howard Johnson and Reid was ineffective and Staple was soon forced to try the spin of Amin and Nasir Javed. Canada reached 57 before the first wicket fell, Chumney giving a catch to Howard Johnson, but they suffered a blow, when, with the score on 66, Davison was forced to retire with a stomach upset. The Americans then took four wickets while Canada added only 40 runs, the visitors finding the spinning ball difficult to master. Fortunately for Canada, Davison was able to return and he and Dhillon put on 88 for the sixth wicket.

The Americans tried seven bowlers before Dhillon hit Lambert into the hands of Aijaz Ali. Nasir Javed then removed the tail. Though lower than perhaps hoped for, the Canadian total of 221 proved competitive as America's batsmen were equally inept at playing spin bowling. Davison took six wickets as the USA struggled to 110/8 at the close.

Davison accounted for the remaining two American wickets on the second morning to finish with 8-61. With a lead of 85 it was expected that Canada would consolidate by batting the rest of the second day and, perhaps, an hour into the third. Instead they tried to score as rapidly as possible but by lunchtime they had lost five wickets for 50 and, by mid-afternoon, were 96/8, a lead of only 181.

Dhaniram showed what should have been done, however, by batting patiently for 161 minutes. With assistance from Hussain and Patel, Canada finally reached 145, enough to set the USA a challenging target of 231 to win. Davison decided to open the bowling with his off breaks and was soon joined by the slow left-arm of Hussain. They picked up a wicket each, but with Mark Johnson and Massiah well set, the home side were 87/2 at the end of the day, and the match was evenly poised.

On the third morning the Americans succumbed feebly to Davison, who took all the remaining wickets, a return of 9-76 for the innings and a match analysis of 36-5-137-17. In terms of the number of wickets, this ranks equal second in first-class cricket to Jim Laker's 19-90 for England against Australia, at Old Trafford, Manchester, in 1956.

Whether the two achievements are anything like equal in merit is a debate that statisticians and cricket enthusiasts will have indefinitely. The American side was undoubtedly of poorer quality than the Australians and Davison was certainly not the equal of Laker as an off-spinner over his career. In four other matches in the Intercontinental Cup, he took only nine more wickets.

UNITED STATES OF AMERICA v CANADA

First-class

ICC Intercontinental Cup – Americas Group

Brian Piccolo Park, Cooper City, Fort Lauderdale FL, 28, 29 and 30 May 2004

Canada won by 194 runs

CANADA

Batsman	Dismissal (1)	R	B	M	4s	6s	Dismissal (2)	R	B	M	4s	6s
D.R.Chumney	c H.R.Johnson b Amin	33	59	73	3	2	c M.R.Johnson b H.R.Johnson	0	6	5	-	-
*J.M.Davison	run out (Reid-Lambert)	84	113		7	3	(7) c H.R.Johnson b Staple	3	8	10	-	-
Z.E.Surkari	c M.R.Johnson b Nasir Javed	1	11	6	-	-	c Blake b Reid	0	4	2	-	-
I.S.Billcliff	c Amin b Nasir Javed	3	15	20	-	-	c Reid b Amin	23	56	64	2	1
+A.Bagai	b Amin	0	7	6	-	-	run out	20	74	92	-	-
N.A.de Groot	c Massiah b Blake	11	43	48	-	-	(2) c M.R.Johnson b Reid	2	24	40	-	-
H.S.Dhillon	c Aijaz Ali b Lambert	69	148		6	2	(6) c M.R.Johnson b Amin	2	17	14	-	-
S.Dhaniram	c H.R.Johnson b Nasir Javed	0	2	3	-	-	not out	65	148	161	4	1
Z.Hussain	lbw b Nasir Javed	0	11	25	-	-	c M.R.Johnson b Lambert	8	45	40	1	-
A.Patel	not out	8	24	15	1	-	c Staple b Nasir Javed	7	50		1	-
E.Sinnathamby	c Blake b Nasir Javed	2	16	18	-	-	lbw b H.R.Johnson	1	9	13	-	-
Extras	b1 lb1 nb6 w2	10					b4 lb1 nb4 p5	14				
Total		**221**						**145**				

USA

Batsman	Dismissal (1)	R	B	M	4s	6s	Dismissal (2)	R	B	M	4s	6s
L.C.Romero	c Billcliff b Davison	33	75	112	2	-	(2) c Bagai b Hussain	14	25	34	-	1
+M.R.Johnson	lbw b Patel	0	1	2	-	-	(1) b Davison	41	70	76	3	2
*R.W.Staple	c Sinnathamby b Davison	30	48	54	4	-	c Surkari b Davison	1	4	2	-	-
S.J.Massiah	c Billcliff b Davison	7	34	36	-	-	c Dhaniram b Davison	37	73	85	1	1
C.A.Reid	c Davison b Dhaniram	4	13	11	-	-	c Dhaniram b Davison	2	15	18	-	-
C.B.Lambert	c Dhillon b Davison	2	3	14	-	-	c Chumney b Davison	11	41	77	-	1
Aijaz Ali	c Hussain b Davison	36	41	48	1	2	c sub (M.Chaudhury) b D'n	4	2	2	1	-
Z.A.Amin	c de Groot b Davison	2	4	3	-	-	c Chumney b Davison	1	7	5	-	-
D.L.Blake	c de Groot b Davison	0	1	1	-	-	c Billcliff b Davison	0	3	1	-	-
Nasir Javed	not out	11	18	36	1	-	c de Groot b Davison	2	9	8	-	-
H.R.Johnson	c Hussain b Davison	2	8	6	-	-	not out	2	17	29	-	-
Extras	b5 nb2 w2	9					b8 lb2 w1	11				
Total		**136**						**126**				

USA	O	M	R	W	nb	w	(ord)	O	M	R	W	nb	w
H.R.Johnson	8	1	25	0	5	-		7.5	2	24	2	3	-
Reid	4	0	22	0	-	-		6	2	10	2	1	-
Amin	20	7	35	2	-	-	(5)	19	7	20	2	-	-
Nasir Javed	23.5	7	78	5	-	1	(3)	13	3	24	1	-	-
Massiah	2	0	11	0	1	-	(6)	3	0	12	0	-	-
Blake	5	1	17	1	-	-	(7)	2	1	4	0	-	-
Lambert	11	0	31	1	-	1	(8)	5	0	9	1	-	-
Staple							(4)	17	4	32	1	-	-

Canada	O	M	R	W	nb	w	(ord)	O	M	R	W	nb	w
Patel	6	1	12	1	-	-							
Sinnathamby	3	0	11	0	1	1	(4)	1	0	7	0	-	-
Hussain	3	0	16	0	-	-	(2)	7	2	15	1	-	1
Davison	14.4	2	61	8	1	1	(1)	21.2	3	76	9	-	-
Dhaniram	14	4	31	1	-	-	(3)	15	6	18	0	-	-

fow	Can (1)	US (1)	Can (2)	US (2)
1	57 (1)	1 (2)	0 (1)	37 (2)
2	67 (3)	43 (3)	1 (3)	38 (3)
3	69 (5)	64 (4)	21 (2)	93 (1)
4	69 (4)	77 (5)	41 (4)	105 (5)
5	106 (6)	83 (1)	45 (6)	107 (4)
6	194 (7)	90 (6)	54 (7)	111 (7)
7	194 (8)	92 (8)	63 (5)	112 (8)
8	209 (9)	92 (9)	96 (9)	112 (9)
9	209 (2)	134 (7)	131 (10)	114 (10)
10	221 (11)	136 (11)	145 (11)	126 (6)

Umpires: B.R.Doctrove (West Indies) and N.A.Malcolm (West Indies)

Referee: J.J.Crowe (New Zealand)

Toss: Canada

Close of play: 1st day – USA (1) 110-8 (Aijaz Ali 24*, Nasir Javed 0*); 2nd day – USA (2) 87-2 (M.R.Johnson 37*, Massiah 25*)

Player of the Match: J.M.Davison (Canada)

In Canada's first innings J.M.Davison (28*) retired ill on 66-1 and resumed on 106-5.

The Emirates excel

After the first year of the Intercontinental Cup, the Asian Cricket Council set up its own multi-innings tournament involving the top five Asian Associates of the time. Initially the venture was called the ACC Fast Track Countries Tournament but after two years, its name was changed to the ACC Premier League. It was then dropped, a reflection that multi-innings cricket was not a priority for the Asian countries.

In its first year the United Arab Emirates and Hong Kong were unbeaten when they met in the last fixture of the competition in February 2005. The match was staged at the Hong Kong Cricket Club ground at Wong Nai Chung Gap, to where they had moved from Chater Road in 1975. The ACC allowed this ground to be used, its requirements for grounds suitable for international cricket being less stringent that those of the ICC, which had ruled that all of Hong Kong's grounds were too small for international multi-innings matches.

Hong Kong and the United Arab Emirates relied heavily on expatriates. Hong Kong had only two players, Roy Lamsam and Sher Lama, who were born in the territory. The remainder of the team comprised six born in Pakistan, two from Australia and one from India. The United Arab Emirates had four locally-born players, three from Dubai and one from Abu Dhabi; the rest of their side were all born in Pakistan.

In sunny and pleasantly warm weather, with temperatures reaching around 20°C in the afternoon and humidity around 70 per cent, conditions were ideal for cricket. Mohammad Tauqeer won the toss and asked the home side to bat first. Ali Asad troubled both openers, who proceeded cautiously to 28, before Tim Smart fell leg-before. Sharma and Lamsam played well and began to dominate the bowling, causing the Emirates' captain to continually change his bowlers. It was somewhat of a surprise when Ali Asad found the outside edge of Sharma's bat to give a catch to the wicketkeeper.

Ilyas Gul and Najeeb Amar gave sufficient support to Lamsam to prevent the innings falling apart. Instead of batting all day, however, Smart, the Hong Kong captain, decided that his bowlers might be better employed in bowling rather than in tail-end batting. He, therefore, declared with seven wickets down and was immediately rewarded. Afzaal Haider proved devastating, taking three of the first four wickets to fall, as the Emirates succumbed to 18/4 in the tenth over. Syed Maqsood, by contrast, seemed oblivious to any problems posed by either the bowlers or the pitch. Once he had reached an impressive hundred the Emirates declared, still 48 runs behind, thereby opening up the game by allowing sufficient time for two further innings.

Hong Kong began poorly, losing two wickets for nine runs. Smart and Tabarak Dar rescued the situation but just as they had placed Hong Kong in a promising position, Tabarak Dar and Gunthorpe were dismissed. Irfan Ahmed batted to the close of the second day, by which time Hong Kong were 163 runs ahead with Smart undefeated on 48. The home side struggled on the last morning against all the Emirates' bowlers, who were supported by some excellent fielding.

Seven chances went to the wicketkeeper and all were taken, giving Mohammad Taskeen a ten-wicket haul for the match. When Hong Kong were all out for 173 the Emirates had a minimum of 81 overs in which to score 222. Asghar Ali and Mohammad Nadeem made the first century stand of the match. Syed Maqsood again played superbly and the target was reached easily in the 54th over. He was the player of the match, scoring 134 runs without being dismissed and taking four wickets.

HONG KONG v UNITED ARAB EMIRATES

Asian Cricket Council Fast Track Countries Tournament

Hong Kong Cricket Club, Wong Nai Chung Gap, Hong Kong, 10, 11 and 12 February 2005

United Arab Emirates won by five wickets

HONG KONG		R	B M 4s 6s		R	B M 4s 6s
*+T.T.Smart	lbw b Ali Asad	6	28	c M'd Taskeen b Javed Ismail	65	200
R.Sharma	c Moh'd Taskeen b Ali Asad	48	141	c M'd Taskeen b Javed Ismail	0	1
J.P.R.Lamsam	c&b Mohammad Tauqeer	89	194	c Mohammad Taskeen b Ali Asad	4	8
A.G.Gunthorpe	c M'mad Taskeen b J Ismail	2	28	(5) c M'd Taskeen b S'd Maqsood	6	41
Tabarak Dar	lbw b Ali Asad	0	5	(4) lbw b Rizwan Latif	31	62
Ilyas Gul	c Moh'd Taskeen b S Maqsood	20	47	(7) c M'd Taskeen b S'd Maqsood	2	14
Najeeb Amar	c R'n Latif b Ahmed N'em	27	45	(8) c M'd Taskeen b S'd Maqsood	8	19
S.B.Lama	not out	8	30	(9) c M'd Taskeen b Javed Ismail	15	18
Irfan Ahmed	not out	17	19	(6) b Ali Asad	23	35
Afzaal Haider				(11) not out	0	1
Nadeem Ahmed				(10) b Javed Ismail	5	6
	b6 lb14 nb10 w4	34		b8 lb4 w2	14	
	(7 wickets declared)	251			173	

UAE		R	B M 4s 6s		R	B M 4s 6s
Sameer Zia	b Afzaal Haider	0	8	(7) not out	4	2
Mohammad Nadeem	c Smart b Afzal Haider	5	25	run out	41	103
Asghar Ali	c Smart b Afzal Haider	4	6	(1) c Lama b Nadeem Ahmed	80	122
Syed Maqsood	not out	100	138	not out	34	37
Fahad Usman	c Smart b Lamsam	1	4	(3) lbw b Afzaal Haider	18	27
Javed Ismail	b Nadeem Ahmed	17	37	(5) c Tabarak Dar b N'm Ahmed	36	28
*Mohammad Tauqeer	c Ilyas Gul b Lamsam	24	32			
+Mohammad Taskeen	c Nadeem Ahmed b Lama	4	18			
Ahmed Nadeem	c Irfan Ahmed b N'm Ahmed	13	41			
Ali Asad	st Smart b Nadeem Ahmed	25	18	(6) c Tabarak Dar b Ilyas Gul	0	1
Rizwan Latif	not out	4	6			
	b4 nb2	6		b1 lb7 w1	9	
	(9 wickets declared)	203		(5 wickets)	222	

UAE	O	M	R	W	nb	w	O	M	R	W	nb	w	fow	HK (1)	UAE (1)	HK (2)	UAE (2)
Ali Asad	25	10	53	3	-	-	16	5	29	2	-	-	1	28 (1)	4 (1)	4 (2)	109 (2)
Ahmed Nadeem	15	2	41	1	2	- (3)	3	1	10	0	-	-	2	117 (2)	8 (3)	9 (3)	147 (3)
Javed Ismail	14.1	3	41	1	8	3 (2)	8.1	2	24	4	-	1	3	129 (4)	17 (2)	73 (4)	149 (1)
Syed Maqsood	9	1	33	1	-	1 (6)	14	3	44	3	-	1	4	130 (5)	18 (5)	89 (5)	205 (5)
Moh'd Tauqeer	14	4	35	1			11	2	31	0	-	-	5	176 (6)	60 (6)	133 (6)	210 (6)
Rizwan Latif	8	3	20	0	-	- (4)	11	2	14	1	-	-	6	207 (3)	102 (7)	140 (7)	
Sameer Zia	2	0	8	0	-	-	4	1	9	0	-	-	7	230 (7)	116 (8)	148 (8)	
													8		151 (9)	160 (1)	
Hong Kong	O	M	R	W	nb	w	O	M	R	W	nb	w	9		180 (10)	164 (9)	
Afzaal Haider	18	4	68	3			12	0	63	1	-	1	10			173 (10)	
Lamsam	10	3	23	2			8	2	25	0	-	-					
Irfan Ahmed	3	0	18	0			8	0	28	0	-	-					
Nadeem Ahmed	13.5	3	63	3		(5)	12	2	51	2	-	-					
Lama	10	3	27	1		(4)	2	1	4	0	-	-					
Ilyas Gul							8.1	2	32	1	-	-					
Sharma							3	0	11	0	-	-					

Umpires: Mahbubur Rahman (Bangladesh) and Sailab Hossain (Bangladesh)

Reserve umpire: S.Gidwani (Hong Kong). Referee: U.C.Hathurasinghe (Sri Lanka)

Toss: United Arab Emirates

Player of the Match: Syed Maqsood (United Arab Emirates)

Close of play: 1st day – unknown; 2nd day – Hong Kong (2) 115-4 (Smart 48*, Irfan Ahmed ??*)

Nepalese supreme

In May 2005, the United Arab Emirates, considered at the time the top Associate country in Asia following the advancement of Bangladesh to Full Membership of the ICC, faced Nepal in the ICC Intercontinental Cup. The two countries had met in the previous year of the competition, in Sharjah, when they drew an uninspiring match in which the Emirates delayed their second-innings declaration too long. Nepal made no effort to win and simply played out time.

In 2005 the fixture was played at Kirtipur, a suburb of Kathmandu. While Nepal were at full strength the Emirates lacked Khurram Khan, Syed Maqsood and Asad Ali, the first two among their best batsmen and the third a bowler who could have taken advantage of the conditions, particularly on the first day which was warm and wet.

The previous two days had seen 13mm of rain fall and a further 1mm fell during the course of the opening day, causing the players and umpires to be on and off the field. Each day, however, the temperature rose to as high as 27°C by mid-afternoon, which, at an altitude of some 1,300m, meant that when the sun did appear it felt quite strong.

Nepal won the toss and batted first but struggled against the visitors' pace attack, losing two wickets for only 19 runs. Chaugai and Gauchan played cautiously and gradually gained the upper hand only for Chaugai to give a tame caught-and-bowled to Rizwan Latif to end a partnership of 65. Vesawkar and Gauchan then gave an assured performance. They entertained the crowd with a partnership of 106, their attractive batting putting Nepal in a strong position. On the departure of Gauchan, Alam scored at a run a ball and hit six fours before being dismissed, leg-before, in the last over of the day.

On the second morning, Nepal added 41 runs for the loss of two more wickets but when Vesawkar was dismissed for 89 and, therefore, not able to reach his hundred, Das declared. He probably expected that he and Alam would be able to exploit the conditions and create problems for the Emirates with their pace attack of right- and left-arm respectively. Alam quickly trapped Ryan Chadha leg-before and the Emirates lost their second wicket to a run-out. However, it was the leg spin of Basnet, Gauchan and Pradhan that caused problems in the afternoon sunshine.

Apart from Arshad Ali, who batted through the innings, no one seemed capable of scoring any runs. All the batsmen chose to defend against the turning ball, with disastrous consequences. The play was tedious for the spectators, a scoring rate of 33 runs per 100 balls, with 25 per cent of the overs bowled being maidens. Arshad Ali's undefeated 81, made off 250 balls with six fours, allowed his team to reach 164, a first-innings deficit of 123. Given the poor batting, it is inexplicable that Nepal used seven bowlers, unless it was Das's wish to let everyone have a share in the wickets. Nepal lost two wickets but, by the close, Chaugai and Gauchan were again looking secure.

Nepal went for quick runs on the last day in order to force an early declaration. Rizwan Latif bowled his slow left-arm spin to good effect, enticing batsmen into errors and picking up three caught-and-bowleds, bringing his total to four such dismissals for the match. Nepal had to bat for 26 overs before Das felt confident enough to declare, by which time only a further 80 runs had been added.

The Emirates were set 249 to win but never got anywhere near. Their batting was even more pitiful than in their first innings. Again Arshad Ali held out while his colleagues fell to Das, who took five wickets. Ahmed Nadeem struck 32 from 38 balls to provide some entertainment but at 29/6 the situation was hopeless and the Emirates were dismissed for a paltry 76 in only 35 overs. Nepal not only did the unexpected in beating the United Arab Emirates. They did it in style by 172 runs.

NEPAL v UNITED ARAB EMIRATES

First-class

ICC Intercontinental Cup

Tribhuvan University International Cricket Ground, Kirtipur, 7, 8 and 9 May 2005

Nepal won by 172 runs

NEPAL		R	B	M 4s 6s		R	B	M 4s 6s
P.P.Lohani	c M'd Taskeen b Zahid Shah	0	15	- -	c Arshad Ali b A'd Nadeem	4	27	- -
K.Chaugai	c&b Rizwan Latif	47	91	7 -	c&b Rizwan Latif	48	103	4 -
D.Chaudhary	lbw b Ahmed Nadeem	3	19	- -	lbw b Ahmed Nadeem	9	13	2 -
S.P.Gauchan	c Asghar Ali b Usman Saleem	68	196	5 -	c M'd Tauqeer b Z'd Shah	26	54	3 -
S.Vesawkar	c Asghar Ali b A'ed Nadeem	89	140	6 -	c&b Rizwan Latif	12	21	1 -
M.Alam	lbw b Zahid Shah	34	34	6 -	c&b Rizwan Latif	2	7	- -
*B.K.Das	c Rizwan Latif b Zahid Shah	17	32	1 -	not out	14	27	- -
+M.K.Baishya	not out	0	2	- -				
R.Basnet					(8) not out	0	5	- -
D.B.Chand								
R.K.Pradhan								
	b5 lb4 nb12 w8	29			b6 lb1 nb2 w1	10		
	(7 wickets declared)	**287**			(6 wickets declared)	**125**		

UAE		R	B	M 4s 6s		R	B	M 4s 6s
Ryan Chadha	lbw b Alam	0	3	- -	lbw b Alam	4	13	1 -
Arshad Ali	not out	81	250	6 -	lbw b Das	18	47	1 -
Usman Saleem	run out	9	10	1 -	(5) c Chaudhary b Das	0	16	- -
Asghar Ali	b Chand	15	29	3 -	c Chaugai b Chand	2	20	- -
Zakir Hussain	c Baishya b Pradhan	18	36	2 -	(6) b Das	8	30	1 -
Sameer Zia	b Basnet	14	64	1 -	(3) b Das	0	12	- -
Ahmed Nadeem	lbw b Basnet	0	1	- -	(8) c Baishya b Gauchan	32	38	4 -
*Mohammad Tauqeer	c Chand b Basnet	8	35	1 -	(7) lbw b Das	0	4	- -
+Mohammad Taskeen	b Gauchan	16	37	2 -	c Gauchan b Das	0	21	- -
Zahid Shah	c Chaugai b Gauchan	0	1	- -	not out	9	7	- -
Rizwan Latif	b Das	0	14	- -	lbw b Gauchan	0	3	- -
	b1 nb1 w1	3			lb1 nb1 w1	3		
		164				**76**		

UAE	O	M	R	W	nb	wd		O	M	R	W	nb	wd	fow	Nep (1)	UAE (1)	Nep (2)	UAE (2)
Ahmed Nadeem	15.3	3	47	2	3	-		17	1	38	2	1	-	1	4	0	12	11
Zahid Shah	19	2	72	3	8	8		11	2	31	1	-	1	2	19	15	38	12
Usman Saleem	10	2	30	1	-	-								3	84	42	97	25
Moh'd Tauqeer	21	1	63	0	-	-(4)		5	0	12	0	-	-	4	190	69	97	25
Rizwan Latif	17	5	41	1	-	-(3)		11.2	2	37	3	1	-	5	246	107	105	29
Sameer Zia	2	0	13	0	-	-								6	286	107	123	29
Arshad Ali	2	0	12	0	-	-								7	287	125		43
														8		152		67
Nepal	O	M	R	W	nb	wd		O	M	R	W	nb	wd	9		156		69
Alam	5	1	17	1	-	-		8	2	10	1	-	1	10		164		76
Das	14.2	4	23	1	-	1		16	7	27	5	-	-					
Chand	12	0	38	1	1	-		6	3	14	2	1	-					
Gauchan	14	6	18	2	-	-(5)		4	1	19	2	-	-					
Pradhan	15	4	35	1	-	-(4)		1	0	5	0	-	-					
Basnet	17	5	27	3	-	-												
Vesawkar	4	1	5	0	-	-												

Umpires: S.S.Prasad (Singapore) and Zameer Haider (Pakistan)

Toss: Nepal

Player of the Match: B.K.Das (Nepal)

The first innings of the match was limited to 90 overs and the total overs for both teams in their first innings was restricted to 180.

Close of play: 1st day – Nepal (1) 246-5 (Vesawkar 73*); 2nd day – Nepal (2) 45-2 (Chaugai 21*, Gauchan 4*)

Battle of the imports

Ryan ten Doeschate was born in South Africa of Dutch parents. He learnt his cricket at school in South Africa but after qualifying as a Dutch citizen he was eligible to represent The Netherlands. As a citizen of the European Union he was also able to play for Essex without being classed as an overseas player.

David Hemp learnt his cricket in England and had a long first-class career with Glamorgan, during which time he played for Wales, and then with Warwickshire. By the mid-2000s, as he was nearing the end of his first-class career, it came to the attention of the Bermuda Cricket Board that he had been born in Hamilton, Bermuda, and could therefore represent the country internationally.

The two faced each other in an ICC Intercontinental Cup match at the L.C. de Villiers Oval in Pretoria in November 2006.

The previous four days had been wet, with 9.9mm of rain falling, but some conscientious work by the ground staff allowed play to start only one hour late on the first day. Van Troost won the toss for the Dutch and decided to bat first. The Bermudan bowling was tight and conditions far from conducive to shot-making. Hurdle bowled six maidens in his opening spell of 11 overs. The Dutch did well to survive and take the score to 83/1 at lunch.

Further rain prevented play after the interval until 3pm and, even then, only three more overs were possible before the umpires decided that the light was too poor and brought the players in for an early tea. More rain meant an additional delay, and when play finally resumed the conditions were so damp that they were not ideal for batting or bowling, though the bowlers suffered more because of the wet ball.

The Dutch struck 40 off five overs and ten Doeschate batted assuredly, scoring runs all round the ground. He and de Grooth took their partnership to 189 before the latter mis-hit a ball into the hands of mid-off. Thirty-three runs later, Dean Minors took an easy running catch behind the wicket to bring to an end ten Doeschate's superb innings. His 138 contained 14 fours and two sixes and had lasted just over five and a half hours.

With the pitch drying out, conditions on the second morning favoured spin. The Dutch lost four wickets before Smits, defending resolutely, helped Stelling and Kashif to take the total to a respectable 378. The Dutch then bowled poorly, being unable to find either line or length. Outerbridge and Kwame Tucker made 44 in the first seven overs and went on to an opening partnership of 105. The introduction of Borren and the two spinners, Kashif and Seelaar, brought some control over the run rate, but Bermuda were strongly positioned at the close, 250 runs behind, despite having lost two wickets.

The third day was a battle between ten Doeschate, who bowled tightly and dismissed Outerbridge and Smith, and Hemp, who batted superbly, particularly in the afternoon session when he just played with the Dutch bowling, hitting it wherever he liked. Bermuda held the advantage all day and the Dutch were somewhat relieved when rain stopped play with 13 overs left.

On the fourth morning, Bermuda achieved the first-innings lead and, with little prospect of either side winning, batted on to reach 620 with Hemp undefeated on 247, made in eight and three quarter hours with 30 fours and two sixes.

The only remaining interest in the match was whether ten Doeschate could make a second century, which he achieved in the penultimate over before being given out leg-before, despite being well down the wicket.

The match was a draw and that was probably true of the battle between ten Doeschate and Hemp. Two centuries and three wickets, with the second century having little meaning in the context of the match by ten Doeschate more or less equalled the double century of Hemp.

NETHERLANDS v BERMUDA

First-class

ICC Intercontinental Cup – Group B

L.C.de Villiers Oval, Pretoria, 21, 22, 23 and 24 November 2006

Match drawn

NETHERLANDS

		R	B	M	4s	6s		R	B	M	4s	6s
B.Zuiderent	b Mukuddem	1	6	5	-	-	not out	56	124	169	1	2
T.N.de Grooth	c Hurdle b Mukuddem	61	185	238	5	-	c Romaine b Mukuddem	4	14	16	-	-
R.N.ten Doeschate	c Minors b Leverock	138	196	273	14	2	lbw b Romaine	100	120	136	8	3
D.L.S.van Bunge	c&b Hurdle	39	92	137	1	1						
A.N.Kervezee	lbw b Leverock	16	46	46	1	-	(4) not out	0	2	2	-	-
P.W.Borren	c K.L.Tucker b Trott	6	12	10	1	-						
*L.P.van Troost	c J.J.Tucker b Leverock	24	66	91	2	-						
W.F.Stelling	c Smith b Trott	33	95	112	3	-						
+J.Smits	b Trott	24	55	93	1	-						
P.M.Seelaar	lbw b Hurdle	1	7	5	-	-						
M.Kashif	not out	13	16	26	2	-						
	b8 lb12 w2	22					b6 lb2 nb2	10				
		378					(2 wickets)	**170**				

BERMUDA

		R	B	M	4s	6s
S.D.Outerbridge	b ten Doeschate	80	175	194	11	-
K.L.Tucker	c ten Doeschate b Borren	33	99	117	4	-
I.H.Romaine	lbw b ten Doeschate	10	30	31	1	-
*C.J.Smith	lbw b ten Doeschate	14	70	90	1	-
D.L.Hemp	not out	247	373	525	30	2
J.J.Tucker	c Borren b Kashif	10	17	19	1	-
+D.A.Minors	lbw b van Bunge	12	23	22	2	-
S.Mukuddem	c Smits b van Bunge	90	191	225	9	-
R.D.M.Leverock	lbw b Borren	51	157	159	8	-
R.J.Trott	lbw b Borren	0	1	2	-	-
K.A.D.Hurdle	c Smits b van Bunge	29	51	50	4	-
	b7 lb19 nb12 w6	44				
		620				

Bermuda	O	M	R	W	nb	w		O	M	R	W	nb	w
Hurdle	29	10	88	2	-	1		4	1	18	0	2	-
Mukuddem	30	7	98	2	-	1		3	0	15	1	-	-
Leverock	47	12	119	3	-	-	(4)	13	5	24	0	-	-
Trott	18.1	1	47	3	-	-	(3)	15	1	86	0	-	-
Hemp	4	1	6	0	-	-							
J.J.Tucker	1	1	0	0	-	-							
Outerbridge							(5)	1	0	5	0	-	-
Romaine							(6)	7	1	14	1	-	-

fow	Net (1)	Ber (1)	Net (2)
1	2 (1)	105 (2)	11 (2)
2	191 (2)	123 (3)	170 (3)
3	224 (3)	154 (1)	
4	255 (5)	181 (4)	
5	264 (6)	203 (6)	
6	285 (4)	219 (7)	
7	309 (7)	438 (8)	
8	351 (8)	570 (9)	
9	352 (10)	570 (10)	
10	378 (9)	620 (11)	

Netherlands	O	M	R	W	nb	w
ten Doeschate	37	8	121	3	4	1
Stelling	11	3	39	0	6	-
Kashif	24	10	57	1	1	1
Borren	44	12	130	3	1	-
Seelaar	24	2	94	0	-	-
van Bunge	37	6	109	3	-	-
van Troost	19	3	44	0	-	-

Umpires: K.H.Hurter (South Africa) and Z.T.A.Ndamane (South Africa)

Reserve umpire: A.Crafford (South Africa). Referee: A.Barnes (South Africa)

Toss: Netherlands

Close of play: 1st day – Netherlands (1) 235-3 (van Bunge 17*, Kervezee 7*); 2nd day – Bermuda (1) 128-2 (Outerbridge 61*, Smith 0*);
3rd day – Bermuda (1) 432-6 (Hemp 143*, Mukuddem 89*)

There were three five-ball overs (41st, 59th, 182nd) and two seven-ball overs (123rd and 190th) in Bermuda's innings.

181

Snyman strikes

In addition to those matches which are effectively a contest between 'imported' players, there are those that reflect rivalry between the top local players. One example of the latter is the Intercontinental Cup match between Kenya and Namibia, held in Sharjah in January 2008. The encounter was originally scheduled as a home fixture for Kenya but with rioting in the country in the aftermath of a hotly-contested general election, the ICC ruled Nairobi unsafe. It was moved to Sharjah where it could be fitted in between Namibia's and Kenya's away matches against the United Arab Emirates.

On winning the toss, Tikolo invited Namibia to bat, thinking this would allow his side to gain the initiative early and, thereby, dominate the match. The decision soon looked justified as Namibia struggled to score. Four batsmen got beyond 20 but only Verwey threatened any dominance. It was as well that the match attracted few spectators since there was little to excite them.

Kenya were even less impressive in reply until Tikolo and Collins Obuya added 66 in a fine partnership and, after Tikolo's dismissal, Odoyo gave sound support. At the close, Kenya were only 35 runs behind with five wickets in hand, and Tikolo's judgement to bowl first still looked good. Obuya and Odoyo continued to score freely on the second day but after Odoyo was leg-before to Kola Burger, Kenya collapsed, moving from 183/5 to 189/9.

Varaiya frustrated Namibia in a last-wicket partnership of 40 before also falling leg-before to give Kola Burger his fifth wicket of the innings. Obuya was undefeated on 76, an uncharacteristically cautious contribution but vital in securing Kenya a 46-run lead.

Kenya pressed home their advantage by taking Namibia's first three wickets for 18, and Varaiya and Tikolo accounted for their middle order to reduce them to 105/6. With disaster threatening, Snyman opted to attack. In a remarkable display he dispatched Kenya's bowlers to all parts of the ground. By the end of the day he had made 194 with 18 fours and nine sixes, a contribution which represented 80 per cent of Namibia's total.

Although Snyman managed to dominate the strike, he could not have succeeded without some support at the other end. This came from the stubborn defence of Durant. In a seventh-wicket partnership of 133, he made 13 to become the only other batsman in the innings to reach double figures. More importantly he survived for 141 balls. Unfortunately he did not last until the close, by which time both he and Kola Burger were dismissed. Nevertheless, Namibia led by 195.

Kola Burger and Klazinga, in turn, stayed long enough on the third day for Snyman to reach his double century and put on 41 runs for the last two wickets. It was Snyman who finally fell, bowled by Collins Obuya, for a magnificent 230, only six runs fewer than Namibia's lead. He had made 81.5 per cent of his team's total at a strike rate of 114.4, with 67 per cent of his runs coming in boundaries; 22 fours and 11 sixes. Tikolo tried eight bowlers without ever being able to control the runs.

Kenya were demoralised and, surprisingly, never came to grips with obtaining what was nothing more than a moderate target of 237. Seven batsmen passed ten but none made 20 as Kola Burger, Kotze and Louis Burger took wickets at regular intervals. The loss of Tikolo, fourth ball without scoring, removed the last vestige of fight from the Kenyan team. Kola Burger took four wickets to finish with 9-105 in the match.

Not only did Kenya lose by a large margin, they did so in three days. Tikolo's decision to bat first still did not seem wrong in hindsight but it backfired due to one outstanding performance. Unfortunately for Kenya, this performance was not a one-off. In October 2012, Snyman scored 201 not out when Namibia beat them at Windhoek by an innings and one run.

KENYA v NAMIBIA

First-class

ICC Intercontinental Cup

Sharjah Cricket Association Stadium, Sharjah, 29, 30 and 31 January and 1 February 2008

Namibia won by 101 runs

NAMIBIA

		R	B	M	4s	6s		R	B	M	4s	6s
A.J.Burger	c Tikolo b Odoyo	9	12		1	-	c D.O.Obuya b Ongondo	5	12		1	-
D.H.Botha	c C.O.Obuya b Ongondo	0	4		-	-	lbw b Odoyo	0	2		-	-
R.van Schoor	b Varaiya	39	114		4	-	c Odhiambo b Ongondo	7	21		-	-
G.Snyman	c D.O.Obuya b Ongondo	24	40		3	1	b C.O.Obuya	230	201		22	11
*L.J.Burger	lbw b Kamande	19	43		2	-	c D.O.Obuya b Odhiambo	4	29		-	-
B.L.Kotze	st D.O.Obuya b Varaiya	23	53		2	1	st D.O.Obuya b Varaiya	7	23		1	-
+T.Verwey	not out	43	43		9	-	c Suji b Tikolo	1	4		-	-
M.Durant	c Suji b Tikolo	0	7		-	-	c Ongondo b C.O.Obuya	13	141		1	-
W.Slabber	st D.O.Obuya b Tikolo	0	1		-	-	c Odhiambo b C.O.Obuya	1	8		-	-
K.B.Burger	c Kamande b Varaiya	1	16		-	-	c&b Kamande	3	14		-	-
L.Klazinga	b Tikolo	7	16		-	-	not out	2	4		-	-
	b7 lb3 nb8	18					b3 lb1 nb4 w1	9				
		183						**282**				

KENYA

		R	B	M	4s	6s		R	B	M	4s	6s
M.A.Ouma	c L.J.Burger b A.J.Burger	32	37		5	-	b K.B.Burger	14	20		2	-
+D.O.Obuya	lbw b Klazinga	0	3		-	-	c&b L.J.Burger	19	69		3	-
A.A.Obanda	b K.B.Burger	0	8		-	-	lbw b K.B.Burger	0	2		-	-
A.O.Suji	b Klazinga	5	25		1	-	c Snyman b Kotze	13	33		2	-
*S.O.Tikolo	c Verwey b Kotze	45	45		7	-	c Klazinga b Kotze	0	4		-	-
C.O.Obuya	not out	76	175		10	-	b Kotze	15	23		1	-
T.M.Odoyo	lbw b K.B.Burger	37	65		5	-	lbw b K.B.Burger	5	17		-	-
J.K.Kamande	lbw b K.B.Burger	0	4		-	-	lbw b K.B.Burger	11	36		1	-
N.N.Odhiambo	c Verwey b Kotze	0	2		-	-	c Botha b L.J.Burger	5	30		-	-
P.J.Ongondo	b K.B.Burger	5	9		1	-	not out	10	30		-	1
H.A.Varaiya	lbw b K.B.Burger	12	30		3	-	c K.B.Burger b A.J.Burger	18	21		2	-
	b7 lb1 nb7 w2	17					b10 lb5 nb8 w2	25				
		229						**135**				

Kenya	O	M	R	W	nb	w		O	M	R	W	nb	w	fow	Nam (1)	Ken (1)	Nam (2)	Ken (2)
Odoyo	9	2	26	1	3	-		5	1	17	1	-	-	1	4 (2)	3 (2)	1 (2)	18 (1)
Ongondo	9	0	30	2	-	-		12	2	35	2	-	-	2	12 (1)	4 (3)	9 (1)	18 (3)
Odhiambo	6	1	26	0	3	-		11	1	73	1	4	-	3	49 (4)	35 (4)	18 (3)	50 (4)
Varaiya	17	8	33	3	-	-		12	2	53	1	-	-	4	82 (5)	42 (1)	42 (5)	50 (5)
Kamande	10	1	34	1	-	-		10	2	24	1	-	-	5	117 (6)	108 (5)	98 (6)	72 (2)
Tikolo	5.5	0	24	3	2	-		7	1	31	1	-	-	6	136 (3)	183 (7)	105 (7)	74 (6)
Suji								3	0	11	0	-	-	7	137 (8)	183 (8)	238 (8)	91 (7)
C.O.Obuya								16.5	3	34	3	-	1	8	137 (9)	184 (9)	241 (9)	100 (8)
														9	163 (10)	189 (10)	270 (10)	109 (9)
Namibia	O	M	R	W	nb	w		O	M	R	W	nb	w	10	183 (11)	229 (11)	282 (4)	135 (11)
K.B.Burger	25	6	68	5	-	1		15	5	37	4	-	-					
Klazinga	14	2	52	2	6	-		5.4	0	24	0	8	1					
A.J.Burger	12	0	56	1	-	-	(5)	0.1	0	0	1	-	-					
Durant	4	0	18	0	-	-												
Kotze	9	1	23	2	1	1	(3)	13	5	22	3	-	1					
Slabber	2	1	4	0	-	-												
L.J.Burger							(4)	12.2	3	37	2	-	-					

Umpires: N.G.Bagh (Denmark) and D.B.Hair (Australia)

Toss: Kenya

Player of the Match: G.Snyman (Namibia)

Close of play: 1st day – Kenya (1) 148-5 (C.O.Obuya 30*, Odoyo 25*); 2nd day – Namibia (2) 241-8 (Snyman 194*).
Match finished in three days.

Tikolo trounces Canada

When Kenya met Canada at King City in August 2009 they were at full strength, whereas the hosts were without any of their Southern Hemisphere imports, John Davison, Ian Billcliff and Geoff Barnett all being unavailable. With Ashish Bagai as captain, both sides were led by their wicketkeepers.

Conditions were far from ideal for cricket, being cool and damp with nearly 60mm of rain having fallen over the previous five days and with rain still falling it was not surprising that the start was delayed. What was surprising, given that Kenya had a good pace attack, was that Ouma opted to bat first on winning the toss, particularly as Canada, in Umar Bhatti and Osinde, possessed what was at the time the best pair of opening bowlers in Associate cricket.

Kenya lost both openers quickly, a wicket each to the opening pair, and a potential recovery was set back when Zahir bowled Obanda. As conditions eased, Tikolo and Ouma began to establish some authority before completely mastering the Canadian attack in an excellent display of batsmanship.

Canada tried eight bowlers in an attempt to break the partnership but without success and Tikolo reached his hundred off 106 balls. As is often the case, a drinks break was enough to disrupt the momentum, Ouma falling leg-before to the slow left-arm of Dhaniram shortly after play resumed, ending a partnership worth 116. Tikolo continued in confident manner but obtained little support from the lower order. He was finally ninth out, caught at the wicket after batting for five hours and 18 minutes. His 158, which was half of his team's total, contained 22 fours.

In six overs before the close Canada lost both openers to finish on 14/2 then batted for most of the second day, but they had few runs to show for it. Most of their batsmen made starts but were dismissed as soon as they tried to raise the scoring rate. Spinners Varaiya and Tikolo were effective in taking wickets and, the more wickets Canada lost, the more defensive they became.

After the tea break, Kamande bowled five successive maidens, conceded two runs in his sixth over, and then bowled another maiden. His lack of penetration, however, forced Ouma to revert to pace in order to bring the innings to a close. The only threat came from nightwatchman Zahir who hit seven fours and two sixes in his 57, but he spent much of his time becalmed. With a lead of 83, Waters and Collins Obuya opted for defence, finishing on 12 without loss at the end of the day.

The third day began with Canada promising a fightback, reducing Kenya to 32/2 before Waters and Tikolo took command of the match. Canada again tried eight bowlers without success until, with the partnership on 330, Tikolo holed out to the long-on boundary, attempting to strike his third six. Tikolo's innings of 169 was made off 207 balls, giving him a total of 327 off 401 balls for the match. Ouma declared as soon as Tikolo was dismissed, leaving Waters undefeated on 157.

Requiring 446 to win, Canada again lost two wickets before the close, leaving Samad, promoted to opener, and Zahir, again coming in as nightwatchman, to lead either their chase to victory or fight for a draw on the last day.

Zahir fell quickly to the pace of Odoyo. Varaiya then produced a classic display of left-arm spin which, Samad excepted, bemused all of the home side's batsmen. Kenya took five wickets in the morning session. In the afternoon, Samad was adjudged leg-before to Odhiambo, leaving Varaiya to take the remaining two wickets to finish with 6-45 and Canada fell at home by 247 runs. Their combined total of 432 was only 105 more than Tikolo made on his own. Not surprisingly, Tikolo was named the player of the match.

CANADA v KENYA
First-class

ICC Intercontinental Cup

Maple Leaf South-West Ground, King City, 14, 15 and 16 August 2009

Kenya won by 247 runs

KENYA

		R	B	M	4s	6s		R	B	M	4s	6s
S.R.Waters	c Cheema b Osinde	10	39	48	1	-	not out	157	268		19	-
D.O.Obuya	lbw b Umar Bhatti	2	7	16	-	-	c Bagai b Osinde	12	35	48	2	-
A.A.Obanda	b Zahir	36	49	79	5	-	c Cheema b Umar Bhatti	3	9	5	-	-
S.O.Tikolo	c Bagai b Osinde	158	194	318	22	-	c Dhaniram b Umar Bhatti	169	207		21	2
*+M.A.Ouma	lbw b Dhaniram	28	71	51	2	-						
C.O.Obuya	c Umar Bhatti b D'ram	7	24	17	1	-						
T.M.Odoyo	lbw b Chauhan	19	45	32	2	1						
J.K.Kamande	c Cheema b Hansra	26	32	45	6	-						
N.N.Odhiambo	c Osinde b Cheema	1	5	3	-	-						
H.A.Varaiya	c Jyoti b Osinde	11	42	46	1	-						
P.J.Ongondo	not out	1	10	13	-	-						
	b13 lb3 nb1 w1	18					b6 lb6 nb9	21				
		317					(3 wickets declared)	**362**				

CANADA

		R	B	M	4s	6s		R	B	M	4s	6s
A.S.Hansra	c Tikolo b Odoyo	0	2	2	-	-	(8) b Odhiambo	17	27	34	2	-
R.A.Cheema	c Odoyo b Odhiambo	6	8	20	1	-	lbw b Odoyo	4	11	21	-	-
S.Jyoti	c D.O.Obuya b Varaiya	39	105	124	4	-	b Varaiya	19	18	32	2	-
M.Z.Zahir	run out (Obanda)	57	131	132	7	2	b Odoyo	1	14	15	-	-
A.M.Samad	c Odoyo b Tikolo	0	18	14	-	-	(1) lbw b Odhiambo	87	152	190	17	-
*+A.Bagai	c Kamande b Tikolo	13	43	43	2	-	(5) b Varaiya	0	4	1	-	-
S.Dhaniram	c Tikolo b Odhiambo	22	17	28	4	-	c D.O.Obuya b Varaiya	24	40	49	5	-
N.R.Kumar	c Ouma b Ongondo	12	83	95	1	-	(6) c Tikolo b Varaiya	0	1	1	-	-
Umar Bhatti	lbw b Varaiya	30	110		5	-	not out	17	76	88	3	-
K.R.Chauhan	c Varaiya b Odhiambo	31	39	55	5	1	c Tikolo b Varaiya	11	37	46	2	-
H.Osinde	not out	3	8		-	-	c D.O.Obuya b Varaiya	6	16	16	1	-
	b9 lb4 nb8	21					b1 lb8 nb3	12				
		234						**198**				

Canada	O	M	R	W	nb	w		O	M	R	W	nb	w	fow	Ken (1)	Can (1)	Ken (2)	Can (2)
Osinde	12.1	3	28	3	-	1		13	1	58	1	9	-	1	2 (2)	0 (1)	29 (2)	14 (2)
Umar Bhatti	14	1	55	1	-	-		15	3	63	2	-	-	2	27 (1)	14 (2)	32 (3)	56 (3)
Chauhan	20	3	73	1	1	-		14	2	68	0	-	-	3	80 (3)	80 (3)	362 (4)	62 (4)
Zahir	9	0	40	1	-	- (5)		6	0	32	0	-	-	4	196 (5)	81 (5)		63 (5)
Jyoti	8	0	37	0	-	- (6)		5	0	18	0	-	-	5	208 (6)	116 (6)		63 (6)
Dhaniram	12	0	42	2	-	- (7)		6	1	23	0	-	-	6	243 (7)	128 (4)		107 (7)
Cheema	10	0	24	1	-	- (4)		23	5	72	0	-	-	7	290 (8)	154 (7)		146 (8)
Hansra	1	0	2	1	-	-		3	0	16	0	-	-	8	294 (9)	181 (8)		161 (1)
														9	312 (4)	221 (10)		188 (10)
Kenya	O	M	R	W	nb	w		O	M	R	W	nb	w	10	317 (10)	234 (9)		198 (11)
Odoyo	17	5	40	1	-	-		10	1	40	2	1	-					
Ongondo	19	8	49	1	1	-		10	3	35	0	-	-					
Odhiambo	20	6	60	3	7	-		11	3	44	2	2	-					
Varaiya	16.4	3	54	2	-	- (5)		20.3	9	45	6	-	-					
Tikolo	13	7	16	2	-	- (4)		3	0	7	0	-	-					
Kamande	7	5	2	0	-	-		11	5	18	0	-	-					

Umpires: K.Bayney (Canada) and N.A.Malcolm (West Indies)

Reserve umpire: R.Sivanadian (Canada). Referee: D.T.Jukes (England)

Toss: Kenya

Player of the Match: S.O.Tikolo (Kenya)

Close of play: 1st day – Canada (1) 14-2 (Jyoti 7*, Zahir 0*); 2nd day – Kenya (2) 12-0 (Waters 5*, D.O.Obuya 3*); 3rd day – Canada (2) 61-2 (Samad 37*, Zahir 0*)

In Canada's first innings there was one seven-ball over.

Afghanistan are champions

When the Intercontinental Cup began in 2004, cricket in Afghanistan was in its infancy. By 2008 the country had gained entry to the World Cricket League Division Five, then the lowest division in the one-day 50-over competition. By April 2009 the team had gained promotion to Division One and thereby qualified to take part in the Intercontinental Cup.

Despite Afghanistan's experience being limited to one-day matches the players quickly adjusted to multi-innings cricket. They won five of their six matches, the other being drawn, to reach the final of the competition against Scotland.

Both teams were surprised by how well conditions favoured the fast bowlers on the first morning. Scotland elected to bat but the frailty of their top order against pace was quickly exposed. Hamid Hassan, arguably the best fast bowler in Associate cricket, proved too lively, and Shahpoor Zadran and Mirwais Ashraf gave excellent support. Scotland lost five wickets in the morning session while scoring only 61 runs. Progress was slowed, however, by Afghanistan's appalling over rate, which produced only 27 overs in the two hours. Hamid Hassan bowled throughout the morning and into the afternoon in an opening spell of 22 overs, a remarkable performance of stamina.

With Scotland on 97/8 the match seemed as good as over but McCallum was batting confidently and, as Afghanistan's bowlers tired, Smith managed to survive. The pair put on 107 for the ninth wicket, defying Afghanistan for two hours and 20 minutes. With the return of Hamid Hassan to the attack, Smith's resistance ended and Lyons became the bowler's fifth victim. McCallum reached his hundred and remained undefeated, having resisted for five hours and 26 minutes. Afghanistan lost one wicket before the close.

Coetzer took over the captaincy for Scotland on the second morning, Drummond being off the field with a rib injury. Without him the pace attack was very ordinary and Karim Sadiq and Mirwais Ashraf added 35 runs in the first six overs. The run rate slowed when Haq and Berrington came on to bowl. Afghanistan lost three wickets but Asghar Stanikzai took 12 runs off Lyons in the penultimate over before lunch and Nowroz Mangal took nine off the next over from Haq, to regain the initiative. Scotland retaliated in the afternoon with Parker conceding only 12 runs in 11 overs and Haq continuing his long spell.

Nowroz Mangal passed his half-century before Afghanistan's innings ended surprisingly quickly, the last four wickets falling for the addition of six runs. Scotland's players and supporters were delighted to have a first-innings lead of 41, but that was before their batsmen gave another inept display as six wickets went down for 64. By the end of day two Scotland's lead had increased to 105, but there were only four wickets in hand.

It took Afghanistan just eight overs to end Scotland's innings but their excellent play was marred by persistent and often wildly optimistic appeals to the umpires for leg-before and close catches. Karim Sadiq and Shabir Noori put on 22 in the first five overs. Parker was again impressive and was rewarded with Karim Sadiq's wicket, a fantastic catch by McCallum running backwards from slip to hold on to a top edge. Parker's reaction was to point Karim Sadiq direct to the pavilion, a gesture for which he was reprimanded by the umpires. Scotland's officials thought this was somewhat harsh given that the umpires had taken no action against Afghanistan's earlier conduct.

Mohammad Shehzad produced one of his characteristic displays, hitting 56 off 62 balls with seven fours, to take Afghanistan to a simple victory by five wickets. They not only won the Intercontinental Cup at their first attempt, but did so on the third day of a match which was scheduled for five days.

AFGHANISTAN v SCOTLAND

First-class

ICC Intercontinental Cup – Final

Dubai Sports City Stadium, Dubai, 2, 3, 4 and 5 December 2010

Afghanistan won by seven wickets

SCOTLAND

Batsman	Dismissal (1st)	R	B	M	4s	6s	Dismissal (2nd)	R	B	M	4s	6s
D.F.Watts	c M Ashraf b S'r Zadran	5	15	23	-	-	c N'z Mangal b S'h Shenwari	28	49	57	4	-
P.L.Mommsen	c N Mangal b H'd Hassan	3	19	15	-	-	lbw b Samiullah Shenwari	9	23	27	1	-
K.J.Coetzer	c M'd Shehzad b H'd Hassan	0	8	21	-	-	run out	11	48	65	1	-
R.D.Berrington	c M'd Shehzad b M's Ashraf	29	53	68	4	-	(7) c A Stanikzai b H Hassan	10	46	71	2	-
N.F.I.McCallum	not out	104	221	326	17	-	c M Shehzad b H Hassan	0	5	7	-	-
G.I.Maiden	lbw b Mirwais Ashraf	3	8	8	-	-	(4) c N Mangal b S Shenwari	4	48	37	-	-
M.A.Parker	lbw b Mirwais Ashraf	9	38	48	-	-	(6) b Hamid Hassan	0	27	41	-	-
R.M.Haq	c S'h Shenwari b H'd Hassan	6	18	23	-	-	c Nowroz Mangal b M Ashraf	3	5	6	-	-
*G.D.Drummond	c M'd Shehzad b S'r Zadran	3	27	36	-	-	(10) b Mirwais Ashraf	4	4	6	-	-
+S.J.S.Smith	c M'd Shehzad b H'd Hassan	36	115	138	4	-	(9) not out	10	29	36	-	-
R.T.Lyons	c S'r Zadran b H'd Hassan	0	12	16	-	-	c M'd Shehzad b M's Ashraf	0	1	3	-	-
Extras	b4 lb6 nb2 w2	14					b1 lb2	3				
Total		**212**						**82**				

AFGHANISTAN

Batsman	Dismissal (1st)	R	B	M	4s	6s	Dismissal (2nd)	R	B	M	4s	6s
Karim Sadiq	lbw b Berrington	34	71	84	5	-	c McCallum b Parker	7	15	24	1	-
Shabir Noori	b Parker	11	11	21	1	-	c Smith b Lyons	35	54	71	5	-
Mirwais Ashraf	c Smith b Haq	21	24	40	3	-						
+Mohammad Shehzad	c Parker b Berrington	10	36	62	1	-	(3) not out	56	62	88	7	-
*Nowroz Mangal	c Smith b Lyons	56	92	167	9	-	(4) lbw b Parker	17	18	23	4	-
Asghar Stanikzai	c Lyons b Haq	26	27	71	3	-						
Mohammad Nabi	c Smith b Parker	1	32	36	-	-	(5) not out	6	11	16	1	-
Samiullah Shenwari	c Smith b Parker	4	32	44	-	-						
Hamid Hassan	c McCallum b Lyons	0	18	20	-	-						
Shahpoor Zadran	b Haq	0	13	19	-	-						
Abdullah Mazari	not out	6	5	6	1	-						
Extras	lb2	2					lb3	3				
Total		**171**					(3 wickets)	**124**				

Afghanistan	O	M	R	W	nb	w	O	M	R	W	nb	w
Hamid Hassan	26.4	10	45	5	-	-	17	6	39	3	-	-
Shahpoor Zadran	20	4	46	2	-	-	3	0	13	0	-	-
Mirwais Ashraf	24	6	53	3	2	2 (6)	6.3	4	8	3	-	-
Mohammad Nabi	6	3	13	0	-	- (5)	2	1	2	0	-	-
Abdullah Mazari	6	3	21	0	-	- (4)	5	3	2	0	-	-
Samiullah Shenwari	6	1	24	0	-	- (3)	14	7	15	3	-	-

Scotland	O	M	R	W	nb	w	O	M	R	W	nb	w
Parker	20	5	56	3	-	-	9.4	1	41	2	-	-
Drummond	2	0	7	0	-	-						
Berrington	9	2	34	2	-	-						
Haq	22.1	9	49	3	-	-	7	0	37	0	-	-
Lyons	7	4	23	2	-	- (3)	8	3	31	1	-	-
Coetzer						(2)	2	0	12	0	-	-

fow	Sco (1)	Afg (1)	Sco (2)	Afg (2)
1	9 (2)	13 (2)	22 (2)	22 (1)
2	13 (1)	54 (3)	41 (1)	79 (2)
3	19 (3)	76 (1)	55 (3)	108 (4)
4	51 (4)	89 (4)	55 (4)	
5	57 (6)	132 (6)	55 (5)	
6	80 (7)	139 (7)	64 (6)	
7	87 (8)	165 (5)	67 (8)	
8	97 (9)	165 (8)	77 (7)	
9	204 (10)	165 (9)	82 (10)	
10	212 (11)	171 (10)	82 (11)	

Umpires: H.D.P.K.Dharmasena (Sri Lanka) and B.B.Pradhan (Nepal)

Reserve umpire: Fidel Jaary (United Arab Emirates). Referee: D.T.Jukes (England)

Toss: Scotland

Player of the Match: Hamid Hassan (Afghanistan)

Close of play: 1st day – Afghanistan (1) 18-1 (Karim Sadiq 2*, Mirwais Ashraf 5*); 2nd day – Scotland (2) 64-6 (Berrington 9*). Match finished in three days.

History revived – again

In August 2011 the organisers of the Etihad Summer Festival of cricket included a two-day fixture between Canada and the USA in an attempt to revive the series between the two countries, yet again, after a gap of 16 years.

The Canadian side was only moderately experienced as the selectors were trying to introduce new players to replace those who had retired and some, like Umar Bhatti, who were being ignored after criticising the way Canadian cricket was being organised. The American team was even less experienced, the selectors again seeking new players in an attempt to overcome the comments that the side was nothing more than expatriates from the Caribbean and Indian subcontinent who were well past their prime.

The venue was the Toronto Cricket, Skating and Curling Club and the weather was warm and dry on both days, with the temperature reaching about 20°C by mid-afternoon. Although programmed as a multi-innings match, each innings was restricted to 45 overs. The United States won the toss and chose to bowl, a decision which was quickly regretted when the American attack found neither line nor length.

Patel and Wadia hit 71 runs before Tummala achieved success and bowled Wadia for 37, an innings which included six fours. Patel and Bhatti, batting surprisingly early at number three, added runs for the second wicket and after Patel was run out there was another productive partnership for the third wicket, which ended when Bhatti nicked a catch to the wicketkeeper.

After 45 overs, Canada had scored 239. The Americans used seven bowlers but could not control the run rate, which averaged 5.3 per over. Patel made 75 from 85 balls with nine fours and one six, and Kumar hit 58 off 45 balls with five fours and one six.

The American innings looked as though it would be a disaster as both openers were run out and Nanjee and Alfred perished to the home side's opening bowlers and four wickets were down with only 24 on the board. Desai and Tummala restored some sanity with a partnership of 61 but they, like Singh and George who followed, could not turn promising starts into a substantial score. Wickets fell regularly, shared between five bowlers, and the visitors were dismissed in 42.4 overs, just before the close, to give Canada a lead of 73 runs.

The Americans removed Wadia, Limbada and Kumar on the second day, the three wickets falling for 39, but they still had Patel to contend with. He was joined by the Canadian captain, Hansra, and the pair added 87. Ghous dismissed Patel, who made 80 from 84 balls with seven fours and two sixes, and Cheema, but Hansra received support from Bhatti in a sixth-wicket stand of 70. Hansra reached his hundred in 110 minutes off only 88 balls, with seven fours and six sixes, a strike rate of 113 runs per 100 balls. When he fell one ball later, he declared.

The American bowlers were even more expensive than they had been in Canada's first innings with the run rate averaging 5.8 an over so the victory target for the United States was 305. Their openers began positively with Alfred and Mohammed putting on 68 in seven overs before the spin trio of Patel, Desai and Siddiqui gained control and the Americans lost six wickets for the addition of only 63 runs.

Tummala and Desai gave the visitors hope and the home side a scare with a partnership of 81. After Tummala fell for a fine 63 off 75 balls and Haider was dismissed one run later, the initiative again rested with Canada. Desai and Ghous made a robust final effort, adding 48, but the task was just too great. Desai was ninth out having made 62 off 45 balls with seven fours and one six, and Ghous last out after hitting 39 from 24 balls, with two fours and two sixes. Desai (slow left-arm), Siddiqui (leg spin) and Hansra (off spin) had three wickets each.

Canada won by 34 runs and retained the K.A. Auty Trophy that they had won in 1995. Although the attendance was disappointingly small, the players enjoyed what turned out to be a close contest and were undoubtedly excited about reviving a piece of history.

CANADA v UNITED STATES OF AMERICA

K.A. Auty Trophy

Toronto Cricket, Skating and Curling Club, Wilson Avenue, Armour Heights, Toronto, 15 and 16 August 2011

Canada won by 34 runs

CANADA

		R	B	M	4s	6s		R	B	M	4s	6s
H.Patel	run out (Adams)	75	85		9	1	c Singh b Ghous	80	84	128	7	2
K.P.Wadia	b Tummala	37	45		6	-	c Dodson b Adams	1	6	12	-	-
+R.A.Bhatti	c Dodson b Ghous	53	83		5	-	(7) not out	12	15	27	1	-
N.R.Kumar	c&b Ghous	58	45		5	1	c&b Tummala	0	5	8	-	-
R.A.Cheema	not out	12	10		1	-	(6) c Tummala b Ghous	21	15	13	1	-
*A.S.Hansra	not out	2	3		-	-	(5) c Desai b Adams	100	89	112	7	6
M.S.Aulakh												
K.R.Chauhan												
P.A.Desai							(3) c Dodson b Tummala	8	26	34	1	-
U.Limbada												
J.Siddiqui												
	b1 nb1	2					b4 lb3 w2	9				
	(4 wickets, 45 overs)	**239**					(6 wickets declared, 40 overs)	**231**				

USA

		R	B	M	4s	6s		R	B	M	4s	6s
+A.L.Dodson	run out (Limbada)	1	10	13	-	-	(6) c Cheema b Hansra	0	1	2	-	-
A.Mohammed	run out (Hansra)	5	17	17	1	-	st Bhatti b Desai	33	27	45	5	1
A.A.Nanjee	c sub (H.S.Baidwan) b Aulakh	2	13	24	-	-	(4) c Bhatti b Patel	3	6	11	-	-
Q.Alfred	b Chauhan	14	11	16	3	-	(1) c Hansra b Desai	38	28	37	5	2
*J.H.Desai	lbw b Chauhan	43	60	86	5	-	(8) c sub (Baidwan) b Siddiqui	62	45	57	7	1
A.Tummala	c Bhatti b Cheema	25	45	57	4	-	(3) b Siddiqui	63	75	88	4	1
C.P.Singh	b Chauhan	20	22	26	4	-	lbw b Siddiqui	0	1	2	-	-
B.George	lbw b Desai	31	32	35	5	-	(5) c Patel b Hansra	26	28	29	3	-
M.A.Ghous	lbw b Siddiqui	16	42	43	-	-	(10) c&b Desai	39	24		2	2
G.M.Adams	b Desai	0	1	1	-	-	(11) not out	2	2			
H.S.Haidar	not out	4	1	7	-	-	(9) c Siddiqui b Hansra	1	2	2	-	-
	b1 nb3 w1	5					lb2 nb1	3				
	(42.4 overs)	**166**					(39.4 overs)	**270**				

USA	O	M	R	W	nb	w		O	M	R	W	nb	w	fow	Ca (1)	US (1)	Ca (2)	US (2)
Adams	4	0	27	0	-	-		12	2	63	2	-	1	1	71 (2)	1 (1)	3 (2)	68 (1)
Tummala	14	1	68	1	1	-		11	2	29	2	-	-	2	138 (1)	10 (2)	33 (3)	75 (2)
Ghous	9	1	44	2	-	- (4)		7	0	56	2	-	-	3	209 (3)	23 (3)	39 (4)	84 (4)
Desai	11	0	53	0	-	-								4	228 (4)	24 (4)	126 (1)	131 (5)
Alfred	1	0	10	0	-	-								5		85 (6)	161 (6)	131 (6)
Haidar	3	1	13	0	-	-								6		113 (7)	231 (5)	131 (7)
George	3	0	23	0	-	- (3)		10	0	76	0	-	1	7		114 (5)		212 (3)
														8		157 (8)		213 (9)
Canada	O	M	R	W	nb	w		O	M	R	W	nb	w	9		157 (10)		261 (8)
Chauhan	11	3	40	3	1	1		5	0	46	0	1	-	10		166 (9)		270 (10)
Aulakh	10	1	46	1	2	-		2	0	16	0	-	-					
Siddiqui	9.4	1	37	1	-	- (5)		10	0	71	3	-	-					
Desai	8	3	24	2	-	- (3)		12.4	1	72	3	-	-					
Cheema	1	0	2	1	-	-												
Hansra	3	0	16	0	-	-		5	0	39	3	-	-					
Patel						- (4)		5	0	24	1	-	-					

Umpires: P.Chettiar (Canada) and H.Rehman (Canada)

Reserve umpire: A.K.L.Brijcoomar (Canada)

Toss: USA

Player of the Match: A.S.Hansra (Canada)

Close of play: 1st day – USA (1) – 166 all out.

Each innings was restricted to 45 overs.

9

One-day wonders

THE EARLY 2000s witnessed the consolidation of an activity that started in 1979 with the first ICC Trophy and expanded through the 1990s with the setting-up of global and regional international one-day tournaments.

The Asian Cricket Council began the trend in 1984 with a south-east Asian tournament held in Bangkok. By 1996 this had developed into an all-Asian tournament held at four-yearly intervals.

The first European Championships were held in 1996. The South American Championships started in 1995 and the first all-American regional tournament took place in 2000. The first African competition was in 2004. Cricket was included in the South Pacific Games for the first time in 1979.

A feature of these early tournaments was the wide range of ability in the competing countries, which often led to mismatches and the establishment of records of high or low scores and major bowling feats. As the number of countries gaining Affiliate membership of the ICC grew the regional tournaments developed a divisional structure with promotion and relegation. This helped to reduce the mismatches because the countries taking part in any given division were more equal in standard. It also meant that the tournaments became more manageable, most being limited to six countries or fewer.

The ICC Trophy was important because it became a pathway for qualification to the World Cup and the chance to play on the world stage against the Full Member countries. For Sri Lanka, Zimbabwe and Bangladesh, success in the tournaments undoubtedly contributed to their rise to Full Membership. In 2007, the ICC Trophy was abandoned and replaced by the World Cricket League (WCL), a competition with a divisional structure and promotion and relegation between the divisions.

Originally there were five divisions, but this was expanded to eight in 2009 before being cut back first to six, and then to five again for 2016. All the countries in Division One and the top two in Division Two took part in the World Cricket League Championships, a separate one-day competition with, for the top two sides, a qualifying route to the World Cup. For 2015 the qualification was direct, but for 2019 the teams will only gain entry into yet another qualifying competition.

For the 2019 World Cup the top eight countries, as at 30 September 2017, from a group comprising the ten Full Members, Afghanistan and Ireland will qualify automatically. The remaining four will go into a qualifying competition with the top four countries from the WCL Championships and the top two countries from World Cricket League Division Two. The latter will comprise the bottom four countries of the WCL Championships and the two countries promoted from WCL Division Three. This brings the qualification route for the men's World Cup roughly in line with that used for the women's World Cup. Since the women's competition was structured in this way, however, no Associate or Affiliate country has qualified. Thus, while seemingly supporting one-day international cricket among the Associates and Affiliates, by setting up a global structure the ICC has made qualification for its leading one-day tournament much harder.

The matches selected here give a flavour of the wide diversity of one-day internationals among the Associates and Affiliates, ranging from those between the top teams and Full Member countries to highly competitive encounters in the WCL and regional leagues and contests of a more recreational nature, where players of more limited ability are just happy to have the opportunity to represent their country. They include exciting, closely-fought matches and those with landmark or record performances by either teams or individuals. All are important in the cricket history of the countries concerned. A few are included for being marked by some strange or quirky event.

Bizarre qualification rules

Wanting to avoid substantial mismatches between weak and strong teams, which had been a feature of previous tournaments, the ICC split the 24 countries taking part in the 2001 ICC Trophy into two divisions, with two groups in each division. The top three countries in each of the Division One groups qualified for a Super Eight stage. In order to provide a pathway for teams from Division Two to progress, the winners of each of the Division Two groups met the fourth-placed teams from the two Division One groups in play-offs.

The standard procedure in the Super Eight stage is that countries do not meet again those they have already played; they carry the result of the matches in the group stage with them. This normally works fine, but, against expectations, Namibia from Division Two beat Bermuda from Division One in the play-offs. The rules meant that Namibia went forward but took with them Bermuda's record of three wins and two defeats. Namibia went on to win all four of their Super Eight matches but, despite being unbeaten in the competition, finished second in the table to The Netherlands because of the two defeats inherited from matches they did not play.

The weather was excellent for the final, held at the Toronto Cricket, Skating and Curling Club's ground at Armour Heights. Conditions were dry and sunny with the temperature rising to 27°C in the afternoon. Keulder won the toss for Namibia and elected to bat. Although there was nothing in the pitch or the atmosphere to aid the bowlers, he had not taken account of the miserliness of the Dutch attack which maintained a consistent line and length throughout.

Most of Namibia's top order made starts and five of the top six passed 20 but there were only two reasonable partnerships, for the second and fourth wickets. Murgatroyd was the most fluent, facing 68 balls before being dismissed for a half-century. Van Troost conceded only 29 runs in his ten overs. Lefebvre, Khan and de Leede all bowled their ten for fewer than 50 runs each. Namibia's total of 195 was competitive but not requiring more than four runs per over to be beaten, it was hardly challenging. Nor was it likely to produce exciting cricket for the spectators.

The Dutch batsmen experienced the same problems as Namibia's, but instead of consolidating with a view to accelerating the scoring rate later they perished early on against the accuracy of van Vuuren, a double international having represented his country at rugby union, and van Rooi. Only van Noortwijk survived with any assurance but when he became the sixth wicket to fall, his half-century had taken 106 balls and the Dutch were scoring at only 2.86 runs per over.

Van Esmeijer decided that the only chance of victory was to hit out and hope for some luck. He did just that and benefitted from three dropped catches. Two possible run-outs were also missed as Namibia's fielding deteriorated and the Dutch added 84 in ten overs, leaving ten still required from the last over with two wickets remaining.

Bjorn Kotze was trusted with delivering this crucial over and restoring some sanity to a somewhat demoralised fielding side. He managed to keep the target down to three runs off the last ball, which he bowled down the leg side. Esmeijer managed to get a bat on it, glancing it down to fine leg for what, at best, should have been a single but what possessed Walters must have been sheer panic.

Instead of picking the ball up and returning it to the wicketkeeper he decided to stop it by diving at it, and missed. By the time he had recovered and chased it to where it had stopped, the batsmen were running like hounds to complete the third run and take their team to victory.

The Dutch were ecstatic. The rest of the players rushed on to the field to congratulate the batsmen, while the Namibians hung their heads in disbelief at their first defeat in the tournament. Both teams, however, had met the goal of qualifying for the 2003 World Cup. The tournament's unworkable qualification rules were never used again.

NAMIBIA v NETHERLANDS

List A – 50 overs

ICC Trophy – Final

Toronto Cricket, Skating and Curling Club, Wilson Avenue, Armour Heights, Toronto, 15 July 2001

Netherlands won by two wickets

NAMIBIA		R	B	M	4s	6s
R.Walters	b Khan	6	4	3	1	-
*D.Keulder	run out (Lefebvre)	24	63	89	2	-
A.J.Burger	lbw b Lefebvre	38	49	56	4	1
B.G.Murgatroyd	c Khan b Lefebvre	50	68	88	7	-
D.B.Kotze	c Lefebvre b van Troost	28	63	76	1	-
+M.van Schoor	run out (Esmeijer-Scholte)	25	33	48	-	-
L.J.Burger	st Scholte b de Leede	3	7	11	-	-
J.L.Louw	lbw b de Leede	10	6	7	2	-
B.O.van Rooi	c Bradley b de Leede	5	7	7	-	-
B.L.Kotze	not out	0	0	1	-	-
R.J.van Vuuren						
	w6	6				
	(9 wickets, 50 overs)	**195**				

NETHERLANDS		R	B	M	4s	6s
R.F.van Oosterom	run out (B.L.Kotze-van Schoor)	13	42	41	1	-
A.Zulfiqar	c Murgatroyd b van Vuuren	6	7	11	1	-
R.R.A.F.Bradley	lbw b van Vuuren	0	1	1	-	-
K.J.J.van Noortwijk	b B.L.Kotze	50	106	118	5	-
T.B.M.de Leede	c L.J.Burger b van Rooi	16	37	41	1	-
L.P.van Troost	c van Schoor b D.B.Kotze	10	22	33	-	-
J.J.Esmeijer	not out	58	51	71	2	2
*R.P.Lefebvre	c Keulder b van Vuuren	19	24	36	1	-
+R.H.Scholte	run out (Keulder-van Vuuren)	6	8	12	-	-
K.A.Khan	not out	3	3	6	-	-
S.F.Gokke						
	b2 lb9 w4	15				
	(8 wickets, 50 overs)	**196**				

Netherlands	O	M	R	W	nb	w
Khan	10	2	47	1	-	1
Gokke	5	1	12	0	-	-
van Troost	10	0	29	1	-	1
Lefebvre	10	1	42	2	-	1
de Leede	10	2	47	3	-	2
Esmeijer	5	1	18	0	-	1

Namibia	O	M	R	W	nb	w
B.L.Kotze	10	2	36	1	-	-
van Vuuren	10	1	35	3	-	1
van Rooi	10	0	38	1	-	3
Louw	8	1	28	0	-	-
D.B.Kotze	10	0	36	1	-	-
L.J.Burger	2	0	12	0	-	-

fow	Na	Ne
1	7 (1)	12 (2)
2	61 (3)	12 (3)
3	79 (2)	32 (1)
4	139 (4)	59 (5)
5	157 (5)	98 (6)
6	167 (7)	106 (4)
7	182 (8)	158 (8)
8	194 (9)	182 (9)
9	195 (6)	
10		

Umpires: R.E.Koertzen (South Africa) and E.A.Nicholls (West Indies)

TV umpire: D.B.Hair (Australia). Referee: J.R.Reid (New Zealand)

Toss: Namibia

Player of the Match: J.J.Esmeijer (Netherlands)

Netherlands innings: One seven-ball over (26th, J.L.Louw's 7th).

Eliaba excellence

The second Pacifica Championships, hosted by Samoa in 2002, produced several mismatches and, as a result, some impressive bowling analyses. The match between the Cook Islands and New Caledonia, played at the No. 1 Ground of the Faleata Oval complex in Apia, was one example.

The weather was dry and warm with temperatures around 25°C in the morning and up to 30° in the afternoon. Conditions were therefore expected to favour the batsmen with nothing in the pitch or the atmosphere to help the bowlers. In the tournament to that point New Caledonia had lost all three matches, with scores of 43, 37 and 74 all out. Their highest total was against Tonga but since it was in reply to 352/7, they were defeated by 288 runs. The question was whether they would be better matched against the Cook Islands.

The toss fell in favour of the Cook Islands, who chose to bat. They lost Kauvai, run out with only 14 runs on the board, but George and Katoa put on 83 for the second wicket before George, trying to force the pace, missed a straight ball from Selefen. Eliaba gave a catch to the wicketkeeper but Katoa and Brown added 86.

The innings wobbled in the middle order as Selefen picked up two further wickets and it looked as though New Caledonia were just about keeping control of events, despite their inability to bowl a consistent line, unless that consistency was wide. That was before Joe and Marurai adopted a typical South Sea Island approach and attempted to strike every ball to the boundary, which was where most balls that were not signalled wides ended up.

Joe hit 40 in as many minutes with two fours and four sixes and Marurai 63 in only half an hour with four fours and six sixes. The bowlers had no answer to the onslaught of the partnership of 91. Joe was dimissed in the 40th over, after which the run rate slowed, but, nevertheless, at the end of 50 overs, the Cook Islands had amassed a formidable 357/7.

There were 66 extras, of which 46 were wides. Selefen was the most successful bowler, with three wickets, but he was guilty of 16 wides in his ten overs. Lalengo went for 31 runs in only two overs, which included seven wides, and Clovis Wassingalu conceded over 100 in his nine overs.

What followed would have been a humiliating performance if New Caledonia's cricketers were not so cheerful and accustomed to it all. Their reply was a disaster. At 30/3 it looked as though they might make a total in excess of 100, but their last seven wickets went down for 13 runs. Not one player reached double figures and their batsmen were barely able to make contact with the ball.

Some form of defence was a possibility and five batsmen stayed at the crease longer than 20 minutes with Simon Wassingalu undefeated after batting for just over half an hour as the whole innings was over in one hour and eight minutes. Altogether New Caledonia made 31 runs from the bat, but when their players did hit the ball, they hit it hard; 20 of these runs came from boundaries.

They were undone by the pace of Deunu Eliaba, who bowled eight overs, taking 9-16. He finished the innings with a hat-trick, all bowled. He was, however, responsible for eight of the nine wides bowled by the Cook Islands.

Eliaba became the first person to take nine wickets in a one-day international innings, in which the bowlers are restricted in the number of overs they can bowl. The only previous instance of a nine-wicket return was the 9-46 by Chris Searson for Jersey against Guernsey in 1993, but, in that match, although each innings was restricted to 55 overs, there was no limit on the number of overs each bowler could bowl and Searson sent down 16.4 overs.

COOK ISLANDS v NEW CALEDONIA

50 overs

Pacifica Championship 2002 – Group B

Faleata Gardens Oval No. 1 Ground, Apia, 4 June 2002

Cook Islands won by 314 runs

COOK ISLANDS		R	B	M	4s	6s
T.Kauvai	run out	13		-	-	-
T.R.George	b Selefen	29		97	3	1
+T.Katoa	c Passil b C.Wassingalu	96		171	10	3
D.Eliaba	c Sinyeue b Folituu	4		-	-	-
C.M.Brown	c Tuakoifenua b Selefen	31		47	2	1
T.Marukore	c S.Wassingalu b Selefen	7				
J.J.Joe	c Xalitre b C.Wassingalu	40		40	2	4
M.Marurai	not out	63		30	4	6
N.Tangimetua	not out	8				
I.Tangimetua						
I.Henry						
	b3 lb6 nb11 w46	66				
	(7 wickets, 50 overs)	**357**				

NEW CALEDONIA		R	B	M	4s	6s
S.Selefen	b Eliaba	7		10	1	-
C.Wassingalu	b Eliaba	7		20	1	-
N.Passil	c Katoa b Eliaba	0	1	2	-	-
M.Tuakoifenua	lbw b Eliaba	4		22	1	-
J.P.Lalengo	b Marurai	1		20	-	-
S.Wassingalu	not out	8		31	1	-
J.Xalitre	b Eliaba	0		3	-	-
B.Waneux	b Eliaba	4		8	1	-
+N.Sinyeue	b Eliaba	0	5	5	-	-
B.Hmeun	b Eliaba	0	1	1	-	-
K.Folituu	b Eliaba	0	1	1	-	-
	b1 lb1 nb1 w9	12				
	(15 overs)	**43**				

New Caledonia	O	M	R	W	nb	w
Tuakoifenua	10	1	35	0	-	2
Passil	9	0	71	0	2	6
Folituu	10	0	46	1	2	6
Lalengo	2	0	31	0	3	7
Selefen	10	0	58	3	4	16
C.Wassingalu	9	0	107	2	-	9

Cook Islands	O	M	R	W	nb	w
Eliaba	8	2	16	9	-	8
Joe	2	0	13	0	-	1
Brown	2	1	5	0	1	-
Marurau	3	1	7	1	-	-

fow	CI	NC
1	14 (1)	14 (1)
2	97 (2)	14 (3)
3	103 (4)	19 (2)
4	189 (5)	30 (4)
5	225 (6)	30 (5)
6	258 (3)	31 (7)
7	349 (7)	37 (8)
8		43 (9)
9		43 (10)
10		43 (11)

Umpires: F.Griffin (New Zealand) and P.D.Jones (New Zealand)

Toss: Cook Islands

In New Caledonia's innings D.Eliaba performed the hat-trick when dismissing N.Sinyeue, B.Hmeun and K.Folituu

Records galore

The Emerging Nations Tournament was established by the Asian Cricket Council (ACC) to remove the weaker countries from the main Asian Cricket Council Cup and thereby avoid some of the mismatches which had characterised previous Asian competitions. Unfortunately the ACC did not appreciate just how great the differences in standards were between even the lower-ranked teams.

The match between the Maldives and Brunei on 4 February 2005 was a prime example. Played at the Polo Club ground in Bangkok, it produced five national records, all of which are still standing.

The Maldives batted first after winning the toss and lost their first wicket quickly as Ismail Nadeem was bowled by Khan with only six runs scored. What followed can only be described as a massacre. The second-wicket partnership produced 244 runs, the highest ever made by the Maldives in international cricket. Brunei tried seven bowlers with little success and their plight was made worse by an injury to Cheema after he had bowled only five overs.

The only way Brunei could get wickets was through mistakes made by the batsmen and these came, but not very frequently. With the score on 250, Ahmed Hussain departed but then Afzal Faiz and Ismail Anil both scored heavily, accompanying Moosa Kaleem in stands of 94 and 49. A further 71 was added for the fifth wicket before Moosa Kaleem was finally trapped, stumped by Mansur Ahmed to give Kamat his only wicket. Moosa Kaleem's 217 is the highest individual international score made by a player from the Maldives and the highest made in one-day internationals by any player from an Associate or Affiliate country.

Neesham Nasir and Abdullah Shahid raised the score to 486, when, undoubtedly to the relief of Brunei, they ran out of overs. The Maldives' total is their highest international team score. All Brunei's bowlers were annihilated. The unfortunate Kamat went for 118 runs off his ten overs and Adnan Bagul conceded 36 in two overs, after which he was removed from the attack.

Brunei never had a chance in their reply. Mansur Ahmed, their captain, wicketkeeper and, by some way, their most experienced player was injured, which meant that neither he nor Cheema were likely to bat. Ahmed was a Bangladeshi who had taken a post with the Brunei Darussalam Cricket Association in 1996, to aid the development of cricket in the country. With his background of an MBA from Dhaka University, he soon found himself doing much of the organisation as well as coaching. He became the manager of cricket development in 2003 and the chief executive officer of the Cricket Association in 2005. He returned to Bangladesh in 2010 to become the CEO of the Bangladesh Cricket Board, but died of a heart attack in January 2012.

Brunei played defensively, seemingly with the aim of seeing how long they could last. With the score on 15 they lost Thomas leg-before to Ismail Anil, but by the time the score reached 30, they had seen off the Maldives' opening attack. Neesham Nasir, however, proved a different proposition. In a performance, the like of which he was never able to repeat, he removed the heart of Brunei's batting as from 30/1 they went to 39/7. After a late partnership of four runs, he then removed Adnan Bagul to finish with six wickets in five overs and three balls, while conceding only one run, the best international bowling analysis for the Maldives and one which is unlikely to be surpassed.

Brunei's innings lasted into the 20th over but accumulated only 43 runs, the country's lowest-ever international team score. Only Thapa and the number of wides reached double figures as the Maldives won the match by an incredible 443 runs, a huge margin for a one-day international, and went on to win the tournament. The result was widely applauded as that country's first major international sporting achievement. Their players returned home to a rousing welcome at the airport and a special presidential reception.

BRUNEI v MALDIVES

50 overs

Asian Cricket Council Emerging Nations Tournament

Polo Club Ground, Bangkok, 4 February 2005

Maldives won by 443 runs

MALDIVES		R	B	M	4s	6s
Ahmed Hussain	c [unknown] b Adnan Bagul	51				
Ismail Nadheem	b Khan	4				
*Moosa Kaleem	st Mansur Ahmed b Kamat	217				
Afzal Faiz	b Thomas	71				
Ismail Anil	b Khan	60				
Neesham Nasir	not out	32				
Abdullah Shahid	not out	5				
+Abdullah Shafeeu						
Hassan Ibrahim						
Mohammed Mahafooz						
Husham Ibrahim						
	b1 lb11 nb2 w32	46				
	(5 wickets, 50 overs)	**486**				

BRUNEI		R	B	M	4s	6s
S.Thapa	c [unknown] b Neesham Nasir	12				
N.Thomas	lbw b Ismail Anil	2				
A.Philip	st Abdullah Shafeeu b Neesham Nasir	3				
S.J.Kamat	c [unknown] b Neesham Nasir	6				
S.Khan	c [unknown] b Neesham Nasir	0				
Johari Noor	c [unknown] b Mohammed Mahafooz	1				
Packir Maideen	b Neesham Nasir	1				
Adnan Bagul	lbw b Neesham Nasir	1				
Kifli Yasin	not out	2				
*+Mansur Ahmed	absent injured					
B.Cheema	absent injured					
	lb1 nb1 w13	15				
	(19.3 overs)	**43**				

Brunei	O	M	R	W	nb	w		fow	Mld	Bru
Khan	10	0	77	1				1	6	15
Cheema	5	0	33	1				2	250	30
Philip	8	0	65	0				3	344	31
Thapa	6	0	52	0				4	393	31
Kamat	10	0	118	1				5	464	38
Adnan Bagul	2	0	36	1				6		38
Thomas	9	0	33	1				7		39
								8		43
Maldives	O	M	R	W	nb	w		9		
Husham Ibrahim	3	0	13	0				10		
Ismail Anil	4	1	10	1						
Abdullah Shahid	4	1	11	0						
Neesham Nasir	5.3	5	1	6						
Mohammed Mahafooz	3	0	7	1						

Umpires: Capt Surinder Singh (Thailand) and S.Sarda (Thailand)

Toss: Maldives.

Fun for aged expatriates

For the 2005 ICC Trophy, 63 countries took part in qualifying rounds with 12 making it through to the competition proper, held in Ireland. Of these, Oman made their debut while the USA maintained their record of having played in every competition. Neither country had much success. Oman lost their first five matches and the USA four out of their five, with one game abandoned because of rain.

The first week of the competition was characterised by cool, wet weather, and many players struggled in the somewhat alien conditions of a typical Irish summer. In the second week the weather improved, becoming dry and, by local standards, hot, with temperatures peaking at 25°C. Oman and the USA both won their next games and found themselves meeting in the ninth-place play-off.

The match was clearly a battle of the aged expatriates. The USA had only two players born in the 1980s but six born in the 1960s. Oman had only one player born in the 1980s and three born in the 1960s. The American team had eight players born in the Caribbean and two born in Pakistan. The 11th player, Leon Romero, though born in New York, learnt his cricket in the West Indies and had represented Trinidad and Tobago, so he, too, could be classed as a cricketer of Caribbean origin. Oman's side comprised eight born in Pakistan and three in India. The American side was the most experienced. It included two West Indian Test cricketers, Clayton Lambert and Hamish Anthony.

Staple won the toss and decided to bat. Opening, however, he lost his wicket with only nine runs on the board. Massiah also failed to contribute much and the Americans found themselves on 31/2. Thereafter, they showed what a good batting pitch existed at the North County Club. Aided by its renowned fast outfield, runs came at pace as Romero and Roopnarine added 136. Apart from Romero, whose 48 took 90 balls to compile, all the Americans scored at a run a ball or faster.

None of Oman's bowlers could exert any control as although wickets fell, the situation just got worse with 97 runs scored in an unbeaten seventh-wicket partnership. Reid hit 61 off only 29 balls with three fours and six magnificent sixes. Not to be outdone, Anthony made 39 off 20 balls with three fours and three sixes. The American total of 345/6 was the highest of the tournament to date and, given their opponent's batting record, looked like an easily defendable target.

Oman began well with a partnership of 47, but once Adnan Ilyas was out, they lost wickets at regular intervals. Most of their batsmen made starts, but none could make the sizeable contribution needed. With half the side gone for 102 an American victory looked only a matter of time before Redkar and Mohammad Aslam gave some respectability to the total in a partnership of 73. Though both were dismissed by the time the score rose to 211, they had done enough to show that the American bowling was far from invincible.

Farhan Khan and Azhar Ali clearly took note of this. Farhan, in particular, was especially severe, striking balls to all parts of the ground. In an incredible innings he reached 94 off only 47 balls, with four fours and nine sixes. It was fortunate that the Americans had so many players who could bowl and they tried seven but none had any idea how to get Farhan out.

Azhar Ali was slightly more sedate in his approach, taking 30 balls to make 44, with three fours and three sixes. Farhan was denied what would have been an outstanding hundred, simply because his team reached their target first with a partnership of 137 from 11 overs and five balls. Oman had the highest team total for the tournament and one of their greatest victories, made with just five balls to spare. Not surprisingly, Farhan Khan was named as the player of the match.

OMAN v UNITED STATES OF AMERICA

List A – 50 overs

ICC Trophy – Ninth-Place Play-off

North County Ground, The Inch, Balrothery, 11 July 2005

Oman won by three wickets

USA

		R	B	M	4s	6s
G.Roopnarine	b Mehta	98	108	149	14	-
*R.W.Staple	c Awal Khan b Farhan Khan	4	7	8	1	-
S.J.Massiah	lbw b Desai	5	10	14	1	-
+L.C.Romero	c Redkar b Mohammad Asif	48	90	108	5	-
B.S.Bartley	c Farhan Khan b Tariq Hussain	28	22	22	2	2
C.B.Lambert	run out	23	16	24	3	1
C.A.Reid	not out	61	29	50	3	6
H.A.G.Anthony	not out	39	20	31	3	3
Aijaz Ali						
Nasir Javed						
H.R.Johnson						
	b4 lb13 nb1 w21	39				
	(6 wickets, 50 overs)	**345**				

OMAN

		R	B	M	4s	6s
Adnan Ilyas	c Nasir Javed b Johnson	14	19	25	2	-
H.P.Desai	c Romero b Anthony	29	21	29	3	2
Mohammad Asif	c Aijaz Ali b Johnson	11	19	23	2	-
Awal Khan	c Romero b Anthony	19	22	35	2	1
H.J.Mehta	b Bartley	9	36	48	1	-
+J.V.Redkar	c Massiah b Staple	38	53	68	4	-
Mohammad Aslam	c Staple b Bartley	58	50	49	8	1
Farhan Khan	not out	94	47	64	4	9
*Azhar Ali	not out	44	30	53	3	3
Tariq Hussain						
Mazhar Khan						
	b1 lb7 nb4 w20	32				
	(7 wickets, 49.1 overs)	**348**				

Oman	O	M	R	W	nb	w
Desai	10	1	69	1	-	4
Farhan Khan	9	2	79	1	-	6
Awal Khan	10	0	56	0	-	1
Mohammad Asif	10	0	46	1	-	3
Mehta	7	1	40	1	-	1
Tariq Hussain	4	0	38	1	-	1

USA	O	M	R	W	nb	w
Reid	6	0	43	0	-	-
Johnson	10	1	48	2	4	3
Anthony	9.1	0	47	2	-	3
Nasir Javed	5	0	32	0	-	2
Bartley	10	0	55	2	-	1
Staple	7	0	85	1	-	2
Massiah	2	0	30	0	-	-

fow	USA	Oman
1	9 (2)	47 (1)
2	31 (3)	48 (2)
3	167 (4)	66 (3)
4	201 (1)	82 (4)
5	203 (5)	102 (5)
6	248 (6)	175 (6)
7		211 (7)
8		
9		
10		

Umpires: R.Dill (Bermuda) and T.Henry (Ireland)

Toss: USA

Player of the Match: Farhan Khan (Oman)

It is not known who bowled the no-ball in USA's innings.

All over in 75 balls

A huge mismatch occurred during the Asian Cricket Council Trophy in Kuala Lumpur in 2006 when Nepal met Myanmar. The Nepalese team were based on that which had finished eighth in the Under-19 World Cup in 2000. They were still a relatively young side, but a successful one. They had won the Plate competition in the 2004 ACC Trophy tournament and, in 2004 and 2005, participated in the ICC Intercontinental Cup, winning two and drawing two of their four matches. These had included a victory over the United Arab Emirates.

In contrast, Myanmar were playing their first internationals since 1927, when Burma, as the country was then known, met MCC in Rangoon (now Yangon). Since that time cricket had declined, despite a visit from the Pakistanis after their tour of India in 1952/53. By the 1990s it had virtually died out, but in the early 2000s an attempt was made at revival. In 1927, Burma's side was largely expatriate, but the new team was 45 per cent ethnic Burmese. It was, however, highly inexperienced and had already been outclassed, losing to Kuwait, Bhutan and Hong Kong. The latter had dismissed them for 20 to win by 422 runs.

On a dry, sunny day, with temperatures hitting 33°C at times, Nepal won the toss and fielded, taking advantage of the slightly cooler or, less hot, period of the day. Alam with his left-arm medium-fast was too pacey for Myanmar's batsmen. Omer was dismissed from the first ball of the innings and Mohammed followed off the fifth to leave Myanmar on 0/2. Zarkariya negotiated the next over, bowled by Das, but two more wickets went down in Alam's second over and Myanmar were 4/4 after only three overs.

Three runs were added by Zarkariya and Ye Myo Tun in overs five and six but in the seventh over, Alam's fourth, two more wickets were lost to leave the score at 6/7. Any semblance of resistance ended when Zarkariya, who had defended stoutly for 20 balls, was leg-before to Das.

The innings was all over on the first ball of the 13th over and Myanmar were all out for ten, still the lowest innings score in men's international cricket. Leg byes top-scored with three, followed by wides with two. Five batsmen made one, the equal top score from the bat, and five failed to score.

Although it was a hapless batting display, Myanmar's cricketers had never played at this level before and were facing one of the best new-ball attacks in Associate cricket. Alam finished with 7-3 from 6.1 overs and Das was relatively expensive by comparison, conceding more runs, four, than he obtained wickets, three.

The only question was how long Nepal would take to achieve victory. No one could have predicted what followed. Chhetri hit Aye Min Than's first ball for three then the next three deliveries were all wides, two of which resulted in additional runs, while the fielders retrieved the ball, and the total stood at 8/0 off one legitimate ball.

The next ball, Aye Min Than's sixth attempt, was struck by Chand and three more runs were scored, meaning Nepal had won by ten wickets off two balls, a result which may be the greatest mismatch ever in an international fixture. Not a single boundary was hit during the whole game. Perhaps it was as well that matches between two teams in a neutral country rarely attract large crowds. At least Myanmar were not humiliated in front of a large audience.

MYANMAR v NEPAL

50 overs

Asian Cricket Council Trophy – Group C

Kelab Aman, Jalan Dampai, Ampang, Kuala Lumpur, 20 August 2006

Nepal won by ten wickets

MYANMAR		R	B	M	4s	6s
+Omer	lbw b Alam	0	1	1	-	-
Zarkariya	lbw b Das	1	20	38	-	-
Mohammed	b Alam	1	3	2	-	-
Abdul Rahman	b Alam	0	4	6	-	-
A.R.A.Sharjeel	c Basnet b Alam	0	4	3	-	-
Ye Myo Tun	b Alam	1	11	14	-	-
*Tin Maung Aye	b Alam	0	3	3	-	-
Zin Min Swe	b Das	1	9	13	-	-
Yusuf	c Gupta b Das	1	11	13	-	-
Aye Min Than	b Alam	0	4	3	-	-
Sai Sai Wunna	not out	0	4	3	-	-
	lb3 w2	5				
	(12.1 overs)	**10**				

NEPAL		R	B	M	4s	6s
+M.K.Chhetri	not out	3	1	4	-	-
D.B.Chand	not out	3	1	4	-	-
A.K.Gupta						
G.Malla						
P.Khadka						
S.Vesawkar						
M.Alam						
B.K.Das						
B.Regmi						
R.Basnet						
R.K.Pradhan						
	w5	5				
	(no wicket, 0.2 overs)	**11**				

Nepal	O	M	R	W	nb	w
Alam	6.1	3	3	7	-	-
Das	6	2	4	3	-	2

Myanmar	O	M	R	W	nb	w
Aye Min Than	0.2	0	11	0	-	3

fow	My	Np
1	0 (1)	
2	0 (3)	
3	4 (4)	
4	4 (5)	
5	7 (6)	
6	7 (7)	
7	8 (2)	
8	9 (8)	
9	10 (9)	
10	10 (10)	

Umpires: S.S.Prasad (Singapore) and A.M.Saheba (India)

TV umpire: Shafizan bin Shariman (Malaysia). Referee: R.J.Ratnayake (Sri Lanka)

Toss: Nepal

Player of the Match: M.Alam (Nepal)

Amini triumph at Amini Park

Papua New Guinea hosted their first women's international tournament in September 2006 at their new facilities at Amini Park, Port Moresby. The occasion was the inaugural East Asia-Pacific women's tournament, which served as a first round qualifier for the Women's World Cup.

Japan were the only other participants in what was the Japanese women's second international outing. They had appeared in the World Cup qualifying competition in The Netherlands in 2003, when they were completely outclassed. The 2006 tournament was therefore an indicator of the level of improvement, if any, in their standard.

A feature of the home team was the number of players who were related to the country's leading male cricketers. Cheryl Amini was the sister of Charles Amini, one of the country's leading players in the late 1980s and early 1990s. Kune Amini, the captain, was the wife of Charles. Their three sons all played for their country. Hebou and Varoi Morea were sisters and Hebou was married to John Ovia, a regular choice for the men's team in the early 2000s.

With only two countries involved, the competition was based on a three-match series. At the start of the third, on 15 September, Japan were 2-0 down and Papua New Guinea were certain of their place in the second round of the World Cup qualifying contest, to be staged in South Africa in 2008.

Japan won the toss and opted to bat first but they started poorly, in both wickets lost and runs made. By the time both openers were out the score was only 22 and Papua New Guinea were bowling their 13th over. Yamauchi, who was the first to go, seemed to maintain most of the strike without being able to score runs. She made three off 51 balls, far from the kind of start any team wants in limited-overs cricket. Kuribayashi, however, played superbly, showing the potential that she was to realise in future years when she became easily Japan's best player. Her strokeplay was impressive, particularly her drives through cover.

She had support from Yamamoto, who found the boundary five times, one more than Kuribayashi achieved. Together they took the score to 131 before Yamamoto gave a catch to Cheryl Amini, and her dismissal caused a slight wobble. Instead of pushing on with the scoring, Takemori was run out after striking one boundary and Chinone was bowled first ball. Nakayama scored in ones and twos, sufficient to give Kuribayashi the strike. By the end of the 50 overs the score had advanced to 156. Papua New Guinea's attack had been steady, but without penetration, relying on mistakes by the Japanese to get their wickets.

Papua New Guinea's batting quickly proved the opposite to their bowling. They attacked from the start, scoring at more than four runs an over. Mea and Hebou Morea put on 65 for the first wicket, giving their side a clear advantage on run rate and laying the foundation from which to reach the target with ease. Both were out leg-before, Mea with the score on 65 and Morea with the total on 74.

David was bowled trying to score quickly, but Kune Amini had no difficulty dispatching the Japanese bowling to the boundary. Cheryl Amini was even more aggressive and together they reached the target in the 36th over with Kune unbeaten on 41 off 75 balls, with six fours, and Cheryl unbeaten on 29, made from 54 balls, with five fours. Like their counterparts, the Japanese bowlers rarely looked like taking wickets. Kuribayashi, though without a wicket, was the most economical with four maidens in her eight overs.

These two countries have remained particularly well-matched. Japan won the equivalent tournament in 2010, and since then 50-over internationals have given way to T20. Japan won the East Asia-Pacific Championship in 2012 and Papua New Guinea in 2014. Japan's greatest achievement to date has been to win the bronze medal in women's cricket at the Asian Games in 2010.

PAPUA NEW GUINEA WOMEN v JAPAN WOMEN

50 overs

East Asia-Pacific Championships

Amini Park, Port Moresby, 15 September 2006

Papua New Guinea won by seven wickets

JAPAN		R	B	M	4s	6s
S.Kubota	lbw b Lumis	1	23	20	-	-
A.Yamauchi	run out (David-Arua)	3	51	55	-	-
*E.Kuribayashi	not out	67	133	165	4	-
M.Yamamoto	c C.Amini b Revaea	46	88	105	5	-
M.Takemori	run out (Heagi)	6	8	10	1	-
+Y.Chinone	b Revaea	0	1	1	-	-
M.Nakayama	not out	10	14	15	-	-
S.Sato						
A.Suda						
Y.Tsukui						
R.Hiroto						
	b1 lb1 nb4 w17	23				
	(5 wickets, 50 overs)	**156**				

PNG		R	B	M	4s	6s
G.Mea	lbw b Takemori	27	46	67	3	-
H.A.Morea	lbw b Hiroto	26	46	50	5	-
*K.R.Amini	not out	41	75	90	6	-
B.David	b Takemori	6	16	18	-	-
C.Amini	not out	29	54	55	5	-
B.Revaea						
K.Heagi						
H.Sam						
+B.Arua						
K.Lumis						
V.I.Morea						
	b1 nb9 w19	29				
	(3 wickets, 36 overs)	**158**				

PNG	O	M	R	W	nb	w
Heagi	10	4	24	0	1	1
Lumis	10	0	26	1	-	8
David	10	3	23	0	-	-
Sam	7	1	29	0	2	5
Revaea	8	1	35	2	-	2
V.I.Morea	5	1	17	0	1	1

Japan	O	M	R	W	nb	w
Sato	8	1	37	0	1	3
Hiroto	7	0	44	1	4	7
Tsukui	5	0	24	0	2	-
Takemori	8	0	36	2	2	9
Kuribayashi	8	4	16	0	-	1

fow	Jap	PNG
1	7 (2)	65 (2)
2	22 (1)	74 (1)
3	113 (4)	92 (4)
4	131 (5)	
5	131 (6)	
6		
7		
8		
9		
10		

Umpires: C.D.Elly (Papua New Guinea) and N.D.Harrison (Japan)

Referee: C.A.Campbell (New Zealand)

Toss: Japan

S.Sato (Japan) became S.Miyaji after she married N.A.Miyaji, the Japanese men's international cricketer.

New Caledonia in record books – again!

Samoa hosted the South Pacific Games in 2007 at their newly-developed Faleata Complex in Apia. While it was expected that Papua New Guinea would, yet again, win the gold medal, the competition was not devoid of interest. For the statistician, the encounter between Papua New Guinea and New Caledonia offered the prospect of another mismatch with records being beaten, unless New Caledonia had improved immensely over their performance in the previous Games in 2003. Then Papua New Guinea had amassed 502/8 off their 50 overs before dismissing New Caledonia for 34, an innings which lasted only ten overs.

In warm, dry conditions, with afternoon temperatures reaching 29°C but tempered by a sea breeze, Papua New Guinea chose to bat after winning the toss. They quickly took the New Caledonian bowling apart as Uda and Ravusiro put on 121 runs and the first wicket did not fall until the 14th over.

Arua missed out, falling leg-before without scoring, to give Kalepo Folituu, the eighth bowler tried, two wickets in two overs. Uda and Pala took advantage of every scoring opportunity, striking the ball to all parts of the ground as Uda reached his century in the 21st over. By the time he was bowled by Fuimaono for 123, in the 24th, a record score for Papua New Guinea looked highly possible.

Although New Caledonia's bowlers tried their hardest and were backed up by some enthusiastic fielding, Pala and Dai were not to be tamed. Both reached their hundreds in a partnership of 245 in 20 overs before offering catches which their opponents were only too pleased to take. Vala then struck 51 from 13 balls and Dikana made ten from only two. Papua New Guinea easily passed their record team score and finished on 572/7, the highest score ever made in a one-day international.

New Caledonia's players were probably relieved that the match had been reduced to 49 overs per side. Ludovic Waneux was their most successful bowler, picking up three wickets, but his ten overs went for 146 runs. The umpires must have made an error in allowing Boaoutho to bowl 11 overs, one more than the maximum allowed.

It was unlikely that New Caledonia would get anywhere near the target but they showed more resistance than four years previously as Papua New Guinea used five bowlers before dismissing them for 62. Their innings lasted 26 overs and two of their batsmen reached double figures. Even so, the margin of victory, 510 runs, was 42 runs greater than before.

Despite perpetually being comprehensively outplayed, the enthusiasm of New Caledonia's cricketers in always coming back for more shows great commitment. When they hosted the 2011 Games they created a new cricket facility at N'Du. Unfortunately, only three other countries chose to send teams, Papua New Guinea, Fiji and Vanuatu. Papua New Guinea won, of course, and, of course, New Caledonia finished last.

NEW CALEDONIA v PAPUA NEW GUINEA

50 overs

South Pacific Games

Faleata Gardens Oval No. 2 Ground, Apia, 31 August 2007

Papua New Guinea won by 510 runs

PNG		R	B	M	4s	6s
A.Uda	b Fuimaono	123				
P.M.Ravusiro	c Selefen b K.Folituu	58				
K.Arua	lbw b K.Folituu	0				
K.Pala	c Kamouda b L.Waneux	146				
M.D.Dai	c Apiazari b S.Folituu	105				
A.Vala	c [unknown] b L.Waneux	51	13			
V.V.Morea	c [unknown] b L.Waneux	29				
M.Kivung	not out	0				
R.Dikana	not out	10	2			
P.Arua						
J.M.Mado						
	b3 lb4 nb10 w33	50				
	(7 wickets, 49 overs)	**572**				

NEW CALEDONIA		R	B	M	4s	6s
K.Folituu	c Morea b Mado	0				
N.Gatuhau	lbw b P.Arua	6				
S.Kilama	c [unknown] b K.Arua	12				
S.D.Kamouda	b P.Arua	0				
F.Fuimaono	lbw b Mado	5				
S.Folituu	b Mado	0				
J.M.Apiazari	c Mado b Dai	17				
E.Waneux	run out	1				
S.Boaoutho	run out	1				
S.Selefen	not out	3				
L.Waneux	run out (Kivung)	0				
	b1 lb1 nb2 w14	18				
	(26 overs)	**62**				

New Caledonia	O	M	R	W	nb	w		fow	PNG	NCal
L.Waneux	10		146	3				1	121 (2)	
Fuimaono	4		39	1				2	121 (3)	
Boaoutho	11		132	0				3	229 (1)	
S.Folituu	3		52	1				4	474 (4)	
Kilama	4		36	0				5	?	
E.Waneux	5		44	0				6	?	
Kamouda	2		28	0				7	?	
K.Folituu	10		96	2				8		
								9		
PNG	O	M	R	W	nb	w		10		
Dai	3		15	1						
Kivung	5		9	0						
Mado	9		21	3						
P.Arua	5		9	2						
K.Arua	4		8	1						

Umpires: [unknown]

Referee: B.Aldridge (New Zealand)

Toss: Papua New Guinea

Match was reduced to 49 overs per side

In Papua New Guinea's innings the bowling is eight runs over; it is not known why Boaoutho bowled 11 overs. In New Caledonia's innings the batting is one run over, the bowling is two runs over and the fall of wickets is not known.

All ten for Alam

In 2007 the ICC introduced the World Cricket League as a competition for the top Associate and Affiliate sides. This provided an opportunity for the top countries to play against others of a similar standard across the world, instead of being confined to regional competitions.

Previously the ICC Trophy had provided that possibility, but only once every four years, whereas the World Cricket League adopted a two-year cycle. The number of teams in each division varied, with most, in the inaugural cycle, being allocated to Division Five, which comprised 12 countries. These included Nepal and the United States, both of which had taken part in the ICC Intercontinental Cup and were recognised as being of reasonable quality, whereas the relative standings of the other participants, Afghanistan, Bahamas, Botswana, Germany, Japan, Jersey, Mozambique, Norway, Singapore and Vanuatu, were then largely unknown.

Nepal and Mozambique met in the group stage on 25 May at Grainville, Jersey. The match was originally scheduled for the previous day when a start was made, but after Nepal had dismissed Mozambique for 70 and had reached two without loss in reply, rain intervened. In the case of an abandonment the tournament regulations permitted the game to be replayed on one of the scheduled rest days. So the teams assembled again the following day in cool, damp conditions, typical of the early part of a British summer.

Nepal made one change from the team that played the previous day, dropping their leg spinner, Pradhan, for a pace bowler, Chand. With Gauchan and both Sanjay and Basant Regmi they still had three spin options. Mozambique kept the same side. Their captain won the toss and, most likely reflecting on their previous efforts, decided to field. Their opening attack of Koliya and Lili were remarkably successful and seemed to enjoy being able to get the ball to move around off the pitch and in the air as they soon had Nepal in trouble at 30/3. First-change bowler Karim was also economical, conceding only 34 runs in his ten overs.

Gauchan and Malla played sensibly, however, taking advantage of scoring opportunities, without trying to force the pace. Their partnership was 73 before Gauchan was dismissed but Khadka continued in a similar fashion, accelerating towards the end. He fell with the score on 183 having made 44 from 50 balls, with two fours and one six. Malla and Alam took the total above 200 but, on 204, Malla's innings ended for 71 off 101 balls with four fours. Alam and Basant Regmi scored rapidly by hitting the ball into the open spaces but neither hit a boundary. Mozambique were unable to stop the runs and, after 50 overs, Nepal had made a comfortable 238.

In the afternoon the temperature struggled upwards to a maximum of 19°C but under cloudy skies with rain threatening and humidity at 80 per cent, Alam, with his experience, was able to exploit the conditions to far greater effect than Mozambique's bowlers. Bowling full and varying between straight deliveries and making the ball swing, he proved devastating to an inexperienced batting line-up.

Beaten for pace and changing line, Mozambique's batsmen were clueless. The only resistance came from Shah, easily their most accomplished cricketer, who survived 41 balls but still made only nine runs. In a superb spell of nearly eight overs Alam took all ten wickets for just 12 runs. Although Mozambique struggled to 19 in 14.5 overs, in many ways their performance was even worse than Myanmar's against the same bowler in 2006. Nine of the batsmen failed to score and three times Alam was on a hat-trick. The last four wickets fell for no runs.

Alam was the fourth Associate cricketer to take ten wickets in an innings, after T.S. Gilbert (Bermuda), J.B. King (Philadelphia) and K. Saker (Malaysia), and the first to do so in the limited-overs format. Not surprisingly, he was named the player of the match.

MOZAMBIQUE v NEPAL

50 overs

World Cricket League Division 5 – Group A

Jersey Island Cricket Club Ground, Grainville, St Saviour, 25 May 2008

Nepal won by 219 runs

NEPAL

		R	B	M	4s	6s
P.P.Lohani	c Karim b Koliya	9	26	43	1	-
+M.K.Chhetri	c Puspussen b Lili	16	29	29	2	-
S.Vesawkar	c Khorava b Lili	1	7	8	-	-
S.P.Gauchan	c Qadir b Patel	34	66	89	3	-
G.Malla	c Ikheriya b Koliya	71	101	152	4	-
P.Khadka	c Ikheriya b Puspussen	44	50	55	2	1
M.Alam	not out	23	13	25	-	-
B.Regmi	c Patel b Koliya	16	10	12	-	-
*B.K.Das	not out	0	0		-	-
S.Regmi						
D.B.Chand						
	lb3 nb2 w19	24				
	(7 wickets, 50 overs)	**238**				

MOZAMBIQUE

		R	B	M	4s	6s
I.I.M.Ikheriya	b Alam	0	6	4		
N.G.Karim	b Alam	0	4	9		
M.Z.Sidat	lbw b Alam	0	8	16		
S.K.R.Shah	c Chhetri b Alam	9	41	42		
Z.G.Patel	lbw b Alam	0	1	6		
+J.M.Khorava	lbw b Alam	0	5	3		
M.K.Qadir	lbw b Alam	0	6	11		
*M.S.Younus	not out	2	12	17		
C.S.C.Puspussen	b Alam	0	1	2		
M.A.A.Koliya	b Alam	0	2	1		
I.S.Lili	b Alam	0	2	1		
	lb2 w6	8				
	(14.5 overs)	**19**				

Mozambique	O	M	R	W	nb	w
Koliya	10	2	49	3	1	3
Lili	10	1	40	2	-	2
Karim	10	0	34	0	-	2
Younus	6	0	31	0	-	6
Patel	8	1	42	1	-	4
Puspussen	6	0	39	1	1	2

Nepal	O	M	R	W	nb	w
Alam	7.5	1	12	10	-	4
Das	3	1	3	0	-	2
Gauchan	4	2	2	0	-	-

fow	Nep	Moz
1	24 (2)	0 (1)
2	30 (3)	1 (2)
3	30 (1)	6 (3)
4	103 (4)	8 (5)
5	183 (6)	9 (6)
6	204 (5)	12 (7)
7	234 (8)	19 (4)
8		19 (9)
9		19 (10)
10		19 (11)

Umpires: M.Carpenter (Jersey) and S.Kad (Finland)

Toss: Mozambique

Player of the Match: M.Alam (Nepal)

Advance Afghanistan

Saturday 31 May 2008 was finals day for the first World Cricket League Division Five competition. Against all expectations it was not Nepal and the USA who took the field, but the hosts Jersey, and the surprise team of the competition, Afghanistan. For Jersey there was the prospect of victory in front of their home crowd in only their second international tournament. For Afghanistan, it would mean winning their first cricket trophy outright. Their previous best had been to share the ACC T20 Trophy with Oman in 2007.

Ball-by-ball commentary was provided on the local radio in Jersey and transmitted worldwide over the internet. It could therefore be followed live in internet cafés in Kabul while 1,000 people crammed into the ground to witness the event, creating pressure on the players of both sides to perform well. Compared to earlier in the tournament, conditions were good for cricket. It was dry and sunny, though not especially warm, with temperatures about 15°C in the morning and reaching 19° in the afternoon.

Hague won the toss for Jersey and chose to bat. The crowd watched expectantly as Peter Gough and Steve Carlyon made their way to the wicket as the day before they had put on 122 for the first wicket in the semi-final against the United States. They found the Afghan bowling a much harder proposition, however, as Dawlat Ahmedzai and Hasti Gul bowled with pace and accuracy. After half an hour, with only 13 runs made, Gough was bowled by Hasti Gul. Hague lasted only six balls and Driver and Dewhurst quickly followed to place Jersey in serious trouble at 25/4.

Jonathan Gough and Steve Carlyon set about retrieving the situation but runs were hard to come by. Each managed only one boundary, the only fours of the innings. They added 42 before Carlyon gave Karim Sadiq another catch behind the stumps to become the only Jersey batsman to fall to spin. Hamid Hassan then showed what an excellent bowler he was with the old ball. He accounted for Jonathan Gough and then ran through the tail, taking four wickets in just under ten overs. The Afghans were ecstatic, having dismissed the opposition for a mere 80 runs in fewer than 40 overs. In contrast, the crowd were stunned by Jersey's disappointing display and by the excellence of Afghanistan's bowling and fielding.

With Jersey's innings finishing so quickly, there was time for Afghanistan to begin their reply before lunch. Their inexperience, combined with their enthusiasm for quick runs, led to the loss of wickets. With Afghanistan on 25/2 at the interval, Jersey were still in the game with a chance. In the afternoon, the medium pace of Driver was far too good for Afghanistan's middle order. He was well supported by Tony Carlyon's economical spell of ten overs for only 13 runs and two wickets.

By mid-afternoon Afghanistan were 42/7 with only Asghar Stanikzai remaining of the recognised batsmen. He was defending stoutly but scoring few runs and a victory for Jersey seemed almost a certainty. However, Hasti Gul managed to survive and 20 runs were added before Asghar Stanikzai was leg-before to Hague. With Dawlat Ahmedzai at the crease and only Hamid Hassan to follow, the Afghan cause now looked hopeless.

Suddenly, Hasti Gul showed an ability with the bat that no one knew he possessed. He steered the ball into the gaps for singles, struck the ball to the boundary for four and hit a huge six over long-on, followed by another over deep square leg.

As Afghanistan moved closer to their target the home side's captain and players seemed at a loss as to what to do. When Hasti Gul turned the ball to fine leg for a single the Afghan players invaded the ground, thinking they had won, forcing the umpires to calm the situation because the scores were only tied. A few balls later, Hasti Gul did hit the winning run, a single past gully, and the Afghan celebration really began. Despite 23 of the possible 100 overs not being needed, the crowd had witnessed a memorable event that showed how exciting a low-scoring one-day international can be.

JERSEY v AFGHANISTAN

50 overs

World Cricket League Division 5 – Final

Jersey Island Cricket Club Ground, Grainville, St Saviour, 31 May 2008

Afghanistan won by two wickets

JERSEY		R	B	M	4s	6s
P.W.Gough	b Hasti Gul	5	22	32	-	-
S.R.Carlyon	c Karim Sadiq b Mohammad Nabi	17	84	126	1	-
*M.R.Hague	c Karim Sadiq b Hasti Gul	0	6	9	-	-
R.C.Driver	c Asghar Stanikzai b Dawlat Ahmedzai	1	5	7	-	-
A.S.J.Dewhurst	c Hamid Hassan b Hasti Gul	4	10	14	-	-
J.M.Gough	b Hamid Hassan	23	56	70	1	-
C.Jones	b Hamid Hassan	0	17	21	-	-
S.M.Patidar	b Hamid Hassan	4	33	40	-	-
T.P.Carlyon	lbw b Hamid Hassan	0	2	11	-	-
B.M.Vowden	run out (Hasti Gul)	0	0	2	-	-
+R.D.Minty	not out	1	7	8	-	-
	b2 lb2 nb4 w17	25				
	(39.5 overs)	**80**				

AFGHANISTAN		R	B	M	4s	6s
+Karim Sadiq	run out (S.R.Carlyon)	3	3	7	-	-
Ahmed Shah	c Minty b Driver	8	34	42	1	-
Noor Ali Zadran	c Patidar b Driver	0	2	2	-	-
*Nowroz Mangal	c Minty b T.P.Carlyon	14	33	27	1	-
Asghar Stanikzai	lbw b Hague	10	65	84	-	-
Mohammad Nabi	b Driver	2	12	14	-	-
Samiullah Shenwari	lbw b Driver	0	3	6	-	-
Raees Ahmedzai	c Minty b T.P.Carlyon	2	18	16	-	-
Hasti Gul	not out	29	40	64	2	2
Dawlat Ahmedzai	not out	3	16	25	-	-
Hamid Hassan						
	lb1 w9	10				
	(8 wickets, 37.4 overs)	**81**				

Afghanistan	O	M	R	W	nb	w
Dawlat Ahmedzai	10	3	17	1	-	4
Hasti Gul	10	3	17	3	-	2
Hamid Hassan	9.5	1	27	4	4	5
Mohammad Nabi	7	3	9	1	-	-
Ahmed Shah	3	0	6	0	-	1

Jersey	O	M	R	W	nb	w
Driver	10	2	26	4	-	5
Jones	6	1	19	0	-	1
T.P.Carlyon	10	4	13	2	-	1
Hague	9	6	8	1	-	1
Dewhurst	1	0	11	0	-	-
S.R.Carlyon	1.4	0	3	0	-	-

fow	Jer	Afg
1	13 (1)	11 (1)
2	13 (3)	11 (3)
3	17 (4)	28 (4)
4	25 (5)	28 (2)
5	67 (2)	38 (6)
6	71 (6)	38 (7)
7	74 (7)	42 (8)
8	78 (9)	62 (5)
9	78 (10)	
10	80 (8)	

Umpires: P.K.Baldwin (Germany) and M.Hawthorne (Ireland)

Toss: Jersey

Player of the Match: Hasti Gul (Afghanistan)

Rwanda ravaged

In the mid-2000s women's cricket in Africa was relatively new and, save for South Africa, was largely concentrated in east Africa, specifically Kenya, Uganda and Tanzania. The first east African tournament was held in 2002 and then played every two years until 2008, when it became an annual event. Namibia made a one-off appearance in 2004 but did not play again until the competition was replaced by an annual African T20 tournament in 2011.

The 2008 competition in Kenya saw the debut of Rwanda who sent an enthusiastic, but highly inexperienced and largely under-19 team. Perhaps not surprisingly, they were completely outclassed. Their match against Uganda was played at the Ngara Sports Club in Nairobi in conditions which should have been familiar to both teams – dry, cloudless skies, low humidity and temperatures of 22 to 29°C.

Uganda batted first and Rwanda seemed to be holding their own, taking the first two wickets for only 32 runs and then adding two more while the score rose to 89. Despite these losses, Uganda had the advantage since typical scores for 50-over matches in women's east African international cricket were in the 120 to 150 range.

Akwenyu and Nanderenga raised Uganda's effort to another level in a partnership of 88 as Rwanda's bowlers were unable to maintain their early promise and became more and more inconsistent in length and direction. As a result it was extras, especially wides, which contributed to Uganda's score rather than the efforts of their individual batters. Only Akwenyu made a sizeable score, her 66 coming from 70 balls, but she hit only two boundaries. Nyiramongi took three wickets to prevent the lower order from adding too many runs and ensure that Uganda did not bat out their 50 overs. She, however, bowled ten wides. Altogether, Rwanda contributed 98 wides, an average 2.3 per over and a record for the most in any one-day international, men's or women's.

Extras made up 36 per cent of Uganda's total. Their 104, however, only equalled the record for the most extras in a one-day international, conceded by Japan's women against The Netherlands at Schiedam in 2003.

Even if their bowling had been more accurate, it is doubtful if it would have made any difference to the result as Rwanda's batters were helpless against Uganda's attack. Ayato was faster than anything Rwanda had previously experienced. She took the first four wickets, three bowled and one leg-before, while Rwanda struggled to reach five on the board. She finished with the remarkable analysis of 4-1 in five overs. Akwenyu and Atim accounted for the middle and lower order as Rwanda were dismissed for 15 on the penultimate ball of the 17th over. Eight of their players failed to score and no one made more than three, with their highest wicket partnership being five. No player survived longer than 15 balls and extras contributed 53 per cent of their total.

Overall, Rwanda had a miserable tournament. Having lost this match by 276 runs, they were defeated by 336 runs by Kenya and 253 runs by Tanzania before losing the third-place play-off to Tanzania by eight wickets. In their four matches they bowled 221 wides.

Despite this performance, Rwanda's women cricketers were not disheartened. They have established a very active women's cricket scene in the country, particularly in schools and clubs. They have participated since in African tournaments at under-19 level with some success. They finished fourth out of six in the 2013 competition, held in Dar es Salaam. In 2015, they returned to international cricket, hosting a tournament against Kenya and Uganda at the Kicukiro Oval in Kigali. Although they lost all their matches, they were no longer outclassed and they bowled only 33 wides in four matches.

RWANDA WOMEN v UGANDA WOMEN

50 overs

East African Championships

Ngara Sports Club, Nairobi, 17 December 2008

Uganda won by 276 runs

UGANDA		R	B	M	4s	6s
+B.Mukankusi	run out (Mukarurangwa)	12	15		1	-
S.Akello	c Uwamahoro b Uwimana	5	7		1	-
S.Atim	c Uwamahoro b Uwimana	11	17		-	-
R.Akwenyu	b Mukarurangwa	66	70		2	-
C.Aryemo	b Mukeshimana	12	15		2	-
M.Nanderenga	lbw b Mukarurangwa	24	37		1	-
F.Najjumba	c Ineza b Nyiramongi	14	15		2	-
M.Ayato	c Byukusenge b Nyiramongi	4	4		1	-
M.Kunihira	c Byukusenge b Nyiramongi	18	9		3	-
G.Adubu	c Uwimana b Umanyana	7	16		-	-
A.Kisaakye	not out	14	22		1	-
	b1 nb5 w98	104				
	(41.1 overs)	**291**				

RWANDA		R	B	M	4s	6s
D.Ineza	b Ayato	2	15		-	-
+V.Byukusenge	b Ayato	2	9		-	-
C.Uwamahoro	lbw b Ayato	0	13		-	-
D.Mukarurangwa	b Ayato	0	1		-	-
V.Gahonzire	c Akello b Akwenyu	3	13		-	-
N.Mukeshimana	b Atim	0	12		-	-
R.B.Ntagozera	run out (Kunihara)	0	14		-	-
A.Umanyana	b Atim	0	8		-	-
S.Uwimana	b Akwenyu	0	5		-	-
E.Mukaremera	not out	0	2		-	-
J.Nyiramongi	c Aryemo b Akwenyu	0	1		-	-
	b2 w6	8				
	(16.5 overs)	**15**				

Rwanda	O	M	R	W	nb	w
Mukaremera	3	0	28	0	-	15
Umanyana	5.1	0	43	1	1	23
Uwimana	9	0	59	2	-	19
Mukeshimana	7	0	54	1	3	9
Mukarurangwa	8	0	53	2	1	16
Nyiramongi	9	0	53	3	-	10

Uganda	O	M	R	W	nb	w
Ayato	5	4	1	4	-	-
Najjumba	5	2	6	0	-	-
Akwenyu	3.5	1	3	3	-	3
Atim	3	1	3	2	-	3

fow	Ug	Rw
1	23	3
2	32	4
3	54	4
4	89	5
5	177	10
6	204	11
7	208	14
8	245	15
9	259	15
10	291	15

Umpires: [unknown]

Toss: Rwanda.

Hat-trick on debut

The years either side of 2010 may come to be seen as the heyday of global international tournaments. The World Cricket League was extended to eight divisions and various regional tournaments extended their breadth to Divisions Three and Four, enabling more countries to take part in international cricket under the ICC's Development Programme. The Americas Division Four tournament, staged in Mexico City in June 2010, was an excellent example, bringing together Mexico, Costa Rica and, playing for the first time internationally, the Falkland Islands.

The Falklands' first match was against Costa Rica whose captain won the toss and, expecting to take advantage of the cloudy conditions, decided to field. The ground of the Reforma Athletic Club, at an altitude of 2,194 metres, is the highest in the world with a grass pitch. Normally, at altitude, the ball does not swing, but Costa Rica thought that the cloud cover might provide some assistance, particularly against a side with no experience of international cricket or high altitude.

Their captain was not disappointed as within four overs Arthur had bowled Summers and Collins and the Falklands were 28/2. Hewitt and Pickup played sensibly but were forced to concentrate on defence rather than run-making, although their partnership of 38 was the highest of the innings before both were out with the score on 66. The remaining batsmen struggled against Smith and Baker and despite three getting into double figures, wickets fell with regularity as the Falklands subsided for 131 in the 39th over.

By failing to bat for 50 overs, the Falklands found themselves in the field before lunch but in the first over, Taylforth had Baker caught in the slips by Collins. Smith, easily Costa Rica's best batsman, scored quickly, finding the boundary four times, but Ashworth was unable to make any headway. A brilliant catch by Barton at mid-off led to the departure of Smith, whose 24 came from 27 balls and with the score on 44/2, lunch was taken.

Despite the cloud clearing and the temperature rising to 27°C after the break, Costa Rica were never quite able to take a grip on the game. Ashworth and Prasad fell soon after the restart and Costa Rica attempted to take advantage of the Falklands' fifth bowler, Hewitt, but while he conceded 16 runs in his two overs he also picked up two wickets as Olivier and Arthur both missed straight balls.

With 132 being a somewhat small target Costa Rica were probably still favourites to win despite their score reaching 92/6 at the start of the 29th over. Taylforth returned to the attack and immediately had Richard Illingworth – not the modern-day first-class umpire of the same name – caught at the wicket. Illingworth is widely regarded as the 'father' of Costa Rican cricket, being instrumental in reviving the game in the early 2000s and organising the Costa Rican Cricket Association. When he played in this match he was aged 69.

With Illingworth's dismissal, captain Taylforth showed his inexperience of one-day customs and went on to the attack, setting two slips, two gullies and all the fielders inside the circle. Tweedale subsequently nicked the next ball to Marlor, one of the gully fielders. Sheriff then faced the hat-trick ball, Taylforth bowled the perfect in-swinger and Marlor, again, picked up the catch.

Armando Foster blocked the next delivery only to glove the fifth of the over to Marlor, giving him his third catch of the innings and Taylforth a remarkable four wickets in five balls and six wickets in the innings as the Falkland Islands won their debut international. The victory would have been even greater if the Falklands had not gifted Costa Rica 30 extras, or 33 per cent of their total score. Not surprisingly, Taylforth took the player of the match award.

Whether their players succumbed to the altitude for the rest of the tournament or whether their opponents grew wiser, the Falklands failed to win another match. To this day this inaugural match remains the country's only victory, although they have not played internationally since 2012.

COSTA RICA v FALKLAND ISLANDS

50 overs

Americas Championships Division Four

Reforma Athletic Club, Naucalpan de Juárez, Mexico City, 15 June 2010

Falkland Islands won by 39 runs

FALKLAND ISLANDS		R	B	M	4s	6s
D.Pickup	b Smith	24	53	82	2	-
M.Summers	b Arthur	2	7	12	-	-
M.Collins	b Arthur	4	20	24	-	-
C.D.Hewitt	c&b Baker	21	50	44	2	-
*D.E.Taylforth	b Smith	12	25	38	1	-
R.Marlor	lbw b Smith	7	13	15	1	-
K.Clapp	c&b Olivier	16	30	32	1	-
M.Barton	lbw b Smith	0	1	1	-	-
C.Paice	b Baker	18	26	28	3	-
D.Biggs	b Baker	5	12	19	-	-
+I.Betts	not out	0	0	1	-	-
	b1 nb3 w18	22				
	(38.3 overs)	**131**				

COSTA RICA		R	B	M	4s	6s
T.Baker	c Collins b Taylforth	0	9	14	-	-
B.Ashworth	b Collins	8	52	64	1	-
B.Smith	c Barton b Pickup	24	27	30	4	-
C.Prasad	b Taylforth	10	27	35	1	-
*+J.Olivier	b Hewitt	4	24	31	-	-
R.Illingworth	c Betts b Taylforth	10	23	35	1	-
O.S.Arthur	b Hewitt	0	1	6	-	-
D.Crisp	not out	6	8	18	1	-
G.Tweedale	c Marlor b Taylforth	0	1	1	-	-
G.Sherriff	c Marlor b Taylforth	0	1	2	-	-
A.Foster	c Marlor b Taylforth	0	2	2	-	-
	b4 nb2 w24	30				
	(28.5 overs)	**92**				

Costa Rica	O	M	R	W	nb	w
Arthur	8	1	15	2	1	4
Prasad	9	0	41	0	1	9
Baker	8.3	1	29	3	1	4
Smith	10	0	32	4	-	-
Olivier	3	0	13	1	-	1

Falkland Islands	O	M	R	W	nb	w
Taylforth	8.5	2	14	6	1	-
Marlor	3	0	12	0	-	2
Pickup	5	0	23	1	1	3
Collins	10	2	23	1	-	9
Hewitt	2	0	16	2	-	10

fow	FI	CR
1	11 (2)	8 (1)
2	28 (3)	44 (3)
3	66 (4)	58 (2)
4	66 (1)	62 (4)
5	80 (6)	77 (5)
6	102 (5)	83 (7)
7	102 (8)	92 (6)
8	106 (7)	92 (9)
9	129 (9)	92 (10)
10	131 (10)	92 (11)

Umpires: A.Nasrullah (Suriname) and K.K.Patel (Canada)

Referee: A.F.G.Griffith (West Indies)

Toss: Costa Rica

Player of the Match: D.E.Taylforth (Falkland Islands)

In Falkland Islands' innings it is not known who kept wicket when J.Olivier bowled.

In Costa Rica's innings D.E.Taylforth took a hat-trick when dismissing R.Illingworth, G.Tweedale and G.Sherriff and took four wickets in five balls when he dismissed A.Foster.

Second string to Ireland's bow

The final of the World Cricket League Division One tournament, hosted by The Netherlands in 2010, was a contest between old rivals Scotland and Ireland. Conditions for the final were excellent as Amsterdam was in the middle of a heatwave, the temperature on the day rising from around 24°C at the start of play to 31°C in the afternoon.

Ireland had done well to make the final undefeated since they were without William Porterfield, Niall O'Brien, Gary Wilson and Boyd Rankin due to their commitments with English counties. Scotland were almost at full strength, missing only Kyle Coetzer, but they were rebuilding their side following the retirements of Gavin Hamilton, Craig Wright and Ryan Watson. Strictly, they were defending the title they had won in Nairobi in 2007, but they were lucky still to be in Division One as its composition had become based on the top six finishers in the ICC World Cup qualifying competition in 2009, in which they had finished sixth.

Ireland won the toss and chose to field, a decision which looked seriously flawed as Watts and Mommsen took advantage of a good batting pitch. They treated Johnston with respect but attacked all the other bowlers and after the first ten overs of power play they had made 30 runs. Despite Johnston, the Irish captain, selecting the next five overs for the second power play of the innings, Scotland increased their scoring rate, adding a further 29. The total reached 100 in the 24th over as Ireland tried seven bowlers in an effort to break the partnership. Mommsen was eventually caught behind in O'Brien's second spell, after making 80 from 107 balls, with seven fours and one six.

The opening stand of 141 gave Scotland an excellent base from which to accelerate to a score well out of Ireland's potential reach, but that was not to be and with Mommsen's departure the innings fell apart. Dockrell partnered Johnston in a spin-pace combination and Scotland lost four wickets while adding only six runs. Watts attempted to steady the innings and finally found support in Drummond, who struck 30 off 26 balls, in a partnership of 57. Drummond could not maintain the effort, however. He played down the wrong line to Cusack and was bowled. Four runs later, Watts was caught at long-on, two runs short of his century, off 112 balls and including eight fours. The innings ended one ball later. A total of 232 was a poor effort from 141/0, particularly as the innings did not last the 50 overs.

Initially Ireland gave Scotland hope. With 37 on the board, Balbirnie was run out, slipping over while taking what would have been a straightforward single. Cusack was then bowled two balls later. Stirling, however, was batting well and the 50 came up in the 12th over but three balls later, he was bowled by Drummond to leave Ireland on 51/3.

At this point the match could have gone either way but O'Brien and White settled its direction with a stand of 160, at more than five runs per over. They made Scotland's bowling look very ordinary and gave only one chance, when White was dropped by Berrington while on 63. The Irish total passed 200 in 39.3 overs, ensuring that victory was almost certain.

When Scotland finally achieved the breakthrough and dismissed White, only 22 more runs were required off 55 balls. White's 79 included a period of four fours in 11 balls and altogether he struck 11 boundaries. Mooney gave Scotland no respite, hitting 12 runs off 17 balls, including one four and a well-connected six over the bowler's head. This effort was enough to prevent O'Brien reaching his century. He was on 97 at the start of the 45th over but opted for his team's performance rather than personal glory. He was content with just a single to take Ireland to a relatively easy victory.

Since they achieved this without their best players, the result confirmed Ireland as the top side in Associate and Affiliate cricket.

IRELAND v SCOTLAND

List A – 50 overs

World Cricket League Division One – Final

VRA Ground, Amstelveen, 10 July 2010

Ireland won by six wickets

SCOTLAND		R	B	M	4s	6s
D.F.Watts	c White b Jones	98	112	209	8	-
P.L.Mommsen	c McCann b O'Brien	80	107	116	7	1
R.O.Hussain	c McCann b O'Brien	2	9	7	-	-
R.D.Berrington	run out (Jones)	0	4	3	-	-
N.F.I.McCallum	c sub (A.van der Merwe) b Johnston	7	15	22	-	-
M.M.Iqbal	c Stirling b Johnston	0	2	3	-	-
+D.R.Lockhart	lbw b Dockrell	0	6	5	-	-
M.A.Parker	c McCann b Dockrell	1	10	8	-	-
*G.D.Drummond	b Cusack	30	26	33	2	-
G.Goudie	b Jones	1	2	6	-	-
R.T.Lyons	not out	0	0	1	-	-
	b5 lb2 w6	13				
	(48.5 overs)	**232**				

IRELAND		R	B	M	4s	6s
P.R.Stirling	b Drummond	32	38	48	3	1
A.Balbirnie	run out (Parker)	6	23	37	-	-
A.R.Cusack	b Berrington	0	2	4	-	-
K.J.O'Brien	not out	98	104	129	4	3
A.R.White	c Berrington b Goudie	79	87	110	11	-
J.F.Mooney	not out	12	14	14	1	1
A.D.Poynter						
N.G.Jones						
+R.D.McCann						
*D.T.Johnston						
G.H.Dockrell						
	w6	6				
	(4 wickets, 44.5 overs)	**233**				

Ireland	O	M	R	W	nb	w
O'Brien	9	1	46	2	-	1
Johnston	10	2	21	2	-	2
Cusack	9	0	53	1	-	-
Dockrell	10	1	42	2	-	1
Jones	2.5	0	20	2	-	-
White	4	0	20	0	-	-
Stirling	4	0	23	0	-	2

Scotland	O	M	R	W	nb	w
Goudie	9.5	0	45	1	-	-
Parker	8	0	44	0	-	3
Berrington	6	0	45	1	-	-
Drummond	9	1	40	1	-	-
Lyons	10	1	39	0	-	3
Iqbal	2	0	20	0	-	-

fow	Sc	Ir
1	141 (2)	37 (2)
2	145 (3)	39 (3)
3	145 (4)	51 (1)
4	163 (5)	211 (5)
5	165 (6)	
6	167 (7)	
7	169 (8)	
8	226 (9)	
9	232 (1)	
10	232(10)	

Umpires: H.P.D.K.Dharmasena (Sri Lanka) and B.G.Jerling (South Africa)

Reserve umpire: B.Hartong (Netherlands). Referee: D.T.Jukes (England)

Toss: Ireland

Player of the Match: K.J.O'Brien (Ireland)

In Ireland's innings there was one five-ball over (31st, Lyons's eighth).

In Scotland's innings A.van der Merwe fielded as substitute for A.D.Poynter.

Irish magic

Despite Ireland's reputation for being able to spring a surprise and England's dismal record in World Cups, the best that most people were expecting in Bengaluru against England in 2011 was that Ireland would give a virtually full-strength English side a competitive game.

In dry, hot conditions, with a mid-afternoon temperature of 30°C, a good batting pitch, fast outfield and short boundaries, Andrew Strauss had no hesitation in batting first after winning the toss. England quickly showed their superiority as captain Strauss and Pietersen struck 72 off the first ten overs and produced an opening stand of 91. The Irish bowlers were unable to control the run rate but the introduction of spin from Dockrell and Stirling removed both openers in quick succession.

There was no respite, however, as Trott and Bell dominated proceedings in a stand of 167. After 43 overs, England were 278/2 and ready to accelerate still further with a score well above 350 in mind. But it was not to be as Mooney picked up four wickets and Rankin, despite being expensive earlier, kept England to three runs from the 48th over. Ireland restricted England to 49 from the last six overs but even so, the total of 327/8 was not expected to be within Ireland's grasp.

Ireland started disastrously when James Anderson bowled William Porterfield with the first ball of the innings. Stirling hit five fours and one six while Ed Joyce played the anchor role, but once Stirling's attempt at a second six ended in the hands of Pietersen in the deep, England's bowlers exerted a stranglehold as Anderson bowled the sole maiden of the match and Ireland managed only six runs from four overs.

Joyce and Niall O'Brien tried to put some momentum into the innings but both fell victim to the spin of Graeme Swann, who then accounted for Wilson, leaving Ireland on 111/5 in the 25th over. Kevin O'Brien began to restore some respectability by attacking the English spinners. With support from Cusack, he gained in confidence and was soon striking the ball to all parts of the ground. The 23,500 spectators were thoroughly entertained as the pair put on 62 in five overs and extended this to a partnership of 162 off 103 balls, with a combination of beautifully timed cricket strokes and mere bludgeoning of the ball to the boundary.

O'Brien should have been run out in the 42nd over but Cusack, sensing the danger, sacrificed himself when only two runs short of his half-century. Mooney, perhaps inspired by the previous partnership, also scored heavily, causing the English attack to disintegrate. He outscored O'Brien in making 28 out of their partnership of 44 in fewer than seven overs. The English attack had no answer and did not know what line or length to bowl. Whatever they tried, the Irish were masters.

England's fielding deteriorated under the onslaught, which served only to aid the increasing run rate. O'Brien reached his century off only 50 balls, the fastest ever made in the World Cup, but after that he seemed to run out of steam. When he eventually fell to a run out, a superb return from the deep by Tim Bresnan over the stumps to Matt Prior, he had batted for 63 balls. O'Brien's 113 included 13 fours and six sixes, the one over long-on off Anderson being measured at 102m. He was given a standing ovation as he left the pitch.

Both sides could have panicked at this stage with victory still possible for either, but Johnston was the calming influence and immediately scored a boundary. With three runs still required off the last over, Mooney struck the first ball for four to give Ireland victory by three wickets.

With an unbeaten 47 and four wickets, Mooney would have done enough in most matches to receive the player of the match award but even he could not quarrel with it going to Kevin O'Brien for an incredible display of batting which turned a likely defeat into a piece of Irish cricket history.

ENGLAND v IRELAND

One-Day International, List A, 50 overs (day/night)

ICC World Cup – Group B

M.Chinnaswamy Stadium, Bengaluru, 2 March 2011

Ireland won by three wickets

ENGLAND		R	B	M	4s	6s
*A.J.Strauss	b Dockrell	34	37	61	2	1
K.P.Pietersen	c N.J.O'Brien b Stirling	59	50	77	7	2
I.J.L.Trott	b Mooney	92	92	126	9	-
I.R.Bell	c Stirling b Mooney	81	86	102	6	1
P.D.Collingwood	c K.J.O'Brien b Mooney	16	11	21	-	1
+M.J.Prior	b Johnston	6	5	7	1	-
T.T.Bresnan	c Johnston b Mooney	4	8	23	-	-
M.H.Yardy	b Johnston	3	6	8	-	-
G.P.Swann	not out	9	5	8	1	-
S.C.J.Broad						
J.M.Anderson						
	b1 lb2 w20	23				
	(8 wickets, 50 overs)	**327**				

IRELAND		R	B	M	4s	6s
*W.T.S.Porterfield	b Anderson	0	1	1	-	-
P.R.Stirling	c Pietersen b Bresnan	32	28	45	5	1
E.C.Joyce	st Prior b Swann	32	61	90	3	-
+N.J.O'Brien	b Swann	29	36	37	2	1
G.C.Wilson	lbw b Swann	3	14	17	-	-
K.J.O'Brien	run out (Bresnan-Prior)	113	63	123	13	6
A.R.Cusack	run out (Collingwood-Broad)	47	58	80	3	1
J.F.Mooney	not out	33	30	40	6	-
D.T.Johnston	not out	7	4	6	1	-
G.H.Dockrell						
W.B.Rankin						
	b5 lb16 w12	33				
	(7 wickets, 49.1 overs)	**329**				

Ireland	O	M	R	W	nb	w
Rankin	7	0	51	0	-	4
Johnston	10	9	58	2	-	-
Cusack	4	0	39	0	-	1
Dockrell	10	0	68	1	-	5
Mooney	9	0	63	4	-	1
Dockrell	10	0	45	1	-	-

England	O	M	R	W	nb	w
Anderson	8.1	1	49	1	-	1
Broad	9	0	73	0	-	2
Bresnan	10	0	64	1	-	2
Yardy	7	0	49	0	-	2
Swann	10	0	47	3	-	-
Collingwood	5	0	26	0	-	-

fow	Eng	Ire
1	91 (1)	0 (1)
2	111 (2)	62 (2)
3	278 (4)	103 (4)
4	288 (3)	106 (3)
5	299 (6)	111 (5)
6	312 (5)	273 (7)
7	317 (8)	317 (6)
8	327 (7)	
9		
10		

Umpires: Aleem Dar (Pakistan) and B.F.Bowden (New Zealand)

TV umpire: M.Erasmus (South Africa). Reserve umpire: R.J.Tucker (Australia). Referee: R.S.Mahanama (Sri Lanka)

Toss: England

Player of the Match: K.J.O'Brien (Ireland)

Papua New Guinea on the rise

Friday 15 April 2011 saw the second meeting that year of two rapidly improving teams with aspirations to threaten the position of the leading Associate and Affiliate countries. Despite their long cricket history, Hong Kong's performances over the previous few years had been disappointing. The departure of many British and Australian players and the retirement of others meant that standards had fallen. But, in the late 2000s, good coaching and investments in cricket infrastructure had led to a crop of enthusiastic young players, who were leading a revival in fortunes.

Hong Kong's opponents were Papua New Guinea. The Pacific countries had been ignored by the ICC when the Intercontinental Cup was set up and this seemed somewhat harsh on Papua New Guinea who were clearly well above the standard of the other countries in the East Asia-Pacific region.

Papua New Guinea and Hong Kong were by 2011 in World Cricket League Division Two and this encounter was the third-place play-off which meant that both were in the top ten of the Associates and Affiliates. Hong Kong, however, were without Jamie Atkinson, who was at university in England; otherwise the teams were at full strength.

Conditions were far from ideal for the match at the ICC Cricket Academy Ground in Dubai. It was hot, with temperatures peaking at 34°C, and the wind was blowing from the desert, creating hazy skies punctuated by occasional dust storms. Dikana won the toss and decided that Papua New Guinea would bat first, even though that committed them to fielding when the sun was at its strongest.

Ura opened with Kent, rather than his usual partner Vala, who came in down the order. Despite some tight bowling, Papua New Guinea batted with confidence. They lost Ura leg-before with the score on 32 and, surprisingly, he was replaced by wicketkeeper Vare whose batting prowess would normally place him at a more than useful number seven or eight. He and Kent kept the score moving but both got out when looking set. Dai quickly followed, bowled by Nizakat Khan to give Hong Kong the advantage with the batting side on 93/4.

Vala and Morea, however, were more than able to meet the challenge, putting on 89. Munir Dar made batting difficult, conceding only 24 runs in his ten overs and he was well supported by Nizakat Khan, with his ten overs going for 37. Loose balls, particularly from the other bowlers, were dispatched with firm strikes, Vala hitting one four and three sixes in his 55 and Morea contributing ten fours and one six in an undefeated 74. After Vala's dismissal, Morea took most of the strike and managed to put on a further 43, first with Kila and then with McIntosh, who contributed only four runs between them. The innings closed on 225, which was a competitive score, but should not have been out of Hong Kong's reach.

Thanks to the efforts of Waqas Barkat, Hong Kong went about their task with fervour and had 20 on the board after just two overs. They lost Kruger, bowled by Haoda, but Khalid Butt continued to score at pace.

Haoda gained a second wicket in the fifth over, removing Waqas Barkat, and Hong Kong's reply just fell apart. Chapman and Butt added 15 but in a display of hit out or get out, eight wickets went down for 47 runs. Haoda accounted for Chapman to give him a third wicket and McIntosh took care of the tail. A total of 98 in 25.3 overs was a pitiful display, showing that Hong Kong's young players still had much to learn about building an innings. In contrast, Papua New Guinea's approach was clinical and demonstrated that cricket in the Pacific region was becoming a force not to be dismissed lightly.

HONG KONG v PAPUA NEW GUINEA

List A – 50 overs

World Cricket League Division Two – Third-Place Play-Off

ICC Cricket Academy Ground, Dubai, 15 April 2011

Papua New Guinea won by 127 runs

PNG		R	B	M	4s	6s
T.P.Ura	lbw b Tucker	11	14		-	-
C.N.Kent	lbw b Nizakat Khan	38	59		6	-
+J.N.T.Vare	c Khalid Butt b Munir Dar	28	53		3	-
A.Vala	c Asif Khan b Irfan Ahmed	55	72		1	3
M.D.Dai	b Nizakat Khan	3	6		-	-
V.V.Morea	not out	74	87		10	1
J.Kila	c Waqas Barkat b Najeem Amar	3	7		-	-
A.McIntosh	not out	1	2		-	-
*R.Dikana						
W.T.Gavera						
R.C.Haoda						
	lb3 w9	12				
	(6 wickets, 50 overs)	**225**				

HONG KONG		R	B	M	4s	6s
+Waqas Barkat	b Haoda	25	16		2	-
C.K.Kruger	b Haoda	1	7		-	-
Khalid Butt	c Vare b Dikana	21	21		4	-
M.S.Chapman	c Ura b Haoda	3	6		-	-
Nizakat Khan	c Kila b Dai	12	24		2	-
Munir Dar	lbw b Gavera	3	13		-	-
Irfan Ahmed	c Dikana b McIntosh	6	16		1	-
*Najeeb Amar	b Dai	19	27		3	-
Nadeem Ahmed	c Dai b McIntosh	0	5		-	-
M.C.Tucker	c Dikana b McIntosh	2	13		-	-
Asif Khan	not out	0	5		-	-
	b4 w2	6				
	(25.3 overs)	**98**				

Hong Kong	O	M	R	W	nb	w
Irfan Ahmed	8	0	55	1	-	2
Tucker	6	0	23	1	-	2
Asif Khan	3	1	10	0	-	2
Nadeem Ahmed	6	0	48	0	-	-
Munir Dar	10	2	24	1	-	-
Nizakat Khan	10	1	37	2	-	1
Najeem Amar	7	0	25	1	-	1

PNG	O	M	R	W	nb	w
Haoda	5	0	40	3	-	-
Gavera	6	0	22	1	-	1
Dikana	4	1	4	1	-	-
Dai	5.3	2	14	2	-	-
McIntosh	5	1	14	3	-	1

fow	PNG	HK
1	32 (1)	20 (2)
2	74 (2)	35 (1)
3	88 (3)	51 (4)
4	93 (5)	55 (3)
5	182 (4)	60 (6)
6	203 (7)	72 (7)
7		72 (5)
8		77 (9)
9		97 (10)
10		98 (8)

Umpires: S.Ganesh (Singapore) and T.G.van Schalkwyk (Namibia)

Reserve umpire: Fidel Jaary (United Arab Emirates). Referee: G.F.Labrooy (Sri Lanka)

Toss: Papua New Guinea

Player of the Match: V.V.Morea (Papua New Guinea)

Khalid Butt is also known as Khalid Hussain Butt and as K.H.Butt. Munir Dar is also known as Munir Ahmed.

Frith outclasses Jersey

In 1950, Guernsey and Jersey met each other for the first in what has since become an annual fixture, known as the Inter-Insular, and the meeting in 2011 was the 60th encounter. With both sides about to take part in Division Six of the World Cricket League in Kuala Lumpur a fortnight later it was decided to give the players in their respective squads for that tournament some practice, the wet summer having restricted the amount of cricket played.

The eligibility criteria for Inter-Insular matches still applied, however, namely that the players had to be resident and have taken part in local club cricket during the season. As a result, Guernsey were without Tim Ravenscroft, a professional cricketer with Hampshire. Jersey were without Steve and Tony Carlyon, Ryan Driver and Chris Jones, all of whom were unavailable for the trip to Malaysia.

Early September coincided with a short, pleasantly warm, dry spell. On the day in question the temperature ranged from 17°C at the start to 20°C in the afternoon, but it was humid, conditions which might have helped the swing bowlers. As always for the Inter-Insular, there was a good crowd with a large contingent of spectators having made the journey from Jersey to support their side at the King George V Sports Ground in Castel.

Guernsey won the toss and opted to bat and in the first over, with eight runs on the board, there was an unfortunate incident. Eager for quick runs, Smit backed up too far and, trying to turn, slipped over and was easily run out. Unfortunately, Faudemer's direct throw hit the stumps and rebounded into the face of Connolly, who was backing up. He was forced to leave the field and seek treatment, thereby depriving Jersey of one of their main bowlers. Savident and Frith entertained the crowd with a wide range of shots, adding 59 for the second wicket in just under 12 overs. Stevens then got one of his left-arm spinners to turn sharply, beating Savident as he advanced down the wicket, and giving Farley an easy stumping. Kneller kept the momentum going with 17 runs from 23 balls before he drove Faudemer straight to extra cover. Le Prevost joined Frith. Instead of trying to hit boundaries past a deep-set field, they pushed the ball only short distances and, through excellent running, made progress in ones and twos.

By the 30th over Guernsey had made 124/3 and were ready to accelerate. Frith then reached his hundred in the 40th over and 20 of his next 29 runs were boundaries, but he holed out to Cooke at midwicket after trying to hook Stevens for a six, ending a partnership of 141. Le Prevost was leg-before to Stevens's next ball, Hooper misjudged the pace of Hawkins-Kay and Nussbaumer became Stevens's fourth victim. Ferbrache and Kimber then hit out, Kimber striking the only six of the day in the last over. The total of 273 was certainly a very fine effort but on what had turned out to be a good batting pitch, would it be enough?

Guernsey's opening bowlers showed better control and looked more menacing than Jersey's had been. Savident beat the bat three times in the first over and van Vliet removed Garton with the first ball of the second. Four overs later, Farley mis-hit a pull shot and gave an easy catch to Hooper. Nussbaumer held a sharp return catch to account for Stevens. When Savident was successful with his leg-before appeal against de la Haye, Jersey were clearly in trouble on 52/4.

Gough and Hawkins-Kay played well in a partnership of 42 but never threatened to bring Jersey within range of the required scoring rate. Both fell to Frith as soon as he was brought into the attack, Hawkins-Kay bowled round his legs and Gough the victim of a superb low diving catch by Nussbaumer at midwicket.

Frith and Rich soon wound up the innings, despite Connolly bravely but for little purpose, deciding to bat and defending for ten balls. Beaten with more than 16 overs remaining and only five of their players making double figures, Jersey were totally outplayed. Their total was three runs fewer than the individual score of Frith who, not surprisingly, was named the player of the match.

GUERNSEY v JERSEY

50 overs

Inter-Insular – Marlborough Trophy

King George V Sports Ground, Castel, 3 September 2011

Guernsey won by 147 runs

GUERNSEY		R	B	M	4s	6s
G.H.Smit	run out (Faudemer)	1	1	3	-	-
L.Savident	st Farley b Stevens	27	33	44	6	-
J.D.J.Frith	c Cooke b Stevens	129	139	144	7	-
R.Kneller	c Gough b Faudemer	17	23	18	2	-
*S.E.Le Prevost	lbw b Stevens	44	73	87	2	-
D.R.Hooper	b Hawkins-Kay	1	2	6	-	-
J.A.J.Nussbaumer	c Gough b Stevens	7	9	14	-	-
L.B.Ferbrache	not out	16	14	17	1	-
+T.C.R.Kimber	not out	14	6	8	-	1
G.J.Rich						
C.A.van Vliet						
	lb4 nb1 w12	17				
	(7 wickets, 50 overs)	**273**				

JERSEY		R	B	M	4s	6s
D.A.Garton	c Frith b van Vliet	1	2	4	-	-
+E.J.Farley	c Hooper b van Vliet	6	18	22	1	-
B.D.H.Stevens	c&b Nussbaumer	10	20	30	-	-
S.J.de la Haye	lbw b Savident	12	20	26	2	-
*P.W.Gough	c Nussbaumer b Frith	31	40	53	5	-
A.W.Hawkins-Kay	b Frith	18	27	30	2	-
A.F.Cooke	c Kimber b Rich	6	20	16	-	-
T.E.Minty	c Smit b Frith	2	11	12	-	-
C.W.Perchard	lbw b Rich	14	20	27	1	-
P.C.Connolly	c Nussbaumer b Frith	1	10	8	-	-
J.A.Faudemer	not out	5	15	15	-	-
	lb7 nb1 w12	20				
	(33.5 overs)	**126**				

Jersey	O	M	R	W	nb	w
Hawkins-Kay	10	0	79	1	1	3
Perchard	4	0	31	0	-	3
Stevens	10	0	35	4	-	1
Minty	9	0	38	0	-	3
Faudemer	10	0	42	1	-	-
Cooke	7	0	44	0	-	2

Guernsey	O	M	R	W	nb	w
Savident	10	0	23	1	-	2
van Vliet	4	0	27	2	1	3
Nussbaumer	4	0	26	1	-	1
Frith	9	1	30	4	-	2
Rich	6.5	0	13	2	-	-

fow	Gu	Je
1	8 (1)	1 (1)
2	67 (2)	23 (2)
3	90 (4)	41 (3)
4	231 (3)	52 (4)
5	231 (5)	94 (6)
6	236 (6)	97 (5)
7	250 (7)	98 (7)
8		103 (8)
9		111 (9)
10		126 (10)

Umpires: M.B.Gray (Guernsey) and R.L.Stockton (Jersey)

Reserve umpire: J.L.Mountford (Guernsey)

Toss: Guernsey

Player of the Match: J.D.J.Frith (Guernsey)

Versatile Vanuatu

Vanuatu played Ghana in the final of the World Cricket League Division Eight tournament, hosted by Samoa in September 2012. This was the second and, unfortunately, the last time that the WCL operated at this level, it being now restricted to five divisions. It is no longer possible for middle-ranking teams across the globe to meet each other and see how they compare to teams outside their own continent. The opportunity for cricketers from countries like Ghana to travel the world, experience different cultures, form friendships with different peoples and learn from playing in different climates and on different pitches does not now exist.

Mansale won the toss for Vanuatu in the match played at the Faleata Gardens Oval in Apia and elected to bat, despite the cloudy conditions. Initially the outcome was disastrous as both openers were dismissed cheaply, leaving Vanuatu on 7/2. Mansale and Dunn began the recovery, first scoring mainly in ones and twos before eventually increasing the run rate with several boundaries. Agbomadzie, the sixth bowler tried, broke the partnership, removing Mansale, normally Vanuatu's best batsman, for an unusually subdued 22.

Nipiko produced some typical South Sea Island sparkle in partnership with Dunn, who was playing fluently. Just as the batsmen were seemingly on top of the bowling, the umpires took the players from the field for a light rain shower. The stoppage was short-lived, however, and did not upset the concentration of the men at the pitch, who continued to play a wide range of drives, cuts and pulls to and over the boundary.

By the 43rd over Vanuatu were in a strong position on 181/3 but with the stand having reached 108, Nipiko gave a catch to the wicketkeeper. His entertaining 59 from 63 balls had included three fours and three sixes. In their attempt to accelerate the scoring rate, Vanuatu lost wickets to a series of poor shots, particularly against the bowling of Aboagye, who picked up three wickets to bring his total for the innings to four. Dunn was the sixth batsman out, after making 78 off 139 balls with six fours and one six. Vanuatu took their total to 222 at the end of their 50 overs, a challenging target on a ground where totals over 200 are unusual. Ghana's task could have been slightly easier, however, if their bowlers had not contributed 21 wides.

Ghana scored at a great rate, posting their half-century in the tenth over despite losing Bakiweyem on the way. Agbomadzie was in great form, hitting seven boundaries in his 33 before falling to Mansale and with his dismissal Ghana lost their way.

Vifah and Awiah were pinned down by the spin combination of Mansale and Chilia as in 12 overs they added a mere nine runs. Vifah vented his frustration by attempting to launch a ball from Chilia over the boundary for six, only to loft a simple catch to Dunn at deep mid-off. Ghana failed to take advantage of two dropped catches and a missed stumping but two more wickets fell to leave them on 92/5 in the 29th over.

Aboagye and Mensah brought Ghana back into the match, striking the spinners for 26 in two overs before a change in the bowling to the pace of Matautaava was rewarded when Aboagye was adjudged leg-before. Short, attractive cameos from Anafie and Bagabena took Ghana to a respectable total but could not prevent Matautaava from cleaning up the tail to give Vanuatu their first and, so far, only international cricket trophy. Dunn was named player of the match but, overall, it was an all-round performance. Without the supporting runs from Nipiko, the wickets of Matautaava and Obed and the miserly bowling of Mansale and Chilia, his effort could easily have been in vain.

GHANA v VANUATU

50 overs

World Cricket League Division Eight – Final

Faleata Gardens Oval Ground No 1, Apia, 22 September 2012

Vanuatu won by 39 runs

VANUATU		R	B	M	4s	6s
L.Natapei	c Mensah b Aboagye	0	9	-	-	
M.J.Avok	run out (Aboagye)	6	5		1	-
J.Dunn	c Ateak b Aboagye	78	139		6	1
*A.Mansale	c Ananya b Agbomadzie	22	51		2	-
N.Nipiko	c Mensah b Bagabena	59	63		3	3
P.K.Matautaava	c Ananya b Aboagye	4	4		-	-
S.H.Obed	c&b Anafie	2	7		-	-
+T.Langa	run out (Agbomadzie-Mensah)	4	6		-	-
S.W.Kalworai	b Aboagye	10	12		1	-
J.W.Chilia	not out	3	4		-	-
K.Tari	not out	2	2		-	-
	b3 lb6 nb2 w21	32				
	(9 wickets, 50 overs)	**222**				

GHANA		R	B	M	4s	6s
F.K.Bakiweyem	c Natapei b Tari	7	15		1	-
O.H.Agbomadzie	b Mansale	33	35		7	-
J.K.Vifah	c Dunn b Chilia	18	48		2	-
S.K.Awiah	c Matautaava b Obed	12	57		-	-
I.K.O.Aboagye	lbw b Matautaava	31	29		2	2
A.Kind-David	c Mansale b Obed	9	14		-	1
+J.H.Mensah	b Obed	23	28		3	-
M.K.Anafie	c Dunn b Nipiko	15	10		1	1
*P.K.Ananya	c Langa b Matautaava	9	10		-	-
K.S.Bagabena	not out	10	11		1	-
V.Ateak	c Langa b Matautaava	1	3		-	-
	b2 lb4 nb3 w6	15				
	(42.5 overs)	**183**				

Ghana	O	M	R	W	nb	w
Aboagye	10	2	39	4	1	2
Bagabena	8	0	39	1	-	2
Ananya	5	0	17	0	1	5
Kind-David	6	0	30	0	-	2
Ateak	10	1	30	0	-	-
Agbomadzie	10	0	54	1	-	2
Anafie	1	0	4	1	-	1

Vanuatu	O	M	R	W	nb	w
Matautaava	6.5	1	27	3	-	1
Tari	7	0	33	1	1	2
Mansale	10	2	37	1	-	-
Chilia	10	2	27	1	-	1
Obed	4	1	17	3	-	-
Nipiko	5	0	36	1	2	1

fow	Van	Gha
1	6 (1)	28 (1)
2	7 (2)	51 (2)
3	73 (4)	75 (3)
4	181 (5)	82 (4)
5	198 (6)	92 (6)
6	198 (3)	131 (5)
7	204 (8)	155 (8)
8	209 (7)	165 (7)
9	219 (9)	181 (9)
10		183 (11)

Umpires: N.D.Harrison (Japan) and S.Hameed (Indonesia)

Reserve umpire: G.A.V.Baxter (New Zealand). Referee: S.R.Bernard (Australia)

Toss: Vanuatu

Player of the Match: J.Dunn (Vanuatu)

O.H.Agbomadzie is also known as O.Harvey.

Iran's women rewarded

Even as recently as the early 2000s, if someone had suggested that the women of Kuwait, an Arab country, and the women of Iran, a country ruled by highly conservative Islamic ayatollahs, would be meeting each other in a cricket match, they would almost certainly have been disbelieved. However, on 27 January 2013, such an event took place during the Asian Cricket Council Women's Championships.

The Kuwaiti side were surprisingly international, comprising expatriates from the Indian subcontinent and including a Jordanian, Maryan Omar, and an Egyptian, Sabreen Zaki. The Iranians were all nationals of their country where cricket is, without too much publicity, being encouraged as a suitable sport for women, since the uniform, accompanied by a head scarf or, when batting, a helmet, meets the country's dress code.

The fixtures in the competition were 25 overs per side, which was probably about the right length. There was a considerable range of abilities between the countries which led to several mismatches, particularly when teams like Kuwait, Iran and Qatar played either China or Thailand.

Kuwait and Iran, however, were of similar standard. The teams met at the Gymkhana Club ground in Chiang Mai, northern Thailand. Iran's captain, Sommayeh Sahrapour, won the toss and, under sunny conditions at 10am local time, invited Kuwait to bat. The decision looked ill-founded as Maryam Omar and Suresh found Iran's bowling to be without threat. Scoring runs freely all round the ground, they put on 72 in 12 overs before Safoura Zivariomid succeeded in bowling Omar with the first ball of the next over.

Thereafter, Kuwait's innings ran out of steam. All their players were too enthusiastic to score quickly and failed. With no one able to give the support Suresh required, only another 57 runs were added in the remaining overs. Suresh finished unbeaten on 68, made from 90 balls, with nine fours. Zivariomid was the most successful bowler with three wickets and Kuwait's total of 129 was helped by the 23 wides contributed by Iran's bowlers, the captain setting the example not to emulate with seven.

Iran's reply followed a similar pattern with a useful opening partnership followed by the loss of wickets. Roya Kaheni dominated the opening stand with Elham Ghorbani. It ended in the ninth over, with 45 runs on the board. While Ghorbani had taken 27 balls to compile ten runs, her successor, Parisa Afzal, scored at nearly a run a ball, before playing across a straight ball. At 86/2 in the 14th over Iran were only slightly ahead of where Kuwait had been at a similar stage, their opponents having reached 80/2 at the end of the 15th over.

Unlike Suresh, Kaheni did not lack support as Masoome Hassani stayed with her until the target had been reached after 21 overs. All three of the wicket partnerships had thus contributed just over 40 runs but, aided by 26 wides and seven no-balls, Iran won with ease. Roya Kaheni was nominated the player of the match for her 56 runs, made from 73 balls, with four fours.

The match resulted in four national records, all of which still stand. These are the highest team totals and the highest individual scores in women's one-day internationals for both nations. Iran were given the Spirit of Cricket Award for the tournament for their general enthusiasm both on and off the field.

The competition comprised teams from 11 countries. These did not include Oman, who had taken part in previous contests, or Japan, who play in ICC's East Asia-Pacific region. Thus, altogether, outside of the Full Member countries of the ICC, 13 countries in the continent of Asia had played women's cricket internationally by 2013, whereas Europe's equivalent competition was still contested only by Ireland, Scotland and The Netherlands. Asia were clearly way ahead of Europe or, indeed, any other continent, in the promotion of women's cricket.

IRAN WOMEN v KUWAIT WOMEN

25 overs

Asian Cricket Council Championships – Group B

Gymkhana Club, Chiang Mai, 27 January 2013

Iran won by eight wickets

KUWAIT		R	B	M	4s	6s
*Maryam Omar	b Safoura Zivariomid	25	29	53	4	-
V.Suresh	not out	68	80	109	9	-
Sabreen Zaki	c Tahereh Miraknezhad b Safoura Zivariomid	2	11	10	-	-
Khadija Khalil	lbw b Nasimeh Rahshetaei	1	4	3	-	-
A.S.Tariq	b Safoura Zivariomid	0	4	7	-	-
+D.Priyarangika	lbw b Somayyeh Sahrapour	0	3	4	-	-
K.Santhoshkumar	lbw b Somayyeh Sahrapour	7	20	30	-	-
Mariyam Khalil						
Maryyam Ashraf						
M.Ranawat						
S.Jayakumar						
	lb1 nb2 w23	26				
	(6 wickets, 25 overs)	**129**				

IRAN		R	B	M	4s	6s
+Roya Kaheni	not out	56	73	91	4	-
Elham Ghorbani	c Sabreen Zaki b Maryam Omar	10	27	37	1	-
Parisa Afzal	b Khadija Khalil	15	16	22	2	-
Masoome Hassani	not out	11	16	31	1	-
Avideh Gilani						
Mahdiyeh Soltaninejad						
Nasimeh Rahshetaei						
Safoura Zivariomid						
*Somayyeh Sahrapour						
Tahereh Miraknezhad						
Zahra Dahmardehzadeh						
	b2 lb3 nb7 w26	38				
	(2 wickets, 21 overs)	**130**				

Iran	O	M	R	W	nb	w		fow	Kuw	Iran
Tahereh Miraknezhad	3	0	28	0	-	4		1	72 (1)	45 (2)
Somayyeh Sahrapour	5	1	18	2	-	7		2	80 (3)	86 (3)
Avideh Gilani	5	0	25	0	1	3		3	81 (4)	
Nasimeh Rahshetaei	5	0	28	1	-	4		4	92 (5)	
Safoura Zivariomid	5	0	21	3	1	4		5	94 (6)	
Mahdiyeh Soltaninejad	2	0	8	0	-	-		6	129 (7)	
								7		
Kuwait	O	M	R	W	nb	w		8		
Sabreen Zaki	5	0	27	0	3	2		9		
Suresh	4	0	31	0	1	7		10		
Tariq	2	1	4	0	-	2				
Maryam Omar	4	0	17	1	-	5				
Ranawat	1	0	15	0	2	1				
Khadija Khalil	4	0	22	1	-	1				
Jayakumar	1	0	9	0	-	1				

Umpires: M.Kamaruzzaman (Thailand) and N.Sirisuan (Thailand)

Reserve umpire: C.Dodd (Thailand). Referee: Aminul Islam (Bangladesh)

Toss: Iran

Player of the Match: Roya Kaheni (Iran)

More magic from O'Brien

Ever since they tied with Zimbabwe and beat Pakistan in the 2007 World Cup, Ireland have developed a reputation of creating surprises when playing against Full Member countries. The match against Pakistan on 22 May 2013 turned out to be another such occasion.

Conditions were appalling. The temperature struggled to get above 10°C all day, there were heavy rain showers and the wind was strong, gusting up to 40kph, but at least the players were able to move around in an attempt to keep warm. The spectators, numbering 2,000 with a strong contingent of local Pakistanis, had no such opportunity.

The toss went Pakistan's way and, to the surprise of many, they chose to bat. Johnston and Murtagh bowled well and Pakistan were forced to adopt a degree of caution. The only serious attacking stroke came from Nasir Jamshed, who clouted Johnston over the pavilion roof for a magnificent six but in the tenth over he was forced to retire after being struck on the knee by a delivery from the same bowler.

In the 13th over, Cusack tempted Imran Farhat with a ball outside the off stump which he hit straight to Stirling at first slip. One batsman out and one hurt was the extent of Ireland's success for some time as Mohammad Hafeez and Asad Shafiq made the bowling look very ordinary. Three breaks for rain failed to upset their concentration with Pakistan giving an exhibition in batting with a wide range of delightful shots all round the wicket.

It took 30 overs before the breakthrough came, by which time the partnership was worth 188, and with the score on 221 and seven and a half overs left the situation was ripe for acceleration. Nasir Jamshed resumed his innings but added only five to his score. Mohammad Hafeez called for a single before deciding against it, by which time Misbah-ul-Haq was too far down the wicket and unable to get back. Kamran Akmal did what was required to take Pakistan to an excellent 266/5. Mohammad Hafeez was undefeated on 122, made off 113 balls, with 12 fours and two sixes. He certainly gave the crowd great entertainment.

With the match reduced to 47 overs per side, Ireland's target was revised by the Duckworth-Lewis method. Since they had all their resources available the target was ten runs more than Pakistan had made and Stirling showed scant respect for the bowling, driving and cutting the ball to the boundary. As in Ireland's innings, it took spin to obtain the first wicket, Mohammad Hafeez dismissing Porterfield. Joyce and Stirling proceeded to score quickly. With the crowd sensing that Ireland were in a strong position and with a chance of winning, there was much disappointment when Joyce inexplicably missed a straight ball to give Mohammad Hafeez a second wicket.

Runs continued to flow as Stirling reached his century off 101 balls, but he was out soon after. Gary Wilson kept Kevin O'Brien company while 59 runs were added before being bowled, playing down the wrong line. Then Niall O'Brien went all too quickly and the initiative had switched to Pakistan.

Johnston, familiar with such situations, struck a four, while Kevin O'Brien kept Ireland in with a chance and at the start of the final over 15 runs were required. O'Brien survived an appeal for leg-before off the first ball and hit the next to long-on for a single. Johnston miscued a full toss, trying to hit it out of the ground, and the batsmen crossed for another single. A win for Pakistan seemed the most likely outcome but O'Brien had other ideas. He struck the fourth ball over long-on for six and clouted the next ball to long-on, but the boundary was saved and only two runs were made.

All three outcomes were possible off the last ball, assuming it was neither a no-ball nor a wide. O'Brien could not manage the six for victory but he was able to flick the ball for four, backward of square, to tie the match. He ended on 84, made off 47 balls with 11 fours and two sixes. The crowd thoroughly enjoyed the occasion which, once again, showed that Ireland could be more than competitive against Full Member opposition.

IRELAND v PAKISTAN

One-Day International – List A – 50 overs

Clontarf Cricket Club, Castle Avenue, Dublin, 23 May 2013

Match tied (Duckworth-Lewis method)

PAKISTAN		R	B	M	4s	6s
Imran Farhat	c Stirling b Cusack	9	34	34	-	-
Nasir Jamshed	c Murtagh b K.J.O'Brien	20	39	57	-	1
Mohammad Hafeez	not out	122	113	150	12	2
Asad Shafiq	c Johnston b Cusack	84	89	107	9	-
*Misbah-ul-Haq	run out (Porterfield)	0	0	1	-	-
+Kamran Akmal	b K.J.O'Brien	13	6	10	3	-
Shoaib Malik	not out	1	1	1	-	-
Ehsan Adil						
Junaid Khan						
Saeed Ajmal						
Mohammad Irfan						
	b2 lb2 w13	17				
	(5 wickets, 47 overs)	**266**				

IRELAND		R	B	M	4s	6s
*W.T.S.Porterfield	c Asad Shafiq b Mohammad Hafeez	19	38	58	2	-
P.R.Stirling	c sub (Umar Amin) b Mohammad Irfan	103	107	149	12	1
E.C.Joyce	b Mohammad Hafeez	32	59	75	1	1
K.J.O'Brien	not out	84	47	71	11	2
+G.C.Wilson	b Junaid Khan	11	16	27	1	-
N.J.O'Brien	c Mohammad Irfan b Junaid Khan	4	6	8	-	-
D.T.Johnston	not out	7	9	19	1	-
A.R.White						
A.R.Cusack						
G.H.Dockrell						
T.J.Murtagh						
	lb8 w7	15				
	(5 wickets, 47 overs)	**275**				

Ireland	O	M	R	W	nb	w		fow	Pak	Ire
Johnston	10	2	53	0	-	3		1	33 (1)	62 (1)
Murtagh	9	0	40	0	-	2		2	221 (4)	158 (3)
Cusack	8	0	50	2	-	2		3	231 (2)	171 (2)
K.J.O'Brien	5	0	43	2	-	-		4	231 (5)	230 (5)
Dockrell	10	0	45	0	-	1		5	261 (6)	240 (6)
Stirling	5	0	31	0	-	-		6		
								7		
Pakistan	O	M	R	W	nb	w		8		
Mohammad Irfan	10	0	57	1	-	4		9		
Junaid Khan	9	1	54	2	-	2		10		
Ehsan Adil	3	0	17	0	-	-				
Mohammad Hafeez	9	0	43	2	-	-				
Shoaib Malik	6	0	34	0	-	1				
Saeed Ajmal	10	0	71	0	-	-				

Umpires: I.J.Gould (England) and R.P.Smith (Ireland)

Reserve umpire: L.Fourie (Ireland). Referee: J.J.Crowe (New Zealand)

Toss: Pakistan

Player of the Match: K.J.O'Brien (Ireland)

In Pakistan's innings Nasir Jamshed (15) retired hurt on 27-0 (9.4 overs) and resumed on 221-2 (42.3 overs).

In Pakistan's innings rain stopped play after 13.3 overs (Pakistan 41-1) and 22.4 overs (Pakistan 87-1) but no overs were lost; when rain stopped play again after 30.4 overs (Pakistan 120-1), three overs were lost. With the match reduced to 47 overs per side, Ireland were set a target of 276 runs.

In Ireland's innings Umar Amin fielded as substitute for Nasir Jamshed.

Advantage Afghanistan

Since 2013, Afghanistan and Ireland have vied for top spot among the Associate countries. By the end of 2015 both sides, however, needed to find younger players to replace those who had served them so well over the previous ten years.

In the autumn of 2015, both countries toured Zimbabwe, Ireland playing three one-day internationals in Harare, and Afghanistan a series of five one-dayers in Bulawayo. Ireland lost their series 2-1 so there was considerable incentive for Afghanistan to do better. Yet they were without some of their best players. Hamid Hassan, arguably the leading Associate bowler of his generation, joined Karim Sadiq on the missing list, as did the more promising Afsar Zazai, Usman Ghani, Javed Ahmadi and Rahmat Shah, whose recent performances had been inconsistent. With the series standing at two matches each, Shahpoor Zadran and Nowroz Mangal were dropped for the decider because of poor form.

Asked to bat, Afghanistan began aggressively with Mohammad Shehzad, in his typical style, striking 26 off 22 balls in an opening partnership of 35. Also typically, he fell clubbing a long hop towards the midwicket boundary that only found the hands of Mutombodzi. Noor Ali Zadran and Mohammad Nabi, the latter promoted to number three for this series, added 97 to place the visitors in an excellent position. But after Raza deceived both with some clever spin bowling the innings inexplicably fell apart and against tight bowling and keen fielding, four wickets fell while only 42 runs were made.

Afghanistan's response was again, typically, to attack, Mirwais Ashraf hitting two sixes in a partnership of 27 with Asghar Stanikzai. Dawlat Zadran also struck lustily but found the boundary only once; it was, however, enough to ensure that Afghanistan's innings lasted the full 50 overs.

Perhaps inspired by their batting, Dawlat Zadran and Mirwais Ashraf removed Zimbabwe's top three batsmen with only 15 runs on the board. Hamza Hotak, with his left-arm spin, then accounted for Mutombodzi and Raza, leaving the home side on 51/5. Meanwhile Williams was batting well and clearly was not experiencing the same problems as his colleagues. While he was finding the boundary for four or clearing it for six, Chigumbura, Chisoro and Jongwe were struggling against the spin of Hamza Hotak and Rashid Khan. They could defend but not score runs. As the run rate required became more desperate, they flailed around and got themselves out.

Chigumbura was completely deceived by a superb leg break from Rashid Khan which drifted into the batsman in the air, before pitching and spinning the other way to hit the off stump. Williams reached his century in the 43rd over but his colleagues were in trouble against Dawlat Zadran, who had returned to the attack and was getting the ball to reverse swing. This was too much for Jongwe and Masakadza, while Panyangara was fortunate to survive the two balls he received. In the next over, Williams advanced down the pitch to Rashid Khan, misjudged the line and was stumped among much excitement by the Afghan players, who had not only won the match by a convincing 73 runs, but also the series 3-2. They, therefore, became the first Associate country to beat a Full Member in a one-day series and achieved what Ireland had hoped, but failed, to do.

While Ireland lacked a bowler with the skill of Dawlat Zadran, the biggest difference between the two sides was probably in their preparation. Afghanistan played two warm-up matches in Bulawayo before the series began whereas Ireland went straight in and were using the series as a warm-up to the Intercontinental Cup match against Namibia, which they duly won with ease. It is far from clear whether it will be Ireland or Afghanistan who will succeed the best in producing the next generation of players.

ZIMBABWE v AFGHANISTAN

One-Day International – List A – 50 overs

Queens Sports Club, Bulawayo, 24 October 2015

Afghanistan won by 73 runs

AFGHANISTAN

		R	B	M	4s	6s
Noor Ali Zadran	b Raza	54	88	163	5	-
+Mohammad Shehzad	c Mutombodzi b Masakadza	26	22	25	5	-
Mohammad Nabi	c Chibhabha b Raza	53	70	101	3	-
*Asghar Stanikzai	c Raza b Masakadza	38	58	87	2	2
Samiullah Shenwari	run out (Chigumbura-Mutumbami)	1	2	7	-	-
Najibullah Zadran	st Mutumbami b Raza	5	9	9	1	-
Shafiqullah Shafaq	b Masakadza	6	20	25	-	-
Rashid Khan	c Masakadza b Jongwe	4	6	9	-	-
Mirwais Ashraf	c Jongwe b Panyangara	21	16	18	1	2
Dawlat Zadran	not out	13	9	10	1	-
Hamza Hotak	not out	0	1	3	-	-
	b3 lb2 nb1 w18	24				
	(9 wickets, 50 overs)	**245**				

ZIMBABWE

		R	B	M	4s	6s
C.J.Chibhabha	c Samiullah Shenwari b Dawlat Zadran	7	7	5	1	-
+R.Mutumbami	b Dawlat Zadran	2	5	20	-	-
C.R.Ervine	c Mohammad Shehzad b Mirwais Ashraf	1	7	7	-	-
S.C.Williams	st Mohammad Shehzad b Rashid Khan	102	124	179	3	4
C.T.Mutombodzi	c Mohammad Nabi b Hamza Hotak	6	20	27	1	-
S.Raza	st Mohammad Shehzad b Hamza Hotak	2	13	13	-	-
*E.Chigumbura	b Rashid Khan	14	36	45	1	-
T.S.Chisoro	c Najibullah Zadran b Hamza Hotak	10	30	46	-	-
L.M.Jongwe	b Dawlat Zadran	16	14	22	2	-
W.P.Masakadza	b Dawlat Zadran	3	8	10	-	-
T.Panyangara	not out	0	2	3	-	-
	nb1 w8	9				
	(44.1 overs)	**172**				

Zimbabwe	O	M	R	W	nb	w
Jongwe	7	0	44	1	-	3
Chibhabha	6	0	27	0	-	-
Panyangara	8	0	45	1	-	-
Masakadza	9	1	31	3	-	-
Chisoro	5	1	20	0	-	3
Williams	4	0	19	0	-	-
Raza	10	0	40	3	-	3
Mutombodzi	1	0	14	0	1	2

Afghanistan	O	M	R	W	nb	w
Mirwais Ashraf	8	1	26	1	-	2
Dawlat Zadran	8	0	22	4	-	2
Mohammad Nabi	8	0	33	0	-	1
Hamza Hotak	10	1	41	3	1	2
Rashid Khan	7.1	0	24	2	-	-
Najibullah Zadran	2	0	21	0	-	-
Samiullah Shenwari	1	0	5	0	-	-

fow	Afg	Zim
1	35 (2)	9 (1)
2	132 (1)	12 (3)
3	160 (3)	15 (2)
4	172 (5)	34 (5)
5	178 (6)	51 (6)
6	197 (7)	103 (7)
7	202 (8)	140 (8)
8	229 (4)	165 (9)
9	240 (9)	172 (10)
10		172 (4)

Umpires: N.J.Llong (England) and L.Rusere (Zimbabwe)

TV umpire: T.J.Matibiri (Zimbabwe). Reserve umpire: L.A.Ngwenya (Zimbabwe). Referee: D.Govindjee (South Africa)

Toss: Zimbabwe

Player of the Match: Dawlat Zadran (Afghanistan) and S.C.Williams (Zimbabwe)

Afghanistan won the series 3-2.

Shafiqullah Shafaq is also known as Shafiqullah Shinwari.

10

The short game

THE CURRENT decade has seen the growth of the short game at international level, otherwise known as T20. The Big Bash, the title of Australia's domestic competition in this format, is probably more evocative of the public's understanding. T20 is generally seen as providing a quick and exciting contest in which a result is guaranteed within either an afternoon or an evening.

The high scoring, with lots of fours and sixes, is great entertainment for spectators. Tactically, greater attention has to be given to field placings in an effort to keep the run rate down. As a consequence, there has been an improvement in the standard of fielding, above that already brought about by the 50-over game.

Producing a short and exciting contest has little value, however, when attendances are no more than a few friends and relatives of the players. A maximum of 20 overs for the length of an innings is largely irrelevant where international teams are little better than moderate English club sides and struggle to bat for more than 15 to 18 overs. T20 merely allows these teams to realise their limitations more often, since it is now possible to play at least two and, in mid-summer in northern Europe, as many as three matches in one day. The format does, however, enable players to take part in more international fixtures, compared to 50-over internationals which take all day or to traditional two-innings matches lasting two or more days. T20 matches are supposed to reduce the gap in standard between the teams. In only 20 overs it is more difficult for one side to dominate.

Sides that are strongest on paper can ill afford to play poorly whereas those who would struggle to maintain consistency over 50 overs may well sustain the effort required for 20. A chance of an upset is more likely to occur. In 48 official T20 men's matches between Associate and Full Member countries the Associates have won eight times, an 18 per cent record. Even so, the argument that T20 will help to minimise mismatches is not strong. In all Associate and Affiliate internationals since the beginning of 2009 to the end of 2015, there have been 39 instances of sides being dismissed for under 50. China have recorded four such dismissals and Japan, New Caledonia and Guatemala three each. The lowest score is 17 by Macedonia against Bulgaria in 2013, a total achieved in 13.2 overs with Bulgaria then requiring only two overs to win by nine wickets. The next lowest score is by Kuwait, who made 20 all out in 13.2 overs in 2014, with Nepal gaining victory by nine wickets in 2.5 overs.

The first international T20 contest outside the Full Member countries took place in Prague in 2004 with a Tri-Nations event involving the Czech Republic, Poland and Slovakia. The first Associate team to play T20 were Bermuda as in April 2006 they met a West Indies XI, an England XI and a South African XI across one week.

The opposition was not of high quality and Bermuda won the first two matches before losing to the South African side in the final of what was described as a T20 World Cricket Classic, which, given the age and quality of many of the players, was certainly a misnomer. Rather than seeing T20 as fulfilling a development role from which countries might move on to 50-over and multi-innings cricket, as their standards improve, it is probably best to view T20 for what it is, namely one format under which cricket is played. T20 matches can then be appreciated for their ability to bring about famous victories or defeats, statistical triumphs, and exciting finishes, as well as help establish cricket in countries with no or little history of the game.

International cricket returns to China

Taking advantage of the shorter format of T20, cricket was included in the Asian Games for the first time in 2010. For the first international matches in China since October 1948 the organisers constructed a purpose-built facility, the Guangdong International Cricket Stadium, with seating for 12,000 spectators, at Guangdong University of Technology. The ground was designed by Chinese architects. Clay was brought in from Shaanxi Province and grass seed imported from the USA to form the only turf pitch in China. The Chinese Cricket Association employed Jasimuddin as the curator, on secondment from the Kinrara Oval in Malaysia. The whole venture was undertaken with the hope that the facility might become the base for a major development of cricket within the country.

With India refusing to take part, Afghanistan were runners-up in the men's event, losing to Bangladesh in the final. Pakistan beat Bangladesh in the final of the women's competition, in which the contest for the bronze medal was between Japan and hosts China. Unlike the men's matches, which were played on grass, the women played on matting laid over one of the playing strips at the edge of the square.

On a breezy but warm day, in front of about 700 spectators, Japan won the toss and chose to field. Experience earlier in the tournament had shown that, perhaps surprisingly, when conditions were warm, the ball tended to swing more. With Ota and Kubota both effecting swing the Chinese players had difficulty getting bat on ball and after four overs they had scored only five runs. Sun Huan then failed to score a run from the 15 balls she faced, an unhelpful scoring rate in a T20 contest with China losing wickets as they tried to increase the run rate by taking quick singles, which were simply not to be had. After ten overs they were 22/4 when Yu Miao and Zhang Mei set about rescuing the situation, the latter striking two boundaries which proved to be the only ones of China's innings. They added 26 runs in the next five overs before Zhang Mei misjudged a ball from Ota. She thought it was a beamer and, in two minds, ducked low enough to be beneath it, but then, seeing that it was not as high as expected, attempted to hit it. She missed and the ball clipped the bail at the top of the leg stump. The umpires conferred to discuss the legality of the delivery. They decided in favour of the bowler and China slipped to 48/5, from where they continued to struggle and ended with a considerably under-par score of 65.

By the time Japan began their reply, the crowd had increased to just over 1,000 and the temperature had risen to 25°C, giving a very pleasant afternoon. Mei Chunhua bowled with considerable pace and had success in her first over, trapping Yamamoto leg-before. Zhou Haijie bowled off spin from the other end with three fielders in the point region. The combination was sufficient to tie down Kuribayashi, easily Japan's best batter. She made only one run off her first 21 balls and after seven overs Japan had reached only 19.

China then gave Kuribayashi a life as Dai Shengnan fluffed a stumping chance. Ten runs were taken off the next over with Iwasaki and Kuribayashi taking the initiative. After Iwasaki was run out, attempting a quick single to a misfield, Wang Meng dropped Kuribayashi at mid-on from a catchable head-high chance.

Ota and Kuribayashi showed good footwork to score runs off the spinners and with ten needed from the last three overs, another stumping chance was missed. With two overs to go there were six runs required, five of which came from the 19th over before, in an anticlimax, Wu Juan bowled a wide to gift Japan the winning run. Despite the interest this match generated at the time, the construction of the Guangdong stadium has not yielded the legacy that was hoped. The Asian Cricket Council used the ground for a women's international T20 tournament in 2012 and since then it has been allowed to deteriorate.

CHINA WOMEN v JAPAN WOMEN

20 overs

Asian Games Women's Competition – Bronze Medal Play-Off

Guangdong International Cricket Stadium, Guangzhou, 19 November 2010

Japan won by seven wickets

CHINA		R	B	M	4s	6s
Sun Mengyao	c Saito b Ota	1	6	-	-	
Zhang Mei	b Ota	26	42		2	-
Sun Huan	lbw b Sudo	0	15	-	-	
Huang Zhuo	run out (Kuribayashi)	3	12	-	-	
Mei Chunhua	run out (sub, F.Kawai)	3	2	-	-	
Yu Miao	c Saito b Kubota	17	30	-	-	
*Wang Meng	not out	5	14	-	-	
Zhang Jingjing						
+Dai Shengnan						
Wu Juan						
Zhou Haijie						
	lb3 nb1 w6	10				
	(6 wickets, 20 overs)	**65**				

JAPAN		R	B	M	4s	6s
*E.Kuribayashi	not out	24	55		1	-
M.Yamamoto	lbw b Mei Chunhua	0	3	-	-	
A.Iwasaki	run out (Sun Mengyao)	10	40		2	-
S.Kubota	run out (Wang Meng/Dai Shengnan)	6	9	-	-	
K.Ota	not out	5	8	-	-	
M.Kanno						
A.Nakayama						
E.Iida						
+Y.Saito						
A.Sudo						
S.Miyaji						
	b5 lb2 w14	21				
	(3 wickets, 19.1 overs)	**66**				

Japan	O	M	R	W	nb	w
Kubota	4	0	8	1	-	-
Ota	4	0	8	2	-	1
Sudo	4	0	18	1	1	2
Kuribayashi	4	0	8	0	-	1
Nakayama	1	0	7	0	-	-
Miyaji	3	0	13	0	-	2

China	O	M	R	W	nb	w
Mei Chunhua	4	2	3	1	-	1
Zhou Haijie	4	0	20	0	-	3
Wu Juan	3.1	0	13	0	-	4
Wang Meng	4	0	12	0	-	-
Yu Miao	2	0	10	0	-	4
Zhang Jingjing	2	1	1	0	-	-

fow	China	Japan
1	1 (1)	5 (2)
2	7 (3)	33 (3)
3	16 (4)	48 (4)
4	22 (5)	
5	48 (2)	
6	65 (6)	
7		
8		
9		
10		

Umpires: V.Kalidas (Malaysia) and N.Sivan (Malaysia)

Reserve umpire: Sun Jianxin (China). Referee: Iqbal Sikander (Pakistan)

Toss: Japan

In the creek at Amini Park

If any region in the world was going to take to T20 cricket it was the South Pacific. Its cricketers had always favoured aggressive batting, sixes being the preferred scoring rather than wasting energy running singles, and fast, attacking bowling.

Up to the early 2000s the hierarchy of the South Pacific was well established. Papua New Guinea were clearly at the top, having won every time that cricket was included in the South Pacific Games. Fiji were the perpetual runners-up even though their standards seemed to be in continuous freefall from those attained in the late 1940s and early 1950s. By 2011 Fiji faced serious competition from Vanuatu and Samoa.

The first East Asia-Pacific T20 Championships, held in Port Moresby in July 2011, saw Papua New Guinea beat Vanuatu in the final. Fiji had to meet Samoa in the third-place play-off and for this, both teams comprised a mixture of youth and experience. Samoa had two players over 40, their captain Geoffrey Clarke (41) and Murphy Su'a (44), the former New Zealand Test cricketer. They had three players under 23 in Pritchard Pritchard, Sean Cotter and Tiafala Alatasi. Fiji's oldest player was Iniasi Cakacaka, aged 42. Four of their side were under 23; captain Josefa Rika, wicketkeeper Maciu Gauna, Vilikesa Nailolo and Viliame Yakabi.

The match was played in the morning as a prelude to the final of the competition in the afternoon. Fiji won the toss and chose to field with Samoa starting cautiously. When they lost their first wicket, Cotter, on the fifth ball of the third over, they had made only 17. Clarke raised his scoring rate to a run a ball but Mailata, Samoa's best batsman, was surprisingly subdued and gave an easy caught-and-bowled to Kida after making only nine runs from 19 balls, without a boundary.

Mulivai showed great power, if little footwork. He simply stood his ground, chanced his arm and slogged. The score mounted from 48 at the fall of the second wicket to 134 in eight overs before he hit a leg break from Yakabi hard and high, into the safe hands of Ravoka. He had made 67 of the 86-run partnership, taking only 35 balls to do so with four fours and an amazing seven sixes.

Pritchard provided the right impetus at the end of the innings with three further sixes, one travelling an estimated 100m before landing in the creek outside the ground at Amini Park. Fiji had no answer to the onslaught of the last ten overs. They tried eight bowlers, six of whom were dispatched for seven or more runs per over as Pritchard's entertaining 28 came from ten balls. Clarke, seemingly stranded as an onlooker at the other end, remained undefeated, but was no slouch when given a chance of the strike. His 43 came off 42 balls, though he failed to hit a six.

Fiji's response suffered a blow in the first over, Mulivai holding a fine diving catch to dismiss Ravoka with no runs on the board. Bulabulavu and Cakacaka played brightly and the score was mounting in promising fashion. The seventh over saw the introduction of Cotter into the attack and, with some seemingly innocuous medium pacers, he was immediately effective, removing Bulabulavu, Cakacaka and Rika in quick time.

With Mulivai taking another, somewhat easier, catch to dismiss Kida, Fiji were 68/5 and the task from there was just too great. Tukana, Gauna, Lomani and Yabaki all made runs at a run a ball or faster, Lomani contributing two huge sixes in his 23 off 14 balls. Yabaki hit four fours in his 24 off only 12 balls and it was all attractive stuff, but to no purpose as Fiji failed to last their 20 overs and fell 30 runs short. Cotter was the most successful bowler, conceding only nine runs from his three overs, and picking up three wickets. This was Samoa's highest place in any cricket tournament to date.

FIJI v SAMOA

20 overs

East Asia-Pacific T20 Championships – Third-Place Play-Off

Amini Park, Port Moresby, 7 July 2011

Samoa won by 30 runs

SAMOA		R	B	M	4s	6s
S.Cotter	c Ravoka b Lomani	14	15		2	-
*G.Clarke	not out	43	42		4	-
F.B.Mailata	c&b Kida	9	19		-	-
F.F.Mulivai	c Ravoka b Yabaki	67	35		4	7
P.Pritchard	not out	28	10		-	3
L.Fuinaomo						
N.Va'asili						
+U.T.Kaisara						
M.L.Su'a						
T.Alatasi						
W.Mariner						
	nb1 w10	11				
	(3 wickets, 20 overs)	**172**				

FIJI		R	B	M	4s	6s
S.Ravoka	c Mulivai b Fuinaomo	0	5		-	-
J.Bulabulavu	c Kaisara b Cotter	37	23		6	-
I.Cakacaka	c Va'asili b Cotter	26	18		5	-
J.V.Kida	c Mulivai b Mariner	4	7		-	-
*J.F.Rika	c Kaisara b Cotter	0	3		-	-
W.Tukana	c Cotter b Alatasi	13	12		1	-
+M.B.Gauna	c sub (F.Fa'aofo) b Alatasi	11	13		1	-
S.R.Lomani	b Mulivai	23	14		-	2
V.Yabaki	c Kaisara b Va'asili	24	12		4	-
V.Nailolo	lbw b Mulivai	0	2		-	-
M.I.Khan	not out	1	1		-	-
	lb1 w2	3				
	(18.2 overs)	**142**				

Fiji	O	M	R	W	nb	w
Khan	4	0	20	0	-	1
Lomani	4	0	36	1	1	1
Tukana	4	0	19	0	-	-
Nailolo	1	0	14	0	-	1
Kida	2	0	32	1	-	2
Rika	1	0	20	0	-	-
Cakacaka	2	0	17	0	-	1
Yabaki	2	0	14	1	-	-

Samoa	O	M	R	W	nb	w
Fuinaomo	2	1	13	1	-	-
Mulivai	3.2	0	22	2	-	-
Alatasi	3	0	36	2	-	1
Mariner	4	0	32	1	-	1
Cotter	3	1	9	3	-	-
Va'asili	3	0	29	1	-	-

fow	Samoa	Fiji
1	17 (1)	0 (1)
2	48 (3)	58 (2)
3	134 (4)	66 (3)
4		66 (5)
5		68 (4)
6		89 (6)
7		109 (7)
8		126 (8)
9		138 (9)
10		142 (10)

Umpires: G.Clelland (Vanuatu) and G.Johnston (Vanuatu)

Referee: G.F.Labrooy (Sri Lanka)

Toss: Fiji

Saint Helena's pioneers

Cricket has been played in Saint Helena since at least the mid-1840s but the country's isolation has meant that the sport has developed with little contact with teams outside the island and, therefore, with no appreciation of how high or low the standard.

April 2012 was therefore the most important month in Saint Helena's cricketing history. It was the first and, so far, the only time that a representative team has left the island to play internationally. The tournament was Division Three of the African T20 Championships, held at Willowmoore Park, Benoni, in South Africa, the ground that has become the headquarters of the African Cricket Association.

Saint Helena's participation at Benoni echoed the pioneering spirit of cricketers in the 18th century. With a population of only 4,000 there is a very limited pool of cricketing talent yet cricket is, arguably, the national sport. The number of players involved in cricket competitions and supervised programmes, introducing cricket to boys and girls, is just over 11 per cent of the island's population, which is one of the highest proportions in the world.

Venturing overseas requires a considerable period away from work and family so outward and return travelling has to coincide with the schedules of RMS *St Helena*, which provides a regular cargo and passenger service between Ascension, Saint Helena and Cape Town, South Africa. The sailings to Cape Town take place about every fortnight and take five days. For the tournament between 25 and 30 April 2012 the cricketers left Saint Helena on 10 April and did not return until 15 May. The cost for the whole squad was around £24,000, most of which was raised by the islanders through subscription.

In their first match they met Cameroon, a country where cricket did not exist until 2005, after which it was promoted through the Commonwealth Students and Youth Development Organisation. Emphasis was given to developing the sport in schools and youth clubs. Cameroon's players were therefore in their late teens and early 20s and with very little experience. Saint Helena's squad, however, was a mixture of older and younger players, the former with many years of experience of playing against each other.

On an unseasonably cool day, with temperatures hovering at 14°C at best, Cameroon won the toss and chose to bat. Conditions were good for pace bowling as inexperience and lack of match practice brought about a quick demise with five wickets soon down for nine runs. Coleman did the damage, taking five wickets in his four overs.

Ngueudam played a defensive role while the lower middle order attempted a recovery, Tchakou helping to add nine runs and Abada a further 17. With the score on 35, Leo completed a hat-trick in his only over, ending Ngueudam's resistance and accounting for Abada and Ndum. When Crowie removed Nyoma with the second ball of his next over, Cameroon were all out for 36. No batsman reached double figures and the innings lasted only 11.2 overs. Although Kidzeeyuf bowled well and proved economical, Nyoma was expensive.

Richards and George had no difficulty surpassing Cameroon's total in the seventh over. This was an encouraging start for Saint Helena who went on to win four out of their eight matches and finish fifth overall.

In recognition of their achievement, the team were given an enthusiastic welcome by the local population on their return and honoured by a reception at Plantation House, hosted by the Governor Mark Capes and his wife. Unfortunately, Saint Helena have not managed any further international cricket since this tournament.

CAMEROON v SAINT HELENA

20 overs

Africa T20 Championships – Division Three

Willowmoore Park Main Oval, Benoni, 25 April 2012

Saint Helena won by nine wickets

CAMEROON		R	B	M	4s	6s
T.B.Nkese	b Coleman	1				
W.N.Teunga	c Thomas b Coleman	0				
+P.B.F.Ngameni	c Yon b Johnson	5				
M.R.Ngueudam	c Coleman b Leo	5				
F.J.Mpegna	b Coleman	0				
N.S.S.C.Kidzeeyuf	b Coleman	2				
I.Tchakou	lbw b Coleman	6				
A.R.G.Abada	b Leo	7				
A.J.B.Nyoma	b Crowie	0				
W.M.Ndum	lbw b Leo	0				
*W.J.C.Solefack	not out	0				
	lb2 nb1 w7	10				
	(11.2 overs)	36				

SAINT HELENA		R	B	M	4s	6s
*+D.Richards	not out	15				
J.Essex	c Ngameni b Kidzeeyuf	0				
G.George	not out	14				
A.Thomas						
S.Crowie						
G.Johnson						
D.O'Bey						
A.Yon						
G.Coleman						
P.Stroud						
D.Leo						
	lb1 nb1 w6	8				
	(1 wicket, 6.1 overs)	37				

Saint Helena	O	M	R	W	nb	w		fow	Cam	St H
Coleman	4	1	8	5	-	-		1	1	3
Johnson	2	1	1	1	-	-		2	7	
Yon	2	0	14	0	1	3		3	7	
Stroud	1	0	7	0	-	3		4	7	
Crowie	1.2	0	3	1	-	-		5	9	
Leo	1	0	1	3	-	1		6	18	
								7	35	
Cameroon	O	M	R	W	nb	w		8	35	
Kidzeeyuf	3.1	0	10	1	-	2		9	35	
Nyoma	3	0	26	0	1	4		10	36	

Umpires: V.R.Angara (Botswana) and W.Dollar (South Africa)

Toss: Cameroon

In Cameroon's innings, D.Leo took a hat-trick when dismissing M.R.Ngueudam, A.R.G.Abada and W.M.Ndum

An evening's entertainment in the Gulf

By the early 2010s, Ireland and Afghanistan had emerged as the leading Associate and Affiliate countries in all three of cricket's formats and a considerable rivalry had developed between them. By the time they met in the final of the World T20 qualifying competition in March 2012 they had played each other five times, Afghanistan winning on three occasions and Ireland twice. The 2012 match was therefore destined to be closely contested.

On a very warm but breezy evening at the Dubai International Cricket Stadium (formerly the Dubai Sports City Stadium), with the temperature just below 30°C, Afghanistan won the toss and elected to bat. The match, which began at 6pm, under floodlights, was Ireland's second of the day. They had beaten Namibia by nine wickets in the morning to qualify for the final.

With a crowd of several thousand, most cheering for Afghanistan, the start was electric and Karim Sadiq clouted the first ball of the match back over Rankin's head for six, then in the next over he struck successive boundaries off Johnston. Rankin responded by bowling a bouncer which hit Karim Sadiq on the helmet, then rebounded on to the stumps to dismiss him for 16 from ten balls and Afghanistan were 18/1.

Mohammad Shehzad then proceeded to dominate events. He lost partners at regular intervals, many to superb catches, but there was no way that Ireland could contain him as he moved into the line of the ball and swung lustily. With a combination of strength and timing he hit two sixes and seven fours before becoming the seventh wicket to fall. His 77 from only 57 balls was 56 per cent of Afghanistan's score at that point. Only O'Brien kept the run rate under control, conceding just 18 runs from his four overs. Otherwise the Irish bowling was somewhat ill-disciplined.

The more Mohammad Shehzad attacked, the angrier the Irish seemed to become, but all they succeeded in doing was bowling more long hops, which were duly dispatched for runs. Once Shehzad fell, Gulbadeen Naib was equally aggressive, finishing the innings with sixes off the last two balls.

Afghanistan's total of 152 was certainly competitive and the start of the Irish innings made it more so. Again it was the first ball that provided the excitement, Dawlat Zadran spectacularly uprooting Porterfield's middle stump. Stirling retaliated almost immediately, sending the first three deliveries of the next over to the boundary. He and Joyce batted superbly and it came as a surprise when the latter hooked Aftab Alam into the safe hands of Mohammad Nabi at deep square leg.

Wilson gave excellent support, allowing Stirling to have the strike whenever possible, and the score rose rapidly to 113 from 76 balls before Stirling's effort ended in another catch at deep square leg, this time by Gulbadeen Naib off the bowling of Dawlat Zadran, before Stirling reached his 50 off only 17 balls and went on to make 79 from 38 balls, with nine fours and two sixes.

Ireland needed fewer than a run a ball but lost another wicket immediately, O'Brien edging his first delivery to the wicketkeeper. Once Dawlat had completed his four overs, however, Wilson took over the scoring role until, with only three runs needed from 12 balls, he failed to reach the boundary at long-off and gave a catch to Mirwais Ashraf. The Irish win came four balls later when Poynter hit a boundary to midwicket.

Although most of the spectators were disappointed not to see Afghanistan win, they had been treated to some excellent entertainment with the batting of Mohammad Shehzad and Stirling, the bowling of Dawlat Zadran and the Irish fielding. Stirling won the player of the match award, Ireland gained revenge for earlier defeats by Afghanistan and both sides had the satisfaction of qualifying for the next ICC T20 World Cup.

AFGHANISTAN v IRELAND
T20 International
ICC World T20 Qualifier – Final
Dubai International Cricket Stadium, Dubai, 24 March 2012
Ireland won by five wickets

AFGHANISTAN		R	B	M	4s	6s
Karim Sadiq	b Rankin	16	10	8	2	1
Javed Ahmadi	c Rankin b Johnston	6	5	14	1	-
+Mohammad Shehzad	c Porterfield b Sorensen	77	57	70	7	2
Mirwais Ashraf	c Porterfield b Sorensen	9	8	15	-	1
*Nowroz Mangal	c Sorensen b O'Brien	10	15	15	-	-
Samiullah Shenwari	c Rankin b Sorensen	11	12	21	-	1
Mohammad Nabi	c Sorensen b Stirling	1	2	5	-	-
Gulbadeen Naib	not out	17	8	10	-	2
Aftab Alam	not out	1	3	5	-	-
Dawlat Zadran						
Izatullah Dawlatzai						
	lb2 w2	4				
	(7 wickets, 20 overs)	**152**				

IRELAND		R	B	M	4s	6s
*W.T.S.Porterfield	b Dawlat Zadran	0	1	1	-	-
P.R.Stirling	c Gulbadeen Naib b Dawlat Zadran	79	38	55	9	3
E.C.Joyce	c Mohammad Nabi b Aftab Alam	11	16	16	2	-
+G.C.Wilson	c Mirwais Ashraf b Aftab Alam	32	39	58	2	-
K.J.O'Brien	c Mohammad Shehzad b Dawlat Zadran	0	1	1	-	-
A.D.Poynter	not out	23	17	24	2	1
A.R.White	not out	1	1	3	-	-
D.T.Johnston						
M.C.Sorensen						
W.B.Rankin						
G.H.Dockrell						
	lb6 w4	10				
	(5 wickets, 18.5 overs)	**156**				

Ireland	O	M	R	W	nb	w
Rankin	4	0	22	1	-	1
Johnston	4	0	41	1	-	-
Sorensen	3	0	26	2	-	1
O'Brien	4	0	18	2	-	-
Dockrell	3	0	26	0	-	-
Stirling	2	0	17	1	-	-

Afghanistan	O	M	R	W	nb	w
Dawlat Zadran	4	0	21	3	-	1
Mirwais Ashraf	1	0	17	0	-	1
Aftab Alam	3.5	0	34	2	-	1
Izatullah Dawlatzai	3	0	33	0	-	-
Samiullah Shenwari	3	0	15	0	-	-
Mohammad Nabi	3	0	25	0	-	-
Gulbadeen Naib	1	0	5	0	-	-

fow	Afg	Ire
1	18 (1)	0 (1)
2	27 (2)	33 (3)
3	56 (4)	113 (2)
4	78 (5)	113 (5)
5	119 (6)	150 (4)
6	131 (7)	
7	137 (3)	
8		
9		
10		

Umpires: C.B.Gaffaney (New Zealand) and B.B.Pradhan (Nepal)

Reserve umpire: I.N.Ramage (Scotland). Referee: D.T.Jukes (England)

Toss: Afghanistan

Player of the Match: P.R.Stirling (Ireland)

Flamingos: a sisterly success

Women's cricket in South America is relatively young internationally with the first South American Championships for women only being held in 2010. The tournament has taken place annually since and has always been in T20 format which Argentina won every year until 2015, when they were beaten by Brazil in the final.

Known as the *Flamingos*, they are today rated fourth in all the Americas, behind the West Indies, Canada and the United States, a much higher ranking than their men's team in equivalent competitions. Not surprisingly, Chile, a side with far less international experience, were no match for them when they met in the South American Championships at St George's College, Quilmes, on 14 February 2013.

The match was played in the afternoon, beginning at 3pm local time, in typical weather conditions for an Argentinian summer, unpleasantly hot and humid. The temperature was just above 30°C with 73 per cent humidity. By early evening, as the match finished, the temperature had dropped to the mid-20s.

Vazquez won the toss and chose to bat, condemning Chile to field in the heat. The visitors' bowlers showed their inexperience by contributing 17 wides and four no-balls, an addition of 21 runs to the total they would need to chase. Dirce Yuli played an outstanding innings, hitting her and her country's maiden international century in women's matches. She finished unbeaten on 113 from 66 balls, with 15 fours. Her partners played a supporting role, scoring in ones and twos, but failing to reach the boundary.

Chile never looked like getting a wicket and the one they obtained, to end the opening partnership on 74, was the result of a misunderstanding between Yuli and Culley, Smith effecting a simple run-out. Sofia Retamales replaced Culley and batted with equal assurance. By the end of the 20 overs the partnership was worth 115 runs with Retamales undefeated on 27, made from 26 balls. All of Chile's bowlers went for seven or more runs per over.

Chile's reply began disastrously with Riquelme falling to a catch at the wicket and Conejeros to one in the slips, both off the bowling of Malena Mustafa and both with the score on three. Smith, who had played in the men's South American Championships for Chile's A team in 2004, showed her experience, and the foundation was slowly laid for a reasonable score. However Budini, although able to defend well, was unable to find shots to pierce the field and when she was forced to retire hurt, she had accumulated a mere two runs off 20 balls.

Moya was more positive as she and Smith managed to find the boundary twice each and the score had risen to 60 when Moya was dismissed off the bowling of del Valle. Three runs later, Stocks accounted for Smith, caught by Eugenia Mustafa. Her 23, made off 61 balls, was Chile's top score. Beltran and Zúñiga batted out the remaining overs but neither was able to make a run.

Apart from gifting 16 wides and four no-balls, Argentina's bowlers were economical with three of their overs being maidens. Although Violetta Yuli did not take a wicket, she conceded only seven runs in her four overs, while her twin sister Dirce took the player of the match award. Although not twins, Sofia and Georgina Retamales are also sisters, and Argentina had three pairs of sisters in their side. Among those who were not selected were Lucia Culley, twin sister of Clara Culley, and Guillermina and Emilia Mustafa, sisters of Malena and Eugenia.

Two days later, Argentina beat Chile again, this time by 139 runs. Dirce Yuli was once more undefeated, scoring 72 out of the Argentine total of 184/3 as Chile put in an even poorer performance. They gave Argentina 45 wides, while scoring only 45 themselves for the loss of eight wickets. Smith top-scored for Chile with eight runs.

ARGENTINA WOMEN v CHILE WOMEN

20 overs

South American Women's T20 Championships

St George's College, Quilmes, Buenos Aires, 14 February 2013

Argentina won by 125 runs

ARGENTINA		R	B	M	4s	6s
+C.Culley	run out (Smith)	20	28		-	-
D.D.Yuli	not out	113	66		15	-
S.A.Retamales	not out	27	26		-	-
*V.M.Vazquez						
G.Retamales						
E.Mustafa						
M.Mustafa						
A.Stocks						
D.Canton						
V.Yuli						
M.del Valle						
	b7 lb1 nb4 w17	29				
	(1 wicket, 20 overs)	**189**				

CHILE		R	B	M	4s	6s
G.T.Budini	retired hurt	2	20		-	-
F.J.Riquelme	c Culley b M.Mustafa	1	7		-	-
N.A.Conejeros	c del Valle b M.Mustafa	0	3		-	-
K.Smith	c E.Mustafa b Stocks	23	61		2	-
+F.A.Moya	c V.Yuli b del Valle	17	19		2	-
Y.Beltran	not out	1	10		-	-
A.M.Zúñiga	not out	0	0		-	-
M.J.B.Saavedra						
A.T.Navarro						
G.C.Barraza						
*J.C.Garcès						
	nb4 w16	20				
	(4 wickets, 20 overs)	**64**				

Chile	O	M	R	W	nb	w
Saavedra	4	0	33	0	-	3
Zúñiga	4	0	34	0	-	4
Riquelme	3	0	37	0	-	6
Garcès	4	0	39	0	1	1
Conejeros	4	0	28	0	-	1
Navarro	1	0	10	0	-	2

Argentina	O	M	R	W	nb	w
M.Mustafa	3	1	9	2	-	2
V.Yuli	4	1	7	0	1	3
E.Mustafa	2	0	6	0	-	5
del Valle	4	0	19	1	3	4
Canton	4	0	19	0	-	1
Stocks	2	1	1	1	-	-
S.A.Retamales	2	0	3	0	-	1

fow	Arg	Chl
1	74 (1)	3 (2)
2		3 (3)
3		60 (5)
4		63 (4)
5		
6		
7		
8		
9		
10		

Umpires: A.Fennell (Argentina) and [unknown]

Toss: Argentina

Player of the Match: D.D.Yuli (Argentina)

It is not known what the team score was in Chile's innings when G.T.Budini retired hurt.

Thai surprise

Women's cricket was unknown in Thailand until 2007 when officials of the Thailand Cricket Association scouted women already playing basketball, softball and hockey and invited them to try cricket. By 2013 Thailand had won the Asian Women's Cricket Championships, a competition for Associates and Affiliates, and gained a place in the World T20 qualifying competition held in July that year in Ireland. After defeat by Pakistan, they faced The Netherlands, arguably the third best women's side in Europe, behind England and Ireland.

The match was played at the Hills Cricket Club, The Vineyard, Milverton, in conditions which were familiar to the Dutch but alien to the Thais. The weather was changeable. After a warm and sunny spell it had rained overnight and much cloud still remained, though, by local standards, the temperatures were still relatively mild, reaching a maximum of 22°C during the afternoon.

The Dutch won the toss and chose to bat. Struggling with the conditions, Chantham bowled three wides but extracted unexpected bounce from the pitch. From the fifth ball, Veringmeier attempted a late cut but hit straight to slip where the chance was dropped. In the next over Tippoch made amends, taking an excellent catch very close to the ground at short extra cover to remove Rambaldo, but Hannema and Veringmeier, striking the loose balls for fours and taking short singles, kept the run rate moving.

In her first over, Sutthiruang conceded a four, bowled a beamer and had a chance dropped at slip. After delivering another full toss above waist height in her next over the umpires intervened, ruled her bowling too dangerous and removed her from the attack.

The Dutch continued to score in boundaries and singles and, after eight overs, had reached 39/1 and were in a good position to accelerate, but the loss of two quick wickets changed that. The ball seemed to slow up on hitting the pitch and the Dutch failed to adjust. With runs limited to singles and the occasional wide, dot balls became as frequent as those scored from. The Dutch struggled on to 84, which contained only three boundaries, and none at all in the last 69 balls.

In Thailand's reply, none of the Dutch bowlers proved menacing. Prathanmitr and Chaiwai scored mainly in singles until taking 12 runs from the sixth over. Then with de Lange getting her off breaks to turn, the opening pair became more watchful. Showing obvious frustration, Prathanmitr got hold of a full toss from Bennett only to hit it straight to Hannema at mid-on. After ten overs Thailand were 33/1 then eight runs came from the 11th over and seven from the 12th, putting them in a strong position. Two wickets fell in the 13th over, both to run-outs which should have been avoided. Chantham and Boochatham also had charmed lives, the former surviving an appeal for a stumping and Boochatham a run-out and a leg-before appeal. Seven runs from each of the 15th and 16th overs brought the run rate closer to what was required.

Despite the loss of another wicket, Thailand continued to advance and, with 18 balls to go, they needed only five runs to win. Four came in the next over before Kornet gifted the winning run by bowling a wide.

Thailand were highly delighted by their best result in international cricket. In contrast, the Dutch lost a match they were expected to win easily. Their bowlers were simply less threatening, Thailand able to strike seven boundaries against three from the Dutch. Chantham was the player of the match.

Despite their victory, Thailand finished behind The Netherlands on run rate in their group and, therefore, failed to qualify for the semi-final stage. Instead they won the Shield with victory over Zimbabwe by 25 runs.

NETHERLANDS WOMEN v THAILAND WOMEN

20 overs

Women's World T20 Qualifier – Group A

Hills Cricket Club, The Vineyard, Milverton, 25 July 2013

Thailand won by six wickets

NETHERLANDS		R	B	M	4s	6s
+M.Veringmeier	run out (Khonchan)	15	29		1	-
H.W.Rambaldo	c Tippoch b Boochatham	0	4		-	-
*D.Hannema	c Boochatham b Sangsoma	25	46		2	-
H.D.J.Siegers	c Saengsakaorat b Padunglerd	1	6		-	-
D.M.Braat	not out	17	22		-	-
E.L.T.de Lange	c Sutthiruang b Sangsoma	5	11		-	-
L.K.Bennett	not out	1	4		-	-
C.H.Hofman						
M.Kornet						
L.Brouwers						
L.Klokgieters						
	b2 nb2 w16	20				
	(5 wickets, 20 overs)	**84**				

THAILAND		R	B	M	4s	6s
+P.Prathanmitr	c Hannema b Bennett	18	31		2	-
N.Chaiwai	run out (Veringmeier)	17	35		1	-
*S.Tippoch	run out (Braat)	9	11		1	-
N.Boochatham	run out (Brouwers)	8	8		1	-
N.Chantham	not out	24	19		2	-
C.Sutthiruang	not out	2	5		-	-
R.Padunglerd						
S.Saengsakaorat						
R.Sangsoma						
N.Khonchan						
W.Liengprasert						
	nb2 w5	7				
	(4 wickets, 17.5 overs)	**85**				

Thailand	O	M	R	W	nb	w
Chantham	2	0	10	0	-	5
Boochatham	4	0	13	1	-	2
Sutthiruang	1.5	0	11	0	2	1
Tippoch	3.1	0	15	0	-	1
Padunglerd	4	0	14	1	-	3
Sangsoma	3	0	11	2	-	2
Khonchan	2	0	8	0	-	1

Netherlands	O	M	R	W	nb	w
Braat	4	0	17	0	-	-
Bennett	4	0	11	1	-	2
Brouwers	4	0	30	0	1	-
Kornet	2.5	0	11	0	1	3
de Lange	3	0	16	0	-	-

fow	Neth	Thai
1	6 (2)	31 (1)
2	41 (1)	50 (2)
3	48 (4)	50 (3)
4	61 (3)	72 (4)
5	77 (6)	
6		
7		
8		
9		
10		

Umpires: Sharfuddoula ibne Shahid (Bangladesh) and R.P.Smith (Ireland)

Reserve umpire: N.Duguid (West Indies). Referee: D.Govindjee (South Africa)

Toss: Netherlands

Player of the Match: N.Chantham (Thailand)

M.Kornet is Mariska Kornet, sister of Mandy Kornet.

Irish joy, Dutch despair

Ireland and The Netherlands contested the third-place play-off in, arguably, the most vital match of the Women's World T20 qualifying tournament as the winners would go through to the World T20 competition proper. The losers would not only fail to qualify but would also lose their official one-day international status.

The match, played at the YMCA Ground, Claremont Road, Dublin, was scheduled for 31 July 2013 but nearly 8mm of rain fell in heavy showers throughout the day. Instead of the scheduled 2pm, the start was first delayed to 2.50pm and at 2.35pm the captains tossed, the Dutch won and asked Ireland to bat only for the rain to immediately return. At 4pm the umpires called off play for the day and the match entered the reserve day, 1 August.

Another 3.5mm of overnight rain meant that any start had to wait for the outfield to dry. The ground staff worked extremely hard on mopping-up operations and, after an inspection at 2pm, the umpires decided that play could begin 45 minutes later. Since this was ruled a separate match from that of the previous day, the captains tossed again at 2.30pm but with the same result.

Ireland lost Shillington in the first over but Isobel Joyce and Garth played sensibly against some very mixed bowling. The Dutch were finding it difficult to control the scoring rate as 13 runs came from the fourth over and by the end of the tenth the score had reached 70. The Dutch continuously changed their bowlers but to little effect until, in the 13th over, Garth fell leg-before. Cecelia Joyce soon followed, placing a long hop into the hands of Rambaldo at short midwicket. With her sister scoring freely and maintaining most of the strike, the Irish total soon passed 100. Although Waldron was needlessly run out and Delany gave an easy caught-and-bowled, runs continued to mount, 12 coming from the 19th over. Ireland finished on 136/5 with Joyce, having reached her 50 off 49 balls, unbeaten on 72 from 64 balls with six fours.

The Dutch reply mirrored the Irish innings with Veringmeier dismissed early and Rambaldo and van der Gun then scoring off almost every ball. Just as the pair were looking dangerous, van der Gun hit the ball high into the covers where Cecelia Joyce fumbled the chance and then held on at the second attempt. Siegers maintained the initiative for the Dutch by striking a full toss over the ropes at deep square leg for the only six of the match. With ten runs coming from the over, followed by seven and five from the next two, the Dutch total was 62 after ten overs, slightly ahead of what would be required by the Duckworth-Lewis method, were rain to bring the game to a halt. By the end of the 14th over the Dutch needed only 46 runs from 36 balls, with their scoring rate increasing all the time.

After Siegers was run out, Rambaldo contrived to hold as much of the strike as she could and the Irish found it hard to stop her scoring. By the start of the final over, 12 runs were required. Delany began with a wide, Rambaldo scored two past point, followed by a leg bye. Braat took a single to long-on. Rambaldo pulled a full toss to deep square leg for two. The fifth ball beat everyone and a bye resulted, leaving four runs to be made off the last ball. A single was taken and Braat stopped running, but Rambaldo, conscious that there might be overthrows, did not. Garth threw directly to the wicketkeeper and Braat was run out, giving a victory to Ireland by a mere two runs.

On such small amounts does the fate of cricket teams sometimes depend. Ireland went through to the World T20 and the Dutch lost their one-day international status. With The Netherlands getting so close, there will always be a question as to whether, well though van der Gun, Siegers and Braat performed, Hannema, as captain, made an error by not coming in above them.

IRELAND WOMEN v NETHERLANDS WOMEN

20 overs

Women's World T20 Qualifier – Third Place Play-off

YMCA Ground, Claremont Road, Dublin, 31 July and 1 August 2013

Ireland won by two runs

IRELAND		R	B	M	4s	6s
C.M.A.Shillington	c Veringmeier b Braat	6	6		1	-
*I.M.H.C.Joyce	not out	72	64		6	-
K.J.Garth	lbw b Bennett	31	31		1	-
C.N.I.M.Joyce	c Rambaldo b Kornet	8	6		1	-
+M.V.Waldron	run out ([unknown]-Veringmeier)	3	4		-	-
L.Delany	c&b Braat	6	8		-	-
M.E.M.O.Scott-Hayward	not out	0	1		-	-
E.A.J.Richardson						
L.N.McCarthy						
E.J.Tice						
L.K.O'Reilly						
	b1 lb3 w6	10				
	(5 wickets, 20 overs)	**136**				

NETHERLANDS		R	B	M	4s	6s
+M.Veringmeier	b McCarthy	3	8		-	-
H.W.Rambaldo	not out	58	54		3	-
T.van der Gun	c C.N.I.M.Joyce b Garth	20	16		2	-
H.D.J.Siegers	run out (O'Reilly-Waldron)	29	30		1	1
D.M.Braat	run out (Garth-Waldron)	12	12		-	-
E.L.T.de Lange						
L.Klokgieters						
M.Kornet						
L.K.Bennett						
S.Bruning						
*D.Hannema						
	b1 lb2 w9	12				
	(4 wickets, 20 overs)	**134**				

Netherlands	O	M	R	W	nb	w		fow	Ire	Neth
Braat	4	0	24	2	-	1		1	7 (1)	10 (1)
Kornet	3	0	30	1	-	5		2	87 (3)	40 (3)
de Lange	4	0	29	0	-	-		3	98 (4)	93 (4)
Bennett	4	0	18	1	-	-		4	109 (5)	134 (5)
Bruning	3	0	14	0	-	-		5	132 (6)	
Klokgieters	2	0	17	0	-	-		6		
								7		

Ireland	O	M	R	W	nb	w		fow		
McCarthy	3	0	14	1	-	-		8		
Richardson	4	0	26	0	-	-		9		
Garth	2	0	14	1	-	1		10		
Scott-Hayward	2	0	14	0	-	-				
Tice	1	0	7	0	-	2				
Delany	4	0	28	0	-	2				
I.M.H.C.Joyce	4	0	28	0	-	-				

Umpires: K.Cross (New Zealand) and Sharfuddoula ibne Shahid (Bangladesh)

Reserve umpire: N.Duguid (West Indies). Referee: D.Govindjee (South Africa)

Toss: Ireland

Player of the Match: I.M.H.C.Joyce (Ireland)

There was no play on the first day because of rain. The reserve day was used.

M.Kornet is Mariska Kornet, sister of Mandy Kornet.

Benvenuti signorie Italiane

In August 2013 Italy hosted a women's cricket tournament in Bologna, involving themselves, Denmark, Gibraltar, Belgium and Estonia. The tournament marked the return of Denmark to international women's cricket and the first appearance of Italy.

Eight of the Italian squad of 13 were of Sri Lankan origin. Like their men's team, the Italian women's side owed much to the links between the Federazione Cricket Italiana and the Board of Control for Cricket in Sri Lanka, whereby the latter sent individuals to help develop cricket in Italy. Also, many of Italy's Sri Lankan immigrants were keen cricket players. Of the others, the captain, Angela Bonora, was the sister of Allesandro Bonora, a past captain of the men's side, and Maneerat Bevacqua, who had previously represented Thailand, was Italian by marriage. In contrast, the Danish squad was entirely Danish, their one player of Asian origin, Andila Jiwani, having been born in Denmark.

Italy and Denmark, the strongest sides in the competition, met at the Centro Sportivo Ca'Nova di Medicina ground, which had matting laid between two football pitches. The result was a rather bumpy outfield which would have challenged most fielding sides. There was no local interest and attendance was limited to the organisers, team squads and officials, but the competition was nevertheless intense. The women cheered every run and every wicket, making enough noise for a crowd of several hundred.

Denmark's captain, Slebsager, won the toss and decided that Italy should bat. With the match beginning at 10am the Danes were able to field in very pleasant conditions, with clear blue skies and a temperature around 22°C. Their bowling was enthusiastic if somewhat variable in line and length and Obris, opening for Italy, took advantage of anything she could cut or hook, but her partner Peddrick was more restrained and concentrated mainly on giving Obris the strike.

Some excellent Danish fielding kept the run rate under control. The fielders pounced on every ball and returned it to the wicketkeeper at the earliest opportunity. They certainly lived up to their name of the Red Foxes.

With a solid start being achieved, Peddrick tried something more ambitious for Italy but played across a straight ball and missed. If there had been any spectators they would have been superbly entertained as Bonora and Obris displayed an excellent array of shots all round the wicket, many of which were cut off by superb ground fielding. Slebsager kept changing her bowling but to no avail.

After 13 overs, 70 runs were on the board and it seemed that only a mistake by the Italians would give the Danes a wicket. Then, with the score on 102, the error came as Bonora tried to cut a ball, missed and was bowled. Dametto soon fell to a run-out, a direct hit by Jiwani.

Samarawickrama settled in quickly and it looked as though she and Obris would bat out the 20 overs but from the last ball of the innings, however, she attempted a second run, which would have given her a half-century, but more good fielding denied her and she too was run out.

Peddrick opened the bowling for Italy, producing a greater level of pace than anything that Denmark had achieved but Juliet Christensen and Line Østergaard were more than equal to what was offered. Their shots pierced the close-in field during the opening overs of power play and the pair ran excellently between the wickets, putting pressure on the Italian fielders.

With 48 runs on the board Christensen was run out, and the Danes never recovered as their final effort fell short by 51 runs. Italy were clearly the more competent side in terms of cricketing skills and their victory ensured that, on their debut, they won the tournament. In Niluka Obris, they had an outstanding cricketer whose achievements were later recognised by the Federazione Cricket Italiana when she was nominated as one of two Players of the Year for 2013, the first Italian woman to be so honoured.

ITALY WOMEN v DENMARK WOMEN

20 overs

Ladies T20 Cricket Festival

Centro Sportivo Ca'Nova di Medicina, Bologna, 17 August 2013

Italy won by 51 runs

ITALY		R	B	M	4s	6s
M.M.N.P.Obris	run out	49				
K.N.Peddrick	b A.L.Østergaard	8				
*A.Bonora	b L.B.Østergaard	33				
D.Dametto	run out (Jiwani)	2				
D.Samarawickrama	not out	10				
D.R.F.Nanayakkara						
+M.Piva						
D.A.K.Karunanayake						
M.Bevacqua						
E.Vezzalini						
N.P.K.F.Diminguwarige						
	nb5 w24	29				
	(4 wickets, 20 overs)	**131**				

DENMARK		R	B	M	4s	6s
J.Christensen	run out	16				
L.B.Østergaard	b Bonora	20				
A.L.Østergaard	lbw b Samarawickrama	0				
+C.Pallesen	c Obris b Samarawickrama	0				
*M.Slebsager	c Bonora b Peddrick	2				
C.Østergaard	c Obris b Bonora	0				
P.Borchersen	c Bonora b Nanayakkara	5				
A.Johansen	c Piva b Bevacqua	4				
A.Jiwani	run out	0				
V.Madsen	not out	3				
L.Christensen	not out	3				
	lb1 nb1 w25	27				
	(9 wickets, 20 overs)	**80**				

Denmark	O	M	R	W	nb	w
Jiwani	2	0	19	0		
L.Christensen	4	0	16	0		
L.B.Østergaard	4	0	26	1		
A.L.Østergaard	4	0	26	1		
C.Østergaard	4	1	24	0		
Slebsager	2	0	20	0		

Italy	O	M	R	W	nb	w
Peddrick	4	0	14	1		
Bonora	4	1	15	2		
Samarawickrama	3	0	13	2		
Karunanayake	3	0	10	0		
Bevacqua	3	0	19	1		
Nanayakkara	3	0	8	1		

fow	It	Den
1	45 (2)	48 (1)
2	102 (3)	50 (3)
3	111 (4)	50 (4)
4	131 (1)	57
5		58
6		58
7		70
8		70
9		72
10		

Umpires: [unknown]

Toss: Denmark

Nepalese delights under lights

For the World T20 Championships in 2014 the ICC allowed six of the Associate and Affiliate countries to qualify for the event, staged in Bangladesh. Unfortunately qualification did not mean that they were permitted to play in the final stages. Instead they were asked to take part in a first round along with Bangladesh and Zimbabwe.

Among those matches was that between Afghanistan and Nepal on 20 March. Although the attendance was good, at just under 2,000, in a stadium built for 22,000, the result was a vast empty space. But the spectators, largely gathered at one end of the stadium, were extremely vocal, so there was at least some atmosphere.

The match was a day/night affair, starting at 3pm local time with Nepal playing under floodlights for the first time. Mohammad Nabi won the toss for Afghanistan and, despite the temperature being around 30°C and humidity around 75 per cent, he followed the customary belief that chasing a target was easier than setting one and decided to field.

Shahpoor Zadran and Dawlat Zadran bowled with good pace on a tight line and managed to get the ball to swing, with Khakurel and Pun reduced to dot balls and singles in order to survive. By the time Nepal lost their first wicket, at the end of the third over, they had scored only 19 runs and benefitted from two lives. But when Afghanistan tried the leg breaks of Samiullah Shenwari, Malla struck him for 18 in one over before Mirwais Ashraf and Mohammad Nabi then regained control and took wickets.

Rather than playing sound cricket shots, Nepal's batsmen just tried to heave the ball over the boundary, albeit with some success. The 15th and 16th overs went for 16 runs each, aided by some atrocious ground fielding. Khakurel passed his fifty before falling to an excellent catch by Asghar Stanikzai, running backwards at midwicket, but Nepal's total of 141/5 was below par and likely to be difficult to defend.

Afghanistan opened their reply with Mohammad Shehzad and Karim Sadiq, both renowned strikers of the ball. Nepal started with spin but Regmi found the new ball hard to control and they had to resort to pace. Kami and Mukhiya bowled well, concentrating on line and length, and scoring runs became difficult. Karim Sadiq was the first to succumb to frustration as Afghanistan's tactics consisted of moving outside the line of the ball and heaving it to leg. Mohammad Shehzad and Najibullah Zadran soon slogged consecutive balls into the safe hands of fielders but Shafiqullah Shafaq prevented the hat-trick, although at the end of the fifth over his side were in difficulty on 21/3.

Nepal rested their pace attack and Afghanistan tried to regroup and, just as they looked to be gaining the advantage, they were set back by a superb piece of fielding. Nowroz Mangal got a top edge, the ball went in the air towards deep square leg, Khadka raced towards it from short fine leg, dived to his left and took an outstanding catch close to the ground. Another excellent catch by Pun then removed the dangerous Shafiqullah before Asghar Stanikzai and Samiullah Shenwari battled on, but 42 runs were still required from the last three overs.

Mukhiya kept the run rate under control and removed Samiullah Shenwari and with 24 runs needed from the last over, Asghar Stanikzai hit two consecutive fours, one through the hands of the fielder at long-on and the next an identical shot, reaching the boundary after the fielder misjudged the bounce. Three balls later, Asghar Stanikzai repeated the shot, Malla took a very simple catch and Nepal's unexpected victory was assured. Nepal fielded far better than Afghanistan, their bowling was more disciplined and, unusually for a T20 match, they did not concede any wides or no-balls.

The defeat was a disappointment for Afghanistan and clearly showed that their players had much to learn about the demands of T20. They gave away too many runs by poor fielding and their batting was unimaginative.

AFGHANISTAN v NEPAL

T20 International (day/night)

World T20 Championship – First Round

Zahur Ahmed Chowdhury Stadium, Chittagong, 20 March 2014

Nepal won by nine runs

NEPAL		R	B	M	4s	6s
+S.P.Khakurel	c Asghar Stanikzai b Shahpoor Zadran	56	53	76	6	1
S.Pun	c Mohammad Nabi b Dawlat Zadran	8	11	18	1	-
G.Malla	c Nowroz Mangal b Mohammad Nabi	22	13	17	3	1
*P.Khadka	b Mirwais Ashraf	1	5	5	-	-
S.Vesawkar	c Mohammad Shehzad b Shahpoor Zadran	37	32	38	5	-
B.Bhandari	not out	4	6	6	1	-
N.B.Budayair	not out	2	3	5	-	-
B.Regmi						
S.P.Gauchan						
S.Kami						
J.K.Mukhiya						
	lb5 nb3 w3	11				
	(5 wickets, 20 overs)	**141**				

AFGHANISTAN		R	B	M	4s	6s
+Mohammad Shehzad	c Kami b Mukhiya	6	17	19	1	-
Karim Sadiq	b Kami	8	7	12	2	-
Najibullah Zadran	c Vesawkar b Mukhiya	5	4	8	1	-
Nowroz Mangal	c Khadka b Gauchan	5	7	16	1	-
Shafiqullah Shafaq	c Pun b Regmi	36	32	38	3	1
*Mohammad Nabi	lbw b Gauchan	1	2	3	-	-
Asghar Stanikzai	c Malla b Kami	49	36	48	4	1
Samiullah Shenwari	c Khadka b Mukhiya	15	13	20	1	-
Mirwais Ashraf	not out	2	2	9	-	-
Dawlat Zadran	not out	0	0	1	-	-
Shahpoor Zadran						
	b4 lb1	5				
	(8 wickets, 20 overs)	**132**				

Afghanistan	O	M	R	W	nb	w
Shahpoor Zadran	4	0	19	2	-	-
Dawlat Zadran	3	0	23	1	1	-
Samiullah Shenwari	3	0	40	0	2	1
Mirwais Ashraf	4	0	14	1	-	-
Mohammad Nabi	4	0	25	1	-	-
Karim Sadiq	2	0	15	0	-	2

Nepal	O	M	R	W	nb	w
Regmi	3	0	28	1	-	-
Kami	4	1	32	2	-	-
Mukhiya	4	0	18	3	-	-
Khadka	3	0	14	0	-	-
Gauchan	3	0	25	2	-	-
Pun	3	0	10	0	-	-

fow	Nep	Afg
1	19 (2)	14 (2)
2	51 (3)	20 (1)
3	53 (4)	20 (3)
4	129 (1)	47 (4)
5	133 (5)	50 (6)
6		83 (5)
7		115 (8)
8		132 (7)
9		
10		

Umpires: Aleem Dar (Pakistan) and S.Ravi (India)

TV umpire: R.J.Tucker (Australia). Reserve umpire: P.R.Reiffel (Australia). Referee: J.Srinath (India)

Toss: Afghanistan.

Player of the Match: J.K.Mukhiya (Nepal).

Shafiqullah Shafaq is also known as Shafiqullah Shinwari.

The Netherlands 2 England 0

The Netherlands, who had surprisingly beaten Ireland to enter the second round of the ICC World T20 competition, met England in Chittagong on 31 March 2014. It was the second time that the two countries had met in a World T20 tournament and in the first, at Lord's in 2009, the Dutch had won by four wickets. The 2014 match was purely for pride since neither side had gained sufficient points to progress to the next round.

Stuart Broad won the toss for England and, as is customary in T20 matches, he decided to bowl. England opened with Moeen Ali, a spinner, but with 13 runs coming from the first over the Dutch were off to an excellent start. They had reached 32 without loss after three overs when Broad brought himself on to bowl and was immediately successful as Swart completely mis-hit and offered an easy catch to Parry at mid-on.

Broad and James Tredwell brought the run rate under control, reducing it from 10.7 to 7.4 per over before The Netherlands regained the initiative in an over from Stephen Parry, which went for 15 runs and gave a life to Barresi when, instead of taking a straightforward catch at deep midwicket, Michael Lumb misjudged the flight, jumped at the wrong time, and parried the ball over the boundary for six.

Tredwell and Ravi Bopara then put England in a strong position by making scoring harder and while the Dutch had made 84 off their first 11 overs, they added only 49 off the next nine. They also lost wickets regularly. Myburgh pulled a full toss into the hands of Alex Hales at deep backward square leg, Tom Cooper fell to a superb catch by Chris Jordan, one-handed and running backwards, and, after surviving a run-out, Borren gave Parry a simple catch at mid-off. The innings ended for a disappointing 133/5 and although Broad picked up three wickets, it was Bopara who exerted most control, bowling four overs for 15 runs.

England were expected to reach the target with some ease and they set off positively but, after three overs, the score was 18 with one wicket down as Lumb drove Bukhari straight to Tom Cooper at cover. The Dutch quickly found that if they bowled slower, the ball did not come on to the batsman as quickly as anticipated, scoring became difficult and there was the chance that the batsman would play too early, mis-hit the ball and offer a catch.

In the fourth over Hales played far too soon to a ball from Bukhari, missed it completely and was bowled. The next over saw Eoin Morgan push hard to a ball outside the off stump to give Borren an easy catch at third slip. The Dutch continued to bowl a tight line, on or just outside the off stump, and full of length. Borren's medium pace was ideally suited to the conditions and, with his first ball, he contrived to get Ali to drive it straight to Tom Cooper, still at cover. Jos Buttler then mistimed a pull to leg where Seelaar took the catch at deep midwicket.

At the end of the tenth over England had made just 42 runs, with five wickets down, and their run rate was 4.2 per over compared to the 9.2 they found themselves needing.

Bopara responded by hitting a full toss from Borren to deep square leg and set off for two runs. He made his ground easily but forgot that his speed between the wickets was not matched by his partner Tim Bresnan, who was easily run out at the bowler's end. Hard as they tried, England's batsmen could not pierce the Dutch field while every bowling change that Borren made worked and the Dutch fielding was a masterclass compared to England's earlier effort. England were all out in the 17th over when a mix-up between Tredwell and Parry left both stranded halfway between the wickets, leading to an easy run-out.

The Dutch completely outplayed England and had beaten them twice in two matches. Only three English players reached double figures and none got as far as 20, while their fielding and running between the wickets were shambolic. Bukhari was chosen as the player of the match for his three wickets for only 12 runs in 3.4 overs.

Even more surprising than England's defeat, was that the result featured strongly in the Dutch newspapers the following day, a rare event since cricket is generally ignored by the Dutch press.

ENGLAND v NETHERLANDS

T20 International (day/night)

World T20 Championship – Second Round Group 1

Zahur Ahmed Chowdhury Stadium, Chittagong, 31 March 2014

Netherlands won by 45 runs

NETHERLANDS		R	B	M	4s	6s
M.R.Swart	c Parry b Broad	13	15	17	2	-
S.J.Myburgh	c Hales b Bopara	39	31	45	6	1
+W.Barresi	b Jordan	48	45	66	2	2
T.L.W.Cooper	c Jordan b Broad	8	15	18	-	-
*P.W.Borren	c Parry b Broad	7	10	14	1	-
M.Bukhari	not out	1	2	5	-	-
B.N.Cooper	not out	0	2	3	-	-
L.V.van Beek						
T.van der Gugten						
P.M.Seelaar						
M.A.A.Jamil						
	b4 lb7 w6	17				
	(5 wickets, 20 overs)	**133**				

ENGLAND		R	B	M	4s	6s
A.D.Hales	b Bukhari	12	17	17	2	-
M.J.Lumb	c T.L.W.Cooper b Bukhari	6	8	11	-	-
M.M.Ali	c T.L.W.Cooper b Borren	3	7	25	-	-
E.J.G.Morgan	c Borren b van der Gugten	6	8	6	1	-
+J.C.Buttler	c Seelaar b van Beek	6	14	20	-	-
R.S.Bopara	c Seelaar b van Beek	18	20	29	-	-
T.T.Bresnan	run out (Bukhari-Borren)	5	6	7	-	-
C.J.Jordan	c Swart b van Beek	14	14	17	-	-
*S.C.J.Broad	c Barresi b Bukhari	4	5	12	-	-
J.C.Tredwell	not out	8	6	8	1	-
S.D.Parry	run out (Swart-Barresi)	1	1	4	-	-
	lb2 w3	5				
	(17.4 overs)	**88**				

England	O	M	R	W	nb	w
Ali	1	0	13	0	-	-
Bresnan	2	0	11	0	-	1
Jordan	3	0	13	1	-	1
Broad	4	0	24	3	-	2
Tredwell	4	0	23	0	-	1
Parry	2	0	23	0	-	-
Bopara	4	0	15	1	-	-

Netherlands	O	M	R	W	nb	w
Swart	1	0	8	0	-	-
van der Gugten	3	0	11	1	-	1
Bukhari	3.4	0	12	3	-	-
Jamil	3	0	14	0	-	-
Borren	3	0	18	1	-	-
van Beek	2	0	9	3	-	-
Seelaar	2	0	14	0	-	2

fow	Neth	Eng
1	34 (1)	18 (2)
2	84 (2)	19 (1)
3	110 (4)	26 (4)
4	131 (5)	32 (3)
5	131 (3)	42 (5)
6		52 (7)
7		74 (6)
8		76 (8)
9		86 (9)
10		88 (11)

Umpires: S.J.Davis (Australia) and B.N.J.Oxenford (Australia)

TV umpire: Aleem Dar (Pakistan). Reserve umpire: R.J.Tucker (Australia). Referee: D.C.Boon (Australia)

Toss: England

Player of the Match: M.Bukhari (Netherlands)

Sauerman strikes for Swaziland

In complete contrast to the highly-publicised and globally-televised events of the World T20 in Bangladesh in 2014 was the Africa T20 Division Three tournament held in Benoni, South Africa, at the same time. Most people were probably unaware that this was part of the first qualifying round for the next World T20 competition.

Sierra Leone, The Gambia, Rwanda and Swaziland were the participants and by the time Swaziland and The Gambia met on 25 March, both countries had played four matches. Swaziland had won two and lost two, while The Gambia had lost all four. The Gambia's problem was that they had only three bowlers who could keep the run rate at eight an over or below.

Overall though, as a cricketing nation they were the more experienced. They had played their first international in 1927, against Sierra Leone, and had taken part in numerous west African tournaments. In contrast, it was not until after independence in 1968 that cricket in Swaziland progressed from being a largely exclusive sport, played in country clubs by white British and South African settlers, to a national multiracial activity, additionally involving the Indian community and an increasing number of Africans.

The Gambia won the toss and elected to field. Greywoode dismissed Idrees Patel, one of Swaziland's best batsmen, for 17 in the fifth over, but his runs had come off only 20 balls and the total was already at 41. Although The Gambia's bowlers were failing to cope, nothing would have prepared their attack for what followed as Sauerman completely dominated the proceedings and not only did he score rapidly, but he kept most of the strike.

Greywoode struck again in the eighth over to remove Bhagubhai for 14, made off 13 balls, but this meant that Sauerman was joined by the Swazi captain, Rashid, and together they blitzed all of Gambia's bowlers in a stand of 132 off ten overs and one ball. Kokal and Williams were each removed from the attack after one over, both conceding 14 runs. Chotrani also suffered, his three overs yielding 47 runs. He was successful, however, in removing Sauerman, whose innings of 101 came off only 54 balls and contained ten fours and five sixes.

With Sauerman's dismissal The Gambia were finally able to exert some control, but it was all relative, the remaining nine balls of the innings producing a mere 21 runs. Rashid ended undefeated on 67 from 36 balls, with eight fours and one six. While in partnership, Rashid and Sauerman matched each other for strike rate with both at over 180.

The Gambia were never in with a chance to reach a target of 222 in 20 overs and runs initially came very slowly, the score at only six when Conteh was out at the end of the third over. Williams decided to take on the task but he had little support from Campbell, whose batting skills were traditionally closer to the lower order than an opener. In 11 overs, the score rose to 75 before Williams departed to a good catch by Rashid off the bowling of Aziz Patel. He had made 54 off only 32 balls, with two fours and four sixes, then Assan Faye went two balls later without scoring. Neither Dumbuya nor Campbell, who was still resisting defensively, were able to add much as both fell in the 17th over. Tamba struck two boundaries in a short cameo but Greywoode and Jarju both failed to score.

With a struggle, The Gambia managed to bat out the 20 overs and take the score above 100, but were convincingly beaten by 117 runs. This was Swaziland's greatest cricketing achievement to date. They went on to win the tournament and qualify for the next round, an Africa Division Two competition, held in September 2014. Despite victories over Mozambique and the Seychelles, they failed to progress further.

GAMBIA v SWAZILAND

20 overs

Africa T20 Championships Division Three

Willowmoore Park Main Oval, Benoni, 25 March 2014

Swaziland won by 117 runs

SWAZILAND		R	B	M	4s	6s
I.A.Patel	b Greywoode	17	20		2	-
E.Sauerman	c Tamba b Chotrani	101	54		10	5
J.A.A.Bhagubhai	b Kokal b Greywoode	14	13		-	1
*H.Rashid	not out	67	36		8	1
A.A.A.Patel	not out	5	2		1	-
A.Khan						
D.Malinga						
+D.Fonseka						
N.Bhaiyat						
S.H.Hassan						
T.Sandeep						
	lb1 nb3 w13	17				
	(3 wickets, 20 overs)	**221**				

GAMBIA		R	B	M	4s	6s
A.M.Conteh	lbw b A.A.A.Patel	4	5		-	-
+P.Campbell	c Fonseka b Rashid	19	54		1	-
M.Williams	c Rashid b A.A.A.Patel	54	32		2	4
P.Assan Faye	b A.A.A.Patel	0	1		-	-
M.Dumbuya	c&b Rashid	4	9		-	-
I.Tamba	lbw b Rashid	12	11		2	-
G.Greywoode	c&b Hassan	0	3		-	-
K.M.Chotrani	not out	8	5		1	-
A.Jarju	run out (sub[unknown]-Fonseka)	0	1		-	-
B.Kokal	not out	1	1		-	-
J.Badjan						
	nb1 w1	2				
	(8 wickets, 20 overs)	**104**				

Gambia	O	M	R	W	nb	w		fow	Swa	Gam
Dumbuya	3	0	25	0	1	7		1	41 (1)	6 (1)
Chotrani	3	0	47	1	1	-		2	68 (3)	75 (3)
Greywoode	4	0	40	2	-	1		3	200 (2)	76 (4)
Conteh	4	0	39	0	1	1		4		82 (5)
Jarju	3	0	31	0	-	4		5		83 (2)
Williams	1	0	14	0	-	-		6		94 (6)
Kokal	1	0	14	0	-	-		7		99 (7)
Assan Faye	1	0	10	0	-	-		8		99 (9)
								9		
Swaziland	O	M	R	W	nb	w		10		
A.A.A.Patel	4	0	15	3	-	-				
Hassan	4	0	22	1	-	-				
Rashid	4	0	30	3	1	-				
Bhagubhai	3	0	15	0	-	-				
Sauerman	2	0	6	0	-	-				
Sandeep	3	0	16	0	-	1				

Umpires: [unknown]

Toss: Gambia

Romania replicate a 'world cup' atmosphere

A large stadium, large crowd, floodlights, televised proceedings and an exciting finish may be the ideal of a T20 World Cup Final. Those conditions cannot always be replicated but the Romanian Cricket Association did its best for the final of the 2014 Continental Cricket Cup. Not only does Romania have a dedicated ground for cricket, instead of having to lay matting on a football field, it has a turf pitch. There is no pavilion as yet at Moara Vlăsiei, 40km east of Bucharest, and a marquee is erected for the purpose on matchdays. For the final against Hungary, national anthems were played before the start, neutral umpires were employed, one from Denmark and one from Luxembourg, and the cricket was streamed live over the internet, with commentary by Chris Croker. The match was watched as far away as England, Australia and Singapore. There was an interview with James Kodor, an Australian who is regarded as the 'father of modern Romanian cricket'. Unfortunately, the attendance was largely restricted to the families and friends of the players and, at best, was only about 35 to 40 people.

With clear blue skies and some fair weather cloud, conditions were extremely hot with the temperature around 30°C. Habib Deldar won the toss for Hungary and decided to bat. They lost their first wicket in the opening over before any runs were scored, but Kheterpal and Khaibar Deldar repaired the damage, Kheterpal striking six boundaries in his first seven scoring shots. He was particularly severe on the bowling of Gondal, who conceded just over ten runs per over.

Deldar, who played a supporting role, was bowled by Thakur for 15, made off 29 balls with only one boundary. When Kheterpal was bowled, playing across the line, he had made 61 from only 40 balls, with 12 fours. Neither Tekauer nor Khan lasted long but Marc Ahuja maintained the impetus with 44 off 33 balls, with five fours and a six. Hungary's total of 138/7 was made at a creditable 6.9 runs per over. Although Mohsin took three wickets, Munawar was the pick of the bowlers, his four overs going for only 11 runs.

Romania's openers survived the first over but a wicket fell in each of the next two. Thakur and Manani steadied proceedings but with Hungary's bowling being more accurate and their field placings more effective, runs were kept to singles rather than boundaries. Bowling changes made little difference as Kheterpal and Kukikhel were just as economical as the Deldar brothers.

Play was temporarily delayed when the Romanians appeared to question the legality of Kheterpal's bowling action. The umpires conferred for several minutes before the match resumed with, seemingly, no decision being forthcoming. Kheterpal was removed from the attack but he returned later to bowl two more overs.

Romania lost their third wicket when Manani was run out by a direct hit by Lovitt-Danks. Satheesan, Thakur and Mircea quickly followed, leaving Hungary looking like clear winners as all they needed to do was keep the run rate under control. However, Mohsin was scoring off every ball he received. Romania still had a chance if he could protect the tail and retain the strike. He proved remarkably inept at doing this and was reliant on Dagla scoring singles from each of the first seven balls he received to give him the strike. Together, they added 32 in just over four overs.

The Hungarian fielding became ragged as Mohsin gained complete control and Romania's run rate went above that of Hungary's for the first time. The loss of Dagla was no setback as Mohsin hit a four, followed by two enormous sixes. With only two runs needed off the last over, the first ball went for a bye and Mohsin struck the next for four to give Romania victory. He was undefeated on 63, made off 27 balls with four fours and five sixes, scoring off each of the last 20 balls he received. Apart from him there was little to choose between the two sides.

The contest was an excellent advertisement for the rise of cricket in eastern Europe, both for the organisation and the enthusiasm of the players.

ROMANIA v HUNGARY

20 overs

Continental T20 Cricket Cup – Final

Moara Vlăsiei, 6 July 2014

Romania won by three wickets

HUNGARY		R	B	M	4s	6s
Z.K.Kukikhel	lbw b Shafaad	0	4	2	-	-
K.Deldar	b Thakur	15	29	40	1	-
A.Kheterpal	b Satheesan	61	40	48	12	-
M.Ahuja	b Mohsin	44	33	38	5	1
E.Tekauer	b Mohsin	1	5	9	-	-
+S.M.Khan	b Shafaad	1	2	2	-	-
S.Ahuja	not out	4	6	14	-	-
*H.Deldar	b Mohsin	0	1	1	-	-
A.G.Lovitt-Danks						
H.Krisztian						
G.Takács						
	b1 lb1 w10	12				
	(7 wickets, 20 overs)	**138**				

ROMANIA		R	B	M	4s	6s
+Z.Mazhar	c Khan b H.Deldar	4	6	13	-	-
A.Topsa	b K.Deldar	1	6	6	-	-
S.Thakur	st Khan b S.Ahuja	31	38	59	3	-
V.Manani	run out (Lovitt-Danks)	16	22	31	1	-
R.Satheesan	b Kukikhel	1	4	3	-	-
*S.Mohsin	not out	63	27	44	4	5
B.Mircea	b S.Ahuja	0	3	3	-	-
R.Dagla	b S.Ahuja	7	9	15	-	-
S.Gondal	not out	1	2	6	-	-
M.Shafaad						
C.Zavoiu						
	b4 lb2 nb1 w11	18				
	(7 wickets, 19.2 overs)	**142**				

Romania	O	M	R	W	nb	w
Shafaad	4	1	11	2	-	1
Manani	2	0	15	0	-	1
Gondal	3	0	31	0	-	2
Mohsin	4	0	37	3	-	2
Satheesan	4	0	28	1	-	1
Thakur	3	0	14	1	-	1

Hungary	O	M	R	W	nb	w
H.Deldar	3	0	15	1	-	-
K.Deldar	3.2	0	26	1	-	2
Kheterpal	3	0	24	0	-	2
Kukikhel	4	0	18	1	-	1
Lovitt-Danks	1	0	10	0	-	-
Tekauer	1	0	7	0	1	2
S.Ahuja	4	0	36	3	-	2

fow	Hun	Rom
1	0 (1)	4 (2)
2	71 (2)	13 (1)
3	91 (3)	56 (4)
4	111 (5)	57 (5)
5	116 (6)	84 (3)
6	138 (4)	87 (7)
7	138 (8)	119 (8)
8		
9		
10		

Umpires: T.Kentorp (Denmark) and B.Lougheed (Luxembourg)

Referee: R.Mitra (Romania)

Toss: Hungary

S.M.Khan is also known as Sufyan Mohammed. V.Manani is also known as M.Veneadri. M.Shaafad is also known as S.Munawar.

Saudara and *Saudari*

Since 1970 the men's teams from Malaysia and Singapore have played each other annually for the Saudara Cup, with the proviso that all the players must be citizens of their country. In 2013 the fixture was cancelled because Singapore were unable to raise a team. Given the increasing number of fixtures that the players of both countries must fulfil in the modern era, it was surprising that this problem had not arisen before. Nevertheless, both countries have not only committed themselves to the competition, but, in 2014, inaugurated an event for their women's teams, the Saudari Cup, *Saudari* being the feminine equivalent of *Saudara* in the Malay language, meaning a close relative or friend.

The arrangements, however, were different to those of the Saudara Cup, which is a multi-innings event held over two or three days. The Saudari Cup consisted of two T20 matches and one 35-over fixture and was not restricted to citizens. Singapore took advantage of this by selecting Annemarie Tanke, a Dutch citizen and former Netherlands international who had been working in Singapore for the previous five years and was therefore eligible to represent them under ICC regulations.

As with the men's teams from both countries, the Chinese element of their populations was poorly represented. Malaysia did not have any Malaysian Chinese in their squad despite those of that origin forming 22 per cent of the country's population. Singapore, where 74 per cent of the population is of Chinese origin, had one player, 48-year-old Lorraine Meyer (née Bee Pheng Chua), the mother of Singapore's former men's international Glenn Meyer.

Historically there had always been players of Chinese extraction who were good enough to represent both countries, but for the last ten or so years they have been absent. Either their cricket associations are not following policies to spread cricket to all their ethnic communities or, if they are, they are not working. In the end, Meyer was not selected by Singapore for this match.

The inaugural match in the Saudari Cup was a T20 fixture, played at the Bayuemas Oval, Kuala Lumpur. Malaysia won the toss and decided to bat. Emylia Eliani and Baret quickly set the tone for the innings, scoring at a run a ball against Maqsood and Sen, before in the fourth over, with the score on 21, Emylia missed a straight ball from Maqsood. Intan Jamahidaya scored more slowly but the run rate failed to decrease as Edmonstone conceded 15 runs in her only over. Since four of these were wides and one a no-ball, she, rather than the Malaysian batting effort, was largely responsible.

Runs from the bat came mainly in ones and twos, which was fine until a misunderstanding occurred between the batters and Intan was run out. Malaysia's captain, Duraisingam, maintained the run rate until she was also run out, by a direct hit from Maqsood. Nur Aishah and Baret put on 45 runs to take the score to 121 at the end of the 20 overs. Baret was undefeated on 37, made off 37 balls. In total, Malaysia's batters struck nine fours.

Singapore began their reply extremely slowly, due, in part, to the inaccuracy of Malaysia's opening attack. Then, with the score on ten, Tanke was leg before to Intan and Singapore just could not get any momentum to their innings, falling from 24/1 to 25/5. Rewina Mohammed took two wickets in two balls, both bowled, and conceded only ten runs in three overs.

Ramesh kept Diviya company and prevented Malaysia from making further inroads but neither could raise the run rate to the level required. Jannadiah Halim bowled two maidens in her four overs as Malaysia's bowlers exerted a complete stranglehold over Singapore, who struggled to 67 at the end of the 20th over. None of their batters managed a boundary as Malaysia completed a surprisingly easy victory by 54 runs. They went on to win the series by two matches to one and therefore won the inaugural Saudari Cup.

MALAYSIA WOMEN v SINGAPORE WOMEN

20 overs
Saudari Cup
Bayuemas Oval, Kuala Lumpur, 29 August 2014
Malaysia won by 54 runs

MALAYSIA		R	B	M	4s	6s
Emylia Eliani	b Maqsood	14	13		2	-
C.N.Baret	not out	37	37		2	-
Intan Jamahidaya	run out (Sreemurugavel-Singham)	11	19		1	-
*W.A.Duraisingam	run out (Maqsood)	16	21		2	-
Yusrina Yaakop	b Diviya	0	1		-	-
Nur Aishah	not out	19	29		2	-
Jannadiah Halim						
Rewina Mohammed						
D.I.Chunam						
Fathinah Nusrah						
+Aina Najwa						
	nb3 w21	24				
	(4 wickets, 20 overs)	**121**				

SINGAPORE		R	B	M	4s	6s
V.Sreemurugavel	lbw b Duraisingam	3	20		-	-
A.S.Tanke	lbw b Intan Jamahidaya	2	11		-	-
*G.K.Diviya	not out	24	41		-	-
D.L.Edmonstone	b Rewina Mohammed	0	5		-	-
+S.A.Singham	b Rewina Mohammed	0	1		-	-
S.Maqsood	lbw b Jannadiah Halim	2	2		-	-
R.Ramesh	not out	18	41		-	-
M.Rangarajan						
A.Moghe						
D.H.Sharma						
T.Sen						
	lb1 nb1 w18	20				
	(5 wickets, 20 overs)	**67**				

Singapore	O	M	R	W	nb	w		fow	Mal	Sin
Maqsood	2	0	13	1	-	2		1	21 (1)	10 (2)
Sen	4	0	27	0	-	6		2	54 (3)	24 (1)
Edmonstone	1	0	15	0	1	4		3	76 (4)	24 (4)
Rangarajan	2	0	13	0	1	2		4	76 (5)	24 (5)
Tanke	3	0	15	0	-	3		5		25 (6)
Diviya	4	0	22	1	-	3		6		
Sharma	4	0	16	0	1	1		7		
								8		
Malaysia	O	M	R	W	nb	w		9		
Nur Aishah	4	0	19	0	-	9		10		
Intan Jamadidaya	4	0	14	1	-	4				
Duraisingam	4	0	14	1	-	2				
Jannadiah Halim	4	2	6	1	-	-				
Rewina Mohammed	3	1	10	2	1	2				
Fathinah Nusrah	1	0	3	0	-	-				

Umpires: B.Ramani (Malaysia) and Nasir Ali (Malaysia)

Toss: Malaysia

Player of the Match: C.N.Baret (Malaysia)

Need a cricket team, turn to baseball

South Korea faced two problems when hosting the cricket competition in the Asian Games in Incheon, in 2014. First, it had no cricket stadium. Second, it had no team. The Korean Cricket Association (KCA) responded by constructing the Yeonhui Cricket Stadium, with a seating capacity of 2,300 people. A seven-wicket cricket square was laid on a foundation of clay, imported from Pakistan, underlain by sand to give an excellent drainage system and seeded with *zoysia* grass, native to eastern Asia, to give a turf pitch with low but even bounce, which favoured spin.

The KCA could not fall back on the squad which had appeared in the East Asia-Pacific Division Two T20 competition in 2011 as Lee Sang-wook was the only surviving player who met the requirement of being a South Korean citizen. The solution was to seek students at Sungkyunkwan University, where cricket is a component of the Sports Science programme, and to invite the country's baseball players to try their hand at cricket. The resulting squad of 14 included four former professional baseballers. Julien Fountain, previously Pakistan's fielding coach, was taken on as head coach. The players were sent on a training camp in India and a pre-Games tour of Fiji.

Despite heavy rain on the morning of 29 September the ground drained within two hours, enabling the afternoon fixture between South Korea and China to take place, though it was reduced to ten overs per side. The hosts quickly took the initiative as Cho Sung-hoon, standing baseball-style at the crease with his bat raised above his shoulder, showed he could swat and time the ball effectively.

He and Sung Dae-sik added 50 for the second wicket in only four overs with Sung particularly proficient, striking two consecutive sixes and reaching 33 off only 16 balls before Cho fell to a superb catch by Hu Gaofeng. With 12 runs coming from the ninth over, a total of over 100 looked possible but Zhong Wenyi took four wickets in four balls with his leg spin to complete the first hat-trick in the Asian Games. For the first time China were on top as the innings closed for 88.

Being the more experienced side, China were expected to reach the target with some ease. They started poorly, however, when Jiang Shuyao gave an easy catch to Cho Sung-hoon in the covers. South Korea kept changing their bowling, using four bowlers in the first four overs, restricting the scoring to ones and twos. When Lee Hwan-hee, aided by some very safe catching in the deep field, picked up two wickets in the sixth over, China were 38/3, scoring at 6.3 runs per over but the required rate was up to 12.8.

It was not until the eighth over that they began to make an impression as Li Jian took 11 runs from the first three balls, only to fall to a foolish run-out when attempting a quick single to keep the strike. China needed 18 off the last over, from South Korea's best bowler, Park Tae-kwan. Trying to score off every ball, they lost three wickets in the first three balls and added only a further 11 runs, giving South Korea victory by six runs.

The result was a remarkable achievement for South Korea who, with little assistance from the ICC, produced a cricket team in two years able to beat a country in which the ICC had actively invested. The KCA now has a dedicated ground, with turf pitches, which can be used for international cricket. Four years previously, China constructed a similar facility at Guangzhou, which is now falling into disrepair through lack of use. How many more grounds must be constructed, only to be ignored by the ICC? The next Asian Games will be in Jakarta, Indonesia. Will we see a third?

SOUTH KOREA v CHINA

20 overs

Asian Games – Group A

Yeonhui Cricket Stadium, Seo-gu, Incheon, 29 September 2014

South Korea won by six runs

SOUTH KOREA		R	B	M	4s	6s
Cho Sung-hoon	c Hu Gaofeng b Zhong Wenyi	23	28	-	-	
Seo Il-hwan	c Hu Gaofeng b Han Minjian	9	8	-	-	
Sung Dae-sik	st Zhao Gaosheng b Zhong Wenyi	33	16	2	2	
Park Tae-kwan	not out	10	6	1	-	
An Hyo-bum	st Zhao Gaosheng b Zhong Wenyi	0	1	-	-	
Lee Sang-wook	c&b Zhong Wenyi	0	1	-	-	
Choi Ji-won	not out	2	1	-	-	
Lee Hwan-hee						
*Kim Kyung-sik						
Cha In-ho						
+Bang Su-in						
	lb4 nb1 w6	11				
	(5 wickets, 10 overs)	**88**				

CHINA		R	B	M	4s	6s
*Jiang Shuyao	c Cho Sung-hoon b Kim Kyung-sik	7	10	-	-	
Song Yangyang	c Sung Sae-sik b Lee Hwan-hee	18	18	1	-	
Zhang Yufei	c Choi Ji-won b Lee Hwan-hee	6	6	-	-	
Lei Sun	not out	14	11	-	-	
Li Jian	run out (Bang Su-in)	15	6	2	-	
Zhong Wenyi	run out (Cho Sung-hoon-Bang Sui-in)	5	4	-	-	
Wang Jing	run out (Park Tae-kwan)	0	1	-	-	
Han Minjian	b Park Tae-kwan	0	1	-	-	
Zhang Peng	not out	5	3	-	-	
+Zhao Gaosheng						
Hu Gaofeng						
	w12	12				
	(7 wickets, 10 overs)	**82**				

China	O	M	R	W	nb	w
Zhang Peng	1	0	13	0	-	2
Wang Jing	2	0	12	0	-	-
Han Minjian	2	0	11	1	-	-
Song Yangyang	1	0	17	0	-	-
Zhang Yufei	2	0	22	0	1	2
Zhong Wenyi	2	0	9	4	-	-

South Korea	O	M	R	W	nb	w
Park Tae-kwan	2	0	15	1	-	1
Cha In-ho	2	0	17	0	-	2
Kim Kyung-sik	2	0	12	1	-	1
Lee Hwan-hee	2	0	20	2	-	-
Choi Ji-won	2	0	18	0	-	3

fow	SK	Ch
1	21 (2)	14 (1)
2	71 (1)	34 (2)
3	83 (3)	38 (3)
4	83 (5)	61 (5)
5	83 (6)	72 (6)
6		72 (7)
7		72 (8)
8		
9		
10		

Umpires: B.Ramani (Malaysia) and M.Kamaruzzaman (Thailand)

Reserve umpire: M.Riaz Chaudhry (Kuwait). Referee: Aminul Islam (Bangladesh)

Toss: China

Match was reduced to ten overs per side

In South Korea's innings Zhong Wenyi completed a hat-trick when dismissing Cho Sung-hoon, Sung Dae-sik and An Hyo-bum and four wickets in four balls with the dismissal of Lee Sang-wook.

Oala outplays the opposition

Women's cricket was included in the Pacific Games for the first time in 2015. Apart from which country would win, the interest was in whether a women's team from New Caledonia, on their first international outing, would fare any better than their men's side, particularly against Papua New Guinea, a much younger and more experienced outfit.

At least seven of the New Caledonian team were over 30 years of age whereas Papua New Guinea had only one such player. They were, therefore, likely to be much more nimble in the field. They also had two players, Konio Oala and Brenda Toi Hau, who were under 20. By the time the match was played, Papua New Guinea were unbeaten in the tournament whereas New Caledonia had already lost to Samoa, Fiji and Vanuatu, so the expectation that they would be outclassed was high.

The home side's captain, Pauke Siaka, wife of Asad Vala, vice-captain of Papua New Guinea's men's team, won the toss and chose to bat. New Caledonia started well, conceding only 12 runs in the first two overs, but their bowlers could not maintain the consistency. Wahmowe bowled four wides and a no-ball in her second over, which went for 12 runs, and Angexetine's second over yielded 21 including three fours and one six. Wahmowe improved, her next over producing only three runs, but Angexetine conceded another 19, again with three fours and a six. Oala and Morea were becoming increasingly confident and ready to treat any loose balls with contempt. With Siwa's first over resulting in a further 16 runs, Papua New Guinea were 83 without loss after the first seven overs.

Some tighter bowling by Elise Kecine, backed up by enthusiastic fielding, produced a quieter period with runs coming mainly in singles and with fewer extras given away. From the fifth ball of the 14th over New Caledonia finally got their breakthrough, Morea missing a straight delivery. The opening partnership of 132 had been made at a strike rate of 159 per hundred balls and Morea's 42 was made at a run-a-ball and included four fours.

Oala took most of the strike for the next five overs and the run rate increased again. Another over from Siwa produced 17 runs, with Oala striking two consecutive sixes. Kaudre and Siwa managed to exert some control in the 18th and 19th overs, which went for 12 runs in total and saw the dismissal of Siaka. Unfortunately Kaudre failed to maintain the pressure in the last over of the innings as she gave away six wides and one no ball, even though, from her third legitimate delivery, she bowled Ruma. Oala finished unbeaten on 108, from 65 balls, with 13 fours and four sixes, the 18-year old making her country's first century in any form of women's international cricket.

New Caledonia were not expected to offer much of a challenge and they made no real effort to reach the target of 195. Instead they chose to bat as long as possible and see just how many runs they could make, and by the end of the eighth over they had scored only 15. They had, however, lost only three wickets.

With Siwa and Wawine both reaching double figures, the score rose to a heady 44/5 with one ball remaining of the 13th over. Three wickets were then lost in three balls. Jeka, Kaudre and Mazeno survived until the end of the 19th over to take the score to 62, the highest team score made by New Caledonia in women's international matches. Although the home side won easily, New Caledonia produced a very creditable performance, despite being outplayed by Konio Oala's superb scoring rate of 166 runs per 100 balls.

PAPUA NEW GUINEA WOMEN v NEW CALEDONIA WOMEN

T20

Pacific Games

Amini Park, Port Moresby, 9 July 2015

Papua New Guinea won by 132 runs

PNG		R	B	M	4s	6s
K.Oala	not out	108	65	91	13	4
+V.I.Morea	b E.Kecine	42	42	60	4	-
*P.Siaka	b Siwa	11	12	20	1	-
T.Ruma	b Kaudre	4	2	5	1	-
K.John	not out	2	3	3	-	-
K.Arua						
B.David						
V.K.Frank						
N.Ovasuru						
B.H.Tau						
H.Philip						
	b2 lb2 nb5 w18	27				
	(3 wickets, 20 overs)	**194**				

NEW CALEDONIA		R	B	M	4s	6s
J.Qaeze	b Ruma	2	11	14	-	-
+R.Angexetine	c&b Philip	4	17	25	-	-
J.Wenevine	c Ruma b Philip	3	13	18	-	-
*R.Siwa	st Morea b David	12	15	23	2	-
L.Wahmowe	c Siaka b David	2	8	7	-	-
L.Wawine	b David	15	10	15	3	-
E.Kecine	b Tau	0	5	5	-	-
L.Jeka	b Ruma	1	10	18	-	-
I.Kecine	b David	0	1	1	-	-
S.Kaudre	b Ruma	4	13	9	-	-
A.Mazeno	not out	3	11	7	-	-
	b6 lb2 w8	16				
	(19 overs)	**62**				

New Caledonia	O	M	R	W	nb	w
Wahmowe	4	0	28	0	1	5
Angexetine	4	0	55	0	-	3
Siwa	4	0	47	1	1	1
E.Kecine	4	0	23	1	1	-
Wenevine	1	0	10	0	-	2
Qaeze	1	0	9	0	-	1
Kaudre	2	0	18	1	1	6

PNG	O	M	R	W	nb	w
Ruma	4	0	9	3	-	4
Philip	4	1	5	2	-	2
Arua	4	0	16	0	-	-
David	4	0	10	4	-	1
Tau	2	0	12	1	-	-
Frank	1	0	2	0	-	1

fow	PNG	NC
1	132 (2)	6 (1)
2	176 (3)	12 (2)
3	189 (4)	14 (3)
4		19 (5)
5		35 (4)
6		44 (7)
7		44 (6)
8		44 (9)
9		56 (10)
10		62 (8)

Umpires: A.Kapa (Papua New Guinea) and C.Thurgate (Japan)

Toss: Papua New Guinea

11

Retrospect and prospect

Since the first international match was played in September 1844, cricket has changed markedly. First, there have been the changes in the laws, the most important of which are the introduction of the third stump and the legalisation of, initially, round-arm, and then over-arm bowling. Second, batsmen have gained the advantage over bowlers, which means that batting and bowling averages are much higher today than they were in the 19th and early 20th centuries. Third, there has been the addition of new formats with their own regulations, so T20 and one-day internationals are now more prevalent than multi-innings matches.

These changes, of course, apply to all forms of cricket, from the first-class game to club and school matches, not just to fixtures between Associates and Affiliates. For the latter, the biggest change is the marked increase in the number of countries participating in international cricket, a change that the world's press and broadcasters have largely chosen to ignore.

With more countries playing internationally, particularly in the one-day and T20 formats, the number of matches per year has increased substantially. As illustrated by Figure 1, in the early years there were generally only one or two matches each year. This

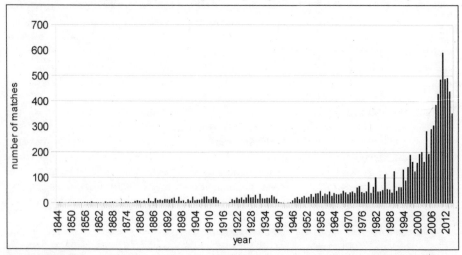

Figure 1: Number of men's international matches played annually by Associates and Affiliates since 1844

increased to the low teens to early 20s in the 1880s and stabilised at that level through to the early 1950s, except for gaps of low activity during the two world wars. In the 1960s and 1970s there were between 30 and 70 matches per year, a pattern that continued into the 1980s and 1990s, except for peaks in the years when the ICC Trophy was contested. Since 1996, over 100 matches have taken place each year, with the number rising to above 200 in the 2000s and above 400 since 2009.

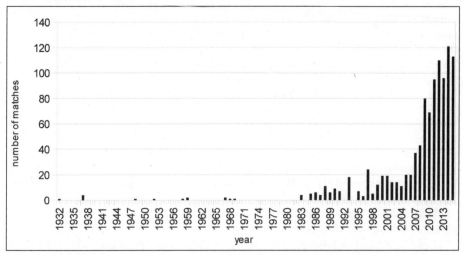

Figure 2: Number of women's international matches played annually by Associates and Affiliates since 1932

The first women's international involving an Associate country was in 1932, when Scotland met England. From then until the 1980s, as seen in Figure 2, one or two matches a year were sometimes played but, more frequently, as during the 1970s, there were none at all. It was not until the 2000s that the number of women's internationals regularly reached double figures and not until 2012 that more than 100 matches were played in a year. Today, women play about a third of the number of internationals each year as the men.

The early matches between the United States and Canada attracted crowds in the low thousands and were graced by the appearance of local dignitaries. Spectators were often entertained by local brass or wind bands while official dinners were given by the hosts to the visitors. In most Associate and Affiliate international matches today, attendances are rarely more than 50 people. Even where Associates and Affiliates play Full Member countries, as in the ODI and T20 World Cups, attendances are low unless the host country is involved.

There are exceptions, the most striking being when Ireland or Scotland play a Full Member country at home, when several thousand may attend. The same is true when Afghanistan play at the Sharjah Cricket Association stadium, which is, at present, their effective home ground, or when Nepal play at home in Kathmandu.

One effect of the greater number of international matches is that countries are better able to rank themselves relative to others. Before the 1970s it was impossible to know how Argentina compared to Fiji, or Scotland to Singapore. Today, the structure of the World Cricket League and the various divisions within regional competitions means that comparisons are possible, at least as far as one-day internationals and T20 formats are concerned.

What has not changed is the role of expatriates in promoting cricket across the world. What the British, supported by smaller numbers of Australians, New Zealanders and South Africans, did in the 19th century, Indians, Pakistanis and Sri Lankans are doing today. The concerns, however, are still the same. These include whether or not cricket will filter down from first-generation migrants to their second- and third-generation descendants and whether these immigrant communities will be successful in developing cricket among the indigenous population. The British failed to bring the latter about in South America but succeeded in places like Bermuda, Ghana, Nigeria, Malaysia, Singapore and the Pacific Islands. Today, migrants from the Indian subcontinent are no more successful in the United Arab Emirates, the USA and Canada, but their efforts seem to be more effective in Europe.

Even so, in countries like Denmark and Germany, the national side is increasingly made up of players of Asian origin, though many have been born in and are citizens of the country. There is a danger though that if these cricketers prove to be more skilled and better players than those from the local population, the latter will be discouraged from taking up cricket, feeling they cannot compete.

Another lasting feature which comes through in the selection of the scorecards made here is that the pioneering spirit, shown by players in the early days of cricket in the United States, Canada and Argentina, is still present. The problems of transport faced by the early cricketers from the United States and Canada were matched by those of Saint Helena when they travelled to South Africa in 2012 for their first internationals. In November 2015, women cricketers from Sierra Leone travelled by road for four days from Freetown to Banjul, via Conakry and Dakar, to take part on the inaugural North West Africa Women's T20. The efforts made by cricketers in Hungary, Romania, Bulgaria and Poland today to obtain land on which to develop new cricket grounds parallels those of the cricketing pioneers in places like Hong Kong, Malaysia and Singapore.

Over the last 20 years, many Associate and Affiliate countries have invested time and money in either upgrading or developing new cricket grounds. For example, Ireland is upgrading the facility at Malahide into an international venue with a capacity of 11,500. Afghanistan has built grounds at Ghazi Amanullah Khan City, Kabul and Khost with respective capacities of 14,000, 6,000 and 18,000. Romania and Hungary have both constructed dedicated cricket grounds. However, such developments should come with a warning.

In 1995 the United States and Canada played an Intercontinental Cup match on a newly-laid turf pitch at the Brian Piccolo Park, in Cooper City, a suburb of Fort Lauderdale, Florida. It was intended that it would become a major cricket venue in the United States but this has not materialised. The construction of another ground at the Central Broward Park in nearby Lauderhill has not helped because, except when both grounds can be used to host tournaments, they are in competition with each other. Further, the United States Cricket Association has been unsuccessful in attracting Full Member countries, like Pakistan and India, to play there. An attempt to stage some of the matches in the ICC World Cup, when it was held in the Caribbean in 2007, failed when the bids from Bermuda, Canada and the United States to host first-round fixtures were rejected.

When China hosted the Asian Games in 2010 and cricket was included as a sport for the first time, the Guangdong International Cricket Stadium was constructed as a purpose-built facility. Part of the legacy of the Games was that the venue would become the base for a major development of cricket in China. This has not happened. There is no longer a curator and the pitches have fallen into disrepair. In 2014, the Korean Cricket Association repeated the exercise when South Korea hosted the next Asian Games in Incheon. The Yeonhui Cricket Stadium was built, yet South Korea plays hardly any international cricket.

The construction of new cricket grounds follows an oft-repeated pattern of development projects. Sponsorship is found for the infrastructure but no money is set aside for maintenance. The National Stadium in Hamilton, Bermuda, was judged unsuitable for internationals by the ICC, forcing Bermuda to play their early matches in the Intercontinental Cup away from home. After an upgrade, the ICC approved the facilities in 2010. The following year, Bermuda lost their official one-day international status. The ground was used during the World Cricket League Division Three tournament in 2013 but has again since been declared unfit for international cricket.

The reason is simple. With Bermuda falling from World Cricket League Division One in 2007 to Division Four today, the country finds it hard to attract international opponents. Without cricket, it is impossible to earn enough money to pay staff to maintain the facility.

Compared to the optimism of the 1990s and early 2000s, when the ICC was actively encouraging the globalisation of the sport, the future for cricket in the Associate and Affiliate countries looks uncertain. Kenya's hopes for attaining Full Membership never materialised. Their one-day international status became increasingly meaningless as they struggled to secure fixtures against Full Member countries. Their cricket went into decline and in 2014, they lost their ODI standing.

Canada, Bermuda, the United States and Argentina have all seen their standards fall and have been relegated into lower divisions of the World Cricket League or, in Argentina's case, demoted from it entirely. Taken with the decline in interest and quality of cricket in the West Indies, these trends imply that there is something seriously amiss in the way cricket in the Americas is being organised and developed.

There are problems in Europe too, where the Dutch have lost their one-day international status and Danish cricket is falling in standard. One positive has been the phenomenal rise of Afghanistan and the success of Ireland, so that both countries are able to compete on level terms with many Full Member countries in both one-dayers and T20. Other countries with improving standards include Papua New Guinea, Hong Kong and Malaysia.

The ICC is giving mixed messages regarding the future of cricket as a global game. On the one hand, new countries are still being admitted to Affiliate Membership such as Hungary in 2012, Romania in 2013 and Serbia in 2015. Against this, four countries have been ejected; Switzerland in 2012, Cuba in 2013, Tonga in 2014 and Brunei in 2015, and five countries have had their membership suspended; Iran, Malawi and Turkey in 2013, and Morocco and the United States in 2015. This is the second time that the United States have been suspended. It happened in 2007 and they were reinstated in 2008. Most of these suspensions and ejections relate to failures in administration. The ICC provides reasonably clear statements of the issues but seems to give little in the way of advice or assistance in how to address them.

Through its High Performance and Development Programmes the ICC has made finance available to enhance the administrative structures, coaching and the expenses of staging matches in the Associate and Affiliate countries. It has supported the ICC Intercontinental Cup and the World Cricket League. Unfortunately, these initiatives have failed on the one key element that could help close the gap in standard between the top Associates and the Full Member countries, namely the opportunity for the former to meet the latter on a regular basis.

Cricketers will only improve their performances if they compete against players who are slightly better than themselves. The present structure allows cricketers from places like Hong Kong, Papua New Guinea, Jersey and Guernsey to do this by playing against the likes of Kenya, Namibia and The Netherlands. Countries like Ireland, Afghanistan, Scotland and the United Arab Emirates each need to be playing six or so matches a year against Zimbabwe, Bangladesh, the West Indies and Pakistan, instead of playing only against each other. Without this, the gap will never close. Ireland and Afghanistan may continue to raise their standards but their cricketers are not aiming at a static target.

Standards in the Full Member countries are rising too. If they rise faster than those in the Associate countries, the gap between will widen, even though all are improving. With Full Member countries receiving much more finance that the Associates, this outcome is a real possibility.

The ambivalence of the ICC towards supporting global cricket is epitomised by the recent reduction in the number of countries involved in international matches. With the World Cricket League being reduced from eight to five divisions and the demise of the lower divisions of the regional tournaments, countries like Israel, Gibraltar, Croatia, Estonia, Finland, Portugal, Myanmar, Brazil, Peru and Chile no longer have the chance to play internationally unless they organise opportunities themselves.

The American regional qualifying tournament for the Women's World T20 was cancelled in 2014, which meant that there was no women's cricket in the region outside of the South American Championships. Not to be thwarted, however, some women from Canada and the United States collaborated to form a combined CANAM side and obtained sponsorship for a tour of Argentina in early 2015. The ICC would like to see these countries direct their resources to what it terms 'grass-roots development', encouraging cricket in schools and clubs. But, if the players at these levels have no international cricket to aspire to, what is the point? Most sports men and women who are any good want to represent their country. If there is no opportunity to do this in cricket, they will simply take up another sport.

The leading Associate and Affiliate countries are faced with unnecessary uncertainty because many decisions of the ICC appear to be made in reaction to events rather than in advance. A simple case is that of The Netherlands after they lost their one-day international status in early 2014. After they beat England and Nepal beat Afghanistan in the World T20 in March that year, the ICC suddenly awarded both countries an official T20 international status. Up to that point, one-day international status also included T20 matches. Now a country can have T20 status but not automatically ODI.

A more complex issue concerns the qualification procedures for the World Cup. In April 2011, the ICC stated that the 2015 World Cup would be restricted to the ten Full Member countries. Two months later, this proposal was changed to permit 14 teams to take part, making room for four Associates. But it was not until September 2011 that the method of qualification was announced. The ICC then stated that the World Cricket League Championships would be used for this purpose, even though this was after one round of the matches had already been played. If the countries had known this beforehand they might have chosen different teams.

In February 2012 the procedure was changed again and the top two in the WCL Championships were to qualify directly for the 2015 World Cup, while the other countries would enter another qualifying competition, along with teams from the Second Division of the World Cricket League. In other words, for all but the top two countries, the WCL Championships became irrelevant. If the ICC continues to change the rules of qualifying competitions while they are in progress, it becomes impossible for the cricket boards of the countries involved to plan anything.

Table 1. Countries where the number of players exceeds 0.4% of the population

Country*	Number of players	Players as % of population
Cook Islands	5,402	36.08
Falkland Islands	595	19.83
Guernsey	8,460	12.85
Gibraltar	3,176	10.69
St Helena	419	10.20
Bermuda	6,440	10.03
Samoa	16,385	8.72
Vanuatu	19,137	7.23

Jersey	6,010	6.07
Suriname	28,591	5.35
Isle of Man	3,015	3.57
Cayman Islands	1,770	3.19
Fiji	25,730	3.00
Papua New Guinea	180,194	2.44
Scotland	68,889	1.29
Seychelles	970	1.08
Namibia	18,207	0.86
Tonga	831	0.80
Bhutan	5,668	0.75
Maldives	2,996	0.75
Ireland	43,838	0.68
Turks and Caicos	195	0.62
Belize	1,841	0.53
United Arab Emirates	47,214	0.50
Swaziland	4,600	0.42

* Affiliate Members are shown in italics.

Data on the number of players are for 2013 (after the International Cricket Council). Population data are for 2014, taken from *Wikipedia*, National Records of Scotland and the Northern Ireland Statistics and Research Agency.

Future development plans for global cricket need to give more attention to the wide variety that exists among the Associates and Affiliates rather than assuming that all countries have the same needs and face the same issues. These differences are most marked in the extent to which, in each country, cricket can be considered a national sport. Although there is no definition of this, a simple measure is to calculate what percentage of the country's population are involved in playing the sport. Depending on which organisations have collected the data, the figures for England and Wales range from 0.5 to 1.5, and for Australia, from 0.7 to 4.0. A slightly lower value of 0.4 per cent is proposed here as a reasonable indicator for Associates and Affiliates.

With this definition there are 25 Associate and Affiliate countries in which cricket can be considered a national sport. These are listed in Table 1. With the exceptions of Papua New Guinea, Scotland, Ireland and the United Arab Emirates, all are small territories, small islands or island groups, with small populations and fewer than 30,000 cricketers. In some cases there are fewer than 1,000. Many of these countries do not rank highly on the world stage in cricket or, indeed, in most other sports.

Having cricket as a national sport does not necessarily mean that it is played to a high standard. Equally, the playing of cricket to a reasonably high standard does not mean that it is likely to be or even become a national sport, or that there are large numbers of participants. As can be seen from Table 2, of the top dozen-ranked Associate and Affiliate countries, only five have cricket as a national sport and in three of these, there are fewer than 20,000 cricketers. Since cricket is largely associated with the educated, middle-class, urban population, it is likely that, in due time, it will become a national sport in Afghanistan and Nepal, as the proportion of the urban population increases. This is less likely to happen in countries like Kenya and Namibia, where cricket has failed to inspire the majority of the urban population and remains mainly an activity of minority ethnic communities.

Table 2. Participation rates in the top 12 Associates and Affiliates

Country	Number of players	Players as % of population
Papua New Guinea	180,194	2.44
Scotland	68,889	1.29
Namibia	18,207	0.86
Ireland	43,838	0.68
United Arab Emirates	47,214	0.50
Canada	73,194	0.21
Uganda	55,388	0.15
Netherlands	19,188	0.11
Afghanistan	24,792	0.10
Hong Kong	5,775	0.08
Nepal	22,802	0.08
Kenya	20,005	0.05

Data on the number of players are for 2013 (after the International Cricket Council). Population data are for 2014, taken from *Wikipedia*, National Records of Scotland and the Northern Ireland Statistics and Research Agency.

Table 3. Participation rates where number of players exceeds 30,000

Country*	Number of players	Players as % of population
Papua New Guinea	180,194	2.44
Scotland	68,889	1.29
Ireland	43,838	0.68
United Arab Emirates	47,214	0.50
Canada	73,194	0.21
Uganda	55,388	0.15
USA	37,338	0.012
China	70,762	0.005

Data on the number of players are for 2013 (after the International Cricket Council). Population data are for 2014, taken from *Wikipedia*, National Records of Scotland and the Northern Ireland Statistics and Research Agency.

A third group of countries comprises those with over 30,000 participants, which should be more than enough to secure the future of cricket, even though these represent only a small proportion of the population. Table 3 lists the eight countries. In two of these, the United States and China, the participation rate is 0.012 per cent or less of the population. In the United States there are over 37,000 participants. For cricket to be considered a national sport this would need to increase to 1.27 million. The challenge for China is even greater. With more than 70,000 participants at present, the country ranks third among the Associates and Affiliates in terms of total number. To become a national sport, however, this figure would need to become 5.47 million.

With limited financial resources available, questions arise as to how the ICC should spend its money. Should it prioritise countries where cricket is played at or near to a first-class level, even if this means discriminating against countries where cricket is established as a national sport? If more funds were made available to countries like the

Cook Islands, Falkland Islands and Saint Helena, how would they be used? Given the very high participation rates in these territories already, how likely is it that they could be increased still further? How much support should be given to countries, like the United States and China, with large numbers of participants, but where cricket is never going to be more than a sport of the minority? Should priority be given to countries which promote cricket across all communities rather than to minority groups, based on either ethnicity or gender? If more money was given to countries like the United States and Namibia to spread cricket more widely across the population, there is no guarantee that large numbers of Americans or Namibian Africans would be interested. If they are not, does it matter?

As migrant communities reach the second and third generations the distinction between the local population and so-called expatriates is surely irrelevant. Why not just concentrate resources on those who want to play cricket? What is not acceptable, however, is to deny resources where there is a demand and interest. Should less support therefore be given to countries like Afghanistan and Saudi Arabia which have yet to field a women's team?

Although all the Associates and Affiliates rely heavily on monies provided by the ICC, it should be remembered that cricket began in many of these countries before the ICC came into existence and certainly before it started to support cricket on a global scale. Also, there are countries like New Caledonia, El Salvador, Latvia and Lithuania which play regular international cricket without being members of the ICC. As long as there are people sufficiently interested to give up their time to become players, officials, coaches or administrators, cricket in the Associates and Affiliates will survive and probably grow, particularly if, as is increasingly the case, local sponsorship can be obtained. Without ICC's support, the level of activity will, however, be much less.

To prevent this, the ICC needs to be less ambivalent in its approach to globalisation and work out a programme of development appropriate to each country's needs and aspirations.

Appendix

A brief history of cricket in Associates and Affiliates

By imposing a restriction of 100 scorecards, it has not been possible to include every country which has played international cricket. This Appendix lists all the countries which are either Associate or Affiliate Members of the ICC and some other countries which have played international cricket. Matches by age-group teams are excluded. For each country, the year of their first international match is listed. Dates of admission to the ICC as Affiliate or Associate Member are shown.

Country	Year of first match Men			Women	Comments
	Multi-innings	*One-day*	*T20*		
Afghanistan	2009			2004	2007
Alderney			2009		
Argentina	1912	1979	2010	2007	Associate 1974
Austria	1992	1990	2010		Affiliate 1992
Bahamas	1998	1994	2011		Affiliate 1987
Bahrain		1994	2009		Affiliate 2001
Belarus		2005			
Belgium	1905	1990	2009	2012	Affiliate 1991, Associate 2005
Belize	1960	2003	2008		Affiliate 1997
Bermuda	1907	1979	2006	2006	Associate 1966
Bhutan		2003	2011	2009	Affiliate 2001
Botswana		1995	2011	2015	Affiliate 2001, Associate 2006
Brazil	1921	1986	2009	2007	Affiliate 2002
Brunei		1996			Affiliate 1992; removed 2015
Bulgaria		2004	2008	2014	Affiliate 2008
Cameroon			2011		Affiliate 2007
Canada	1844	1974	2008	2006	Associate 1968
Cayman Islands	2005	2000	2006	2012	Affiliate 1997, Associate 2002
Chile	1920	1995	2009	2010	Affiliate 2002
China	1866	2009	2009	2007	Affiliate 2004
Colombia		2001	2014		
Cook Islands		2001	2009	2012	Affiliate 2000
Costa Rica		2002	2008		Affiliate 2002
Croatia		2000	2008		Affiliate 2001
Cuba					Affiliate 2002, removed 2013
Curaçao	1961	2006			
Cyprus		2006	2011		Affiliate 1999
Czech Republic	2001	2002	2008		Affiliate 2000
Denmark	1932	1974	2008	1983	Associate 1966
East Africa	1956	1972			Associate 1966, ceased 1989
East & Central Africa		1990			Associate 1989, ceased 2001
Ecuador		2007			
Egypt	1907				Last match 1951
El Salvador		2007	2008		

Estonia		2000	2008	2012	Affiliate 2008
Falkland Islands		2010	2010		Affiliate 2007
Fiji	1895	1979	2009	2010	Associate 1965
Finland		2000	2009	2013	Affiliate 2000
France	1906	1990	2009	2011	Affiliate 1987, Associate 1998
Gambia	1927	1975	2011	2015	Affiliate 2002
Germany	1992	1989	2009	2012	Affiliate 1991, Associate 1999
Ghana	1904	1991	2011	2015	Affiliate 2002
Gibraltar	1927	1982	2011	2012	Associate 1969
Greece		1977	2011	2014	Affiliate 1995
Guatemala			2012		
Guernsey	1922	1978	2011	2013	Affiliate 2005, Associate 2008
Hong Kong	1866	1980	2007	2006	Associate 1969
Hungary		2007	2008	2013	Affiliate 2012
Indonesia		2004	2009		Affiliate 2001
Iran		2004		2009	Affiliate 2003, suspended 2013
Ireland	1856	1974	2008	1983	Associate 1993
Isle of Man		2005	2011		Affiliate 2004
Israel		1979	2011		Associate 1974
Italy	1991	1989	2011	2013	Affiliate 1984, Associate 1995
Japan	1991	1996	2009	2003	Affiliate 1989, Associate 2005
Jersey	1922	1978	2011	2011	Affiliate 2005, Associate 2007
Kenya	1914	1978	2007	2002	Associate 1981
Kuwait		2000	2007	2009	Affiliate 1998, Associate 2005
Latvia		2005	2008		
Lesotho	1986	1995	2010		Affiliate 2001
Lithuania		2012	2010		
Luxembourg	1991	1990	2010		Affiliate 1998
Macedonia			2010	2014	
Malawi	1982	1981	2011		Affiliate 2003, suspended 2013
Malaysia	1890	1977	2007	2006	Associate 1967
Maldives		1996	2010		Affiliate 2001
Mali		2007	2011	2015	Affiliate 2005
Malta	1970	1977	2011		Affiliate 1998
Mexico		2006	2008		Affiliate 2004
Morocco		2003	2011		Affiliate 1999, suspended 2015
Mozambique		2004	2011		Affiliate 2003
Myanmar	1894	2006			Affiliate 2006
Namibia	1992	1990	2009	2004	Associate 1992
Nepal	2004	1996	2007	2007	Affiliate 1988, Associate 1996
Netherlands	1901	1978	2008	1937	Associate 1966
New Caledonia		1979	2011		
Nicaragua		2002	2008		
Nigeria	1904	1991	2011	2011	Associate 2002
Norfolk Island		2001			
Norway		2000	2007		Affiliate 2000
Oman		2002	2009	2009	Affiliate 2000, Associate 2014
Panama		2000	2009		Affiliate 2002
Papua New Guinea	1973	1975	2009	2006	Associate 1973
Peru	1927	1995	2011	2011	Affiliate 2007
Philippines		2011	2011		Affiliate 2000
Poland		2012	2004		
Portugal	1895	1992	2011		Affiliate 1996
Puerto Rico		2004			
Qatar		2002	2007	2009	Affiliate 1999
Romania		2014	2008		Affiliate 2013
Russia			2008		Affiliate 2012
Rwanda		2004	2011	2008	Affiliate 2003
Saint Helena			2012		Affiliate 2001

Country					
Samoa		1979	2009	2010	Affiliate 2000
Saudi Arabia		2004	2007		Affiliate 2003
Scotland	1849	1975	2007	1932	Associate 1994
Serbia			2010		Affiliate 2015
Seychelles			2011		Affiliate 2010
Sierra Leone	1927	1991	2011	2011	Affiliate 2002
Singapore	1890	1977	2007	2006	Associate 1974
Slovakia		2002	2004		
Slovenia	2001	2000	2006		Affiliate 2005
Solomon Islands	1977	1991			
South America	1932				Last match 1932
South Korea			2011	2014	Affiliate 2001
Spain	1993	1990	2010		Affiliate 1992
Suriname		2004	2011		Affiliate 2002
Swaziland	1981	2008	2011		Affiliate 2007
Sweden		1993	2007		Affiliate 1997
Switzerland		1990	2010		Affiliate 1985, removed 2012
Tajikistan		2013	2013		
Tanzania	1951	1981	2011	2002	Associate 2001
Thailand	1909	1991		2007	Affiliate 1995, Associate 2005
Tonga		1979	2009		Affiliate 2000, removed 2014
Turkey		2009	2011		Affiliate 2008, suspended 2013
Turks and Caicos Islands		2001	2008		Affiliate 2002
Tuvalu		1979			
Uganda	1914	1993	2009	2002	Associate 1998
United Arab Emirates	2003	1976	2007	2007	Affiliate 1989, Associate 1990
United States	1844	1979	2010	2009	Associate 1965, suspended 2007-2008 and again in 2015
Uruguay	1926				Last match 1960
Vanuatu	1977	1979	2009	2011	Affiliate 1995, Associate 2009
Venezuela	1961	1999			
Wales	1923	1979	2008	2002	
West Africa	1976	1982			Associate 1976, ceased 2002
Yemen	1964				Last match 1964
Zambia	1930	1981	2012		Associate 2003
Zanzibar	1956				Merged with Tanzania 1964

For men's matches the dates show the first match played against either another country or a team from a Full Member country which contained at least seven players with previous first-class experience.

Multi-innings matches include one-day matches played to standard multi-innings rules. Matches against A teams are included if the opposition is a country of higher standing, e.g. an Affiliate country versus the A team of an Associate country.

One-day matches are one-innings matches of more than 20 overs per side played to the one-day international regulations prevailing at the time. For women's matches, the date is that of the first match played regardless of format.

In some countries, representation is by surrogate teams for certain periods of their history: China includes matches played by Shanghai; Kenya by the British East Africa Protectorate; Malaysia by the Federated Malay States; Peru by Lima; Singapore by the Straits Settlements; Wales by the Cricket Board of Wales; and Yemen by Aden.

Cambodia, Taiwan and Tajikistan were elected as Associate Members of the Asian Cricket Council in 2012, though they are not members of the International Cricket Council. Their present status is uncertain since the ACC merged with the ICC in June 2015.

Andorra, Iceland and the Vatican City have played representative matches against visiting club sides, but have yet to play another country.

Sources

Annuals, journals and magazines
Cricket
Cricket World
History Today
Indian Cricket
New Zealand Cricket Almanack
South African Cricket Annual
The Cricket Statistician
The Cricketer
The South African Non-European Cricket Almanack
Uganda Cricket
Wisden Cricket Monthly
Wisden Cricketers' Almanack

Books
Bone, D.D. *Fifty Years' Reminiscences of Scottish Cricket*. Aird & Coghill, 1898.
Bowen, R. *Cricket: a History of its Growth and Development Throughout the World*. Eyre and Spottiswoode, 1970.
Bridger, K.E. *North and South: A History of the Annual Cricket Classic in Argentina*. Talleres Gráficos, 1976.
Frith, D. *The Golden Age of Cricket 1890–1914*. Lutterworth, 1978.
Hall, J.O. and McCulloch, R.O. *Sixty Years of Canadian Cricket*. Bryant, 1895.
Hargreaves, P.S. *Derbyshire's Dane*. Privately printed, 1983.
James, A. *Oldfield's Australian Cricket XI in Malaya and Singapore 1927*. Privately printed, 1998.
James, A. *Cricket Matches Played by Australian Teams in Canada and the United States of America 1878 to 1995*. Privately printed, 1999.
Labouchère, P.G.G., Provis, T.A.J. and Hargreaves, P.S. *The Story of Continental Cricket*. Hutchinson, 1969.
Major, J. *More Than a Game. The Story of Cricket's Early Years*. Harper, 2007.
Marder, J.I. *The International Series: The Story of United States versus Canada at Cricket*. Kaye and Ward, 1968.
Morgan, R. *ICC Intercontinental Cup*. Association of Cricket Statisticians, 2011.
Snow, P.A. *Cricket in the Fiji Islands*. Whitcombe and Toombs. 1949.
West, W. *50 Years of Irish Cricket 1940 to 1990*. Lindis, 1991.

Newspapers
Bangkok Post
Bermuda Colonist

Buenos Aires Herald
Daily Nation
Hong Kong Daily Press
Lagos Daily News
New York Times
Nigerian Daily Times
North China Daily News
North China Daily Press
North China Herald
Royal Gazette
Saint Helena Telegraph
South China Morning Post
Straits Echo
Sunday Nation
Syonan Shimbun
The Gold Coast Times
The Irish Times
The Philadelphia Inquirer
The Scotsman
The Star
The Straits Times
The Times
West African Times

Websites

www.abc.net.au
www.asiancricket.org
www.cricketarchive.com
www.cricketargentina.com
www.cricket.com.hk
www.cricket.dk
www.cricketeurope.net
www.crickitalia.com
www.cricketmalaysia.com
www.cricketscotland.com
www.dreamcricket.com
www.espncricinfo.com
www.foxsportspulse.com
www.gocricketgocanada.com
www.guernseycricketstats.co.uk
www.iceap.com
www.sthelenaonline.org
www.times.co.sz
www.tutiempo.net/en/Climate

Index of matches